UNWILLING EX

Unwilling Executioner

Crime Fiction and the State

ANDREW PEPPER

Great Clarendon Street, Oxford, OX2 6DP,
United Kingdom

Oxford University Press is a department of the University of Oxford.
It furthers the University's objective of excellence in research, scholarship,
and education by publishing worldwide. Oxford is a registered trade mark of
Oxford University Press in the UK and in certain other countries

© Andrew Pepper 2016

The moral rights of the author have been asserted

First published 2016
First published in paperback 2019

All rights reserved. No part of this publication may be reproduced, stored in
a retrieval system, or transmitted, in any form or by any means, without the
prior permission in writing of Oxford University Press, or as expressly permitted
by law, by licence or under terms agreed with the appropriate reprographics
rights organization. Enquiries concerning reproduction outside the scope of the
above should be sent to the Rights Department, Oxford University Press, at the
address above

You must not circulate this work in any other form
and you must impose this same condition on any acquirer

Published in the United States of America by Oxford University Press
198 Madison Avenue, New York, NY 10016, United States of America

British Library Cataloguing in Publication Data
Data available

Library of Congress Cataloging in Publication Data
Data available

ISBN 978–0–19–871618–1 (Hbk.)
ISBN 978–0–19–883112–9 (Pbk.)

Links to third party websites are provided by Oxford in good faith and
for information only. Oxford disclaims any responsibility for the materials
contained in any third party website referenced in this work.

For the translators, the unacknowledged heroes
of the global book trade

Preface and Acknowledgements

There is a fascinating revelation in David Peace's new foreword to Jean-Patrick Manchette's 1977 crime masterpiece *Fatale*. In his diary, Manchette reveals how he added 'a completely crazy scene' and that 'the long quote from Hegel is likely to drive people at Série Noire totally bats'. He signs off with a phrase that is at once gleeful and dismissive—'Ah, well!'—as though he already knows the negative repercussions it will have. Later we learn that Série Noire turned down the novel and that it was picked up by the imprint's publisher Gallimard as a 'regular novel'—and that in the early years of its life as a book it never really found a sizeable audience, perhaps because Manchette, by his own admission, tried 'to desiccate the crime thriller as much as I could… by applying to my subject matter a very carefully crafted "Marxist" architecture'.[1]

The anecdote and what it tells us about Manchette and crime fiction in general is significant for a number of reasons: it demonstrates Manchette's commitment to furthering some kind of political agenda through his crime stories and at the same time the difficulty of incorporating radical politics into his lean, pulsating tales of violence and revenge; it shows us the cost, to Manchette, of trying to do so and indicates that most readers did not react especially favourably to his Marxist inclinations. But most of all it underlines the struggle between commerce and politics that informs Manchette's own literary production and that has shaped, and continues to shape, the genre's character and development. To entertain *and* to provoke, to critique *and* perhaps also to reassure, have always been part of the genre's DNA but this small incident shows us how daunting the challenge is. The more you have to say, or the further you want to push, the harder is the challenge and the more you risk. For writers like Manchette the cost, in terms of commercial and hence financial success, was considerable.

This is not a story we hear very often these days. Instead, the relentless global march of best-selling crime novelists like Michael Connolly, Harlan Coben, and Lee Child, coupled with the idea that these same writers are using the genre as a vehicle for social and political criticism, suggests that contemporary practitioners can have their cake and eat it. I am not so sure. This is not to dismiss their novels outright or indeed to downplay the ongoing significance of drawing readers into crime novels by giving them what they want: excitement, suspense, tension, mystery, and a frisson of social and political engagement. But to do all this, and still find a way of properly exposing the ills of capitalism, the inadequacies of our liberal–democratic framework, the failures of the policing and justice system, the interconnectedness of the worlds of law, business, and crime, and even to tell us that everything won't be ok in the end, is a prodigiously difficult and perhaps nigh-on impossible task.

---

[1] Jean-Patrick Manchette qtd in David Peace, 'Foreword', in Manchette, *Fatale* (London: Serpent's Tail, 2015), pp. v–vii.

Dashiell Hammett did so, even if his novels were never wildly popular at the time of their publication; Georges Simenon—one of the best-selling crime novelists of all time and yet politically much more complex than he is often given credit for—remains, for me, the most influential figure in the global march of the genre in the twentieth and twenty-first centuries; and Maj Sjöwall and Per Wahlöö quickly found a sizeable international audience for their Marxist-inflected police procedural novels.

But even here, with these ostensible 'successes', the struggle to bring the disparate elements of the crime story, its assaults on the rottenness of the existing order, and its necessary defences of the law, into effective tension or conflagration would not be easily achieved; and would lead to accusations—self-accusations in Manchette's case—of failure, even when success, defined in terms of remaining absolutely true to one's political beliefs and also finding huge numbers of readers, was at best a distant hope rather than an expectation. In writing about figures like Simenon, Hammett, Manchette, and Sjöwall and Wahlöö who strived, and sometimes failed, to marry the commercial and political imperatives of the genre, because it could not be otherwise, I am hoping to tell a larger story about the genre. Too often, I think, we limit this narrative to a self-selecting group of American crime novels published between the 1920s and 1950s under the designation 'noir' or 'hard-boiled', and one of my main ambitions here in this book is to argue that the impetus to politicize and popularize the writing of crime as fiction has a much longer historical lineage and a much broader geographical trajectory than we sometimes seem to want to admit—and that this impetus should be seen as having an international dimension rather than as something confined to discrete national traditions.

I am not alone in this belief of course and my book is a small contribution in a much larger effort to unsettle some of the critical orthodoxies that have calcified around the genre. As such, I am deeply indebted to the excellent critical work that precedes and makes possible my book; and the following list of names, though by no means an exhaustive one, indicates the interventions I have found most helpful: Bill Alder, Clive Bloom, Chris Breu, Leonard Cassuto, Jonathan Eburne, Robin Truth Goodman, Claire Gorarra, Cynthia Hamilton, Dominique Kalifa, Martin Kayman, Stewart King, Stephen Knight, Sean McCann, Andrew Nestingen, Barbara Pezzotti, David Platten, Charles Rzepka, and Ronald Thomas.

I would particularly like to acknowledge my debt to Lee Horsley, both for her excellent work and the friendship and support she has shown me during the long gestation of this project, and to Pete Messent, who has written clearly and with genuine insight about the crime fiction genre and who first encouraged me down this path when I was an undergraduate student at the University of Nottingham. My own thinking about what crime fiction is and does is just as indebted to Paul Cobley, and the friendship and many beer-themed conversations I have shared with him over the years, and to David Schmid, with whom I have greatly enjoyed collaborating on another project and from whom I have learned a great deal.

At Queen's University Belfast, where I have taught since 2001, I have been supported by the sabbatical leave programme which remains the single most important means of gaining the time and space to attempt large-scale academic projects. At Queen's, I have been fortunate enough to enjoy the support and friendship of colleagues in the School of English and elsewhere, notably Fran Brearton, Mark Burnett, Marilina Cesario, David Dwan, Catherine Gander, Gail McConnell, Philip McGowan, Paul Simpson, Bal Sokhi-Bulley, Adrian Streete, Caroline Sumpter, and Ramona Wray. Of these I would like to pick out David, whose typically challenging but always generous insights into the philosophical and political foundations of my book were key to shaping it at an early stage of the project. In addition to the numerous students I've taught on my many crime fiction modules over the years, I would especially like to acknowledge Clare Clarke whose doctoral thesis I was lucky enough to supervise and who has gone on to write an award-winning book on Victorian crime fiction. Last and certainly not least, one of the most important and helpful influences on my thinking about crime fiction, especially its international dimensions and its reception and circulation in France, has been Dominique Jeannerod, who teaches French at Queen's, with whom I have shared conversations and insights too numerous to mention and who has helped to shape the direction and scope of this book in more ways than I am sure he realizes.

Parts of Chapter 1 were first published as 'Early Crime Writing and the State: Jonathan Wild, Daniel Defoe and Bernard Mandeville in 1720s London' in *Textual Practice*, 25:3 (June 2011), pp. 473–91; parts of Chapter 5 were published as '"Hegemony Protected by the Armour of Coercion": Dashiell Hammett's *Red Harvest* and the State', in *Journal of American Studies*, 44:2 (May 2010), pp. 333–49. I would like to thank Routledge and Cambridge University Press for their permission to reproduce this material.

My greatest debt of gratitude goes to Debbie Lisle, my partner in crime and life, a brilliant scholar of International Relations in her own right who has read numerous parts of this book and who has brought her typical generosity, wisdom, insight, and disciplinary perspective (and red pen) to what I've written. She has also endured, with more grace and patience than I've been able to reciprocate, my teeth-gnashing despair and catastrophizing over the years when it seemed like this project was neither feasible nor possible. Without her love, friendship, and support, this book quite simply wouldn't have been started, let alone finished. I won't offer the patronizing and wholly untrue claim that my kids have also influenced the outcome of this book, except in the negative sense of depriving me of sleep and time, but this is exactly as it should be, and I like to think that their current "superheroes" and 'bad guys' predilections may one day blossom into a finer appreciation of the nuances and ambiguities of the crime genre. Or not—because these stories do also tell us 'bad guys' need to go to jail. This book is dedicated to the translators, the unlikely superheroes of the impetus to share and understand crime fiction across national and linguistic borders, and as a linguistic neophyte my debt to their trailblazing work should be self-evident but probably still needs to be acknowledged.

Table of Contents

Introduction: Crime Fiction as Unwilling Executioner	1
1. 'A Life of Horrid and Inimitable Wickedness': Crime, Law, and Punishment in Early Eighteenth-century London and Paris	19
2. 'Let Us Attack Injustice at Its Source': Crime Literature in an Era of Revolution and Reform	50
3. 'A Mysterious Power Whose Hand is Everywhere': Imagining the State and Codifying the Law in the Mid-nineteenth Century	77
4. Crime, Business, and Liberty at the Turn of the Century: The Individual, the State, and the Emergence of Modern Capitalism	104
5. 'No Good for Business': States of Crime in the 1920s and 1930s	131
6. 'On the Barricades': Crime Fiction and Commitment in an Era of Radical Politics	166
7. From Sovereignty to Neoliberalism: Crime Fiction in the Contemporary World	206
Conclusion	248
Select Bibliography	253
Index	265

Introduction
Crime Fiction as Unwilling Executioner

This book is founded upon a modest central proposition: that the development of crime fiction as a genre is bound up with the consolidation of the modern, bureaucratic state; that is to say, with the policing, governmental, and judicial apparatuses set up to enforce law, and with the new techniques and technologies of governing established to produce a more secure world.[1] The development of crime fiction as a genre is propelled by the contradictions that ensue when the state assumes control of the justice system. Crime fiction, then, explores the connections and the elisions between what Jean and John Comaroff aptly describe as 'modernist state power' on the one hand and 'popular fantasies of law and order'[2] on the other. If the state is not easily seen and remains an oblique presence in much fiction, crime stories thematize and make visible the institutional bodies, policing practices, legal processes, and judicial norms that make up the criminal justice system. In doing so, they give tangible shape to the state's labyrinthine operations and multiple institutional forms. Typically, the stories feature a figure directly appointed by the state or an auxiliary, a private individual for example, who performs a related function. Their enquiries, which give the narrative its archetypal shape and form, draw attention to the failures, flaws, and coercive capacities of the state's crime control mechanisms, and in doing so are animated by popular or populist opposition to institutionalized power. But their investigations and the resolutions they bring about, perhaps partial or inadequate, also aim to create a more secure world, and ideally, though not always in practice, facilitate a move from disorder to order. As such they underscore the socio-political good of combatting crime—what Loader and Walker call security as a 'thick public good' and an 'indispensable constituent of any good society'[3]—and draw attention to the ethical dimension of the state.

These stories, therefore, move from or between an account of the state as impartial or standing above society, and hence capable of acting in the general good, to one where the state acts to safeguard the interests of the wealthy and oversee the surrender of public interests to private concerns. Crime fiction—or rather the kind

---

[1] My deployment of Foucauldian language here to describe the operations of the state is deliberate. As will become apparent, the aim is to situate an understanding of the political dimension of crime fiction in a field of tension between Marxist and Foucauldian conceptions of power.

[2] Jean and John Comaroff, 'Criminal Obsessions after Foucault: Postcoloniality, Policing and the Metaphysics of Disorder', *Critical Inquiry*, 30:4 (Summer 2004), p. 805.

[3] Ian Loader and Neil Walker, *Civilizing Security* (Cambridge: Cambridge University Press, 2007), p. 4.

of crime fiction that comprises the field of study for this book—tends to produce a contradictory account of the state as both necessary for the creation and maintenance of collective life and central to the reproduction of entrenched socio-economic inequalities, to the point that this tension becomes the constitutive and foundational feature of the emerging genre.[4]

It is not my intention to suggest that the crime story willingly performs the role of state henchman or executioner, hence the title of the book. If there is a populist scepticism in crime fiction from its earliest incarnations towards traditional modes and figures of authority, any overt political radicalism is contained by the accommodations crime stories must make towards the articulation of law and the restitution of order. In the same way, this conservative impulse is itself undermined by the crime story's typical refusal to turn a blind eye to institutional failure and corruption. Lee Horsley puts this best when she writes: '[t]he genre is neither inherently conservative nor radical: rather, it is a form that can be co-opted for a variety of purposes'; or indeed that a 'dialogic' approach to reading and understanding the genre is preferable, one that emphasizes 'the ambiguity, or indeed contradictoriness, of individual texts'.[5] Hence critical approaches that pay too much attention to the genre's capacities for imposing and advocating dominant ideologies or disciplinary norms,[6] or, for that matter, those that overplay its political radicalism or deviancy or indeed its willingness to service politically progressive agendas,[7] cannot do justice to the specificity of the genre's ambivalent relationship to the justice system, which in turn gives exemplary crime stories their particular shape and dramatic form.[8]

Despite this general thesis, my book is not seeking to offer a totalizing theory of crime fiction or make a series of sweeping generalizations about all crime stories. Rather my aim is to delineate the richness and complexity of a long tradition of crime writing in which crime, and indeed policing, is seen as rooted in the social

---

[4] This builds on a claim made by Sean McCann, who argues that detective fiction articulates a 'more complex and plausible view of the problem of law'; namely that 'on the one hand...laws and norms are the basis of ethical claims and the grounds for any vision of social justice; and, on the other hand, that laws are nevertheless often rigidly bureaucratic and the means of abuse or exploitation'. *Gumshoe America: Hard-Boiled Crime Fiction and the Rise and Fall of New Deal Liberalism* (Durham, NC and London: Duke University Press, 2000), p. 310.

[5] Lee Horsley, *Twentieth-Century Crime Fiction* (Oxford: Oxford University Press, 2005), pp. 158, 2.

[6] Here I am deliberately conflating Marxist and Foucauldian positions because both underscore, albeit in different ways, the repressive logic of the genre. Examples of the latter include Michel Foucault, *Discipline and Punish: The Birth of the Prison*, trans. Alan Sheridan (London: Penguin, 1991), pp. 67–9; D.A. Miller, *The Novel and the Police* (Berkeley, CA: University of California Press, 1988); Marie-Christine Leps, *Apprehending the Criminal: The Production of Deviance in Nineteenth-Century Discourse* (Durham, NC and London: Duke University Press, 1992). Examples of the former include Ernest Mandel, *Delightful Murder: A Social History of the Crime Story* (London: Pluto, 1984); Dennis Porter, *The Pursuit of Crime: Art and Ideology in Detective Fiction* (New Haven, CT: Yale University Press, 1981).

[7] Examples of works that, I think, slightly overplay the genre's radicalism and deviancy include Jim Collins's *Uncommon Culture: Popular Culture and Post-Modernism* (London and New York, NY: Routledge, 1992) and Tony Hilfer's *The Crime Novel: A Deviant Genre* (Austin, TX: University of Texas Press, 1992).

[8] I am not staking out entirely new ground here but rather building on work that similarly emphasizes the genre's ambivalent status as, to quote Ronald Thomas, an 'enforcer of legitimate cultural authority and a force of resistance too'. See *Detective Fiction and the Rise of Forensic Science* (Cambridge: Cambridge University Press, 1999).

and economic conditions of its time. Not every crime story will be amenable to this kind of analysis. Those resolutely focused on disruptions to the ordered surfaces of the domestic realm tend to feature less prominently than those which trace and interrogate the complex workings of power in the public *and* private domains. I suspect that those who see the crime story solely as a form of popular entertainment will bridle at the claims of my book and its preoccupation with the political underpinnings of the crime story. I do not dispute that crime fiction is a form of popular writing that in part operates according to long-established codes and archetypes, e.g. detective and criminal. But it is precisely by unsettling and moving beyond these archetypes and the assumptions that underpin them that the crime story—the crime story under investigation here—assumes its exemplary form. For example, by moving beyond an individualist focus on detective and criminal to provide what David Schmid calls 'politically-engaged critiques of capitalist, racist and patriarchal spatializations of power',[9] this kind of crime fiction cannot help but explore how individual action is always socially and economically situated. And precisely because of their engagement with the complex workings of power, these stories necessarily move beyond straightforward accounts of sovereignty, i.e. as the legal expression of the state's authority. Even as the genre establishes the state's legitimacy and exceptionality, it also shows how intimately this authority is intertwined with capital and the logic of the productive forces, how sovereignty is as much about projection or performance as it is about power, or indeed how the state, as Gramsci implies, must encompass not just the realm of politics and government but also of civil society as well.[10]

The ongoing transfer of public power to private interests might reach a crescendo in the contemporary era but even here the passage between sovereignty and what we might call 'neoliberalism' is never straightforward and draws attention to the inadequacy of both in what Lauren Berlant calls 'world-homogenizing' systems 'with coherent intentions' that in turn produce 'subjects' who serve their interests[11] (see Chapter 7). In any case, as the rest of the book demonstrates, the intertwining of public and private interests, of state institutions and commercial businesses, has a long and complicated history: Jonathan Wild's role as thief-taker in early eighteenth-century London, and his self-conscious usurping of a policing mandate for personal enrichment, is an early example of this move (see Chapter 1).

THIS IS NOT A HISTORY

It is perhaps easier to say what this book is not, than to set out exactly what it is. For a start, this is not an authoritative and comprehensive history of crime fiction:

[9] David Schmid, 'Imagining Safe Urban Space: The Contribution of Detective Fiction to Radical Geography', *Antipode*, 27:3 (1995), p. 243.
[10] Antonio Gramsci famously asserted: 'the state = political society + civil society'. See *Selections from the Prison Notebooks of Antonio Gramsci*, ed. Quintin Hoare and Geoffrey Nowell-Smith (London: Lawrence & Wishart, 1971), p. 263.
[11] Lauren Berlant, *Cruel Optimism* (Durham, NC and London: Duke University Press, 2011), p. 15.

a seamless narrative that explains how the different stories we understand as crime fiction link together and move from a single point of origin to the multiplication of the genre in the twentieth century. Such works do exist. Stephen Knight's *Crime Fiction 1800–2000* (2004) offers the best narrative history of the Anglo-American tradition, while Lee Horsley's (2005) *Twentieth-Century Crime Fiction* is the most incisive account of the diversity of the genre in what she calls the long twentieth century.

Instead, the book's foundational claim—that the emergence of crime fiction is linked to consolidation of the modern state—produces its own historical framework. All points of origin are to some extent arbitrary but there are good reasons for tracing the crime story, with its ties to the state, back to, say, the Treaty of Westphalia (1648) and the establishment of the modern state system or to the publication of Thomas Hobbes's *Leviathan* (1653) and certainly to the stories of crime and punishment that were regularly circulated in London and Paris from the late seventeenth century onwards. My own decision to start the book in London and Paris in the 1720s is not without foundation because, as I show in Chapter 1, this is the moment when writers like Daniel Defoe began to approach for the first time the subject of crime and punishment in a self-conscious manner. In other words, they demonstrated an awareness of the tensions between the right and need to punish, and inadequacies and failures of the bodies charged with this task—and hence, as Mary Evans outlines in her book *The Imagination of Evil: Detective Fiction in the Modern World* (2009), the complex 'relationship of morality to the law'.[12] This is not to suggest that Defoe and others ever identified themselves as crime writers or at least as writers working according to a set of predetermined formal and thematic patterns. Rather it is to argue that their engagement with the subject of crime and the law's response to crime gradually and perhaps organically established literary conventions that would over time come to characterize what we now understand as crime fiction (i.e. a popular genre with a self-consciously ambivalent stance towards the exercising of state power and the subtle intertwining of public office and private enterprise).

This is not a history of crime fiction, then, but it does have a historical chronology: it offers an account of crime writing's transformation into what Peter Messent calls 'an ongoing serial enquiry into the state of the nation, its power structures and its social concerns'[13] at various junctures in this process. Rather than providing a coherent and comprehensive account of this transformation, my aim is to build on excellent work already undertaken by Maurizio Ascari, Martin Kayman, and Charles Rzepka to disrupt the typical narrative of the genre's origins and development, i.e. moving seamlessly from Poe to Doyle to Christie, as though the genre, to quote Paul Cobley, is to be seen as 'a gift of its "brand leaders"'.[14] Kayman, for

[12] Mary Evans, *The Imagination of Evil: Detective Fiction and the Modern World* (London and New York, NY: Continuum, 2009), p. 2.
[13] Peter Messent, 'The Police Novel', in Charles J. Rzepka and Lee Horsley (eds) *A Companion to Crime Fiction* (Oxford and Malden, MA: Wiley-Blackwell, 2010), p. 178.
[14] Paul Cobley, *The American Thriller: Generic Innovation and Social Change in the 1970s* (Basingstoke: Palgrave Macmillan, 2000), p. 55.

example, is rightly suspicious of 'a retrospective theory which situates every event in its appropriate place in an orderly and totalizing narrative... [and] which presents Conan Doyle as the model of the genre and in consequence treats earlier writing as a simple anticipation of his "classic"'.[15]

As I argue in Chapter 4, the centrality of Doyle to a particular account of crime fiction would take the genre, at least in England, down something of a political dead end: the Sherlock Holmes stories secure, rather than unsettle, the public/private dichotomy, and therefore the assumption that the free market, with small adjustments by Holmes, is capable of creating a fair society *without* the intervention of the official police and that the police play a neural, if slightly incompetent role in the ongoing quest for public order. Rather than putting Doyle at the centre of a familiar story of the genre's panoptic capacities, my approach here is more closely aligned to what Foucault calls a 'genealogy': not the 'flow of causally connected events, each of which has a discrete significance and forms part of an overall pattern or meaning of history' but a 'method of analysis which traces the uneven and haphazard process of dispersion, accumulation and overlapping that are constitutive of the event'.[16]

What links Dashiell Hammett's Personville of the 1920s, Eugène-François Vidocq's Paris of the 1820s, and Defoe's London of the 1720s is a desire to assimilate complex, ambivalent critiques of state power, and society as it is organized under capitalism, into narratives which imaginatively weigh up the competing and overlapping claims of the individual, morality, community, justice, and the law. The point is not to diminish the radically different contexts and stages of development which in turn produce narratives that are as distinctive from one another as they are similar. Rather it is to draw attention to the multiple influences and constituent parts and indeed elasticity of the form, something that encourages variety and allows writers to inflect their narratives in different ways and in relation to different political ends and different historical contexts.

If one point of departure for this book is the efforts of writers like Defoe to self-consciously think about crime and punishment as a way of reflecting upon the claims of morality, justice, and the law, another is the instrumentalizing of policing away from 'the art of managing life and the well-being of populations' towards the more specific goal of preventing disorder, which Foucault sees as symptomatic of the modern era.[17] This, in turn, meant that the functioning of the institutions responsible for policing, in this narrower sense, became, arguably for the first time, a subject for wider discussion. For Foucault such a move produces a more standardized crime literature: the complex articulations of, and struggles between, narratives of popular rebellion and official power yielding, at some point in the

[15] Martin A. Kayman, *From Bow Street to Baker Street: Mystery, Detection and Narrative* (Basingstoke: Macmillan, 1992), p. 3. Also see Maurizio Ascari, *A Counter-History of Crime Fiction: Supernatural, Gothic, Sensational* (Basingstoke: Palgrave Macmillan, 2007) and Charles Rzepka, *Detective Fiction* (Cambridge: Polity, 2005).
[16] Foucault, 'Nietzsche, Genealogy, History', in Paul Rabinow (ed.) *The Foucault Reader* (New York, NY: Penguin, 1991), pp. 88, 89.
[17] Foucault, *Security, Territory, Population: Lectures at the Collège de France 1977–1978*, ed. Michel Senallart, trans. Graham Burchell (Basingstoke: Palgrave Macmillan, 2007), p. 354.

nineteenth century, to a less fractious, more mannered form, exhibiting the disciplinary tendencies of society and culture more generally.[18]

Foucault's influence on the study of crime fiction has been significant and has produced a body of work that has tended to problematically characterize the crime story as 'too singular and monolithic an ideological force'.[19] My aim is to bring to bear Foucault's more nuanced and interesting assessment of Vidocq's *Memoirs*—'the direct, institutional coupling of police and delinquency...the disturbing moment when criminality became one of the mechanisms of power'[20]—on other examples of the genre, and to focus on those crime stories which do indeed unsettle the distinction between policing and criminality and require us to think about the rootedness of both in the same socio-economic reality. In a larger sense, while Foucault's insistence upon studying power 'outside the field delineated by judicial sovereignty and the institution of the State'[21] may limit his usefulness to a study which seeks to do precisely what he cautions against, my attempt to explore the complex intersections between the state and capitalism permits a reading of power where, as Antonio Negri puts it, 'government is unified in the will of capital' and where 'the unity of power is diluted'—i.e. where Foucauldian and Marxist accounts of the operations of power and the implications for subjects or citizens are perhaps not as far apart as some might think.[22]

CRIME FICTION AS WORLD LITERATURE

When staking out the territory for a critical account of crime fiction's development over a three hundred year period, the general problem of historical teleology and the specific one of imposing an overly-schematic reading upon the genre (e.g. eighteenth-century, subversive; nineteenth-century, conservative) are both exacerbated by a tendency to draw conclusions from a limited corpus of self-selecting crime fiction 'classics' (e.g. Poe, Doyle, etc.). In this sense, the genre's inherent complexities, its capacities for confronting and buttressing power, can only be fully appreciated if it is grasped as a trans-Atlantic circuit connecting Britain, the United States and continental Europe, primarily France.[23] A narrow Anglo-American frame, especially one that insists upon pursuing the development from 'classic'

---

[18] Foucault, *Discipline and Punish*, pp. 68–9.
[19] Thomas, *Detective Fiction and the Rise of Forensic Science*, p. 14.
[20] Foucault, *Discipline and Punish*, p. 283.
[21] Foucault, *Society Must be Defended: Lectures at the Collège de France, 1975–76*, trans. David Macey (London: Penguin, 2004), p. 34.
[22] In looking for areas of commonality as well as difference between Marx and Foucault, Negri also states: 'it is possible to assume that Marx's concept of capital, especially when if in its historical development from "manufacture" to "large scale industry", from "social capital" to "financial capitalism", is strictly connected to the concept of power that Foucault defined as the result of a relation of forces'. See Antonio Negri, 'A Marxist Experience of Foucault', trans. Arianne Bove, http://www.generationonline.org/p/fp_negri25.htm, accessed 18 August 2015.
[23] Pim Higginson, for example, makes the excellent point that, following Poe, 'the genre follows a circuit connecting the United States, Great Britain and France'. See 'Mayhem at the Crossroads: Francophone African Fiction and the Rise of the Crime Novel', *Yale French Studies*, 108 (2005), p. 162.

writers like Poe and Doyle to hard-boiled writers like Hammett and Raymond Chandler, produces an inadequate, lop-sided understanding of the ways in which the genre has challenged social and political norms: what Horsley describes as 'existing social and racial hierarchies, the assumed power structure, establishment values'.[24]

An expanded historical and geographical frame puts to the sword some of the lazier critical orthodoxies that have coalesced around the genre and that have proved surprisingly hard to dislodge. Just as the notion that Poe immaculately conceived the crime story with the publication in 1841 of 'The Murders in the Rue Morgue' will not do, the idea that the genre's development can be described in terms of a move from the 'classical' crime story of the nineteenth century (characterized as 'conservative') to the 'radical' hard-boiled crime novel of the twentieth century falls apart if a wider historical and geographical lens is deployed.[25] John Gay's account in *The Beggar's Opera* (1728) of the interpenetration of business and policing is just as far-reaching as Bertolt Brecht's in *The Threepenny Opera* (1928), hardly a surprise given that Brecht used Gay's play as his source material; Arthur Morrison's short story 'The Affair of the Avalanche Bicycle and Tyre Co., Limited' (1897) offers in many ways a more pointed and bleaker assessment of the effects of finance capital than Dashiell Hammett's *The Maltese Falcon* (1930); William Godwin's condemnation of state violence in *Caleb Williams* (1794) is as forceful as Chester Himes's in *The Heat's On* (1966); the account of the absurdity of reason is as developed in Marcel Allain and Pierre Souvestre's *Fantômas* (1911) as in Friedrich Dürrenmatt's *The Pledge* (1958) and Vidocq's thematization of bureaucratic intransigence and the limits of political reform in *Memoirs* (1828) looks ahead to the treatment of these same subjects in the police novels of Maj Sjöwall and Per Wahlöö.

There are dangers of course in seeking to make connections between writers and national traditions across time and space, and in a book that sets out to explore the genre's inherent transnationality over a three hundred year period it is inevitable that much of the valuable contextualization carried out by studies of particular writers or periods or national traditions will be lost. Still my overarching claim remains a pressing one: i.e. that the crime story has a much richer, longer, and more radical lineage that some critics are prepared to cede.

At stake here is the very real issue of the genre's intrinsic transnationality. As such, a focus just on the relationship between English and American archetypes overlooks the extent to which the production and circulation of crime fiction has always been a transnational phenomenon. For example, the coincidental but synonymous

[24] Lee Horsley, *Twentieth-Century Crime Fiction* (Oxford: Oxford University Press, 2005), p. 102.
[25] The critical move to address the first problem has been successfully negotiated by studies such as Kayman's *From Bow Street to Baker Street* (1992), Knight's *Crime Fiction 1800–2000* (2004), and Ascari's *A Counter-History of Crime Fiction* (2007). But the tendency to see US hard-boiled crime writing as a moment of rupture in the genre's emergence has weakened otherwise excellent books such as Christopher Breu's *Hard-Boiled Masculinities* (2005) and Sean McCann's *Gumshoe America* (2000). Studies that successfully, and rightly in my opinion, resist this temptation include Knight's *Crime Fiction 1800–2000* (2004) and Clare Clarke's *Late Victorian Crime Fiction in the Shadows of Sherlock* (2014).

rise and fall of Wild in London and Louis-Dominique Cartouche in Paris was simultaneously documented by Daniel Defoe; Godwin's *Caleb Williams* was, in part, a response to continental debates about penal reform; Vidocq's *Memoirs* were simultaneously translated into English and circulated in London, influencing writers on both sides of the Channel; Poe read Vidocq, Emile Gaboriau read Poe, and Doyle read Gaboriau; Simenon and Hammett read each other's work and both were championed by André Gide; Brecht and Walter Benjamin, avid readers of crime fiction, admired Simenon's early crime novels; Himes only wrote his Harlem crime stories once he emigrated to France and only then at the urging of his Parisian editor; and works by Jean-Patrick Manchette, Sjöwall and Wahlöö, and David Peace owe a debt to Hammett. Despite this reality, the critical tendency has been to overlook connections between Anglo-American crime fiction and other national crime fiction traditions, especially in continental Europe.[26] As Claire Gorrara astutely notes: 'European crime fiction in languages other than English has received relatively little critical attention in the Anglophone critical world', and that most companions to crime fiction

> tend either to treat European crime fiction as an umbrella term, providing short generalized surveys of different national traditions, or to view the whole notion of crime writing traditions outside the 'big two' of Britain and America as minor tributaries whose interest derives mainly from a select group of iconic figures.[27]

The most useful intervention in this emerging field of study, to explore the international dimensions of crime fiction, both historically and as a contemporary phenomenon, has come from Stewart King and it is worth pausing on his (2014) essay 'Crime Fiction as World Literature' for a moment to think over his main claims. King points to the growing number of works exploring the emergence and significance of 'nonmainstream' and 'non-Anglophone' crime fiction but insists that 'these studies have not been able to break the monopoly of the Anglo-American canon'.[28] More pointedly, King claims that these works, which ostensibly want to break up this monopoly, in fact 'contribute to their own marginalization in crime fiction criticism by tending to limit their object of analysis to specific national or regional literary tradition'.[29] Instead, he proposes 'we read crime fiction as an example of world literature to gain greater insights into the global reach of the genre' or at the very least to explore 'international connections between works'.[30] Usefully too King marshals arguments made by David Damrosch's *What is World Literature* (2003) in order to limit the potential field of study: not simply every crime novel published anywhere in the world but those works that 'circulate

---

[26] This point is made very well by Vincenzo Ruggiero in a review of Martin Priestman's edited collection, *The Cambridge Companion to Crime Fiction*. See Vincenzo Ruggiero, 'Review of *The Cambridge Companion to Crime Fiction*', *Modernism/modernity*, 11:4 (November 2004), pp. 851–3.

[27] Claire Gorrara, 'Introduction', in Gorrara (ed.) *French Crime Fiction* (Cardiff: University of Wales Press, 2009), p. 2.

[28] Stewart King, 'Crime Fiction as World Literature', *Clues: A Journal of Detection*, 32:2 (Fall 2014), p. 9.

[29] King, 'Crime Fiction as World Literature', p. 9.

[30] King, 'Crime Fiction as World Literature', p. 10.

beyond their culture of origin' and make direct interventions in literary systems and cultures 'beyond that of [their] original culture'.[31] King's insights are so useful for my own study for a number of reasons: they draw attention to the need to dislodge the Anglo-American tradition from its typically dominant position in most accounts of the genre's development; they argue for the opening up of this account to other, non-Anglophone crime fiction traditions; and they encourage comparative and transnational studies of the crime novel's production, circulation, and reception within and across national boundaries. If there is something disappointingly 'first world' about my focus here on works produced in England, the United States, and continental Europe, I am happy to accept the resultant criticisms and claim this book as a small step in the direction that King rightly urges us to go.

There are obvious impediments to this kind of move, notably the thorny question of linguistic difference, and in terms of the international circulation of crime fiction criticism in English, I am indebted to colleagues in French studies such as Gorrara, Margaret Atack, David Platten, and Dominique Jeannerod who have written about French crime fiction in English; or Dominique Kalifa whose work has been translated into English, and to critics in Italian and Scandinavian studies (e.g. Barbara Pezzotti and Andrew Nestingen) who similarly develop their critiques of Italian and Swedish crime fiction traditions in English. Another impediment has been the unavailability of translated crime novels, but the success of publishing imprints like Europa and Bitter Lemon in translating and circulating French and Italian crime fiction in the UK and the US and the phenomenal popularity of Scandinavian crime fiction internationally (following Henning Mankell and of course Stieg Larsson) has prompted much greater critical reflection on categories like international or global crime fiction and on the historical roots of the genre's transnational circulations.[32]

My book is part of this new critical move to map and interrogate the historical roots of crime fiction's transnationality, initially focusing on France and England and then on links between continental Europe and the US, and finally on this transnationality in an era of globalization. To even attempt this kind of work, I am indebted to the excellent translations of the French, Italian, Swedish, German, and Japanese crime novels on which I have offered assessments. This, of course, raises other, thornier issues related to translation in general—i.e. the appropriateness of using translated texts in the first place. One approach here would be to emphasize

---

[31] King, 'Crime Fiction as World Literature', p. 9.
[32] New studies exploring the international or global dimensions of the contemporary genre include Marieke Krajenbrink and Kate Quinn (eds), *Investigating Identities: Questions of Identity in Contemporary International Crime Fiction* (Amsterdam: Rodopi, 2009) and Christine Matzke and Susanne Mühleiser, *Postcolonial Perspectives: Crime Fiction from a Transcultural Perspective* (Amsterdam: Rodopi, 2006). It should be noted that scholars in French studies have been quicker to appreciate these transnational dimensions than their Anglophone counterparts. See, for example, Higginson, *The Noir Atlantic: Chester Himes and the Birth of the Francophile Crime Novel* (Liverpool: Liverpool University Press, 2011); Alasdair Rolls and Deborah Walker, *French and American Noir: Dark Crossings* (Basingstoke: Palgrave Macmillan, 2009); Jonathan Eburne, *Surrealism and the Art of Crime* (Ithaca, NY and London: Cornell University Press, 2008).

what is lost in translation. Or, to put this another way, since I cannot provide my own translations, and since the translations provided by, among others, Donald Nicholson-Smith, Lawrence Venuti, and others are so successful on their own terms, all I can do is acknowledge that I am not basing my analysis solely on the original work but a hybrid creation of novelist and translator—and that something essential is lost in the translation and circulation of the original work in another language.

Another approach, following Damrosch's *What is World Literature*, is to point out what is gained by translation: the reinvigoration of formerly discrete national literatures as they are brought into contact with counterparts from elsewhere so that literature, or for the purposes of this book, crime fiction 'not only survives in translation but gains new meanings and relevance every time it crosses geographical, cultural, and linguistic borders'.[33] If my own approach favours the latter over the former, I am wary about wholeheartedly embracing Franco Moretti's concept of 'the global atlas of the novel' as a 'complex, centreless map in which difference reigns'.[34] The point is not to deny or overlook national particularities, local contexts, and historical framing or indeed to see the transnational as what Berlant calls a 'world-homogenizing' system 'whose forces are played out to the same effect, or affect, everywhere'.[35] Rather it is to combine a sustained focus on individual texts and their particular local and national contexts with a broader, comparative approach that explores the ways in which the translation, circulation, and reception of crime fiction in, and between, Britain and France in the first instance, then including the US and continental Europe, and finally incorporating the globe, produces a richer, more complex and indeed nuanced portrait of the genre than would be possible if one just focused on, let's say, British or French or American crime fiction as a discrete entity; or worse still excluded works by crime writers from France, Ireland, Italy, Sweden, Switzerland, and Japan altogether.[36]

Drilling down into the detail, producing this kind of portrait of the genre, or particular examples of the genre, requires more than simply looking at crime stories by US, British, French, and Italian authors in separation from one another. Perhaps the designation of 'crime fiction as world literature', as set out by King, or 'the global atlas of the novel'[37] as used by Moretti, is too broad for my purposes, at least insofar as my field of study is for two-thirds of the book limited to French, English, and to a lesser extent American examples. Nonetheless as a method or an approach, which requires or presupposes the circulation and translation of ideas,

[33] Karen-Margrethe Simonsen and Jakob Stougaard-Nielsen (eds), *World Literature, World Culture: History, Theory, Analysis* (Aarhus, DNK: Aarhus University Press, 2008), p. 15. Also see David Damrosch, *What is World Literature?* (Princeton, NJ and London: Princeton University Press, 2003); Pascale Casanova, *The World Republic of Letters*, trans. M.B. DeBevoise (Cambridge, MA: Harvard University Press, 2004).

[34] Simonsen and Stougaard-Nielsen (eds), *World Literature, World Culture*, p. 11.

[35] Berlant, *Cruel Optimism*, p. 9.

[36] This approach broadly dovetails with Damrosch's preference for 'close' as opposed to what Moretti calls 'distant' reading: described by Simonsen and Stougaard-Nielsen as 'a reading of world literature through the study of heterogeneously combined microcanons' (see *World Literature, World Culture*, p. 13).

[37] Franco Moretti, 'Conjectures on World literature', *New Left Review*, 1 (2000), pp. 55–68.

themes, and concerns about crime and policing across and between national traditions, while trying to pay due attention to specific sociocultural and institutional contexts, it speaks very well to my intention here: a thoroughgoing, sustained, *comparative* analysis, whereby the preoccupations of crime novelists from different national traditions are brought to bear on each other, in the hope of arriving at synthesized positions. For example, in Chapter 5, the move to consider Hammett, typically viewed as a leftist radical, in light of Simenon, often perceived as a social conservative, and vice versa, and both in light of the consolidation and transformation of the state and capitalism in the first three decades of the twentieth century, produces a more nuanced and entangled understanding—formally *and* politically—of both writers and their works, and indeed of the national traditions they belong to and emerge out of.

THE POLITICS OF CRIME

All of the figures addressed in this book, whatever their nationality, could be considered to be political crime writers—and this ambition or preoccupation, in turn, gives dramatic shape and structure to their work, albeit not in a uniform or prescriptive manner. By political, I do not mean that their work propagandizes for any particular cause or that they necessarily espouse a left or right political orthodoxy. Nor even should we think of the crime writers examined in the book as politically 'committed', though many are exactly this; committed to confronting the injustices of state power; committed to revealing the exploitation of capitalism; committed to furthering social and economic equality or simply revealing what is rotten in the society they belong to.[38] For as I have already argued, the anger that such commitment produces must, and is, weighed up against a realization, typically from an insider's perspective, that the state cannot simply be dismantled and that the law performs a necessary and fundamentally important social function. Moreover, despite this political commitment, where and when it is expressed, there is no expectation or indeed hope, in most works considered, that it will directly affect social or political change, i.e. that its effects will be so explicitly felt. As Jacques Rancière nicely puts it, 'literature...does not perform political action, it does not creative collective forms of action, it contributes to the reframing of forms of experience'.[39]

In terms of the crime novel, and indeed the political crime novel, one of the ways it reframes experience is to ask, though without any compunction to answer, some of the most pressing questions about the character of society (i.e. of individual and collective existence) as it is governed by the state and organized under

---

[38] While right-wing crime novelists are by no means unheard of—James Ellroy often describes himself as a Tory for example, even if his work demonstrates the corrosive effects of capitalist business practices—the majority of crime writers considered here, at least in the twentieth century, would identify with the left, albeit in complicated and often disaffected ways (see Chapter 6).

[39] Jacques Rancière, 'A Few Remarks on the Method of Jacques Rancière', *Parallax*, 15 (2009), p. 122.

capitalism. How is society ruled and for whose benefit? Is the justice system fair? Does the pursuit of self-interest lead to the betterment of society as a whole? What can the individual do in the face of injustice and exploitation? Can the needs of security and the desire for liberty ever be reconciled? Can crime ever be seen as a legitimate form of political protest? To what extent should we see the distinctive realms of crime, business, and politics as linked? If so, linked how? And what might the implications of this be?

If this runs the risk of making the crime novels themselves seem dull—or too concerned with the 'big' questions—it should be made clear that these preoccupations are not imposed on the novels from above, so to speak, but emerge organically from the unfolding of the plot and the unravelling of mystery. Dominique Manotti's claim about *Lorraine Connection* (2006)—that she 'wanted to make a novel about the links between factory and finance'[40]—is not plonked down on the narrative but is teased out via her intricate portrait of a strike at a Daewoo factory in eastern France and its implications both for those men and women caught up in the action and for the context of global corporate malpractice (see Chapter 7). Regarding terminology, I prefer crime fiction to detective fiction not because I agree with Ascari that the former is the more 'comprehensive' and in turn should be differentiated from the more 'conservative' subcategory or designation of detective fiction,[41] but in the sense that Kayman conjoins the terms: 'the links between modern detection and its corollaries are, to my mind, best established through the prior object that each presupposes, a *mystery*.'[42] If this brings us closer to Umberto Eco's account of the appeal or fascination of the crime novel as 'a kind of conjecture'—i.e. that 'the fundamental question of philosophy...is the same as the question of the detective novel: who is guilty?'[43]—my point is that the mystery to be unravelled in what I am calling political crime fiction is not simply the question of who is guilty, for sometimes we know this from the start or the question is irrelevant in plot terms, but more pertinently *what* is to blame: what has caused this problem called 'crime' in the first place? Why is justice such an elusive and even problematic concept? As such, the systemic is always privileged over the subjective: there may be a specific crime to solve or a problem to unravel, where a specific figure may be culpable; but the *mystery*, what keeps us reading, typically opens out to interrogate the nature of society itself, and of the systems—of state power and capitalism—which simultaneously envelop and govern us, and those in the stories, as subjects.

Of course not all crime fiction is interested in pursuing this kind of expansive and politicized line of enquiry and my decisions about what to include and what to exclude are based on how incisively and persuasively the novels speak to, and

---

[40] Dominique Manotti qtd in Anissa Belhadjin, 'From Politics to Roman Noir', *South Central Review*, 27:1&2 (Spring, Summer 2010), p. 75.
[41] Ascari, *A Counter-History of Crime Fiction*, p. xiv.
[42] Kayman, *From Bow Street to Baker Street*, p. 4.
[43] Umberto Eco, *Postscript to The Name of the Rose*, trans. William Weaver (New York, NY: Harcourt, 1984), p. 54.

about, this question of who and what is to blame.[44] There may be notable absences, and eyebrow-raising inclusions, but since this is not seeking to be an authoritative history of the genre's development, there should be no need for me to justify my crime fiction corpus beyond this. Nor am I much interested in exhausted and banal debates about high and low, serious and popular, which seem to do nothing more than calcify the terms that are apparently being scrutinized. In another sense, of course, the choice of what to look at was determined by the structure and frame of the book itself: a genealogy of crime fiction's complex relationship with power, whereby comprehensiveness is sacrificed for specificity—i.e. this is not a comprehensive account of the genre's development from the 1720s to the contemporary, which in Foucault's terms aims to capture the 'essence of things' but rather a genealogy which traces 'the uneven and haphazard process' of the genre's emergence vis-à-vis 'particular stages of force'.[45] Hence my focus is on the consolidation of the justice system in the 1720s, reforms to the penal code before, during, and after the French Revolution, the rise of state bureaucracy in the nineteenth century, the ever closer interpenetration of government and capitalism in the 1920s and 1930s, the radical protests against the state and capitalism in the 1960s and 1970s, and the simultaneous intensification and waning of sovereignty in relation to the challenges of neoliberalism in the contemporary era.[46] The extent to which the crime stories I have chosen to look at are able to offer critical reflection on these processes (and their own historical moment of production) and on corresponding thematizations of power by political theorists, themselves responding to similar circumstances, constitutes one of the major jumping-off points for the book.

There are of course inevitable and necessary limits (i.e. temporal, geographical, and conceptual) to the scope and reach of my book. If my historical frame is quite expansive, this means I've had to think very carefully about how widely I can set my geographical lens, without losing or sacrificing all specificity, or rather the specificity that emerges from 'close reading'. While writers from Switzerland, Germany, Ireland, South Africa, Japan, and Italy are considered here, the touchstone for my developing account of crime fiction remains the 'big three' of France, England, and the United States. This of course runs the risk of replicating the problem of over-identifying crime fiction in general with the authors working in these same countries (even if it doesn't preclude the move to examine the circulation and translation of crime stories across national borders); but there are, of course, important historical precedents, tied to compelling questions of significance or value, that require or produce such a focus. As the genre becomes more and more international and transnational in the contemporary era, meanwhile, the move to push beyond the crime novels produced in France, the UK, continental Europe,

---

[44] I am not necessarily making a value judgement about the writers I have chosen to look at and those I have chosen to omit, i.e. that the former are somehow better, either in terms of style or the artfulness of their character studies or the excitement generated by their stories.

[45] Foucault, 'Nietzsche, Genealogy, History', pp. 89, 83.

[46] I couldn't find the space to include a chapter on the 1940s and 1950s which meant there was no place for crime writers such as Raymond Chandler, Patricia Highsmith, Jim Thompson, and Josephine Tey, whose work very much opens itself out to the central preoccupations of my book.

and the US will inevitably gather pace—something I wholeheartedly welcome. And—thinking about the conceptual frame of the book—while the gendered and racial implications of state and capitalist power relations, and of public and private spheres, are explored vis-à-vis specific writers (e.g. Braddon, Green, Himes, Orford, Beukes, Kirino, Manotti) mostly in the twentieth century, I would be the first to admit that much more work is needed than I have been able to manage here.[47]

THE STATE OF SOVEREIGNTY

My book's main concern—how crime fiction at different times and places and under different historical conditions negotiates and interrogates the complex relationship between capital and the state—requires a conceptual framework which draws upon a range of theories of the state and of the state's relationship to civil society. As the book unfolds, a debate between what we might call liberal and Marxist accounts of the state and of power emerges; but crucially it isn't one that is anachronistically and arbitrarily imposed on the novels themselves. Hence Hobbes and Mandeville are deployed to interrogate almost contemporaneous work by Defoe and Gay; Mill's elucidations on individual liberty shed important light on Conan Doyle's crime fiction; and Gramsci's claim that 'the state = political society + civil society'[48] allows us to see how deeply entwined public power and private enterprise, or the state and civil society, are for writers such as Hammett, Brecht, and even Simenon. What emerges on the one hand is, I hope, an account of modern liberalism as a variegated stream of competing and overlapping ideas, whereby the differences between, for example, Hobbes, Mandeville, Beccaria, Bentham, and Mill become as important as their commonalties. On the other hand, the Marxism I predominantly draw on owes less to Marx himself, though Marx's insights into civil society, the relative autonomy of the political classes, and the nature of fictitious capital, shed important light on certain aspects of the nineteenth-century crime story. Rather Engels's *The Condition of the Working Class in England* (1843), and contemporary works of Marxist historiography and criminology by E.P. Thompson and Peter Linebaugh that are informed by Engels's insights, are more helpful in showing how crime should be treated not as the product of individual deviancy but rather as a symptom of prevailing social and economic conditions—and that crime control is never a politically neutral activity.[49]

Yet we perhaps need to be careful about how we talk about the relationship between liberal and Marxist conceptions of the state (either as, to quote Weber's

---

[47] The best example of a critical study of the contemporary genre that has successfully brought together race, gender, sovereignty, and globalization into a single field of analysis is Robin Truth Goodman's excellent *Policing Narratives and the State of Terror* (Albany, NY: State University Press of New York, 2009).

[48] Gramsci, *Selections from the Prison Notebooks*, p. 263.

[49] See, especially, E.P. Thompson, *Whigs and Hunters: The Origin of the Black Act* (London: Allen Lane, 1975); Peter Linebaugh, *The London Hanged: Crime and Civil Society in the Eighteenth Century* (London: Verso, 2003); David Greenberg (ed.), *Crime and Capitalism: Readings in Marxist Criminology* (Palo Alto, CA: Mayfield, 1981).

seminal definition, 'a human community that [successfully] claims monopoly of the legitimate use of physical force within a given territory'[50] or, drawing on Marx's throwaway remark in *The Communist Manifesto*, as 'a committee for managing the affairs of the whole bourgeoisie'[51]) and sovereignty, typically understood as the legal expression of the state's authority within its territorial and jurisdictional limits. If the liberal state, as Wendy Brown points out, is 'necessarily legitimated through the language of sovereignty' so that sovereignty becomes the foundation of individual autonomy, and the state, as interpreted by Marx, is understood in terms of both bureaucratic consolidation and 'the organization of the social order by capital'[52] so that sovereignty and capitalism become hard to disaggregate as forces that determine and subjugate individual bodies, the crime stories under consideration here pose some difficult questions against both conceptions of sovereignty. To the former, they question what individual freedom means in the context of the massive consolidations of governmental power in the modern era and how far this power in fact limits, rather than produces, this freedom. To the latter, they ask whether or to what extent the effects of power, conceived of as impersonal and totalizing, are really so determining and if not what implications this has for our understanding of sovereignty. In both cases sovereignty as a kind of gleaming monolith, either to be defended or dismantled, begins to yield and we start to see its contingent, anxious, performative, dimensions—what Berlant calls 'a fantasy misrecognised as an objective state'.[53]

In the face of the messy, complicated, ambivalent, unruly lives of those tasked with upholding the law or those determined or compelled to transgress its authority, or those who do both, willingly or unwillingly, sovereignty becomes less about the projection of absolutes, or the overcoming of these absolutes, than a set of practices, some effective, others not, aimed at creating some degree of order.[54] Not un-coincidentally, as we will see, this is also the account of the everyday experiences of crime and policing that we find in many of the crime stories under consideration in this book.

As such, crime fiction performs more than a passive, illustrative role, e.g. illustrating Marxian or indeed liberal ideas, and stakes out its own intellectual and political positions, at times *contra* Mill, Hobbes, Marx, and others. To McCann's claim that the 'detective story has always been a liberal genre, centrally concerned with a fundamental premise of liberal theory—the rule of law—and with the tensions fundamental to democratic societies that constantly threw that principle into

---

[50] Max Weber, *From Max Weber: Essays in Sociology*, eds H.H. Gerth and C. Wright Mills (London: Routledge and Kegan Paul, 1985), p. 78.
[51] Karl Marx, *Essential Writings of Karl Marx* (St Petersburg, FL: Red and Black, 2010), p. 163.
[52] Wendy Brown, *States of Injury: Power and Freedom in Late Modernity* (Princeton, NJ: Princeton University Press, 1995), pp. 17, 16.
[53] Berlant, *Cruel Optimism*, p. 97.
[54] Brown argues that while 'the liberal state is necessarily legitimated through the language of sovereignty its primary function has never been sovereignty'. Rather, as I think I'm suggesting here and she puts it, 'the state rises in importance with liberalism precisely through its provision of essential social repairs, economic problem solving, and the management of a mass population' (see *States of Injury*, p. 17.

it',[55] the crime stories examined here, or at least most of them, would agree and disagree. Most strive again and again to delineate the procedural and juridical rules and norms by which the state seeks to govern, and to see the law, ideally, as an unqualified human good, a potential check on the interests of the powerful, while at the same time posing far-reaching questions about the interpenetration of public and private and the flimsiness of the state–civil society separation, moves that would undermine the very basis of liberalism's account, from Hobbes onwards, of the autonomy or separateness of the state. The idea that the state's justice system might be in hock to those with the deepest pockets, or that the laws of organized crime might also be the laws of capitalism, and vice versa, or even that crime might be 'viewed as a creative act of protest against oppression'[56] would steer these novels into Marxist territory; but at the same time a residual commitment to the rule of law and individual freedom, and an uneasiness about reducing the entire justice system to a claim about class power, would always make this affinity an awkward one.[57] Moreover, these crime stories, in whatever form, would never embrace the teleological certainty of classic Marxism, with its faith in the emancipatory potential of the downtrodden, and time and time again would find ways of reimposing the law and returning society to what it had been before, even if this ended up being an unremittingly bleak statement about the failure of individuals and institutions to reform the system for good from within or indeed via intervention from the outside.

If this account of the crime story's ambivalence in the face of different forms and modalities of power (institutional, economic, class, etc.), and its willingness to portray the political and economic realms as both autonomous and complicit, runs the risk of imposing a uniformity on the multiple and highly distinctive examples of what I am calling crime writing, one needs to remember a couple of things. First, I am *not* making a generalized claim about the genre as a whole; just those examples, as already stated, that explicitly situate their individual dramas in relation to larger questions about how society is ruled and about what crime means in this context. Second, insofar as we are talking about 'political' crime fiction where ambivalence, compromise, and at times failure are emphasized over individual heroism and uncomplicated struggles of good against evil, the stories considered here may not even be that popular, i.e. in the sense of attracting a large readership. Or indeed that their popularity owes itself to factors extrinsic to their political 'message': for example the bawdy humour, catchy songs, and the energetic debunking of officialdom in all of its guises made John Gay's *The Beggar's Opera* a runaway success when it was first staged in London in 1728 but

[55] McCann, *Gumshoe America*, p. 6.
[56] Greenberg, 'Crime and Revolution' in Greenberg (ed.), *Crime and Capitalism*, p. 414.
[57] Perhaps surprisingly the Marxist historian E.P. Thompson comes closest to articulating this ambivalence, stating about the justice system in eighteenth-century England: 'We reach, then, not a simple conclusion (law = class power) but a complex and contradictory one. On the one hand, it's true that the law did mediate existent class relations to the advantage of the rulers...On the other hand, the law mediated these class relations through legal forms, which imposed, again and again, inhibitions upon the actions of the rulers' (see *Whigs and Hunters*, p. 264).

its account of the interpenetration of law, crime, and business and of the individual's growing incorporation by resulting networks of power is unremittingly bleak (see Chapter 1).

Certainly the crime stories considered here do not always or often give us comforting, uncomplicated answers to the problems they raise. Finally, insofar as I am referring to a field of tension between different or opposing political polarities and arguments, rather than trying to impose some kind of generic straightjacket on different crime stories across time and space, such a formulation would allow us to consider examples with different formal characteristics and political sympathies. For example, Conan Doyle's Sherlock Holmes stories, with their sanctification of a J.S. Mill-derived celebration of individual liberty and the small or laissez-faire state and their accompanying formal logic, are set against, and operate in entirely different fashion from, the bleakness of Morrison's Dorrington stories and their Marxist denunciations of finance capitalism (see Chapter 4).

In his illuminating book *Philosophies of Crime Fiction* (2013), Josef Hoffman argues that the 'mutual influence of philosophy and crime fiction is manifold' and that this can be identified in terms of 'argumentation, themes, narrative styles or aesthetic reflections regarding literary form',[58] but while he does a good job of bringing particular philosophical approaches to bear on particular crime novels, we need to be careful about how far we are prepared to push this link. While philosophy or political philosophy is typically concerned with developing claims about power, truth, aesthetics, reality, and language based on reasoned argument, fiction, and in this case crime fiction, need not overly concern itself with such rigour; and indeed this can be a strength rather than a weakness, as Michael Cohen argues about *Caleb Williams*: 'In the novel, Godwin [who also wrote *Enquiry Concerning Political Justice*] confronts the genuine incompatibility of human experience in a way that his theoretical political treatise cannot.'[59]

The crime story may contradict itself, and may vulgarize or even debase complex political arguments, but its constitutive and foundational tension—based upon competing and indeed incompatible accounts of the law and the justice system—means that it is just as well suited as theory for the task of mapping the ambivalences of state power. More importantly, these stories show us the messy, contingent effects of this power on the lives of those caught up in its midst: typically sceptical representatives of the system and the perpetrators and victims of crime. Furthermore, insofar as the focus of the crime story—the crime story considered here—is always outward, always on the ways in which individual lives are shaped by the push and pull of larger social, political, and economic forces, always on the nature and adequacy of the justice system and on the reasons why crimes are committed, it remains the most politically minded of all the literary genres. It is from

---

[58] Josef Hoffman, *Philosophies of Crime Fiction*, trans. Carolyn Kelly, Nadia Majid, and Johanna da Rocha Abreu (Harpenden: No Exit Press, 2013), p. 11.

[59] Michael Cohen, 'Godwin's *Caleb Williams*: Showing the Strains in Detective Fiction', *Eighteenth-Century Fiction*, 10:2 (January 1998), p. 208.

this simple claim that *Unwilling Executioner* as a whole emerges: not necessarily that the crime story is an uncomplicated vehicle for radical social and political criticism, but that it is interested in the ways in which individuals try, and often fail, to seek out their own fates in the face of a conjunction of different modes or forms of power.

1
'A Life of Horrid and Inimitable Wickedness'
Crime, Law, and Punishment in Early Eighteenth-century London and Paris

All exact points of literary origin are arbitrary. The question of where and when a particular genre of literature first appeared has vexed and will continue to vex critics. Still, the central claim of this book—that the emergence of the crime story is bound up with the consolidation of the modern state—narrows the frame a little; i.e. sometime after the Treaty of Westphalia (1648) which established the modern state system, and Hobbes's *Leviathan* (1653) which theorized, arguably for the first time, what was distinctive about the authority of the modern state. If Martin Kayman is right, and I think he is, that *Leviathan* is where 'our story of modern crime and detection must begin',[1] my aim in this first chapter is to argue for the 1720s as the first significant moment in the early development of crime writing, and that these developments were equally centred in London and Paris. Tales of crime and punishment were commonplace in Britain and France from the late seventeenth century onwards but what makes London and Paris in the 1720s significant is the confluence of a number of related historical and cultural phenomena. For a start, capital crimes (i.e. crimes punished by public execution) significantly increased in this period. Pascal Bastien details how the Parliament of Paris issued 112 *arrêts criminels* (official accounts that offered a description of and justification for the judicial decisions reached) in the years 1721–30, compared with just five in the previous decade.[2] Meanwhile the historian Gerald Howson describes how 'a great wave of crime' gathered pace in the south of England, especially London, from about 1715 onwards and reached a climax in the early 1720s, and E.P. Thompson agrees: 'if that unsatisfactory term [i.e. crime wave] could ever be used with conviction, it might possibly be applied to the early 1720s.'[3]

The reasons for this crime wave are numerous and include endemic poverty, economic uncertainty, and official corruption, but by far the biggest factor in the explosion of capital crimes in Paris and London relates to the coincidental but

---
[1] Martin Kayman, *From Bow Street to Baker Street: Mystery, Detection and Narrative* (Basingstoke: Macmillan, 1992), p. 140.
[2] Pascal Bastien, 'Private Crimes and Public Executions: Discourses on Guilt in the *Arrêts Criminels* of the Eighteenth-Century Parliament of Paris' in Amy Gilman Srebnick and René Lévy (eds) *Crime and Culture: An Historical Perspective* (Aldershot and Burlington, VT: Ashgate, 2005), p. 146.
[3] E.P. Thompson, *Whigs and Hunters: The Origin of the Black Act* (London: Allen Lane, 1975), p. 196.

oddly symmetrical career paths of Jonathan Wild and Louis Dominique Cartouche. Rather than being individual opportunists, both men set up and controlled complex hierarchies of criminal operatives and spies, with themselves at the helm. Wild's network of spies and informers was thought to span much of the country while contemporary accounts estimated that, by the time of his capture, Cartouche's gang or troop numbered eight hundred.[4] The sheer scale and reach of these operations threatened the state's monopoly on policing (defined here in its broadest sense not as a distinctive institution but rather as a mode of government) and produced an orchestrated response on the part of the authorities to confront and dismantle these gangs. Cartouche's gang included soldiers and serving police officers, and owed its success to a scheme of systematic bribery whereby profits from robberies were used to pay off certain police officers. Wild, meanwhile, took advantage of a perceived vacuum in policing to set himself up as thief-taker—actually a scheme to gain advantage over rivals and those who crossed him by giving them up to the authorities—and played up this role to such effect that he was able to call himself, without too much exaggeration, Thief-Taker General of Great Britain. Still, despite the seeming freedom with which Wild and Cartouche were able to operate, it would be wrong to assume that both states' criminal justice systems were wholly bankrupt. Criminality may have been ubiquitous but the era was also marked by the presence of the scaffold: for Foucault, the most obvious marker of the spectacular power of the sovereign to punish by means of execution.[5]

The stage would be set for reflections on the majesty and omnipotence of the state and on its inadequacies and failure; and the fact that, in Wild's case at least, the head of the police was, as the historian Gerald Howson points out, 'the same man as the head of the underworld',[6] afforded essayists and writers even more opportunity to assess contradictions and tensions in the justice system. Indeed, the instrumentalizing of policing and justice away from 'the art of managing life and the well-being of populations' towards the more specific goal of preventing disorder, which Foucault argues is symptomatic of the era,[7] meant that the functioning of the institutions responsible for policing, in this narrower sense, became, arguably for the first time, a subject for wider discussion. Moreover the complex tangle between state power and private enterprise, characterized in terms of illicit or criminal organizations nonetheless established along the lines of government institutions, with their own hierarchies and systems, and mimicking the practices of legitimate business, provided additional scope to assess whether the state was a necessary force in the fight against criminal gangs or a corrupt institution wholly or partially in league with these same gangs. The state's response, exemplified in

---

[4] See Daniel Defoe, *The Life and Actions of Lewis Dominique Cartouche Who was broken Alive upon the WHEEL at PARIS Nov.28 1721 Relating at Large His Remarkable ADVENTURES, desperate ENTERPRIZES and various ESCAPES* (translated from the French) 2nd edn (London: J. Roberts, 1722), p. 8.

[5] Michel Foucault, *Discipline and Punish: The Birth of the Prison*, trans. Alan Sheridan (London: Penguin, 1991), pp. 47–50.

[6] Gerald Howson, *It Takes a Thief: The Life and Times of Jonathan Wild* (London: Cresset, 1987), p. 6.

[7] Foucault, *Security, Territory, Population: Lectures at the Collège de France 1977–1978*, ed. Michel Senallart, trans. Graham Burchell (Basingstoke: Palgrave Macmillan, 2007), p. 354.

Britain by the passage of the Black Act of 1724 which increased the number of capital crimes to more than three hundred and fifty, may have been intended to reassert the might and majesty of the sovereign. But to some writers, notably Gay, it underscored the extent to which the law serviced the rights of property[8] and at the same time opened up the chance for crime, arguably for the first time, to be seen as a form of primitive rebellion.

Given these activities and tensions, and given the richness of the source material, it is perhaps unsurprising that this period was also marked by a surge in interest on the part of writers and publishers of crime-related texts, notably, in Britain, the novelist Daniel Defoe, the essayist–philosopher Bernard de Mandeville, and the playwright John Gay; and, in France, the legal historian and former government insider Nicolas Delamare, whose four-volume *Traité de la police* (1705–38) showed how painstaking historical research into the activities and nature of policing could influence debates about how best to secure the streets of Paris.[9] The centrality of crime, punishment, and the law as subjects to early eighteenth-century writing in France and Britain is confirmed by contemporary research into the period. In French Studies, Sarah Maza's *Private Lives and Public Affairs* (1993) examines the significance of judicial memoirs and *causes célèbres* published in the pre-revolutionary era. In a British context, just as David Punter argues that 'eighteenth-century fiction is obsessed by the law'[10] and Thompson claims that 'the rhetoric of eighteenth-century England is saturated with notions of the law',[11] Hal Gladfelder points to 'the virtual inescapability of popular discourses of criminality in eighteenth-century England'.[12] Ian Bell, meanwhile, agrees that eighteenth-century literature 'is suffused with crime' but makes the useful point that 'it handles [this material] in a wholly different way from that of the twentieth'.[13] Arguably Bell overstates this distinction and part of what my book is seeking to do is reconnect crime writing of the nineteenth and twentieth centuries with its eighteenth-century antecedents, but it is true that most writing about crime in the 1720s was not confined 'to a single generic or conventional form, designed for a particular audience'.[14]

It may be too early, then, to talk about crime writing as a dedicated literary genre with its own conventions and readily identifiable audience, but the criminal

---

[8] As Thompson argues, the Black Act both reiterated the primacy of the 'Bloody Code' and the scaffold as the key weapon in the state's disciplinary arsenal and demonstrated the extent to which the rule of law confirmed and consolidated class power (*Whigs and Hunters*, p. 259).

[9] Foucault sees the scope and range of Delamare's vision of 'policing' as an instance of a more general concern for 'managing populations' rather than part of a trend from the eighteenth century onwards that identified policing simply with eliminating disorder. See *Security, Territory, Population*, pp. 333–5.

[10] David Punter, 'Fictional Representations of Law in the Eighteenth Century', *Eighteenth-Century Studies*, 16 (1982–3), p. 47.

[11] Thompson, *Whigs and Hunters*, p. 263.

[12] Hal Gladfelder, *Criminality and Narrative in Eighteenth-Century England* (Baltimore, MD and London: The Johns Hopkins University Press, 2001), p. xi.

[13] Ian A. Bell, 'Eighteenth-century Crime Writing', in Martin Priestman (ed.) *The Cambridge Companion to Crime Fiction* (Cambridge: Cambridge University Press, 2003), p. 7.

[14] Bell, 'Eighteenth-century Crime Writing', p. 8.

biographies, *mémoires judiciaries* (judicial memoirs), gallows pamphlets, and criminal court judgements (*arrêts criminels*) published in the early eighteenth century establish what would become one of the defining characteristics of crime writing as it developed later in the nineteenth and twentieth centuries: an ambivalent account of the state and its legal apparatus, both as institutional forms and as 'particular rules and sanctions which stand in a definite and active relationship...to social norms'.[15] In making these arguments, my theoretical touchstones are the political philosophy of Hobbes and Mandeville and more recent work carried out on eighteenth-century crime and punishment by Marxist historians like Thompson and Peter Linebaugh.[16]

In arguing for an affinity between dense theoretical treatises and/or politically inflected histories and what might on first reflection seem slight tales of criminality, it is not the case that the latter are necessarily replicating the complexities of the formers' arguments. Some—like Defoe's account of Wild's life, or the 1722 translation of *The Life and Actions of Dominique Cartouche* (accredited to him), and Gay's *The Beggar's Opera*—do demonstrate genuine political and aesthetic sophistication while others, such as the gallows pamphlets that J.M. Beattie argues were in Britain 'published regularly from the 1670s'[17] instinctively and maybe naively groped towards political insight. Others still, like the *arrêts criminels* published by the Parliament of Paris and *causes célèbres* like François Gayot de Pitival's *A Select Collection of Singular and Interesting Histories* (1734, trans. 1744) offered interesting, sometimes quite self-aware, reflections of the relationship between legal and literary frames. In all cases the texts apprehend and condense incipient anxieties in early eighteenth-century British and French societies relating the efficacy of the law and the reach and authority of the state. What marks the 1720s as being significant in the early development of the crime story is that it is the first moment when writers such as Defoe and Gay began to address the subject of crime and punishment in a deliberately and identifiably self-conscious manner: i.e. that an awareness of the tension between the right and need to punish and the inadequacies of those bodies charged with this task is deliberately written into the work itself.

One of the central claims of my book as a whole is that the development of the crime fiction genre throughout the eighteenth and nineteenth centuries should be understood in the context of an emerging debate between what might tentatively be characterized as liberal and Marxist accounts of state power and the relationship between the state and civil society. It is not difficult to see how, in crude terms, the aforementioned tension might map onto this schema; i.e. the disinterested omnipotent state acting as neutral umpire might correspond with an illiberal liberalism originating with Hobbes and the state as perpetrating entrenched social and economic inequalities might correspond with what we now recognize as a Marxist position. Still, all kinds of caveats and qualifications need to be made before such

---

[15] Thompson, *Whigs and Hunters*, p. 260.
[16] See especially Douglas Hay, Peter Linebaugh and E.P. Thompson (eds) *Albion's Fatal Tree: Crime and Society in Eighteenth-Century England* (London: Allen Lane, 1975).
[17] J.M. Beattie, *Policing and Punishment in London, 1650–1750: Urban Crime and the Limits of Terror* (Oxford: Oxford University Press, 2004), p. 59.

an assertion can be sanctioned. For a start, liberalism is an extremely broad variegated tradition and hence very difficult to reduce to a handful of key thinkers and ideas. Hobbes's account of the state in *Leviathan* may establish its neutral, disinterested status and hence provide a frame or basis for later thinkers such as Bentham to develop a more focused reading of bureaucratic rationality; and Hobbes's claims that the state establishes the conditions for civil society to exist presupposes the kind of state–civil society distinction which would be developed by theorists of individual liberty like J.S. Mill.

That said, there is much that separates Hobbes's account of the asymmetrical relationship between sovereign and individual (who willingly gives up some of their liberty in exchange for their security) from Mill's denunciation of state intrusion into the private lives of its citizens and from Mandeville's claims about the social utility of greed as a necessary means of ensuring social stability. My use of Hobbes and Mandeville to interrogate this new writing about crime, and indeed vice versa, implicitly draws attention to the multiple interpretations of liberalism that were already in circulation in the early 1800s. My use of Marx, meanwhile, owes as much to the work of Marxist historians of the eighteenth century like Thompson and Linebaugh as to Marx, especially in the way these figures have used Marx's insights into land enclosure and primitive rebellion to illuminate the relationship between criminality and law: the idea that the state existed to preserve property and law was an instrument of the ruling class.[18] Still, while such claims are clearly incompatible with Hobbesian assertions about state neutrality, we should perhaps be careful about casting this division in absolutist terms. Just as an anxiety that some thinkers have read back into Hobbes's work draws attention to the state's precariousness and its illiberal, repressive capacities (thereby nudging it towards a Marxist account of state power), Marxist thinkers like Thompson are happy to admit that the notion of 'the rule of law' is 'an unqualified human good' even 'if the actuality of the law's operation in class-divided societies has, again and again, fallen short of its own rhetoric of equality'.[19] Crucially, writing about crime and punishment during this period, whether intentional or not, found useful ways of opening up and interrogating this tension; between an account of the state as omnipotent and transcendent and in its policing provision as piecemeal and impotent, and of the law as an inhibition on the arbitrary powers of the rich and mechanism for ensuring the reproduction of class inequalities.

HOBBES' *LEVIATHAN*, GALLOWS CONFESSIONS, *ARRÊTS CRIMINELS*, AND *MÉMOIRES JUDICIARIES*

Kayman may want to see *Leviathan* as 'where our story of crime and detection' must begin but he is careful not to read Hobbes's most famous work itself as a story of modern crime and detection. In other words, a move from the intolerable

---

[18] See Thompson, *Whigs and Hunters*, pp. 21, 259.
[19] Thompson, *Whigs and Hunters*, pp. 266, 267.

freedom of the state of nature characterized by its war of all against all to the security offered by the social contract is not necessarily analogous to the shift that takes place in most crime stories from the disorderly scene of criminal excess to the orderly scene of the law's eventual triumph. Rather, it is more helpful to think about how or to what extent these stories, even in their crudest formulations, end up responding to the threat of social anarchy by justifying a Hobbesian move from the state of nature into the social contract while at the same time hinting, intentionally or otherwise, at the inadequacies of the state's provisions for law enforcement when confronted by exactly the kind of excessive crime and lawlessness that a move into the social contract was intended to deter.

For Quentin Skinner, Hobbes is the quintessential theorist of the modern state because he is the first to properly characterize it as autonomous and above society. In its pre-modern incarnation, status (where the term state is derived from) is linked to the interests of charismatic rulers. Skinner describes the first move away from this pre-modern formulation as a Republican one and links it to thinkers like Machiavelli. The essence of the Republican case, he tells us, is that governmental authority is no longer linked to the power of individual rulers but is embedded in laws and institutions which these rulers, as proxies of the people, 'are entrusted to administer in the name of the common good'.[20] But this, Skinner reminds us, constitutes only one of two moves towards the establishment of what we now recognize as the modern state. We distinguish the state's authority from that of its rulers but, as Skinner maintains and as Hobbes shows us, 'we also distinguish its authority from that of the whole society...over which its powers are exercised'.[21] This lifting out of political authority so that it sits apart from and above both ruler and ruled, as Skinner argues, best expresses our modern concept of the state. The gallows speeches, judicial memoirs, and court judgements circulated before, during, and after state-sanctioned executions are best understood as depictions, accurate or otherwise, of the consequences of a move from the state of nature into the social contract. Crucially, though, what they seek to project is not the bleak conditions of existence experienced by those living in poverty and abjection (either inside or outside the social contract) but to all intents and purposes Hobbes's uniform, unassailable and, above all, impartial system of law and punishment in which capital crimes inevitably lead to the scaffold. Still, while it might be their intention to underscore the rightness of the judgement imposed on the condemned, even these tales end up betraying some anxieties about the fairness and adequacy of the justice system.

Meanwhile, the *arrêts criminels* and *mémoires judiciaires* produced in France from the early eighteen hundreds, as Biet, Bastien, and others have argued, drew attention to, often in quite sophisticated ways, the cut and thrust of legal claims and counterclaims and in so doing demystified the judicial process (in a way that ran counter to the obfuscating ambitions of the religious dignitaries). Certainly all

---

[20] Quentin Skinner, 'The State', in Terence Ball, James Farr, and Russell L. Hanson (eds), *Political Innovation and Conceptual Change* (Cambridge: Cambridge University Press, 1989), p. 108.
[21] Skinner, 'The State', p. 112.

these narratives demonstrated how seeming cut-and-dried legal treatises and factual biographies utilized the same rhetorical devices and linguistic registers as works of fiction. The result, Biet argues, was the emergence of a new type of writing 'which produces an intermediary fiction between judicial and literary fiction' and that shows 'how the same themes, narrative procedures and aesthetical systems are summoned in both judicial and literary contexts'.[22]

In his important study of the form and function of criminal biographies in late seventeenth- and early eighteenth-century England, Lincoln Faller notes how each account and individual figure was 'made to conform to a pre-existing type, as certain features of their lives was emphasized, played down or suppressed, and "facts" were often invented'.[23] The messy exigencies of individuals, often forced by circumstances into criminal acts, are exorcized from these tales. The crime itself is usually glossed over, as is the investigation and capture of the offender. Instead the narrator, often the Ordinary of Newgate (a clerical figure attached to Newgate prison where many of the condemned were held prior to execution) provides a brief account of the person's fall from grace, only obliquely allowing them to address readers in their own words. The point is not to dwell on the crime or even the trial and execution but to focus on the confession which tends to acknowledge the fairness of the sentence and asks for God's forgiveness. 'The Ordinary of Newgate's Account of the Behaviour, Confession and Last Dying Speech of Matthias Brinsden' (1722) is exemplary.[24] There is a very brief description of the crime—Brinsden, we are told, mortally wounded his wife by 'giving her (with a Knife of 7 inches in Length), a Wound under the left Pap'—and a perfunctory account of Brinsden's 'Savageness and Barbarity of Nature' and his un-Christian attitudes: that while waiting for his trial he 'never once appear'd at Prayers' and refused to throw himself 'on the Mercy of the Court'. Thereafter emphasis is placed on ceaseless and ultimately successful efforts of the Ordinary, Thomas Purney, to persuade Brinsden to see the error of his ways. In the end, the condemned kept 'constantly to Prayers' until 'Death was very acceptable to him' and his last act is to receive the sacrament.

In this instance, Brinsden's confession is framed and controlled by the Ordinary. Elsewhere malefactors are permitted to address the reader directly but only to underline the fairness and appropriateness of the state's action against them. In 'Memoirs of the Right Villainous John Hall, the Late Famous and Notorious Robber Penn'd from his own mouth' (1708), Hall acknowledges his failings and, underlining the link between narrative, morality, and power, warns the crowd waiting for his execution against following his example.

> I desire you all, good people, to pray for me: I confess I have been a very wicked offender, and have been guilty of many heinous Sins, especially Whoring, Drunkeness,

---

[22] Christian Biet, 'Judicial Fiction and Literary Fiction: The Example of the Factum', *Law and Literature*, 20:3 (Fall 2008), p. 405.
[23] Lincoln B. Faller, *Turned to Account: The Forms and Functions of Criminal Biography in Late Seventeenth- and Early Eighteenth-Century England* (Cambridge: Cambridge University Press, 1987), p. 2.
[24] Thomas Purney, *The Ordinary of Newgate's Account of the Behaviour, Confession and Last Dying Speech of Matthias Brinsden* (London: John Applebee, 1722), BL/515.I.2/227.

Sabbath-breaking and the rest, which has brought me to this shameful end; therefore pray take example by me, that you may mend your lives.[25]

Not all malefactors acknowledged their guilt, of course; and in some accounts, it is possible to identify different voices struggling to assert their authority over the narrative. In 'The Ordinary of Newgate's Account of the Behaviour of the Last Dying Words of Edward Bird, Gentleman, who was executed at Tyburn on Monday 23rd February 1718 for the Murder of Samuel Coxton' (1718), Bird refuses to yield to the admonishments of Paul Lorrain, the Ordinary of Newgate, and proceeds to write his own account insinuating his innocence which the Ordinary, as the controlling narrator, rejects and that we, as the readers, do not see.[26] 'I told him plainly, that the Draught of that Paper, being to insinuate that he had not Justice due to him at his Trial, he must not think that the World would believe him to be (as he endeavour'd to appear) innocent of the Murder he was condemn'd for,' the Ordinary writes, adding for our purposes: 'I thought him justly convicted of that Murder.'[27]

The ostensible intention of these accounts was, of course, to try to close down any anxieties relating to the committing of violent crimes and the general practice of the criminal justice system. If such crimes were perceived as a threat to the moral and religious schema of the church—for as Faller points out, unreasoning murder could be seen 'to impugn God's justice' and at least raise the question of how such acts could 'be allowed to happen in a justly ordered universe'[28]—they also raised doubts about the ability of the state to provide adequate security for its citizens, especially those with property (i.e. if these provisions were adequate, why did people continue to commit crimes?) Hence execution narratives had a related function: to reiterate the 'natural' order of God's justice and to articulate a vision of power and authority seemingly compatible with a Hobbesian account of the state as acting consistently, fairly, and in the general good. Though the tales themselves offer almost no insight into the everyday practices of policing and justice, perpetrators are always caught, tried, and made to reflect on the fairness of their sentence; and even when they refuse to do so, the Ordinary intervenes to note that justice has been done. The public nature of the execution affirms the omnipotence of the state which, in the context of its legal apparatus, is seen to be neutral and standing above or apart from ruler and ruled. As such, what distinguishes the violence sanctioned by the state from the violence enacted by individuals is that it is,

---

[25] Anonymous, *Memoirs of the Right Villainous John Hall, the Late Famous and Notorious Robber Penn'd from his own mouth* (London: H. Hills, 1708), BL/515.I.2/214.

[26] Philip Rawlings writes: 'In 1719 Paul Lorrain, the Ordinary of Newgate, noted that Edward Bird had shown him the draft of a paper he intended to have published and which, Bird hoped, would clear his name' (which Lorrain thought inappropriate). See *Drunks, Whores and Idle Apprentices: Criminal Biographies of the Eighteenth Century* (London and New York, NY: Routledge, 1992), p. 7.

[27] Paul Lorrain, 'The Ordinary of Newgate's Account of the Behaviour of the Last Dying Words of Edward Bird, Gentleman, who was executed at Tyburn on Monday 23rd February 1718 for the Murder of Samuel Coxton' (London: J. Jeffries, 1718), BL/515.L2/224.

[28] Lincoln B. Faller, *Crime and Defoe: A New Kind of Writing* (Cambridge: Cambridge University Press, 1993), pp. 10–11.

to quote Ryan's assessment of Hobbes's *Leviathan*, 'regular, predictable, lawful and public'.[29]

Still, while the *intention* of these accounts might have been resolutely conservative, the presence of narrative inconsistencies and even contradictions left open the possibility to read them in alternative ways or, as Gladfedler astutely points out, subversive messages can 'break out even from the most determinedly conservative forms'.[30] In some instances, such as 'A Full and True Account of a most horrid and barbarous Murder committed yesterday, April 24th, in St James's house, by Elizabeth Smith' (1711), the crime—the stabbing of 'poor innocent Babe' by his mother and her attempt to hide the corpse in 'an odd hole in the ceiling'—is sufficiently gruesome to limit or even negate any reassurance readers may gain from the description of her confession and execution, especially as no motive for the crime is provided.[31]

In other instances, such as 'An Account of the Behaviour, Confession and Last Dying Words of Arundel Cooke Esq and John Woodman, Labourer' (1722), the gaps in the narrative raise troubling questions—even about what has actually taken place—which are never adequately addressed or resolved. In the full title of the piece, we are told that Cooke and Woodman are executed for attempting to kill Edward Crispe, who is described merely as a 'gentleman' but initially at least we are not told why an attempt on Crispe's life was made or how it involved Cooke's servant, Woodman. Rather the narrative describes Cooke's failed efforts to secure a pardon, despite spending a considerable sum of money, and the forgiveness of his accomplice. Typically the focus is on the execution itself and Cooke's eventual demonstration of sorrow and contrition; the fact he not only asks for God's pardon 'for his wicked life' but also begs the crowd 'to take warning of his sad example'. But disquieting truths are alluded to without being fleshed out; Woodman, for example, admits to giving Crispe's children sugar plums but denies knowing they were poisoned, whereupon we are told that both children died, without any sense of why Cooke might have wanted to do them harm. Later, too, Cooke denies poisoning 'Mr Durrant's horse, Mr Salisbury's swine etc.' thereby suggesting some kind of larger plot that he has no knowledge of.[32] Having finished the account, one is left to ponder the way in which a messy, complicated tale is corralled into a narrative straightjacket that is not, in the end, able to contain it.

Later in the eighteenth century, the legal reformer Cesare Beccaria would argue that the authority of the state is in inverse proportion to the violence it is compelled to use in order to secure its laws and its boundaries, and that one can tell

---

[29] Alan Ryan, 'Hobbes's Political Philosophy', in Tom Sorrell (ed.) *The Cambridge Companion to Hobbes* (Cambridge: Cambridge University Press, 1996), p. 238.

[30] Gladfelder, *Criminality and Narrative in Eighteenth-Century England*, p. 9.

[31] R. Newcomb, 'A Full and True Account of a most horrid and barbarous Murder Committed Yesterday, April 24th, in St-James's-house, by Elizabeth Smith, upon the Body of her own Male Child' (1711), BL/515.I.2/214.

[32] Anonymous (court proceedings), 'An Account of the Behaviour, Confession and Last Dying Words of Arundel Cooke, Esq., and John Woodman, Labourer, who were Executed at Bury St. Edmunds in the County of Suffolk on Saturday March 31 1722 for the Barbarous Attempt on the Life of EDWARD CRISPE, gentleman' (London: T. Payne, 1722), BL/515.L2/232.

how insecure a state is by the nature and extent of the force it uses in reaction to perceived threats.[33] As such, it is possible to see the state, as it is analogized in these crude execution narratives, not as an institution of irresistible power but rather as inherently unstable, precisely because of the staged and very public nature of the execution spectacle; i.e. the idea that its might has to be projected or amplified in this manner is an indication of its weakness rather than of its strength. This is undoubtedly a subtext of these tales; that the state, despite the theatrical staging of its own authority, is always on the verge of disintegration, something that in turn throws useful light on, and corroborates, a particular reading of Hobbes: namely that the violence practised by the state shouldn't be understood, to paraphrase Norberto Bobbio, as 'oppression which derives from an excess of power' but rather as a marker of insecurity 'which derives, on the contrary, from the lack of power'.[34]

If this is one counter-reading of these tales and of the spectacle of public execution in general, another might draw attention to their combined ineffectiveness as deterrents and indeed their capacity for encouraging audiences to see criminality as a form of justified rebellion. This point, made by Foucault in *Discipline and Punish*,[35] is developed by Hans-Jürgen Lüsebrink's *Kriminalität und Literatur* (1983) in relation to French criminal biographies or *causes célèbres* in which he sees some evidence of a popular tradition of social banditry emerging. Likewise, in the context of their early eighteenth-century British equivalent, Gladfelder poses the question: 'if the criminal's body and voice were seen as potentially encoding rebellion and potential resistance, what was the cultural resonance of a genre of fictions (disturbingly claiming to be true) written in the assumed voices of the outlaw poor, upstart servants and rootless adventurers?'[36]

We need to be careful about how far we push this point (i.e. the potential to read these criminal memoirs as potential sites of popular rebellion[37]), just as there are dangers in overstating the inadequacies of the criminal justice systems in France and Britain; and the ways these flaws are encoded in the texts themselves. Better to argue that, whether intentional or not, these tales offer us a fascinatingly ambivalent account of early eighteenth-century law and justice. A brief look at what Biet calls 'factums'—an emerging genre in France located somewhere between judicial writing and literary fiction—and Bastien identifies as *arrêts criminels* (criminal court judgements) confirms this position. Factums are the written conclusions of the defence lawyer and 'contain the facts and circumstances of a case that is to be judged',[38] while *arrêts criminels*, published by the Parliament of Paris and typically read out in public prior to executions, are the conclusions of the prosecutor. It's no surprise, then, that the latter sought to uphold the trial verdict and provide justification for the punishment. As Bastien notes, 'The private and public reading of the

---

[33] See Cesare Beccaria, *On Crimes and Punishments*, ed. David Young (Indianapolis, IN: Hackett, 1986), p. 81.
[34] Norberto Bobbio, *Thomas Hobbes and the Natural Law Tradition* (Chicago, IL and London: University of Chicago Press, 1993), p. 29.
[35] Foucault, *Discipline and Punish*, pp. 31–69.
[36] Gladfelder, *Criminality and Narrative in Eighteenth-Century England*, p. xi.
[37] Faller points to the limits of this argument; see *Turned to Account*, p. 11.
[38] Biet, 'Judicial Fiction and Literary Fiction', p. 405.

arrêts placed the criminal within a Manichean moral system by forcing him to assume, alone, the responsibility for his condemnation.'[39] Still, in so far as the *arrêts* utilized the same rhetorical and linguistic devices as both the defence lawyers in their factums and more significantly writers of fiction, and since, as Bastien demonstrates, they implicitly drew attention to tensions in the justice system between the imperatives of monarchy and Parliament,[40] we need to be careful about seeing them simply as forms of propaganda. This complexity is evident in the factums themselves, notably one involving a civil case taken up by a woman, wrongly punished, against her accuser. Published in 1710, the account exhibits this complexity so well and provides a useful point of comparison with François Gayot de Pitaval's *Causes Célèbres*, first published in France in 1734 and translated into English ten years later, which offers an account of the same incident but, as I explore in the final section, Pitival's 'Singular and Interesting Histories...' with a markedly different tone and perspective.

A brief description of the affair will have to suffice. On 23 September 1687 the Count of Montgommery was robbed of a considerable sum of money (the equivalent of £30,000 sterling) and based on the guilty behaviour exhibited by his recently ennobled neighbours Sir and Lady d'Anglarde, they were charged and tried for the crime, and found guilty. D'Anglarde, who was sentenced to nine years as a galley-slave (his wife dispatched to prison for the same length of time), died in 1689 just before an anonymous letter was circulated suggesting their innocence and naming Montgommery's priest and an accomplice as the 'real' perpetrators of the theft. The factum relates to a civil case brought by the wife against Montgommery, both to sue for damages and to prove that Montgommery was complicit in pursuing what he knew to be an unsafe conviction. If the intention of these factums in general was to attack the position of opposing council, it is not the case that they impugned the entire legal system—far from it, in fact. As with the *arrêts*, the larger ambition was to underscore good practice and the effective working out of due process.

That said, any case that dealt in a serious miscarriage of justice couldn't help but reflect upon the ills of the justice system. For Biet, the significance of this particular factum lies in the way in which the defence lawyer, using rhetoric common to fiction, challenged and overturned a commonly held view of the 'daring, cunning, greedy, hypocritical and self-interested' unfairly attacking a respected aristocrat and by extension the entire legal system to 'build the case of this amazing and paradoxical "honest widow"' and by doing so requiring that the judge 'break free from both the ties of class consciousness that join him to the count and the social image attached to the widow'.[41] Hence while the factum and what Biet calls narrative judicial fiction both seek to resolve opposing views 'into a particular solution', the accounts themselves, with their claims and counterclaims, are 'sufficiently complex for the judgments on them to be particular, multiple and contradictory'

---

[39] Bastien, 'Private Crimes and Public Executions', p. 156.
[40] Bastien, 'Private Crimes and Public Executions', p. 154.
[41] Biet, 'Judicial Fiction and Literary Fiction', p. 413.

i.e. that they demonstrate both the rigours of due process and significant flaws in the judicial system.[42]

BERNARD MANDEVILLE'S PRIVATE VICES AND PUBLIC BENEFITS

Bernard Mandeville is a fascinating if slightly perplexing figure in early eighteenth-century thought; someone committed to the rule of law and keen to push capital punishment as a proper means of deterring criminal excesses and yet at the same time a dedicated libertarian and someone who believed, foreshadowing the work of Adam Smith, that rational self-interest could be a useful stabilizing force, even if his account of greed as a manifestation of this self-interest would be disagreeable to Smith's more finely-tuned sense of moral purpose. Some commentators at the time, and subsequently, mistook him for a Hobbesian: 'little more than a minor Hobbesian acolyte' wrote one critic, and later in the nineteenth century his best known work *The Fable of the Bees: or, Private Vices, Publick Benefits* (first published in 1714 and revised throughout the 1720s) was said to be 'occasioned by the doctrines of Hobbes'.[43] There are some superficial similarities. Like Hobbes, Mandeville has a jaundiced view of human nature and humans' propensity for selfishness. 'All untaught Animals', he declares at the start of a revised version of *The Fable of the Bees*, 'are only solicitous of pleasing themselves, and naturally follow the bent of their own Inclinations.'[44] And like Hobbes, too, he argues that the visible, consistent exercise of public power is necessary for the maintenance of social order: not least because 'no Species of Animals is, without the Curb of Government, less capable of agreeing long together in multitudes than that of man'.[45] In *Enquiry into the Causes of Frequent Executions at Tyburn* (1725), Mandeville confirms his Hobbesian credentials most forcefully arguing for a shift away from a culture of reform and a return to firm rule as a proper deterrent to potential wrongdoers. What keeps man from breaking the law, he claims, echoing Hobbes, 'must be some mighty Principle of vast Force and Efficacy; for if he acts consistently, he despises not only Death but the Wrath of Omnipotence, and a Punishment just at Hand, that shall be everlasting'.[46]

Unlike Hobbes, however, Mandeville is not a systematic theorist of public power, and *The Fable of the Bees*, for example, is less concerned with the problem of public order as with the consequences of economic prosperity. In other words, despite his seeming interest in the scaffold as a visible manifestation of sovereign power, his

---

[42] Biet, 'Judicial Fiction and Literary Fiction', p. 420.
[43] See E.J. Hundert, *The Enlightenment's Tale: Bernard Mandeville and the Discovery of Society* (Cambridge: Cambridge University Press, 1996), pp. 176, 241.
[44] Bernard Mandeville, *The Fable of the Bees or, Private Vices, Publick Benefits* (London: J. Tonson, 1725), p. 27.
[45] Mandeville, *The Fable of the Bees*, p. 28.
[46] Mandeville, *An Enquiry into the Causes of Frequent Executions at Tyburn* (London: J. Roberts, 1725), p. 33; reprinted by the Augustan Reprint Society, publication 105, William Andrews Clark Memorial Library, University of California, Los Angeles, CA (1964).

attention, as a thinker, is directed not at Hobbes's artificial man but at the realm of civil society and the social utility of self-interest or greed. For whereas man may be 'subdued by a superior Strength' it is 'impossible by Force alone to make him tractable and receive the improvements he is capable of'.[47] Eschewing the principle of goodness for its own sake, Mandeville argues that men should indulge rather than try to conquer their appetites. And while Hobbes argues that, unchecked, vanity and competition over scarce resources would inevitably lead to violent conflict, Mandeville claims that selfishness, unregulated but in a well-ordered society and economy, may serve the public good because it enables 'every body, who in some thing or other will be serviceable to the publick, to purchase the assistance of others'.[48] In other words, he argues that greed has an important social function and that in a fast-growing mercantile society where opportunities for self-advancement were manifold, the unvirtuous instincts of envy, vice, and even at a push corruption could, as Hundert puts it, 'unintentionally' but in a practical way contribute, as much as the visible and uniform exercise of public power, to 'the stability of the modern state'.[49]

The case of Jonathan Wild presents Mandeville with a potential problem and points perhaps not to a contradiction in his thought but certainly to an unresolved tension, one that in turn offers us a useful way of situating and thinking about subsequent efforts by writers like Defoe and 'H.D.' to narrate Wild's life. Mandeville's *Enquiry into the Causes of the Frequent Executions at Tyburn* was originally published as a series of letters to the *British Journal*, the first of which appeared on 27 February 1725, just twelve days before Wild was arrested on charges which would lead to his execution in May 1725. As receiver of information about stolen goods, Wild is named by Mandeville as one of the causes of the unacceptable lawlessness that blighted early eighteenth-century life:

> But I think it unpardonable that a Man should knowingly act against the Law, and by so doing powerfully contribute to the Increase, as well as Safety and Maintenance of Robbers, from no other Principle, than a criminal Selfishness, accompany'd with an utter Disregard to the Publick: Yet nothing is more common among us. As soon as any Thing is missing, suspected to be stolen, the first Course we steer is directly to the Office of Mr. *Jonathan Wild*.[50]

Later in the same pamphlet, Mandeville argues that the main threat to public order comes not from 'the mischief that one man can do as a Thief' but rather from criminal organizations, and that 'all Gangs and Knots of Thieves should be broke and destroy'd'. It is Wild's duplicity, just as much as his organization, which enrages Mandeville. 'A profess'd Thief-Catcher,' he claims, doubtless with Wild in mind,

> above all, ought to be severely punish'd, if it can be proven that he has suffer'd a known Rogue to go on in his Villainy, tho' but one Day, after it was in his Power to apprehend and convict him, more especially if it appears that he was a Sharer in the Profit.[51]

---

[47] Mandeville, *The Fable of the Bees*, p. 28.
[48] Mandeville qtd in Thomas A. Horne, *The Social Thought of Bernard Mandeville: Vice and Commerce in Early Eighteenth-Century England* (London and Basingstoke: Macmillan, 1978), p. xi.
[49] Hundert, *The Enlightenment's Tale*, p. 177.   [50] Mandeville, *Enquiry*, p. 3.
[51] Mandeville, *Enquiry*, p. 9.

Yet, in spite of Mandeville's indignation, it is not clear how Wild's endeavours depart from the practices of self-interest that elsewhere and particularly in *The Fable of the Bees* are offered as socially useful. Certainly Wild's greed operates in excess of or even in opposition to the law, such as it is, and we must be careful about collapsing the perceived corruption that Mandeville argues flows from increased commercial opportunities and expanding the wealth-base of a nation, and the kind of systematic lawbreaking enacted by Wild (even if Wild's own exploits, as we shall see, mimic those of the police). That said, one cannot get away from the fact that the kind of 'criminal selfishness' and 'utter disregard to the Publick' demonstrated by Wild are small steps from the equally unvirtuous pursuit of luxury and vice that Mandeville explicitly does not condemn in *The Fable of the Bees*.[52] There are undoubted strengths and weaknesses in Mandeville's arguments. In so far as Mandeville is looking at the mechanics of state power as it operates in the economy, he is able, better than Hobbes, to pose the question of whether the economy should be understood as part of the public realm and hence subject to state regulation, or the private realm and hence to be left alone. Still, the issue of whether the expansion of commercial and private interests that Mandeville to some extent welcomes should be seen as just a stabilizing force remains a moot one.[53] Precisely because these private and/or commercial interests result in the conglomeration of power and money in the hands of the most devious and capable citizens (e.g. Wild), this process must, as Mandeville implicitly acknowledges in *Enquiry*, throw into doubt the ability of the supposedly impartial state to act in the general good.

The problem for Mandeville may be his partial account of the state and state power. For Hobbes, '[t]he Obligation of Subjects to the Soveraign, is understood to last as long, and no longer, than the power lasteth, by which he is able to protect them'.[54] In other words, a theory of the inadequate state is only possible where the sovereign cannot protect his subjects. As Bobbio tells us, what 'makes Hobbes's moral theory one of the most daring, though not always consistent, expressions of ethical legalism' is the idea 'which holds that the sovereign...does not command what is just, but that what is right is what the sovereign commands'.[55] For Mandeville, the state may be the only body capable of instilling sufficient terror in people to deter them from committing crimes but, in more practical terms, his disregard for Sir Robert Walpole, the prime minister at the time and someone compared by his critics to Jonathan Wild, meant he could never wholly subscribe

---

[52] For a fuller assessment of Mandeville's account of virtue and vice, see M.N. Goldsmith, *Private Vices, Public Benefits: Bernard Mandeville's Social and Political Thought* (Cambridge: Cambridge University Press, 1985), pp. 34–5.

[53] In so far as Mandeville is looking at both the mechanics of state power and the role of the economy in the pursuit of social stability, he poses, if not answers, the question of whether the economy should be understood as part of the public or private realm and what might be the relationship between the state and civil society: an issue that, in turn, would exercise nineteenth-century thinkers like Marx and Mill.

[54] Thomas Hobbes, *Leviathan*, ed. Richard Tuck (Cambridge: Cambridge University Press, 1996), p. 153.

[55] Bobbio, *Thomas Hobbes and the Natural Law Tradition*, p. 57.

to Hobbes's absolutist vision of state power and this idea that rightness is what the sovereign declares.[56] At the same time this inability or unwillingness to endorse absolutist positions and a concern about what was happening in the streets—a concern for the practicalities and compromises of everyday life—means that Mandeville's ideas are more useful for interrogating early crime stories than Hobbes.

What we are left with, then, is a fascinating and from my perspective highly productive tension between competing views of the state (as omnipotent and nearing collapse) and of the world of commerce (as a useful social glue and a snake-pit of greed and self-interest). It's in this context I'd like to consider *The Life and Actions of Lewis Dominique Cartouche* whose second edition was published anonymous by J. Roberts in 1722 and translated into English, allegedly by Defoe; and two accounts of Wild's rise and fall—*The True and Genuine Account of the Life and Actions of Jonathan Wild* published anonymously by John Applebee in 1725 but thought to be penned by Defoe also; and the other, *The Life of Jonathan Wild*, published in the same year by Warner and authored by 'H.D., the late clerk to Justice R—'. Following one strain of Mandevillian thought, the state and the law enforce order, if necessary by force (or the threat of force). Following another, the authorities are permissive and even corrupt, in so far as Cartouche and Wild are permitted to prosper. Similarly, unfettered economic activity is the best way of ensuring prosperity and stability and at the same time unfettered economic activity inevitably favours those like Wild who are able to criminally manipulate the system to suit their own ambitions. It would take Gay's *The Beggar's Opera* to fully expose the partiality of the law and directly connect the figure of the criminal to the outwardly respectable man, perhaps even the prime minister himself, but what these texts manage to do so well is bring these various, perhaps even contradictory elements into productive tension. In doing so they give us a surprisingly nuanced and starkly modern account of the nature and limitations of state power and also give an emerging body of crime writing or writing about crime its most sophisticated manifestations to date.

LOUIS DOMINIQUE CARTOUCHE, JONATHAN WILD, AND THE AMBIVALENCE OF STATE POWER

In light of the self-evident symmetries between their respective rise to power—their determination to bring the anarchic elements of the criminal underworld under their control and organize their respective enterprises according to rational principles and their eventual and perhaps inevitable fall (Cartouche was executed in Paris in November 1721, Wild in May 1724)—it is something of a surprise that

---

[56] Gunn, for example, discusses Mandeville's efforts 'to run down the capacities of Walpole as prime minister, probably to better serve the interests of Lord Macclesfield, Mandeville's patron'. See J.A. Gunn, '"State Hypochondriacks" Dispraised: Mandeville versus the Active Citizen', in Charles Prior (ed.) *Mandeville and Augustan Ideals: New Essays* (Victoria, BC: English Literary Studies, University of Victoria, 2000), p. 26.

their treatment as historical figures and of the various literary works produced about their lives hasn't paid much attention to the comparative context. Cartouche has been claimed by French literary critics seeking to establish a lineage of banditry and social rebellion in France from the early 1800s to the appearance of *Fantômas* at the start of the twentieth century. Wild, meanwhile, is interpreted as an example of the perceived lawlessness of early eighteenth-century English life. Part of the impulse here, and in the book as a whole, is to break down this obsession with national particularity and to see the efforts to narrate their respective lives as occasioned by a set of anxieties circulating in both countries about the adequacy of the criminal justice system and by extension the nature and reach of state power. This task is made a lot easier by the apparent involvement of Daniel Defoe in both endeavours; he is assumed to be the author of *The True and Genuine Account of the Life and Actions of Jonathan Wild*, published by John Applebee in 1725, and is alleged to have translated *The Life and Actions of Lewis Dominique Cartouche* for London publisher J. Roberts in 1721.[57]

Some further contextualization is needed. By the early 1720s, John Applebee had what Richard Holmes calls a 'virtual monopoly in the publishing of "True Confessions"' at least in London. Applebee paid Newgate ordinaries and often even prisoners for their stories, and hired journalists to write them, and then sold these accounts as two-penny broadsheets, six-penny pamphlets, or one shilling bound pamphlets.[58] Defoe joined *Applebee's Original Weekly Journal* in June 1720, where 'for the next five years, he would write all the Letters Introductory, as well as various other news items'.[59] Because Defoe was one of Applebee's leader-writers and because Applebee enjoyed this virtual monopoly as publisher of criminal biographies, it is sometimes assumed that Defoe wrote most, if not all, of these works published by Applebee in the first half of the 1720s. Furbank and Owens suggest this wasn't necessarily so, although they concede that 'it would not be absurd to suppose "The True and Genuine Account"' was penned by Defoe, even if there is 'no positive evidence to suggest it'.[60] The case is much less clear-cut with the translation of *The Life and Actions of Lewis Dominique Cartouche*, especially as Defoe had no formal association with its London publisher. Furbank and Owens are willing to cede *The True and Genuine Account* to Defoe because it demonstrates 'the sort of idiosyncratic and purposeful thinking or polemical edge one expects in Defoe'.[61]

---

[57] The edition which I consulted *The Life and Actions of Lewis Dominique Cartouche* (translated from the French) second edition (London: J. Roberts, 1722), gives no indication of original authorship but the British Library catalogue ascribes the translation to Daniel Defoe. See http://explore.bl.uk/primo_library/libweb/action/search.do?dscnt=0&vl(174399379UI0)=any&frbg=&scp.scps=scope%3A%28BLCONTENT%29&tab=local_tab&dstmp=1355312117222&srt=rank&ct=search&mode=Basic&dum=true&tb=t&indx=1&vl(freeText0)=Defoe+Cartouche&vid=BLVU1&fn=search, accessed 12 December 2012.

[58] Richard Holmes, 'Introduction', *Defoe on Sheppard and Wild* (London: Harper Perennial, 2004), pp. xv–xvi.

[59] P.N. Furbank and W.R. Owens, 'The Myth of Defoe as "Applebee's Man"', *The Review of English Studies*, 48:190 (May 1997), p. 199.

[60] Furbank and Owens, *The Review of English Studies*, p. 203.

[61] Furbank and Owens, *The Review of English Studies*, p. 202.

This polemic is noticeably absent from *The Life and Actions of Lewis Dominique Cartouche* and as such I have chosen to situate it alongside a work about Wild's life penned by 'H.D., the late clerk to Justice R—' not least because both texts adopt a markedly similar tone and stance towards their subjects. But let us return for a moment to Defoe. By the mid-1720s, he was in his sixties and had already enjoyed considerable success with *Robinson Crusoe* (1719) and *Moll Flanders* (1723) and one can see something of the complexity of tone and voice ably demonstrated in these novels in *The True and Genuine Account* of Wild's life. Subtitled 'not made up of Fiction and Fable but taken from his Own Mouth, and collected from PAPERS of his own writing', the account makes much of its claims to the truth. 'The following tract does not indeed make a jest of [Wild's] story, or present his history, which indeed is a tragedy of itself, in a style of mockery and ridicule, but in a method agreeable to the facts.'[62] What underscores this imperative to be agreeable to the facts, Defoe implies, is the seriousness of the subject. Because of what is at stake, Defoe is not content to play the role of impartial observer, in spite of the disingenuousness of his expressed intent to 'leave history to those who know how to distinguish good from evil' (p. 72). If the truth, for Defoe, is appalling, then he cannot but condemn the practices he describes and therefore when he is told stories—'which I have particular reasons to believe are true' (p. 109)—about, say, Wild's exploitation of children for personal gain, he is not able to hold back his moral outrage. 'Horrid wickedness! His charity has been to breed them to be thieves; and still more horrid! several of these, his own foster children, he has himself caused to be apprehended and hanged for the very crimes which he first taught them how to commit' (p. 109).

The polemical intention behind *True and Genuine Account* is, in part, given shape and form by the criminal biographies and gallows reports produced by the ordinaries of Newgate. As such, the moralizing tone adopted by the narrator towards Wild would appear to serve a similar function as the judgements handed out by the ordinaries: to remind readers about the authority of God and the law. The shape of the narrative, too, follows those accounts, in so far as Wild's exploits ultimately lead him to the scaffold and result in the visible demonstration of state power. Wild is humbled before the law and reduced to a laudanum-addled state before a crowd that, we're told, universally recognizes the fairness of the judge's sentence; but there is a qualitative difference between the moralizing accounts of the Newgate ordinaries and what Novak calls the impressively 'consistent moral tone of the narrator'[63] in *True and Genuine Account*. While the intention of the former is both to draw attention to the consequences of a fall from God and reiterate the authority of the state, it is harder to ascribe a straightforward, univocal ambition to the narrator of *True and Genuine Account*. Certainly there is outrage at Wild's exploitative practices but Defoe's is a far more sophisticated narrative

---

[62] *The True and Genuine Account of the Life and Actions of the Late Jonathan Wild* (London: J. Applebee, 1725). Subsequently reprinted as Daniel Defoe, *Defoe on Sheppard and Wild*, ed. Richard Holmes. This citation is taken from *Defoe on Sheppard and Wild*, p. 72.

[63] Maximilian E. Novak, *Daniel Defoe: Master of Fiction* (Oxford: Oxford University Press, 2003), p. 641.

than the crude accounts produced by the ordinaries of Newgate. *Moll Flanders* is exemplary. Defoe's novel would seem to set Moll's rough, immodest language against her mature, self-conscious voice in a way that contains and neutralizes the disruptive possibilities inherent in the former, but the rough, toxic Moll cannot be entirely expunged from the narrative and what Defoe ultimately gives us is a sophisticated, self-conscious deployment of competing voices and moral claims. Schornhorn's claim for Defoe's writing as propaganda *and* political theory (it is concerned both with 'this or that... point of political policy' and 'with the origins of government, the reasons for the successes and failures of political society, and the nature of leadership'[64]) suggests a complexity of tone and ambition that is present not just in *Moll Flanders* but also in his account of Wild's rise and fall. For instance, as much as Defoe wants to condemn Wild, his account is beset by anxiety regarding the privatization of law enforcement that is wholly absent from the didactic, one-dimensional accounts of the Newgate ordinaries. One can see this in the conclusion:

> Thus ended the tragedy, and thus was a life of horrid and inimitable wickedness finished at the gallows, the very same place where, according to some, above 120 miserable creatures had been hanged, whose blood, in great measure, may be said to lie at his door... and many of them at last betrayed and brought to justice by his means, upon which worst sort of murder he valued himself, and would have had it passed for merit, even with the Government itself. (pp. 116–17)

Unlike the criminal tales and gallows sermons compiled by the ordinaries of Newgate, which provide clear, unequivocal closure, Defoe's attempt to bring his narrative to resolution raises more potentially troubling questions than it answers. For what differentiates the state-sanctioned murder of Wild and the executions of as many as '120 miserable creatures... brought to justice' by Wild's nefarious means, especially as such executions 'would have passed for merit, even with the Government'? If the authority of the state, as envisioned by Hobbes, is distinguished both from the authority of its rulers and from society as a whole, then Wild's interventions as thief and thief-taker constitute a debasement of this double move precisely because they are personally motivated. But might we still argue that Defoe, here, is acknowledging an affinity between Wild's practices and the activities of government? Early in the narrative, Defoe states, '[t]he life of Jonathan Wild is a perfectly new scene' (p. 74) but new in what sense? Certainly Wild's 'inimitable boldness' and 'brutal courage' (p. 74) catch Defoe's eye and elicit grudging admiration, and what merits considerable authorial scrutiny is the deviousness of Wild's practice: 'encouraging rogues to rob and plunder, and then demanding money for them to bring back what they had stolen, out of which he always secured a share for himself' (p. 86). What also sets Wild apart is his careful refusal to handle the stolen goods himself and hence his ability to skirt around the edges of law. But is this exactly what makes Wild's life a perfectly new scene?

---

[64] Manuel Schornhorn, *Defoe's Politics: Parliament, Power and Kingship* (Cambridge: Cambridge University Press, 1991), p. ix.

The difficulty for Defoe, and for us as readers, is that mechanisms for containing or controlling crime are the same ones that are implicated in the crime spree that Wild's endeavours have set in motion. It is not the case, then, that Wild's presence and actions underline the abjection of the justice system and the lawlessness of 1720s London but that Wild's organization is, at times, indistinguishable from the institutions of state, hence the notion that the *result* of Wild's efforts (i.e. the execution of 'career' criminals) 'would have passed for merit, even with the government itself'. In effect, Wild's technical expertise, organizational prowess, and hierarchical system mimic the emerging logic of statehood and this is what most unsettles Defoe and makes Wild's life a 'new scene': not that Wild steals, cheats, and even murders but that his actions, irrespective of intent, are to some extent synonymous with government and 'the public good in taking and apprehending the most open and notorious criminals' (p. 91).

In some ways, H.D.'s *The Life of Jonathan Wild* is, from my point of view, the more interesting narrative because, shorn of Defoe's conflicted tone of moral condemnation, it is better able to explore the implications of this tension. H.D. is the 'late clerk to Justice R—' who, Cross tells us, is Chief Justice Raymond, before whom Wild was tried and sentenced.[65] He is the consummate insider, therefore, rather than a dispassionate observer; not a judge, but a recorder and hence his account isn't as condemning of its subject as Defoe's (i.e. it is structured by a more self-consciously ambiguous attitude towards Wild than is found in *True and Genuine Account*). While Defoe tries to downplay, not always convincingly, the link between Wild's organization and the logic of statecraft, H.D. readily acknowledges the association, both directly evoking the language of statecraft to describe Wild's practices and demonstrating how it is his activities in the private realm that allow him to act as self-appointed thief-taker:

> The Reader will imagine, by what has been here related, that Jonathan must be a Person of no uncommon Parts—To govern a Commonwealth already fixed and establish'd, is no more than what may be done by any common Capacity; but to form and establish a Body of such lawless people into what we call a form of Government; to erect a Commonwealth like that of the Bees... in which every Member was oblig'd to go forth and labour, and bring an Offering to him the King... and to be able to many Years evade the Punishments appointed by the Laws of all Nations, and to live not only in toleration, but even in a kind of Credit, amongst people he was robbing every Day, and to accept the Plots and Conspiracies of his own treacherous Subjects—I say, to be able to manage all this, must proceed from an admirable Wit and Cunning.[66]

Wild, then, is operating in contravention to the 'Laws of all Nations' but doing so in such a manner as to maintain order in an environment where order is not usually maintained (i.e. he is doing *more* than simply governing a Commonwealth 'already fixed and establish'd'). As such, we might say the primary point of reference

---

[65] Wilbur Lucius Cross, *The History of Henry Fielding Vol. 1* (New Haven, CT: Yale University Press, 1918), pp. 407–8.

[66] *The Life of Jonathan Wild from his Birth to Death by H.D., late Clerk to Justice R—* (London: T. Warner, 1725), pp. 21–2.

is Hobbes, and that the establishment of a body of lawless people into 'a form of Government' with Wild himself as de facto monarch is evocative of the move from the disharmony of the state of the nature to the harmony of the social contract. Intriguingly, it's Machiavelli rather than Hobbes to whom Wild is consistently likened (e.g. as the 'Machiavel of Thieves', p. 31) but this analogy, I suspect, is the product of a crude rendering of Machiavelli's *The Prince* (i.e. a statement about the cunning and cruelty one needs to rule) rather than carefully nuanced comment on the differences between Republican and monarchical forms of government. More importantly, the link between criminality and good governance both unsettles the Manichean world of right and wrong conjured by the scaffold and paradoxically evokes Bobbio's account of Hobbesian morality; i.e. the sovereign doesn't do what is right but right is what the sovereign does. Wild's legitimacy is underscored by his effectiveness as thief-taker *and* keeper of order (and indeed his wit and cunning), even as his legitimacy, moral or otherwise, is fatally undermined by the self-interestedness of his ambitions. If we are meant to see Wild's gang as a kind of dark mirror held up to the respectable world (and police force), this self-interest would in turn pose serious questions about the neutrality of the justice system and the extent to which the implementation of state power and pursuit of personal gain are, even in such early articulations of the crime story, intricately bound up with each other.

Like H.D.'s text, *The Life and Actions of Lewis Dominique Cartouche* offers its readers a fairly perfunctory admonishment at the outset—i.e. to 'convince us how fatal it may prove to begin with small Crimes which if once made habitual, never fail to draw Men into the most abominable Villainies'[67]—and ends, typically, with its subject begging for repentance before being broken on the wheel. But if these framing devices are imposed on the account, by the demands of conventionality, morality, and historical truth (i.e. Cartouche *was* put to death on 27 November 1721), when it gets going, the narrative, like H.D.'s account, treats its subject in an instructively ambiguous manner, though the ambiguity is deployed in a slightly different way or form and has a correspondingly different effect. Superficially there is the same sense of Cartouche working both sides of the law in order to further his own ambition (e.g. 'discovering Thieves and bringing them to Justice' in order to knock out the competition) and, as with the accounts of Wild's life, this one is keen to underscore Cartouche's organizational abilities and the close links between organized crime and business. 'The money they took was not divided amongst them', we are told, drawing attention to the virtues of sound business administration and deferred gratification, 'for some of it was disposed to Spies, and even to the Officers of Justice themselves; who were to be treated and paid punctually every Quarter' (p. 34). If this draws attention both to potential corruption and Cartouche's facility for assimilating former and serving soldiers and police officers into his ranks, it also requires us to think about what actually distinguishes the activities of the state and the affairs of Cartouche's gang.

[67] *The Life and Actions of Lewis Dominique Cartouche*, p. 4.

But despite clear efforts to deploy the language of statehood to describe the former—for example, we're told, echoing Hobbes, 'He required of [his Comrades] a despotick Power to punish with Death any who should infringe the Laws' (p. 33)—this is not quite the same thing as H.D.'s efforts to yoke together Wild's ambitions as thief-taker and the affairs of government, even if the result is the same: a challenge to the state's authority and hence its monopolistic control within its own territory. Rather what we see in here is an unfolding war between the forces of the state (e.g. the police and army) and Cartouche's gang, a war that initially draws attention to the state's inability to impose law and order in Paris and beyond, but that, as the story develops, underscores the reach and determination of the authorities to stamp out this threat to its dominion. In other words this is not an instance of the pre-modern state with its crumbling policing provision but a concerted and ruthless crackdown on criminality, one that plays out as a fascinating, cat-and-mouse struggle between Cartouche and the apparatus of the police and judiciary which, given the early eighteenth-century context, comes across as surprisingly joined up and effective. Efforts to control the territorial space of the city and the sale of pistols and weapons in general within that space (i.e. we're told about 'an order for all Vagabonds, and People who followed no Trade, to depart the City; and the Gun-smiths and Sword-Cutlers were forbid to sell Arms to any Person, without a particular Leave in Writing from one appointed by the Government', p. 38) are followed by the mass circulation of Cartouche's likeness 'to every Market-Town in the Kingdom' (p. 43) and an official order to all 'Magistrates in the Country, to make strict search for him in all Places, under their Jurisdiction, and to take him dead or alive' (p. 51).

Returning to H.D.'s account of Wild's life for a moment, the emphasis here is less on the state's reach and effectiveness than, following Mandeville (whose magnum opus *The Fable of the Bees* is referenced—Wild's ambition is 'to erect a Commonwealth like that of the Bees'), on the claims of the state and the law on the one hand, and of civil society and commerce on the other. The issue for H.D. would not seem to be Wild's criminality or his duplicity—the fact that he tricks his wards into stealing for him and then gives them up for arrest—but rather how well he exercises control over his increasingly sizeable dominion. As we will also see in *The Life and Actions of Lewis Dominique Cartouche* the tone of H.D.'s narrative is largely admiring, though in this case (and unlike *Cartouche*) it is due to Wild's skills as a surrogate policeman and the efficiency of his office as a clearing house for information regarding stolen goods: a move which threatens the sanctity of any public/private distinction (i.e. as both spheres become indistinguishable). In one extended passage, H.D. describes how Wild and three constables, acting for the Chief Justice, go to a house on Billingsgate Street to serve a warrant on a suspected thief, and how Wild apprehends the man after he flees the scene and hides in the coal cellar beneath a nearby linen-draper's house (pp. 33–7).

In the end, Wild is put to death by the same authorities he, on occasions, serves but H.D.'s narrative complicates rather than re-inscribes the state's authority. While Defoe's account attempts, not always successfully, to close down some of the more troubling conclusions to be derived from Wild's life, H.D.'s text embraces and opens up these tensions: Wild's criminality is openly connected to his statecraft. Three further conclusions can be reached. First, Wild's role as thief-taker is evidence of the privatization of policing that was a feature of early eighteenth-century life and of the complex and overlapping relationship between public and private realms and by implication the state and civil society. Second, Wild's activities do not simply mimic police work but *are* in fact police work; the fact that he has been able to claim that title of 'THIEF-CATCHER-GENERAL OF GREAT BRITAIN' draws attention to the effectiveness of hierarchical organization in the fight against criminal gangs and also to the inadequacy of existing law enforcement provision and, by extension, the weakness of the state even as the power of the state is reaffirmed by Wild's eventual death at Tyburn. And third, the fact that Wild's police work and his self-interest are shown to be entirely synonymous gives credence to Mandeville's claims and undermines them from within. For what if the demands, or the coercive imperatives, of statehood and the kind of greed or self-interest that, according to Mandeville at least, could be harnessed for public benefit were *best* reconciled in a man like Wild? What did this say about both the efficacy of private vices and the supposed impartiality of the state and its ability to act in the general good?

The political implications of the ambiguous relationship between criminality and the law may not be as developed in *The Life and Action of Lewis Dominique Cartouche* but the way that *Cartouche*—arguably more so than H.D.'s text—complicates our identifications and deploys literary devices such as point-of-view shifts to generate tension, draws attention to the growing literary sophistication and indeed literary self-consciousness of the early crime story. Certainly the fact that Cartouche is treated not as type but rather as a complex, three-dimensional figure in his own right, someone capable of reflection and despite his self-evident boldness prone to anxieties regarding his fate, is evidence of this move. It may not be the case that we infer this from the narrative, a case of showing, but are told it by the narrator (Cartouche, we are told, began to reflect seriously on the conditions he would be in, 'if he were taken' and that these reflections 'daunted him, notwithstanding his courage', p. 48) although elsewhere the portrait is impressively nuanced. Cartouche may be talented, bold, and capable of acts of breathtaking courage but he is also presented as vain, capricious, hubristic, and cruel. In the absence of any real moralizing sentiments, we are left to ruminate on the man's violence and ruthlessness; the fact he assassinates companions in cold blood he imagines might betray him and, in one instance, castrates and facially disfigures a man he suspects of conspiring against him (in full view of other gang members in order to deter them from doing likewise).

He is no social bandit, then, a man whose rebellion is rooted in the inequalities of the system that has produced him, but nor is he a one-dimensional marker of villainy, someone characterized as 'evil' or beyond the bounds of normative behaviour and whose eventual execution by the state is intended—unequivocally—to console readers. Indeed, when captured and with his courage beginning to falter, Cartouche's desperation—embodied by his efforts to 'knock is Brains out against the Fetters' (p. 74)—humanizes him, in spite of the violence he's perpetrated and that the narrative has unflinchingly depicted. This ambiguity is signalled most obviously in the narrator's concluding remarks, so that Cartouche is described as both 'a Man of Wit and Vivacity' and of 'extraordinary presence of Mind, sound Judgment and intrepid Courage' and at the same time someone ruined by 'false notions of Honour, an excessive Love of Shew, join'd with a ridiculous Ambition' (p. 87). More intriguingly, it is also woven into the narrative, i.e. those parts where Cartouche's imperilled status vis-à-vis the forces of the state is signalled by a rapid point-of-view switch. The knowledge that Monsieur Pacome of the Regiment of French Guards takes thirty soldiers to a place where Cartouche is thought to be hiding makes the subsequent shift in perspective to a still sleeping Cartouche a fraught one, especially as it gives readers no indication of whether we should be rooting for the soldiers or Cartouche.

This ambiguity also extends to the narrative's treatment of the state; for in the same way that it is left up to the readers whether to identify with Cartouche, the various arms and agents of the state are represented neither as tyrannical and indulging in arbitrary excesses nor as wholly fair-minded and acting only in the interests of the common good. The sometimes sadistic and cold-blooded violence practised by Cartouche bestows legitimacy on the authorities and their determination to bring him to trial. But the torture exercised by the state against Cartouche to elicit a confession threatens this legitimacy, as does the violent nature of the sanctioned punishment (i.e. whereby he 'received eleven blows on his Body' before being 'expos'd upon the Wheel, till he died', p. 83). The result, augmented by the self-conscious deployment of literary devices (i.e. the framing of Cartouche in highly ambiguous terms as someone to be admired and feared), is a narrative where clear-cut moralizing is noticeably absent and where the boundary between fact and fiction is hard to discern. In place of straightforward claims about telling the truth, we are given a biography that serves not to warn or deter but to situate a flawed, compelling figure in a recognizable social context and where the state's actions don't necessarily lead to the restoration of order (all characteristics that would become central to the emerging crime fiction genre later in the nineteenth century). It is significant that immediately following the execution, Cartouche's accomplices held 'a General Meeting at the Gate of St Anthony' and 'proceeded to the Election of a Leader' who then 'assign'd every one their respective Offices' (p. 87). The tale ends not with the state's triumph but with a return to 'normality' that equates the activities of a criminal gang with the status quo.

THE PROBLEM OF CRIME AND PRIVATE PROPERTY: *THE BEGGAR'S OPERA*

The ambiguous character of authorial treatment of criminality and state authority, and hence of readerly identification, is deepened and extended by John Gay's *The Beggar's Opera*, first performed at the playhouse in Lincoln Inn's Field on 29 January 1728. In the case of Gay's play, this dilemma—of how to disentangle the related impulses of crime and law enforcement—is developed in more systematic manner and with clear political intent: not necessarily to celebrate the criminal but rather to lay bare the threadbare claims of the state to speak for everyone while simultaneously passing law after law to shore up the interests of private property. As E.P. Thompson puts it,

> Since property was a thing, it became possible to define offences as crimes against things, rather than as injuries to men. This enabled the law to assume, with its robes, the postures of impartiality: it was neutral as between every degree of man, and defended only the inviolability of the ownership of things.[68]

Vincenzo Ruggiero makes an insightful comparison between Locke and Defoe, arguing that Defoe 'represents the popular counterpart of the moral philosophers of his time, who engage in the elaboration of a theory of property with a view to making the new economic system acceptable to themselves and others'.[69] As such, he could not have been expected to critique one of the cornerstones of the 'Second Treatise of Government' (i.e. government had a duty to protect private property). But by directly linking Wild's organization and the business of statecraft, Defoe's account of Wild's life necessarily betrays some anxieties about the supposed impartiality of the law, even as the rule of law and indeed the equality of the law are, in principle, defended as unqualified goods. Gay is a good deal more willing than Defoe to question the fairness of this new economic system and its correlative in the law but what links *The Beggar's Opera* and Defoe's *True and Genuine Account* and *Cartouche* is a willingness to create what Kayman calls 'allegories of state' which conflate 'commerce and politics' to imagine 'a regime in which the codes of political government are structured by the new master-codes of contemporary economic organization: "trade," the division of labour, cut-throat competition and obsessive accumulation, self-interest, profit and cartels'.[70]

The opening refrain of *The Beggar's Opera*, repeated throughout, is a ballad that sees no difference between the practices of criminal and respectable societies. 'All professions berogue each other,' an old woman professes. 'The priest calls the lawyer a cheat / The lawyer be-knaves the divine / And the statesman, because he's so great / Thinks his trade as honest as mine.'[71] The kicker is in the final line, a sly dig at the then prime minister, Sir Robert Walpole, who was often referred to as the Great Man and who, in this rendition, is reduced to the status of rogue, or perhaps even lower, since at least rogues earn their keep through their own graft. 'What we win, gentlemen, is our own by the law of arms, and the right of conquest,' Jemmy Twitcher declares (p. 68). On a rung or two below statesmen, meanwhile, are the lawyers who, as Peachum says, 'don't care that anybody should get a clandestine livelihood but themselves' (p. 60). Peachum is modelled on Jonathan Wild, a thief-taker and receiver who, as we discover in the first act, also stands at the helm of the city's sprawling underworld and who trades or impeaches gang members no longer

---

[68] Thompson, *Whigs and Hunters*, p. 207.
[69] Vincenzo Ruggiero, *Crime and Markets: Essays in Anti-Criminology* (Oxford: Oxford University Press, 2000), p. 176; also see Schornhorn, *Defoe's Politics*, p. 3.
[70] Kayman, *From Bow Street to Baker Street*, p. 52.
[71] John Gay, *The Beggar's Opera* (London: Penguin, 1986), p. 43.

useful to him for a forty pound reward. The collision here of the law, criminality, and capitalism offers a timely reminder of the rottenness of a quasi-privatized justice system. But the fact that Peachum and Lockit, gatekeeper at Newgate prison and the *Opera*'s sole police representative, arbitrarily carve up the territory to best suit their ambitions—and pockets—does not mean that Gay is presenting us with an anachronistic vision of law enforcement that is wholly disconnected from the practices of the modern state.

The Beggar's Opera would appear to pit the Peachum–Lockit axis, with its dependence on bookkeeping and numbers, against the dashing highwayman Macheath and his gang who, at first glance at least, operate perhaps not as 'social bandits' in the way Eric Hobsbawm uses the term (bands of men who violently confront 'the economic, social and political order by challenging those who hold or lay claim to power, law and the control of resources'[72]) but seemingly with more honour than their counterparts in the civilized world. 'Who is there here that would not die for his friend?' one such figure boasts. 'Who is there here that would betray him for his interest?' another pipes up (p. 69). While Peachum and Lockit trade poor people's lives for profit, highwaymen like Macheath rob from those who can afford it and put the resulting spoils to better use: for as Matt the Mint states, 'where is the injury of taking from another, what he hath not the heart to make use of?' (p. 69). On the one hand, Peachum's set-up is established and run according to the related logic of organized crime and trade. As Ruggiero points out, Peachum's organization 'displays a particular division of labour among its members, based on the growing separation between the task of planning and that of executing' and that, as a result, 'there is a low degree of cooperation among its members'.[73] On the other hand, Macheath's gang would seem to act as a properly 'independent' group whereby 'tasks are collectively planned, profits shared and further activities collectively attempted'.[74] In part, the antagonism between Peachum and Macheath dramatizes what Ruggiero calls 'the attempt of organized groups to subject independent criminal groups and professional individuals to their control, and to turn them into pure employees with no decision-making role'.[75]

Michael Denning extends this line of argument into the play's treatment of the law. He argues that two types of law correspond to two types of honour; that of Peachum which is the 'law of counting and contracts' and of naked self-interest, and that of Macheath's gang which is the 'law of personal bonds'. The latter, he says, 'are not bound by contract, but by paternalism, customs, ancient rights, [and] a discretionary system of law'.[76] In reading the play as a struggle between two types of law and two meanings of property—'the common rights and customary perquisites, and the absolute ownership of property'—Denning argues that Peachum's

---

[72] Eric Hobsbawm, *Bandits* (London: Abacus, 2003), p. 7.
[73] Ruggiero, *Crime in Literature: Sociology of Deviance and Fiction* (London and New York, NY: Verso, 2003), p. 46.
[74] Ruggiero, *Crime in Literature*, p. 46.   [75] Ruggiero, *Crime in Literature*, p. 46.
[76] Michael Denning, 'Beggars and Thieves: *The Beggar's Opera* and the Ideology of the Gang', *Literature and History*, 8:1 (Spring 1982), pp. 52–3.

system (which would replace common rights 'with counting...[and] rationalized law') must inevitably triumph, even if the play ultimately shows the rottenness and moral bankruptcy at the heart of this mode of socio-political organization.[77] Both analyses of the play are astute and build on work undertaken by Thompson and Linebaugh exploring the gradual incorporation of the law in the early eighteenth century as an ideological weapon in the defence of property. Still, in so far as Ruggiero and Denning come close to characterizing Macheath and his gang according to Hobsbawm's social bandit formulation (i.e. as some kind of pre-political or primitive rebellion against the existing order) a few qualifications are needed. For a start, the eventual actions of some of Macheath's gang belie this notion of collectivity and communitarianism. As the play makes clear, the fact that Jemmy Twitcher is involved in the 'peaching' of Macheath suggests that this quasi-romantic reading of the gang has always been a fiction. ''Tis a plain proof that the world is all alike,' Macheath laments, upon learning of his friend's treachery, 'and that even our gang can no more trust one another than other people' (p. 118). Nor is Macheath quite the socially conscious bandit he at times tries to pass himself off as. The hierarchy of Peachum's organization is, to some extent, mirrored by the set-up in Macheath's gang (i.e. everyone is equal but some are more equal than others), and the initial disagreement with Peachum arises because Peachum fears, with justification, that Macheath's intentions towards his daughter Polly are mercenary; i.e. that he 'may hang his father and mother-in-law, in hope to get into their daughter's fortune' (p. 57). Certainly Macheath is willing to prey upon and exploit Polly's overblown romanticism—and to use her to help him escape from Newgate prison.

Here, then, the law is not an unqualified good, capable of imposing constraints on the ruling elites, but rather an apparatus that can be traded just like any other commodity in order to further particular claims and vested interests. Lockit and Peachum use a corrupted law to profit from human misery and in doing so perform what Linebaugh calls 'the relationship between the organized death of living labour (capital punishment) and the oppression of the living by dead labour (the punishment of capital)'.[78] 'Can it be expected that we should hang our acquaintance for nothing, when our betters will hardly save theirs without being paid for it?' Peachum points out. 'In one respect indeed, our employment may be reckoned dishonest, because, like great statesmen, we encourage those who betray our friends' (p. 85). The unseen 'statesmen' of the play are not neutral arbiters capable of fairly adjudicating between competing factions, but men with their snouts well and truly in the trough. But in this they are no different, no better, and no worse, than Peachum, Lockit, or Macheath who have long adjusted themselves to the logic of the marketplace, and who think nothing of pursuing monetary gain above all other imperatives.

---

[77] Denning, 'Beggars and Thieves', pp. 52–3.
[78] Peter Linebaugh, *The London Hanged: Crime and Civil Society in the Eighteenth Century* (London: Verso, 2003), p. xvii.

In this respect at least, *The Beggar's Opera* is a bleak, cynical play, one that suggests not simply that all human nature is fundamentally self-interested but more pertinently that the unfairness of the social contract and the growing interpenetration of the state and the marketplace have, if not caused then certainly contributed to this situation. In terms of its status as a play about crime, it raises the question, without necessarily answering, what would become of some of the foundational concerns of the genre. In the face of near-universal corruption, what actually constitutes crime and what, if anything, distinguishes a thief who steals 'your goods and plate' and a lawyer who steals 'your whole estate' (p. 60) is up for grabs. What, too, can be done in the face of so much disorder and is it possible to imagine not just a more ordered world but a fairer one as well? Gay offers no obvious palliatives and, in a world where everyone is complicit, there is no one who stands above or outside of the fray in order to put right perceived wrongs. That said the very fact that the play dramatizes the rottenness of the system and corruption of the law, as Denning points out, means that rebellion against the authority manifest in the scaffold cannot be ruled out.[79] But, as Denning also points out, what distinguishes the play is its political insights as well as its light-heartedness and comic energy, perhaps one reason why it was so popular and ran for an unprecedented sixty-two performances following its debut in January 1728.[80] More even than its rendering of place, or its social critique, or its twinning of crime and politics, what makes *The Beggar's Opera* significant as a precursor to the kind of crime tales that will be explored in this book is its populist energy and willingness to debunk the codes and imperatives of what was considered to be a bourgeois form. Denning notes that Gay's 'place within the genteel literary system' prevented him from wholeheartedly embracing 'the canting vocabulary used by Grub Street productions' and that his play is not *necessarily* 'about the people and by the people';[81] but by drawing upon the language of the street ballad, he was able to harness some of its nascent anger at the injustice of poverty. More to the point, by embracing rather than trying to deodorize the nastiness of his milieu, Gay's play puts down an important marker: if they were to have any political traction, stories about crime would have to show some of the unpleasantness and unruliness of what it was like to commit crime or to be a victim of crime or to detect crime, even as they wrapped up this vision in a popular narrative form that appealed to readers' desire for danger and excitement, and yes, also resolution. One must not forget that Gay gives us a 'happy' ending in which Macheath lives not because the story or poetic justice demands it (in fact, as we are told, poetic justice demands the opposite, that he dies on the scaffold) but because a play like this one needs 'to comply with the taste of the town' (p. 121).

---

[79] Denning, 'Beggars and Thieves', p. 53.
[80] Denning, 'Beggars and Thieves', pp. 48–9; for performance detail see Bryan Loughrey and T.O. Treadwell (eds), 'Introduction', in John Gay, *The Beggar's Opera*, ed. Bryan Loughrey (London: Penguin, 1986), p. 7.
[81] Denning, 'Beggars and Thieves', pp. 49, 50.

PITAVAL'S 'SINGULAR AND INTERESTING HISTORIES' AND FIELDING'S 'WILD'

The basic claim of this chapter is not that the emergence of writing about crime has its origins in this era, the first two and a half decades of the eighteenth century, but rather that the 1710s and especially the 1720s see the first real articulations, in England and France, of a markedly self-consciousness and ambivalence in the treatment of crime and its relationship to state power and commerce. A willingness to treat crime as a social and political problem—in texts like H.D'.s *The Life of Jonathan Wild* or Defoe's translation of the *The Life and Actions of Lewis Dominique Cartouche* or indeed Gay's *The Beggar's Opera*—means that these examples are able to ask searching questions about the interpenetration of organized crime (as a metaphor for trade) and the private realm of individual initiative and the public realm of the state and state power; and hence how fundamental shifts in the economic organization of society in turn raised troubling questions about the impersonality and indeed legitimacy of the criminal justice system. The resulting ambiguity, whether this is manifest in the characterization of the criminal or the police or indeed in a more general awareness of the irreconcilable tensions in their accounts of the state as both necessary and inadequate and/or corrupt, would become a key feature of the crime story, as it would develop later in the nineteenth and twentieth centuries. Still, not all writers would embrace or open up this tension in formally or politically instructive ways and if the 1720s marks both a useful point of origin and a high 'early' moment in the thematization of crime, the 1730s and 1740s would see a more cautious approach to the subject.

In *A Select Collection of Singular and Interesting Histories* (first published in France in 1734 and translated into English in 1744), François Gayot de Pitaval revisits and recounts particular cases from the previous century, mostly from the 1630s and 1640s; these cases typically detail the ways in which excessive behaviour characteristic of the unreformed world (e.g. devil-worshipping monks and evil and/or promiscuous aristocrats) is eventually brought to book by and under the law. The fact that Pitaval is going back into the historical archive, so to speak, could be construed as a conservative move; a form of displacement intended to obscure rather than illuminate problems of his own present. The misdeeds of M. de Cinq Mars (who plotted against Louis XIII); or the Marchioness de Gange (who, we're told, 'barbarously assassinated her Husband's Brothers';[82]) or Urban Grandier (who apparently tried to 'possess' the Nuns of Loudon); or the dissolute, upwardly mobile Madam Tiquet (who is 'condemned for attempting the Assassination of her Husband', p. 136) are all conceived of in terms of individual deviancy, rather than as social problems, and all are treated as part of relics of the distant past, even if the judiciary which inevitably passes sentence on them must be seen to be acting in a

---

[82] François Gayot de Pitaval, *A Select Collection of Singular and Interesting Histories. Together with The Tryals and Judicial Proceedings to which the Extraordinary Facts therein recorded gave Occasion (translated from the Original French)* (London: A. Miller, 1744), p. 138.

fair and impartial manner (i.e. in a manner compatible with the reformed, hence modern rather than pre-modern, justice system).

In these 'singular and interesting histories' murderers are punished, challengers to the monarch are put to the sword, and tyrannical despots are exposed. The only affair that causes the author any problem is the final one in the collection and it is instructive, for my purposes, that it recounts the same case—of a husband and wife wrongly accused of theft—that formed the basis of a legal factum (based on a hearing in 1692 but published in the 1710s) described by Christian Biet and assessed in the earlier section Hobbes' *Leviathan*, Gallows Confessions... Biet's account is illuminating because it draws attention to the struggles involved in presenting such a case as this before a judge; of having to reverse the typical image of the money-grabbing widow and instead present such a woman as wronged and paradoxically honest (paradoxically because it goes against custom to view such a figure in a positive light, especially as her case rests on challenging the word of a nobleman). The widow in question, Lady Langlade, has, along with her husband, the ennobled Sir Langlade, been tried and convicted of stealing from the Count of Montgommery, and having seen her husband perish in prison, she is exonerated when new evidence comes to light supporting their innocence and then takes out a civil suit against the Count for falsifying charges against them. The original factum is instructive, for Biet, because it draws upon the conventions of literary fiction to explore and open up 'the contradictions not only of society but also of its laws, the multiple legal systems, full of holes, gaps and possible interpretations, with no code and no constitution'.[83]

Pitaval's re-narration of this case, however, strips it of its inherent ambiguities (for example the need to recognize the Langlades as innocent and yet at the same time buttress existing hierarchies of class and privilege which in turn requires defending the Count) and turns it into a straightforward instance of two innocents being treated despicably by the judicial process. 'What is more effectual to deter Judges from giving Judgment rashly, than the following History of the Condemnation of the Sieur d'Anglarde and his Wife, who were condemned upon mere Conjectures?' (p. 290). It is the miscarriage of justice that most vexes the narrator rather than the contradictions the case throws up.[84] The knotty tensions implicit in the original case and legal factum are smoothed away and this becomes a grievous instance of judicial failure and nothing else. Moreover, instead of asking or requiring us to choose between Lady Langlade and the Count, the narrative resolves the dispute by affirming the rightness of both parties: while the Langlardes' conviction is deemed 'injurious, wrongful and illegal' (p. 346) the Count, we are reassured, simply made an honest mistake. The fact that a new judgement is reached, and a fair one at that, shows us, or is meant to show us, that the system is capable of making good on its failings.

---

[83] Biet, 'Judicial Fiction and Literary Fiction', p. 404.
[84] For example, we're told that 'The Verdict... is one of the most deplorable Instances of Error, into which the human mind is capable of being surprised', de Pitaval, *A Select Collection*, p. 299.

The same recuperative tendencies are evident in Henry Fielding's *The Life of Mr Jonathan Wild the Great* (1743). While Gay thrusts us directly into the grubby, Hogarthian world of the gin shop, Fielding recreates Jonathan Wild as an upwardly mobile bounder and crucially adopts a heavily ironic register which allows us to sneer at, rather than feel unsettled by, his protagonist's gestures towards 'greatness'. The result is a more comfortable, less politically incisive vision of statecraft, business, and the law, where the complexities and contradictions of Gay's play and H.D.'s narrative are glossed, Fielding using the figure of Wild to satirize Walpole or, if not Walpole, then other supposedly 'great' men. The skills required to run a criminal enterprise and the affairs of state are, at first glance, similar. But when challenged, Wild is quick to distinguish between 'a legal Society' where 'the Chief Magistrate is always chosen for the public Good' and doesn't sacrifice this good for 'his own Wealth or Pleasure' and 'an illegal Society' where absolute submission to a Head is all that staves off dissolution.[85] The reference to the Chief Magistrate is heavily ironic but by insisting on this distinction at all, Wild (and by implication Fielding) is acknowledging that the criminal world does in the end operate according to a different set of rules. This, in turn, sets the stage for his own demise, for while the state can only be toppled by revolution, a common criminal need only be subject to the rule of law, however imperfect this may be. Ultimately Wild is put to death and the authority of the law, with its attendant links to private property, is reinforced. As Denning concludes, 'Fielding's novel turns the contradictions of the Wild story as written by Gay into a bourgeois morality piece much like the original criminal pamphlets. We are given the vicarious thrill in the life of an aristocratic villain ... and are then gratified to see the villain brought to justice.'[86]

If E.P. Thompson sees the '"sub-culture" of the Hanoverian Whig and the "sub-culture" of Jonathan Wild' as 'mirror-images of each other'[87] we should reflect, by way of a conclusion, on these different appropriations of Wild's life and what they suggest about the newly emerging preoccupation with crime. Perhaps the dark ironies and subversive energies of the 1720s, fuelled by anxieties surrounding rampant criminality and the bursting of the South Sea bubble, had run their course by the time Fielding published his novel about Wild. Certainly the ambiguous morality of H.D.'s account of Wild's life and *The Life and Actions of Lewis Dominique Cartouche* is, in Fielding's novel, replaced by a satirical impulse which in the end yields to a more conventional bourgeois morality. Still, the influence of these earlier examples should not be undersold, especially their willingness to bring crime, politics, and trade into messy but ultimately productive tension. It may be too far-sighted to claim that Gramsci would make a similar move two centuries later (see Chapter 5) and argue for the state's increasing penetration of civil society.

But it is significant, I think, that Bertolt Brecht, a Marxist sympathizer and a contemporary of Gramsci, would go back to Gay's *The Beggar's Opera* and the

---

[85] Henry Fielding, *The Life of Mr Jonathan Wild the Great*, ed. Hugh Amory (Oxford: Oxford University Press, 2003), p. 122.
[86] Denning, 'Beggars and Thieves', p. 47.   [87] Thompson, *Whigs and Hunters*, p. 218.

figure of the thief/thief-taker as the source for *The Threepenny Opera* (1928). Brecht takes an idea that is implicit in *The Beggar's Opera*—i.e. that Peachum's form of commercial endeavour is parasitic on the everyday practices of the criminal underclass and working poor—and develops it into a full-blown critique of capitalism. More particularly, and looking ahead to the kind of work that would come to be categorized as crime fiction later in the nineteenth century, these texts—in different ways—end up (unwillingly) reiterating the authority of the state, while raising troubling questions about the adequacy and fairness of the justice system as a whole. In doing so, works by Defoe, H.D., and Gay establish a tension that would become constitutive and foundational of crime writing as an emerging genre: that the state is necessary for the creation and maintenance of public life and central to the reproduction of the socio-economic inequalities that lead to crime in the first place.

2

'Let Us Attack Injustice at Its Source'
Crime Literature in an Era of Revolution and Reform

In the spring of 1762 the French writer and philosopher Voltaire read about the trial and planned execution of Jean Calas in Toulouse. Already opposed to the unreformed justice system, and all too aware of the potential for error or abuse, the case—what Voltaire perceived as an obvious miscarriage of justice—gave him the chance to intervene in order to demonstrate this opposition. In October of the previous year, Marc-Anthony Calas was found hanging in his father's shop. Initially the family tried to have the death treated as murder (since suicide, the more likely explanation, was outlawed and carried a great social and religious stigma) and claimed an unidentified intruder was responsible. The authorities, however, decided to focus their suspicions on the father, Jean, believing that as a Huguenot Protestant he had murdered his son in order to stop him from converting to Catholicism. There was little physical evidence to support this accusation but the magistrate was convinced of his guilt and on 9 March 1762 the appellate court condemned Calas to die at the stake.[1] When news of the verdict reached Voltaire, he decided to look into the affair, focusing on the magistrate's botched investigation. Committed to the principle of penal reform, the case seemed, for Voltaire, to embody all that was wrong with the French justice system: the power invested in individual magistrates, the lack of openness, the undue influence of the Catholic church, and the apparent ease with which conjecture and bias could influence the judicial process. Assuming the role of detective, Voltaire set about trying to overturn the verdict: he interviewed the family, made inquiries in Toulouse, and looked into claims that Marc-Anthony had been about to convert. 'It is useful to investigate matters thoroughly',[2] he told a friend. Convinced of the father's innocence, Voltaire widened his search and found further cases where religious prejudice may have influenced the legal process and where Calvinist 'imbeciles' had been wrongly imprisoned. Enraged by these and other miscarriages of justices, he petitioned at the highest levels to have the Calas conviction reassessed and finally in 1765, after a protracted judicial review, Jean Calas was pardoned and the family cleared of any wrongdoing in the death of the son.

---

[1] Peter Gay, *Voltaire's Politics: The Poet as Realist* (Princeton, NJ: Princeton University Press, 1959), p. 275. My subsequent account of Voltaire's investigation is largely derived from this source. For further details, also see Theodore Bestman, *Voltaire* (London and Harlow: Longmans, 1969) and A. Owen Aldridge, *Voltaire and the Century of Light* (Princeton, NJ: Princeton University Press, 1975).

[2] Gay, *Voltaire's Politics*, p. 276.

The crime story would not be brought into existence, at least as a recognized genre with its own codes and readers, for another hundred years but it is significant how closely the reasons informing Voltaire's inquiries, the investigation itself, and the positive outcome mirror the preoccupations and yearnings of the two most important late eighteenth- and early nineteenth-century crime fiction archetypes: William Godwin's *Things As They Are; or, The Adventures of Caleb Williams*, hereafter referred to as *Caleb Williams* (1794), and Eugène-François Vidocq's four-volume *Memoirs* (1828). Godwin, the political anarchist, may not have found much in common with the more conservative Voltaire but both were appalled by the arbitrary horrors of state-sanctioned punishments and the extent to which 'due process' could be hijacked by particular interests (e.g. the church and the aristocracy). Both also understood that reform, and not revolution, was the best way to bring about a fairer, more egalitarian society. The successful outcome of Voltaire's campaign to free Jean Calas demonstrated a number of important lessons that subsequent writers, including Voltaire himself, would try to heed when addressing the subjects of crime and punishment: that the archaic judicial system could be challenged and that larger scale penal reform was, by implication, possible; that power and privilege didn't always win out and vested interests could be exposed and to some extent checked; that careful, methodical detective work could play its part in improving social conditions; and that such work might in turn bring morality, the law, and justice into closer proximity. But time and time again the works themselves, while ostensibly committed to such ideals, ended up demonstrating the opposite: that reform was impossible, ineffective, or both and privilege too embedded in the system to be swept away; that investigative efforts, even where they were methodical and painstaking, could not bring the truth, whatever this was, into focus; and that moral claims about 'good' and 'evil' were irrelevant for most people's 'lived' realities.

Voltaire's practical interventions in the penal reform debate may have shown that the rational individual could act to expose and even rectify glaring abuses of power (anticipating an important strain in crime fiction where the detective would attempt a similar end). Similarly the 'penetrating and subtle power of discernment' demonstrated by Zadig in Voltaire's novel of the same name at being able to infer from the marks and tracks left behind on the ground certain truths about the horse that made them is an early, perhaps even the first, example of the kind of inductive logic that would become central to the detective's approach to crime solving.[3] But in his most famous work of fiction, *Candide* (1759), Voltaire asks whether rationality and righteousness are linked and if so whether the distinction between right and wrong has any rational basis. At the start of the tale Candide, Voltaire's eponymous hero, is presented as being 'quite sound in his judgement' and possessing 'the most straightforward of minds'.[4] He occupies a stable and secure world where he is aware of his inferior social rank (at least compared to the Baron and his two

---

[3] Voltaire, *Candide and Other Stories*, trans. and notes Roger Pearson (Oxford: Oxford University Press, 1998), p. 133.
[4] Voltaire, *Candide and Other Stories*, p. 1.

children) and where the teachings of Pangloss confirm the orderly nature of the universe ('there is no effect without cause' so that 'everything having been made for a purpose, everything is necessary for the best purpose', p. 2). However, the sacking of the Baron's Westphalian home scatters the various protagonists across the globe and wrenches Candide from his secure moorings. Later, when reunited with the Baron's son, whom he thought dead, joy for Candide quickly turns to blind rage, when the son rails against the idea of Candide, the commoner, marrying his sister, and Candide 'drew his own [sword] and plunged it up to the hilt into the Jesuit Baron's gut' (p. 39). Notable is his lack of insight into the relationship between cause and effect (e.g. that he was provoked and had reason to lash out in such a manner) and his insistence that, despite what he's done, he remains good. 'I am the best fellow in the world and already that makes three men I've killed' (p. 39). In other words, in spite of Voltaire's faith in the capacity for rational thought to intervene in the world for positive and even 'good' ends, what we see in *Candide*, and what confronts Candide at the end of the story, is not the orderly, benevolent universe promised by Pangloss but a Hobbesian world where 'the weak execrate the strong while they grovel at their feet' (p. 58) or at best one of metaphysical confusion where good intentions do not necessarily yield positive outcomes.

The lesson of Voltaire's tale would not be lost on Godwin and on subsequent generations of crime novelists later in the nineteenth and twentieth centuries. As Michael Cohen puts it, 'suspicion that judgements about right and wrong follow money and power' conceal, though barely so 'a deeper and more disquieting suspicion that right and wrong are not discoverable... that guilt can face it out without being discovered and that innocence has no power to make itself known'.[5] Godwin and Voltaire would love this not to be so and both actively pursue the goal of creating a fairer world but their work, especially their fiction, asks awkward, potentially unanswerable questions about the practicality of such efforts: whether privilege can be dislodged, what good and evil mean, and whether disorder can ever be contained. It is the resulting 'powerful phantasmagoria of anarchy versus order'[6]—or the irreconcilable tension between individual freedom and the demands of law—that would give the emerging crime story its narrative shape and political thrust. As a political radical and self-professed anarchist, and author of a treatise entitled *Enquiry Concerning Political Justice*, published in 1793, a year before *Caleb Williams*, Godwin may have been instinctively and systematically opposed to entrenched privilege and the consolidation of state power but his work—fiction and non-fiction—betrays considerable anxieties about abandoning a world organized around private property (and indeed tradition) and embracing the revolutionary unknown. The same could be said of Cesare Beccaria's *On Crimes and Punishment* (1765), which sets out its case for penal reform in a clear, methodical manner but also demonstrates, consciously or not, the same doubts and anxieties that plague Godwin's *Caleb Williams*. Indeed it is worth looking closely at Beccaria's

---

[5] Michael Cohen, 'Godwin's *Caleb Williams*: Showing the Strains in Detective Fiction', *Eighteenth-Century Fiction*, 10:2 (January 1998), p. 216.
[6] Roger Caillois qtd in Robin Walz, 'Vidocq, Rogue Cop', in François-Eugène Vidocq (ed.) *Memoirs of Vidocq: Master of Crime* (Oakland, CA and Edinburgh: AK Press/Nabat, 2003), p. xv.

work, and not just because of its immediate impact on debates about penal reform across Europe, particularly in France where it was recruited by Voltaire to aid his own campaign against the unreformed judicial system and in Britain where Bentham credited Beccaria with being 'the father of Censorial Jurisprudence'.[7]

Beccaria's short book, an uneasy synthesis of contractarian claims derived from Hobbes and Locke and utilitarian arguments developed from Helvetius, wants to take on vested interests and conglomerations of wealth and privilege, and use penal reform as a means of instigating social change, but in a progressive rather than revolutionary manner. Evoking a Hobbesian argument about the benefits of swapping the intolerable freedom of the state of nature for the socially useful security of the social contract, Beccaria claims that '[l]aws are the condition by which independent and isolated men, tired of living in a constant state of war and of enjoying a freedom made useless by the uncertainty of keeping it, unite in society'.[8] But whereas Hobbes argues that the transfer of power, and the surrender of rights, from the people to the sovereign has to be permanent and absolute, Beccaria's account of the social contract, like Locke's, is more limited and arguably more aware of the potential abuses that can accrue from the unnecessary concentration of power. People, he remarks, only need sacrifice 'a portion of this liberty to enjoy the remainder of it in security and tranquillity'.[9] For Beccaria, just punishments—administered by a fair-minded and well-regulated judiciary—enhance rather than curtail liberty and private individuals should be encouraged to give up a small portion of this liberty not for some notional public good but rather because it benefits them to do so. '[F]or there is no enlightened man who does not love the open, clear and useful contracts of public security,' Beccaria writes, 'when he compares the slight portion of useless liberty that he has sacrificed to the total sum of all the liberty sacrificed by other men'.[10] In other words, Beccaria's defence of an individual's interests does not rest on the idea of natural rights but on the principle of utility and maximizing individual happiness. This is achieved by minimizing the state's capacity to inflict harm on others or rather by limiting punishments to what is necessary in order to maintain social cohesion and security in the face of internal and external threats: 'All punishments that exceed what is necessary to preserve this bond are unjust by their very nature.'[11]

Godwin would pursue a similar line of argument in both *Caleb Williams* and *Political Justice*. The collective target is the archaic, irregular, semi-feudal system of justice that predominated in the second half of the eighteenth century throughout Europe. But the question of how to address and even rectify this problem and particularly the role that the state would play in this task is a good deal more contentious; and Godwin, arguably more than Beccaria (perhaps because he wrote

---

[7] Richard Bellamy, 'Introduction' in Cesare Beccaria, *On Crimes and Punishments, and Other Writings*, ed. Richard Bellamy (Cambridge: Cambridge University Press, 2003), p. xvii.
[8] Cesare Beccaria, *On Crimes and Punishments*, notes and intro. David Young (Indianapolis, IN: Hackett, 1986), p. 7.
[9] Beccaria, *On Crimes and Punishments*, p. 7.
[10] Beccaria, *On Crimes and Punishments*, p. 76.
[11] Beccaria, *On Crimes and Punishments*, p. 9.

these two texts in light of the British government's post-1789 crackdown against political dissenters), is all too aware of the damaging consequences for individual liberty of the 'dangerous and excessive' consolidation of power by the state—a position that sets him against Hobbes. Beccaria and Godwin both recognize that laws, to quote Beccaria, are 'often dictated by the powerful out of greed and endured by the weak';[12] that tyrannies perpetrated by the rich and powerful in the name of law have a more damaging effect on society as a whole than crimes committed by the poor because their influence 'works at a wider distance and with greater force' by 'destroying the idea of justice and duty among subjects and substituting the right of the strongest'; and that crime itself could be the product of 'misery and deprivation'.[13] In this respect, Beccaria argues that the right of property, which he also refers to as 'a terrible and perhaps unnecessary right', potentially leaves 'only a bare existence'[14] for those who do not benefit from this right. As Cohen points out, Godwin had a similar unease about private property ownership, arguing for a collective right to property, in line with his communitarian instincts.[15] But just as Godwin prevaricates on this issue, by also claiming that individuals are entitled to the fruits of their own industry,[16] Beccaria, more of an enlightened absolutist than Godwin, sees private commerce as a benefit to social stability rather than as a cause of unrest—as long as trade takes place in an open, well-regulated environment where everyone is equal under the law. While security and freedom under the law, for Beccaria, are 'the true foundations of happiness', the lure of wealth and luxury, if pursued in a thriving and open economy, also 'opposes despotism because it stimulates men's industry and activity'.[17] Godwin's *Caleb Williams* wants to attack the domain of privilege, of which property ownership is an integral feature, and is deeply suspicious about the role of the marketplace in instrumentalizing literature as a form of control; but the novel can't quite throw its weight behind those, like Captain Raymond and his band of outlaws, who commit crimes to show up the iniquities of private ownership and who would seem to embody some kind alternative to the status quo.

The extent to which the marketplace is a free realm is also a contentious issue for Beccaria and Godwin and if it is not, then equally contentious is the relationship between property, ownership, and the state. Godwin's anti-statist rhetoric is a good deal sharper than Beccaria's. While Godwin is angered that 'the spirit and character of the government intrudes itself into every rank of society',[18] Beccaria cedes that the state is the only authority capable of representing 'all of society united by a

---

[12] Beccaria, *On Crimes and Punishments*, p. 65; also see pp. 47, 78.
[13] Beccaria, *On Crimes and Punishments*, pp. 18–19.
[14] Beccaria, *On Crimes and Punishments*, pp. 39–40.
[15] Cohen, 'Godwin's *Caleb Williams*', p. 208.
[16] See William Godwin, *Enquiry Concerning Political Justice*, ed. K. Codwell Carter (Oxford: Oxford University Press, 1971), pp. 108–9. For a fuller account of Godwin's complicated views on property, see Godwin, *Enquiry Concerning Political Justice and its Influence on Morals and Happiness*, Vol. 2, ed. F.E.L. Priestley (Toronto, ON: University of Toronto Press, 1946), pp. 420–53.
[17] Beccaria, *On Crimes and Punishments*, p. 62.
[18] Godwin, 'Preface', *Caleb Williams*, ed. David McCracken (Oxford: Oxford University Press, 1998), p. 1.

social contract'.[19] And while Godwin is primarily concerned with coercion and the role that the state plays in perpetuating coercion, Beccaria wants to argue for the state, anticipating the position adopted by nineteenth-century liberals like von Humbolt, as night watchman, a neutral arbiter between theoretically free and equal competitors.[20] Beccaria's interest, as a jurist, is primarily in the law and as such he argues that a properly calibrated legal system, with proportionate punishments directly relating to the severity of crimes committed, a more efficient and much prompter judicial process, and a scaling back of capital punishment, would reduce the need for institutions of the state, such as the police, to directly intervene in society.[21] What results from this, according to Beccaria, is an orderly, secure state where a less draconian, some might say more *enlightened* penal regime reflects positively on 'the condition of the nation itself',[22] but he qualifies this with a warning that has a direct bearing on Godwin's depiction of the cosy, perhaps even corrupt relationship between squire and magistrate. 'If... the sovereign accustoms his subjects to fear the magistrates more than the law, then the magistrates will profit from this fear more than the personal and public security will gain from it.'[23] In this scenario, as Richard Bellamy points out, where the benefits of the legal system are not equally distributed and the state's partiality is made clear, the resultant failure 'would not only justify but also positively promote crime'.[24]

The idea that the law, in Godwin's novel, promotes the happiness of some rather more than others raises the prospect of, and indeed legitimizes, popular dissent, and the desire on the part of the authorities to crush this dissent, via a highly visible show of force, allows us to see the state in *Caleb Williams* not just as coercive but also anxious, threatened, and divided. But the fact that Godwin's own dissident instincts are kept in check, and Caleb Williams acquiesces in the novel's final courtroom scene to Falkland's enlightened despotism, and the attendant world of privilege, would have important implications for the development of the genre as a whole. For the type of crime story that will become central to my account of this development, e.g. *Caleb Williams*, opposes conglomerations of privilege and vested interests, is suspicious of unchecked, arbitrary power, supports due process and the idea of all being equal under the law, and wants to counter the surrender of public bodies to private interests. But equally, as we see in Godwin's novel, such sentiments

---

[19] Beccaria, *On Crimes and Punishments*, p. 9.
[20] David Held describes the character of classical nineteenth century 'English liberalism' as follows: '[T]he state was to have the role of umpire or referee while individuals pursued, according to the rules of economic competition and free exchange, their own interests.' See 'Central Perspectives on the Modern State', in Gregor McLennan, David Held, and Stuart Hall (eds) *The Idea of the Modern State* (Milton Keynes and Philadelphia, PA: Open University Press, 1984), p. 43.
[21] Emphasizing consent over coercion, or public opinion over force, Beccaria—anticipating a claim that Hegel would make in *The Philosophy of Right*—argued that 'the magnitude of punishment ought to be relative to the condition of the nation' and that 'to the extent that human spirits are made gentle by the social state, sensibility increases; [and] as it increases, the severity of punishment must diminish if one wishes to maintain a constant relationship between object and feeling' (Beccaria, *On Crimes and Punishments*, p. 81).
[22] Beccaria, *On Crimes and Punishments*, p. 81.
[23] Beccaria, *On Crimes and Punishments*, p. 78.
[24] Bellamy, 'Introduction', *On Crimes and Punishments*, p. xxiv.

run aground on the truculent 'reality' of things as they are: where state coercion, if not brutality, persists, where everyone is not equal under the law and the benefits of the legal system are not equitably distributed, where the public good is hocked to private interests, and where viable alternatives flounder before our eyes.

CALEB WILLIAMS: 'GOVERNMENT ... IS A QUESTION OF FORCE'

In the preface of *Caleb Williams*, Godwin announces the repressive capacities of the state: 'It is now well known to philosophers that the spirit and character of the government intrudes itself into every rank of society.'[25] Still, with Godwin's novel as a whole in mind, we need to be careful how far we push this claim, especially in the particular context of its publication and reception. Godwin may have had an instinctive sympathy for the Jacobins and opposed the state-sponsored crackdown against dissenters in Britain in the 1790s but *Caleb Williams* is largely silent about the events of the French Revolution itself. Where the subject of revolt is raised, for example in the preface in which Godwin comments, '[w]hile one side pleads for reformation and change, the other extols... the existing constitution of society',[26] the implications and inferences are by no means clear. Is change here a good thing or are there merits in supporting the existing constitution of society? Godwin's political instincts may put him on the side of the dissidents but this support is always qualified and any revolutionary fervour is always tempered by a utilitarian pragmatism. More to the point, as Cohen argues, if Godwin's political writing displays a degree of ambivalence regarding the competing claims of tradition and change, these gaps or fissures are opened up or exposed even more effectively in *Caleb Williams*. This in turn draws attention to what the novel—and the proto-crime novel—is able to do, vis-à-vis the drier, more precise idiom of the political treatise: '[In the novel] Godwin confronts the genuine incompatibility of human experiences in a way that his theoretical... treatise cannot' and hence 'grapples with the problems of truth and justice in ways that specifically anticipate the approaches of later popular fiction'.[27]

At the heart of the literature of penal reform and Godwin's political and fictional work (and indeed the emergent crime story) is a preoccupation with the law; with the law's ability, even when applied humanely, to confront and remedy society's problems, notably its glaring inequalities. If Godwin had a good deal less faith than a jurist like Beccaria or Bentham in what could be achieved by reforming the criminal justice system, he was also unconvinced by the revolutionary claims of the French Jacobins, precisely because of the absence of a proper legal infrastructure. 'Revolution is instigated by a horror against tyranny, yet its own tyranny is not without peculiar aggravations.'[28] Apparently endorsing a jurist position, Godwin

---

[25] Godwin, *Caleb Williams*, p. 1.   [26] Godwin, *Caleb Williams*, p. 1.
[27] Cohen, 'Godwin's *Caleb Williams*', p. 208.
[28] Godwin, *Enquiry Concerning Political Justice*, p. 136.

cedes that lasting social improvement can only be sustained 'when the improvement of our institutions advances',[29] and as such comes close to replicating Bentham's argument against Revolutionary France which he calls 'a country without government; a pretended legislature without powers to make laws'.[30] Only strong, central government, Bentham writes, can create the rational, uniform legal frameworks that are necessary to ensure public utility. However, it is over this question of utility and the role of government that Bentham and Godwin part ways. For Godwin, some form of limited government is necessary for the provision of security and as a bulwark against out and out anarchy, but by extending its reach into all areas of existence even this type of limited government ends up 'regulat[ing] behaviour which ought to be left to individual discretion'.[31] In the same way, the authority of the government wanes as soon as it wavers 'in the smallest degree from the line of justice'[32]—and once individuals see this injustice and withdraw their support for the state 'the fabric which it built upon it falls to the ground'.[33] Therefore proper utility, for Godwin, cannot result from legal reform alone (as it can for Bentham) but rather from an individual's natural propensity for justice which is defined as 'that mode of action, which constitutes the best application of the capacity of the individual, to the general advantage'.[34]

This tension between the claims of individual liberty and the acknowledgement of the role of government is a foundational one for Godwin's novel, and for the crime story as a genre that would follow later in the nineteenth century. On the first page Godwin introduces his novel as 'a general review of the modes of domestic and unrecorded despotism by which man becomes the destroyer of man' (p. 1) and thereafter he offers two instances of this despotism, and of the poisonous effects of arbitrary tyranny and by extension the unreformed legal system. The first culprit is Barnabus Tyrell, a crude, atavistic landowner who 'arbitrarily uses power that results from his economic station, ruining his tenant Hawkins and killing his poor relative Emily Melville'.[35] Tyrell's animus is directed primarily at his aristocratic neighbour Fernando Falkland who initially at least would seem to be everything he's not: urbane, intelligent, and sufficiently virtuous to argue that 'the rich must do every thing in our power to lighten the yoke of these unfortunate people' (p. 77). The conflict between the two landowners comes to a climax at the end of the first volume when Tyrell is found murdered and Falkland emerges as the chief suspect. The fact that Falkland is quickly exonerated by an official investigation is not a surprise, given his elevated social rank. The law, Godwin suggests, always protects the powerful. The fact Falkland sets out to persecute his secretary

---

[29] Godwin, *Enquiry Concerning Political Justice*, p. 138.
[30] Jeremy Bentham, *Rights, Representation and Reform: Nonsense upon Stilts and Other Writings*, eds Philip Schofield, Catherine Pease-Watkin, and Cyprian Blamires (Oxford: Clarendon Press, 2002), p. 265.
[31] See K. Codell Carter, 'Editor's Introduction' in Godwin, *Enquiry Concerning Political Justice*, p. xxix.
[32] Godwin, *Enquiry Concerning Political Justice*, p. 116.
[33] Godwin, *Enquiry Concerning Political Justice*, p. 77.
[34] Godwin, *Enquiry Concerning Political Justice*, p. 14.
[35] Cohen, 'Godwin's *Caleb Williams*', p. 209.

Caleb Williams once Williams initiates a private investigation into his affairs is more of a problem for readers, especially as Falkland's benevolence has already been established.

Two tentative conclusions can be drawn. First, this portrait of Falkland points to Godwin's ambivalence regarding a Burkean squirearchy and that Falkland, at once noble and yet cruel and vindictive if cornered, is 'as close to his utilitarian aristocrat'—described and to some extent defended in *Political Justice*—'as a flawed society will allow a man to be'.[36] As we will see, this ambivalence comes out most significantly in the final courtroom passage where Falkland's guilt and yet also his 'good' character is simultaneously affirmed. Second and more importantly, this reversal—Falkland's transformation from liberal protector to illiberal despot—serves to remind readers that individuals matter far less than the system itself, especially since individual tyrants are 'a copy of what monarchs are, who reckon among the instruments of their power prisons of the state' (p. 177) and since Caleb's righteous anger extends to 'the whole machine of society' (p. 183). In other words, if Falkland is no better than Tyrell, then our attention needs to shift to what, if anything, can be done to reform the system as a whole, so that the fate of men like Caleb does not depend on the whims of the rich who will always look to shore up their positions.

This urgent imperative to reform the archaic justice system would seem to steer *Caleb Williams* towards the positions staked out by Beccaria and Bentham. Just as Beccaria argues against draconian punishment regimes, seeks to rein in the arbitrary power of magistrates, and draws attention to unreformed laws that inevitably favour the clergy and nobility, *Caleb Williams* demonstrates how existing legal statutes are used by the wealthy to secure their own interests. The Black Act of 1724 is used by Tyrell to silence a just complaint from his tenant, while Falkland's familial association with the local magistrate Forrester means that Caleb's plea for a fair trial (once he has been wrongly accused by Falkland of theft) falls on deaf ears. Caleb here falls victim to the kind of 'legal despotism' (p. 184) highlighted by Beccaria. His trial is indefinitely postponed while he is allowed to rot in prison, and when it does take place he is not given any opportunity to set out his defence. In an implicit retort to continental thinkers like Montesquieu and Voltaire who praised aspects of the English criminal justice system (e.g. trial by jury and *habeas corpus*), Godwin exposes the hollowness of the English refrain that 'we have no Bastille!' and 'no man can be punished without a crime!' (p. 181). Assuming Godwin's political anger, Caleb scolds these assumptions, declaring 'Go, go, ignorant fool! and visit the scenes of our prisons!...witness their unwholesomeness, their filth...After that show me the man shameless enough to triumph, and say, England has no Bastille!' (p. 181).

The social contract envisaged here is less totalizing than its Hobbesian incarnation and implicit in Godwin's exhortations is the realization or acceptance that unfairness, when it is so self-evident, is enough to sanction a concerted programme of individual and perhaps even collective resistance. Godwin's call to arms mirrors

[36] Cohen, 'Godwin's *Caleb Williams*', p. 209.

or approximates Beccaria's at least in so far as both equate ostensible criminality—being designated as criminal by an unfair system—with social rebellion. The following is Beccaria's attempt to imagine the reasoning of a justified thief:

> What are these laws that I must respect and that leave such a great distance between me and the rich man? He denies me the penny I ask of him, and he excuses himself by exhorting me to work, something with which he himself is unfamiliar. Who made these laws? Rich and powerful men who have never deigned to visit the squalid hovels of the poor... Let us break these bonds that are so ruinous for the majority and useful to a handful of indolent tyrants; let us attack injustice at its source. I shall revert to my natural state of independence, and for a time I shall live free and happy from the fruits of my courage and industry. (pp. 50–1)

The technique employed is similar to that of a novelist—i.e. trying to get inside the mind of a character—and it is evident how closely this section of *On Crimes and Punishments* resembles a corresponding passage from Godwin's novel in which Caleb discusses the 'perfidiousness exercised by the powerful members of the community against those who were less privileged than themselves' with a renegade or outlaw called Reynolds who seeks to justify the fact that he steals in explicitly political terms. 'Who that saw the situation in its true light would wait till their oppressors thought fit to decree their destruction, and not take arms in their defence while it was yet in their power?' (p. 220). Still, both Beccaria and Godwin eventually back away from Hobsbawm's social bandit thesis (whereby *certain* criminal acts are understood as 'a cry for vengeance on the rich and oppressors, a vague dream of some curb upon them, a righting of individual wrongs'[37]), though perhaps for different reasons. For Beccaria, the jurist, the solution to such ills lies in comprehensive reform rather than rebellion, whatever form it takes, while it is Godwin's utilitarianism that causes him to reject what the robbers stand for, despite praising their 'good qualities' and 'their uncommon energy, ingenuity and fortitude' (p. 226). The case against theft is convoluted and involves a tortuous, conflicted defence of property, but it rests upon what is best for the whole:

> The man who risks or sacrifices his life for the public cause is rewarded with the testimony of an approving conscience; but persons who wantonly defy the necessary, though atrociously exaggerated precautions of government in the matter of property, at the same time that they commit an alarming hostility against the whole, are as to their own concerns scarcely less absurd and self-neglectful, than a man who should set himself up as a mark for a file of musqueteers to shoot at. (pp. 226–7)

If some form of limited government is necessary for the general good, even if its precautions in the matter of property are 'atrociously exaggerated', and if potentially violent crime, even where it takes the form of protest, can commit 'an alarming hostility against the whole', the specific issue of how to protest against unfairness and oppression and how effective such protest might be becomes pertinent. In *Political Justice*, Godwin falls back on the nebulous concept of an individual's

---

[37] E.J. Hobsbawm, *Primitive Rebels; Studies in Archaic Forms of Social Movement in the 19th and 20th Centuries* (Manchester: Manchester University Press, 1971), p. 5.

natural propensity for justice (i.e. 'the best application of the capacity of the individual, to the general advantage'). But in *Caleb Williams* whether this individual propensity for justice can bring about a general good, exactly how or under what circumstances this propensity is produced, and what happens when it comes up against an all-pervasive power that stubbornly refuses to acknowledge it is less clear.

For jurists like Beccaria and particularly Bentham, there is a clear relationship between cause and effect. The will to reform and the careful drawing up of plans for preventative policing, pauper management, or judicial organization is based upon what L.J. Hume calls 'the expectation that one could make institutions more efficient by imposing on them uniformity, simplicity and clarity'.[38] In other words, by carefully studying and observing the unreformed world and coming up with a series of rational deductions based upon these observations you could hope to create a coherent body of thought which in turn might help to produce a fairer, more efficient system. It is no coincidence that the detective in crime fiction might want to claim a similar method but it is equally revealing that Caleb Williams, once he turns his hand to detecting, for example trying to gather evidence and to use principles of observation and rational deduction to arrive at the truth and expose Falkland's culpability in the matter of Tyrell's death, falls apart or is made to fall apart.

Caleb's instincts as a detective are unerring. Having witnessed his master's secretive behaviour, and his total transformation following Tyrell's death, Caleb's suspicions that Falkland may have been responsible are confirmed by Falkland himself, after he catches Caleb snooping for evidence in his private quarters. As Cohen points out, Caleb makes much of evidence;[39] of gathering and processing the material evidence at hand in order to prove or disprove particular theories. He only becomes convinced of his master's guilt 'after having carefully examined the different kinds of evidence of which the subject was susceptible, and recollecting all that had passed on the subject' (p. 123). But this faith is dashed in a number of ways. First, Caleb does not actually find any physical evidence proving his master's guilt and the 'truth' is only revealed when Falkland confesses to him on the understanding that Caleb keeps this information to himself. Second, when Falkland decides he cannot trust Caleb and when Caleb is forced, or chooses, to flee his master's home, Falkland concocts evidence in order to prove that Caleb stole from him. Godwin manages to undermine the basis of legal rationalism in other ways too. The application of a rationalist methodology assumes the presence of a figure able to think and act in these terms: that is to say, a rational, coherent and knowable subject. Caleb Williams might believe himself to be such a figure but faith in his observational prowess and evidence gathering techniques quickly yield to something less comfortable. 'The spring of action, which more than any other, characterised the whole train of my life was curiosity', he informs us initially, consciously or otherwise evoking Bentham. 'It was this that gave me my mechanical turn; I was

---

[38] See L.J. Hume, *Bentham and Bureaucracy* (Cambridge: Cambridge University Press, 1981), pp. 11–12.
[39] Cohen, 'Godwin's *Caleb Williams*', p. 211.

desirous of tracing the variety of effects which might be produced from given causes' (p. 4). But rather than producing proof and perhaps even truth, this curiosity leads Caleb into much darker territory, a move that underscores Godwin's more typical reputation as a Gothic rather than crime or detective writer.[40] Indeed when he addresses his capabilities as detective at finding proof of Falkland's guilt, the result is not the production of this proof but his own abyssal descent into a nightmarish world of flight, anxiety, and paranoia.

In part Caleb's plight is a consequence of not paying sufficient deference to the master–servant relationship and hence of not accepting his own subservient position vis-à-vis Falkland. The spectre of the zealous, over-watchful servant activated a particularly English fear of social and/or class transgression. But Caleb's plight is not simply the result of overstepping his class role. Rather, Godwin suggests, it is because he has been *too* curious and that his curiosity, rather than being a condition of his function as detective, is some kind of fatal flaw. 'The reader can with difficulty form a conception of the state to which I was now reduced', Caleb tells us, indicating how far he has unravelled. 'My act was in some sort an act of insanity; but how indescribable are the feelings with which I looked back upon it' (p. 132). In other words, it is his impulse to find out, to unearth his master's secret, the very *raison d'être* of the detective story, that is figured as weakness rather than strength. As Stephen Knight argues, Caleb is neither just 'the poor clever youth' who 'will expose the older, decadent authority' nor a 'tragic victim of [that authority's] power' but rather a man 'who must face up to the fact that there might be something evaluatively wrong with [his] desire to inquire'.[41]

Here, the rationalist epistemology of the emerging crime story comes fatally unstuck. Even before we can talk about the crime story as its own literary genre, Godwin is suggesting not simply that the application of rational thought to specific problems may not yield the right answers but even more daringly that the inquirer's failure to find justice requires us to examine what constitutes justice in the first place and whether it can be achieved or even known. The ending of the novel is indicative, but only if we see Caleb's doggedness and ultimately his efforts to force a confession from his master and chief tormentor as failure rather than success. It is quite possible to argue the opposite: to see Falkland's confession in the climactic courtroom passage as vindication for Caleb or even as his triumph. Patrick Bratlinger pursues this claim in relation to what he identifies as Caleb's growing literacy: 'it is only through the ability to read and write', he maintains, 'that Caleb is finally able to rectify the situation, demonstrate his innocence and bring Falkland to justice'.[42] In order to challenge the logic of Falkland's malicious

---

[40] See, for example, David Punter, *The Literature of Terror: A History of Gothic Fictions from 1765 to the Present Day* (New York, NY: Longmans, 1996); Ronald Paulson, 'Gothic Fiction and the French Revolution', *English Literary History*, 48:3 (Autumn 1981), pp. 532–54; Ingrid Horrocks, 'More than a Gravestone: Caleb Williams, Udolpho and the Politics of the Gothic', *Studies in the Novel*, 39:1 (Spring 2007), pp. 31–47.

[41] Stephen Knight, *Crime Fiction 1800–2000: Detection, Death, Diversity* (Basingstoke: Palgrave Macmillan, 2004), p. 11.

[42] Patrick Bratlinger, *The Reading Lesson: The Threat of Mass Literacy in Nineteenth-Century British Fiction* (Bloomington, IN: Indiana University Press, 1998), p. 47.

account of his apparent criminality, which is hawked on London's streets for a halfpenny, Caleb must scribe his own account of his life in order to clear his name and damn Falkland. 'I will use no daggers!' he promises. 'I will unfold a tale –! I show thee for what thou art, and all men that live shall confess my truth! –' (p. 314).

Bratlinger emphasizes—overemphasizes, I think—the threat that Caleb's literacy poses to the established order, maintaining that it 'expresses Godwin's belief in the revolutionary power of democratic literacy and the enlightenment to correct Gothic abuses of power and injustices of the past'.[43] Bailey, too, picks up on Godwin's interest in the politics of writing but instead of suggesting that Caleb wields his pen as weapon, more tellingly, he posits the written word as part of an increasingly sophisticated apparatus of control:

> the obvious powers of the state—the police and the penal system—are only the visible tip of the "extraordinary powers" available to the regime... the real power lies in the ability of those in control—in this case, Falkland—to manufacture consent among the populace through a sophisticated and integrated use of prisons, police and literature.[44]

My point is that Caleb's ability to upset the establishment and punish his former master is by no means as settled as Bratlinger seems to imply. In the context of the violent excesses of the French Revolution and anxieties relating to the breakdown of social order in England, it is questionable how much social upheaval the middle-class Godwin wanted to endure, in spite of his utopian, anti-statist yearnings. For all its righteous anger at judicial injustice, there is little evidence of populism or radicalism at work in Godwin's novel. As a self-educated man 'born of humble parents' (p. 1) but enjoying an existence 'somewhat above middle stature' (p. 4), Caleb is no revolutionary and in spite of what happens to him, he sees no profit in tearing down the system and arguing for the kind of genuine shift in power from the state to its citizens imagined by Rousseau in *The Social Contract* (1762). Rather than agitating for revolution, and articulating his role as unwilling advocate of a system already identified as fundamentally flawed, Caleb chooses to tackle Falkland in court. In doing so, he successfully elicits a confession not because the evidence he presents is overwhelming but only because Falkland decides to unburden himself, a move that rescues him in the eyes of the reader and suggests a softening in Godwin's attitudes towards the social elite.

An alternative ending, written by Godwin prior to the preferred one and then discarded, gives an indication of the author's vacillations about what to do with Falkland: i.e. whether to condemn or rescue him. In the discarded ending, Falkland doesn't waver from his promise to destroy his former servant and Caleb quite literally falls to pieces under the weight of his own rage and impotence. Caleb's legal action fails and faced with jail and ruin, even the power to write, language itself, deserts him. As the text breaks up and blank spaces pepper his narrative, Caleb unravels as a person and becomes nothing. 'HERE LIES WHAT A MAN ONCE

---

[43] Bratlinger, *The Reading Lesson*, p. 48.
[44] Quentin Bailey, '"Extraordinary and Dangerous Powers": Prisons, Police and Literature in Godwin's *Caleb Williams*', *Eighteenth-Century Fiction*, 22:3 (Spring 2010), p. 547.

WAS' (p. 334). Of the two endings, this one is bleaker and in one sense more satisfying, not least because it fulfils the grim promise of previous events and actions and underlines the extent to which the system protects class privilege: the malignant Falkland triumphs, the virtuous Caleb is annihilated. But the ending that Godwin eventually favoured is the more ambiguous. When Falkland declares himself to be 'completely detected' (p. 324) he would seem to be attesting of the power of the proto-detective to uncover, to exculpate. But what exactly, we might ask, has been revealed here and does Caleb in fact triumph? Certainly there is no *volte face* in Godwin's damning attitude towards the law, i.e. Falkland doesn't confess because he is compelled to do so by the law. Rather Caleb's move from outsider to unwilling executioner and his support, consciously articulated or not, for a justice system exposed throughout the novel as archaic and corrupt, speaks to or about the crime story's deeply ambivalent attitude towards the institutions of the state. Falkland's eleventh hour confession, meanwhile, suggests that Godwin's rejection of the possibility that 'moral excellence' might accompany 'hereditary privilege' needs to be revised, further indication of his conflicted attitude towards authority.[45] As a powerful cultural fantasy of law against disorder, *Caleb Williams* looks ahead to Vidocq's *Memoirs* and further into the nineteenth century to both affirm and undercut the logic of legal rationalism and the authority of the state. The novel also proposes a figure, a rational thinker and would-be detective, who is not able to mask the contradictions in his self and who, despite his best efforts, is not able to bring the complex relationship between truth, justice, and morality into proper focus.

CRIMINAL TO/AND POLICEMAN: *MEMOIRS OF VIDOCQ*

Eugène-François Vidocq is a pivotal figure—perhaps *the* pivotal figure—in the emergence of crime writing in the nineteenth century, more so even than Poe's Dupin who according to some accounts is based on Vidocq's self-creation and whose centrality to the unfolding genealogy of the genre (as I'll argue in Chapter 3) has sometimes been overstated.[46] Vidocq too is a pivotal figure in this book, both a throwback to Wild and Cartouche, a rambunctious presence, thief, and thief-taker adept at moving across the legal/illegal divide, and in his role as the first head of the Parisian Brigade du Sûreté a reform-minded individual eager to apply the systematic logic of procedure and jurist principles of legal rationalism to the task of apprehending criminals. Crucially these positions are not as distinct or antithetical as we might imagine. There has been a tendency, at least in Britain, to dismiss Vidocq—and for that matter Wild—as self-promoting rogues (in a theatrical production of his life that opened in London in 1860 Vidocq was described as 'THE

---

[45] Cohen argues this point very well, pointing out that despite Godwin's apparent anti-establishment rhetoric, in his conception of Falkland as what he calls 'benevolent man', he has 'reinvented the aristocracy according to its own self-description as the moral class' ('Godwin's *Caleb Williams*', p. 208).

[46] J. Gerald Kennedy, 'The Limits of Reason: Poe's Deluded Detectives', *American Literature*, 47:2 (May 1975), p. 185.

FRENCH JONATHAN WILD'[47]) but this move blinds us to the significance of Vidocq's *Memoirs* vis-à-vis the emerging crime genre: here, then, Caillous's conception of the crime story as a 'powerful phantasmagoria of anarchy versus order'[48] achieves its most fulsome articulation to date. Vidocq's narrative takes this logic, or this tension, and for the first time brings it to bear on the system of policing and law from an insider's perspective. In turn, this would show us the benefits and more importantly the limits of a Benthamite overhaul of the bureaucratic and administrative apparatus of government, especially when overseen by a figure as unstable, conflicted, and self-interested as Vidocq. This double move whereby Vidocq is figured, or figures himself, as recidivist and reformer—a former criminal who is also capable of pragmatic action based on empirical observation, to see and present things as they are—means his vision of statecraft is closer to Machiavelli's than to that of a liberal jurist like Bentham or Beccaria, something that puts further pressure on the already strained relationship between the crime story and reformist thinking.

The narrative trajectory of Vidocq's four-volume *Memoirs*—which tells of his journey from petty criminal, army deserter, and prison escapee to police spy and first head of the Parisian Brigade du Sûreté—allows us to frame the work as a straightforward tale of progress and transformation: an Enlightenment parable in which the depraved rogue finds salvation via his engagement with the values and ideologies of bourgeois society. This move reinforces the sanctity of private property (i.e. the reformed thief sees the harm that theft causes) and supports—and even enacts—a facile account of the genre's historical development. In this reading, the disappearance of the criminal–bandit who was, as Foucault points out, 'against the law, against the rich, the powerful, the magistrates, the constabulary or the watch, against taxes and their collectors',[49] and his replacement by the detective is symptomatic of a loss of freedom and the emerging disciplinary power of a new social and political order.[50] Vidocq's incorporation into the state apparatus would appear to be the embodiment and inevitable culmination of what Foucault calls 'the intensive development of police networks' in the nineteenth century that contributed to 'a new mapping and close surveillance of urban space' and a 'more systematic and efficient prosecution of minor delinquency'.[51] However, this reading fails to do justice to the ambiguities of the *Memoirs* and to Vidocq himself, a figure who casts himself as a reluctant criminal whose effectiveness as a policeman nevertheless depends on insights and associations gathered from his delinquent life and on a willingness to transgress the moral authority of his office. Furthermore, it also constitutes a partial misreading of Foucault's position in *Discipline and Punish*. Here Foucault is quick to acknowledge the complexities of crime literature of the

---

[47] See James Morton, *The First Detective: The Life and Revolutionary Times of Vidocq* (London: Ebury Press, 2005), p. 326.
[48] Caillois qtd in Walz, 'Vidocq, Rogue Cop', p. xv.
[49] Foucault, *Discipline and Punish*, p. 67.
[50] Foucault, *Discipline and Punish*, pp. 65–9.
[51] Michel Foucault, 'The Dangerous Individual', in Lawrence D. Krizman (ed.) *Politics, Philosophy, Culture: Interviews and Other Writings 1977–1984* (London and New York, NY: Routledge, 1988), p. 142.

early eighteenth century ('neither...a spontaneous form of "popular expression", nor...a concerted programme of propaganda' but rather 'a locus in which two investments of penal practice met'[52]) but he is less impressed by a post-Gaboriau turn whereby 'the great murders had become the quiet game of the well behaved'.[53] Vidocq's *Memoirs*, however, are a more intriguing proposition for Foucault—and for me—because they detail the collision of policing and criminality, where delinquency is not expunged but 'invested by power and turned inside out': i.e. the 'disturbing moment when criminality became one of the mechanisms of power'.[54] Rather than an aberration, as Foucault seems to regards it, this 'disturbing moment' in fact constitutes a key foundational move in the emergence of crime writing as a whole.

Before we turn to the content, it is worth saying a few things about the text itself—I am using the 1828 translation, *Memoirs of Vidocq, Principal Agent of the French Police Written by Himself*, published in London by Whittaker & Co.[55] The reliability of the text, and of Vidocq's presentation of himself and of what we might call reality, has been the subject of much debate. Vidocq uses the preface to the first volume to distance himself and his narrative from his criminal background and accusations that he might be trying to play up these sensational elements to promote his work. He explains in a convoluted and unconvincing fashion that he broke his arm in five places while preparing the manuscript and had to employ a freelance writer to revise the content. Unbeknown to Vidocq and at the behest of his enemies, this man embellished certain passages in order to turn the textual Vidocq into 'the scoundrel of the age...without one redeeming point of sensibility, conscience, remorse or repentance'.[56] Vidocq claims that this revised material made it into the published manuscript only because of time pressures and publication deadlines: 'contrary to my own interests and to satisfy the public impatience, I accept now as my own, a production which at first I would have rejected.'[57] It is true that Vidocq had many enemies in the Parisian police following his departure from the Sûreté, but we need to treat these claims with suspicion. One explanation for the qualification is simply that Vidocq wanted to have his cake and eat it: to wallow in the bawdiness of his early life while also underscoring his commitment to personal and social reform. James Morton makes the point that Vidocq hoped to use his memoirs to relaunch his public image and perhaps recapture his old job as head of the Sûreté; and that openly flaunting his criminality 'would have ruined the image he had so carefully built'.[58] The English publisher may have been willing to support this agenda up to a point but they were also keen to exploit the

---

[52] Foucault, *Discipline and Punish*, p. 67.
[53] Foucault, *Discipline and Punish*, p. 69.
[54] Foucault, *Discipline and Punish*, p. 283.
[55] François-Eugène Vidocq, *Memoirs of Vidocq, Principal Agent of the French Police Written by Himself (translated from the French in Four Volumes)* (London: Whittaker & Co, 1828). This version was published almost simultaneously in France and Britain thereby underscoring the extent to which the circulation of crime fiction even at the start of the nineteenth century was a transnational affair.
[56] Vidocq, *Memoirs of Vidocq*, Vol. 1, p. xv.
[57] Vidocq, *Memoirs of Vidocq*, Vol. 1, p. xvii.
[58] Morton, *The First Detective*, p. 91.

picaresque, sensationalist elements of the work, especially the youthful, unreformed Vidocq.[59]

If it is instructive to assess the ways in which Vidocq, consciously or otherwise, plays off the unreconstructed voice of his early self against his mature and reform-minded self, it is important not to get unnecessarily sidetracked by claims and counterclaims about the veracity of what we are being told. In spite of anxieties about the interference of his enemies, Vidocq makes much of his work's truthfulness, declaring in the preface that 'I speak, and will speak, without reserve, without restriction, and with all the frankness of a man who has no longer cause to fear'.[60] At the end of the second volume, he reiterates this claim: 'now it is Vidocq, the free citizen, who freely narrates the truth, the whole truth and nothing but the truth'.[61] At the same time Vidocq's numerous detractors, including his successor, Louis Canler, sought to denounce *Memoirs* as a self-serving fabrication,[62] while subsequent critics have pointed to its deliberate exclusions. Schütt observes that Vidocq's editor, Tenon, wanted the chronicles to 'reveal the extent of the tyranny and abuse exerted by [Charles V's] political police',[63] a claim substantiated by the English editor who even went to the trouble of inserting a 'sequel' at the end of the fourth volume in which he accused Vidocq of refraining 'from making those disclosures which you had pledged to the public at large you would make'[64] and speculated Vidocq had been bought off. Rather than playing off the various truth claims against one another, I am more interested in the way in which Vidocq's self-presentation invokes a particular, highly pragmatic tone which, in turn, offers an important clue about the complicated nature of his reformist ambitions.

At the start of the first volume, Vidocq claims he 'was brought into the world on the 23rd July 1775 in a house adjoining that in which Robespierre was born sixteen years earlier'[65] but he displays little enthusiasm for his neighbour's revolutionary politics and makes a point of mocking the Sans Culottes and their portable guillotine and bloodthirsty justice and only takes an oath of fidelity to the Republic when it is sensible to do so. Nor, though, is Vidocq a standard bearer for the *ancien regime*, a supporter of the irregular, custom-bound rule of the aristocracy. He is a reformer of sorts, though not a jurist in the mould of Beccaria or Bentham, a fellow liberal committed to freedom and social progress through legal and economic reform. It would be easy to see Vidocq as an opportunist, someone, as Morton

---

[59] The English publisher was at pains to emphasize the picaresque, unreformed Vidocq—the daring rogue, the courageous bandit, embodiment of an earlier, untamed epoch. 'In these days, when the hand of improvement, so called (God save the mark!) macadamizes the hoary relics of antiquity to smooth the path along which civilisation progresses; when the age of chivalry is gone; and daring deeds and adventurous exploits are superseded by mere commonplace and matter-of-fact details; it is a thing of marvel to read the incident of a life so full of romance, so teeming with the wild and wonderful' (Editor, 'Foreword', François-Eugène Vidocq, *Memoirs of Vidocq*, Vol. 1, p. vi).

[60] Vidocq, *Memoirs of Vidocq*, Vol. 1, p. viii

[61] Vidocq, *Memoirs of Vidocq*, Vol. 2, p. 266.

[62] See Morton, *The First Detective*, pp. 151–2.

[63] Sita A. Schütt, 'French Crime Fiction', in Martin Priestman (ed.) *The Cambridge Companion to American Crime Fiction* (Cambridge: Cambridge University Press, 2003), p. 61.

[64] H.T.R., 'Sequel', Vidocq, *Memoirs of Vidocq*, Vol. 4, p. 275.

[65] Vidocq, *Memoirs of Vidocq*, Vol. 1, p. 1.

points out, who 'changed political direction, favouring whoever was in power at the time'.[66] Certainly Vidocq lived through remarkable times—the overthrow of Louis XVI and the Revolution, the Terror, Napoleon, the Bourbon restoration, and the July Revolution of 1830. As a protean figure, he adapted himself well to changing situations, Republican or Royalist depending on prevailing circumstances. Yet there is something more interesting about his pragmatism than mere opportunism—not least because it describes an anti-essentialist modus operandi based on rigorous empiricism, the use of observation and inductive logic to arrive at the most effective policing strategy, and the careful collation and analysis of disparate pieces of information. As such, Vidocq's method, if it can be called that, closely mirrors Machiavelli's and in making this link, I am characterizing the sixteenth century Florentine consort neither as a cynical manipulator of people nor as an enlightened civic humanist but rather as an anti-essentialist, political realist who, as Joseph Femia argues, was primarily 'concerned with the practical principles of statecraft'.[67] It is hard to see a figure as slippery and ostensibly untrustworthy as Vidocq as political pragmatist. But when Machiavelli writes in *The Prince*,

> I have thought it proper to represent things as they are in real truth, rather than as they are imagined... the gulf between how one should live and how one does live is so wide that a man who neglects what is actually done for what should be done moves towards self-destruction rather than self-preservation[68]

he is, as Femia points out, setting out three foundational propositions that are, consciously or otherwise, assimilated into Vidocq's modus operandi. First, that 'humans are not what they seem' and are 'generally wicked'; second, that 'ideal projections... are... absurd and harmful'; and third, that 'security... often requires actions at odds with traditional Biblical morality'.[69]

Taking these propositions together, Vidocq is no believer in human goodness and his own criminal background, and his awareness of other's people duplicitousness and greed, means he is better able to do his job as policeman—i.e. better able to see through pretence and discern the reasons why people steal, cheat, and even kill. Seeing things and people as they are, of course, presupposes an anti-idealistic mindset and while Vidocq isn't consciously hostile, in *Memoirs*, to idealistic modes of thought, he demonstrates, through his practical interventions, how bringing criminals to book requires adopting duplicitous and sometimes even violent practices that are wholly incompatible with Biblical morality. Still, to cast Vidocq in this light doesn't mean we can't also see his reformist impulses as genuine and in some way principled. Again, Femia's assessment of Machiavelli is useful here and not just because he points out that 'a commitment to certain political ideas and principles is not incompatible with an... attachment to objective methods of analysis'.[70] It is also useful because Femia sees Machiavelli's 'utilitarian justification for

---

[66] Morton, *The First Detective*, p. viii.
[67] Joseph V. Femia, *Machiavelli Revisited* (Cardiff: University of Wales Press, 2004), p. 11.
[68] Niccolo Machiavelli, *The Prince*, trans. George Bull (London: Penguin, 1999), p. 49.
[69] Femia, *Machiavelli Revisited*, p. 63.   [70] Femia, *Machiavelli Revisited*, p. 57.

unpleasant procedures' and his identification of law as a means to an end (the end being security rather than justice) as in some way foreshadowing Bentham. As such Bentham and Machiavelli (and I would also include Vidocq in this formation) belong to a tradition of anti-metaphysical empiricism and utilitarianism whereby means (i.e. procedures) are related to ends (i.e. security) according to rational principles. This is not simply the belief that 'one could make institutions more efficient by imposing on them uniformity, simplicity, clarity... and a preference for legal-rationalism'[71] but that, as Femia puts it, 'moral judgements and concepts are resolvable into a form of utility; that justice is a means of obtaining security for life and property, and so of securing the greatest utility or happiness of society as a whole'.[72]

If Bentham's reformist ambitions arose from the rapid expansion of government in Britain in the early nineteenth century and the need to reorganize departments and institutions to cope with this growth, the same situation could be said to apply in France, only more so because by the 1820s France had a far more established and wide-ranging (though not necessarily efficient) policing apparatus.[73] As such, Vidocq's move to establish the first specialist department of plain-clothed policeman—the Brigade de Sûreté—in 1809 could be seen in the context of this wider rationalization. Some further contextualization is needed before this connection is developed. At the same time as Vidocq was setting up this new detective force, Bentham was drawing up a systematized rationale for the reorganization of government according to utilitarian principles, though importantly for this comparison Bentham gave his utilitarianism an individualist complexion. Individuals could pursue their own self-interest, he intimated, without interference from the state but state sanction, through the law, was the best and indeed only way of ensuring an individual's actions didn't unduly harm the general happiness, a position not that dissimilar from that staked out by Godwin's *Political Justice*. Thus state power, regulated by a reformed bureaucracy and supported by the law, could be reconciled with individual liberty. Institutional reform, for Bentham at least, could 'make a democratic constitution more effective... establish and preserve positive rights for individuals and... universalize the responsibilities of officials within a world of autonomous individuals'.[74]

Vidocq's *Memoirs* do not provide the same thoroughgoing critique of existing procedures but by situating the role and function of the state and its justice system at the heart of the narrative and by intimating what could be achieved by applying rational thinking to the practice of apprehending criminals, the work ends up grappling with some of the same concerns. However, as with *Caleb Williams*, there

---

[71] Hume, *Bentham and Bureaucracy*, p. 11.
[72] Femia, *Machiavelli Revisited*, p. 99.
[73] An official police presence had existed as far back as the sixteenth century, with the establishment of the *maréchaussée* and later the *gendarmerie nationale*, and by the early nineteenth century the policing apparatus had evolved into an extensive but piecemeal network of magistrates, government administrators, city officials, soldiers, uniformed police officers, and spies. See Clive Emsley, 'The Origins and Development of the Police', in Eugene McLaughlin and John Muncie (eds) *Controlling Crime* (Milton Keynes and London: Open University, 2002), pp. 41–4; Alan Williams, *The Police of Paris 1718–1789* (Baton Rouge, LA: Louisiana State University Press, 1979).
[74] Hume, *Bentham and Bureaucracy*, p. 258.

are important differences which in turn point to the capacity of the crime story to put pressure on some of the positivist assumptions of a reformist agenda. Bentham's work draws upon the idea derived from Adam Smith that self-interested individuals pursuing their own advancement within an expanding marketplace could contribute to the moral as well as financial well-being of the nation. In such an environment, the enlightened bureaucrat instigating greater efficiencies becomes a crucial figure in bringing about this well-being. Vidocq's *Memoirs* ostensibly support the idea that preventative policing can be made more efficient and that being good or appearing to be good—i.e. a general 'moral sense'—is resolvable into a form of utility but, as with Machiavelli, this formulation requires us to pay some attention to the idea of appearance. Machiavelli is under no illusions about our capacity for deceit, aggression, and greed but argues that outward demonstrations of conformity, i.e. to moral norms, are often enough to bring about a desired order. Vidocq may share Machiavelli's jaundiced view of human nature but it is much harder, I think, to reconcile the brute force and native cunning he demonstrates as a policeman with claims about the utility of the new security provisions he puts into place.

Like Bentham (and for that matter Voltaire and Beccaria) Vidocq is aware of the iniquities of the unreformed justice system and, from first-hand experience, speaks with authority about the brutalizing effects of prison, especially on the impressionable. Of his own experience, he remarks: 'Cast at twenty-four years of age amongst the most abandoned wretches, and necessarily in contact with them...compelled only to see and hear degraded human beings, whole minds were incessantly bent on devising evil schemes, I feared the dire contagion of such vicious society'.[75] Later, in the fourth volume, an older, wiser Vidocq is able to comment dispassionately on the ills of an apparently *correctional* system in which ends and means are wildly out of kilter. 'How is it that we go on in a mode inverse to our aim?' he asks, implying that utilitarianism and pragmatism may not be the same thing. 'It is because to ill use is not to correct, but contrariwise to pervert and corrupt more and more weak human nature.'[76] In these sections, Vidocq sounds like every bit the jurist. Evoking Beccaria, for example, he proposes that punishments should be 'graduated by necessity in proportion to the greater or inferior understanding of the delinquent' and that laws 'should be made, like the soldier's dress, of three sizes, with a great latitude to the judge's discretion to decide according to the circumstances of the case'.[77]

Still, we should be wary of characterizing Vidocq as a jurist and reformer, someone committed to social progress through the application of judicial discretion and regular, uniform standards across the justice system. For a start, his transformation from lawbreaker to enforcer is not precipitated by his concerns about antiquated penal codes or the arbitrariness of the legal system but rather because his personal circumstances have become intolerable. Moreover, his initial decision to turn police informer is primarily a self-interested one and his motivation here is to shore up his own position

---

[75] Vidocq, *Memoirs of Vidocq*, Vol. 1, p. 220.   [76] Vidocq, *Memoirs of Vidocq*, Vol. 4, p. 3.
[77] Vidocq, *Memoirs of Vidocq*, Vol. 4, p. 5.

vis-à-vis his superiors and to demonstrate his cunning by outsmarting his former associates, even if Paris is safer as a result of his interventions. Similarly while Vidocq's successes as police spy and then as detective owe a great deal to the new practices he institutes, especially after the establishment of the Sûreté, just as significant is his encyclopaedic knowledge of the underworld—and the 'criminal' boldness of his interventions. As such, greater security is achieved not via the promulgation of regular, uniform legal codes but through Vidocq's intimate knowledge of illicit customs and practices and because, unlike uniformed gendarmes, he ventures unafraid and 'without hesitation into the midst of the herd of miserable beings'.[78]

There is a Machiavellian element in this formulation of course: the eponymous prince doing whatever is necessary in order to secure a virtuous end, e.g. the arrest and capture of hardened criminals, by whatever means. Indeed this practice is not necessarily at odds with what we might call procedural regularity. One particular incident brings this point out clearly. A butcher called Fontaine is robbed of fifteen hundred francs by two men who try to befriend him, and he is then beaten and left at the side of the road where he is discovered by the attorney-general. Anticipating the use of forensic science, the crime scene is meticulously searched by Vidocq and other investigators and potential clues are collected:

> Nothing had been neglected which might lead to the discovery of the assassins. Accurate impressions were taken of the footmarks; buttons, fragments of paper dyed and blood were carefully collected. On one of these pieces, which appeared to have been hastily torn off to wipe the blade of a knife found at no great distance from it, was observed some written characters, but they were without any connecting sense, and consequently unable to afford any information likely to throw a light on the affair.[79]

Nonetheless Vidocq is able to deduce an address from the fragments of paper, that of a wine merchant who, he discovers, is in league with a man called Raoul, already known to Vidocq as 'one of the most daring traffickers in contraband goods',[80] and Court who has just served a six-month prison sentence. Vidocq pinions Court and searches his apartment, finding two loaded pistols and some knives. Later he befriends Raoul, disguised as Monsieur Jules, and finds in his possession the other part of the paper from which the scrap found at the crime scene had been torn. Raoul and Court are arrested and held separately for interviewing and while Court is quick to admit his guilt, and name his accomplice, Raoul initially refuses to confess, despite being subjected to Vidocq's persuasions. 'I worked him,' Vidocq tells us, 'as it is called, in every possible way, lured every species of argument to convince him that it was in his own interest to make a full avowal.'[81] Eventually, after the victim has identified both men as his attackers, Raoul confesses and both men are tried, sentenced, and executed. Intriguingly, though, Vidocq suggests that in the course of the pursuit, he has forged a fraternal bond with the men and when he visits them in prison, prior to their execution, a reconciliation of sorts takes place. 'They assured me that my visit afforded them the greatest pleasure they were

---

[78] Vidocq, *Memoirs of Vidocq*, Vol. 2, p. 189.
[79] Vidocq, *Memoirs of Vidocq*, Vol. 3, pp. 197–8.
[80] Vidocq, *Memoirs of Vidocq*, Vol. 3, p. 199.   [81] Vidocq, *Memoirs of Vidocq*, Vol. 3, p. 211.

capable of receiving, and entreated me to bestow on them one friendly embrace, in token of my forgiveness of their past, and satisfaction at their present conduct.'[82] After the execution, Vidocq implicitly invites comparison between his unreformed self and the men by commenting that their villainy 'was less the effect of natural depravity than the consequences of having associated with dissolute characters'.[83]

This particular incident may foreground Vidocq's boldness, and his choice to include a reference to the kinship he feels towards the condemned men underscores how his criminal background continues to inform his practice as police detective. But just as significant, though less exciting from a reader's perspective, is the emphasis on effective evidence gathering and processing and on the importance of establishing proper procedures, honing interview techniques, and sharing information across different departments and institutions. Indeed there is something explicitly modern about the preciseness of the data that Vidocq is able to produce for the year 1817, detailing the arrests made and the offences committed:

Assassins or murderers	15
Robbers or burglars	5
Ditto with false keys	108
Ditto in furnished houses	12
Highwaymen	126
Pickpockets or cut-purses	73
Shoplifters	17
Receivers of stolen property	38
Fugitives from prisons	14
Tried galley-slaves having left their exile	43
Forgers, cheats, swindlers etc.	46
Vagabonds, robbers returning to Paris	229
By mandates from his Excellency	46
Captures, seizures of stolen property	39
	811[84]

Making a connection between modernity and statistics, Joan Copjec argues that '[e]ntire bureaucracies grew up around these numbers to count, cross-reference and analyse them'[85] and also that this interest in numbers was central to the consolidation of the modern state. Copjec claims that the statistical tabulation and analysis of crime produced an expectation that risk could be calculated and that crime could be understood and even controlled, even if particular crime stories showed this not to be the case.[86] *Memoirs*, I would argue, is an early example of this manoeuvre. In one sense, Vidocq is at pains to emphasize how successful his new methods are in imposing law and order. 'Such have been, at the utmost, the

---

[82] Vidocq, *Memoirs of Vidocq*, Vol. 3, p. 245. [83] Vidocq, *Memoirs of Vidocq*, Vol. 3, p. 250.
[84] Vidocq, *Memoirs of Vidocq*, Vol. 2, p. 246.
[85] Joan Copjec, 'The Phenomenal Nonphenomenal: Private Space in Film Noir', in Copjec (ed.) *Shades of Noir: A Reader* (London and New York, NY: Verso, 1998), p. 170.
[86] Copjec, 'The Phenomenal Nonphenomenal', p. 170.

effective force and the expense of the Brigade de Sûreté... I have maintained security in the bosom of the capital, populated by nearly a million inhabitants.'[87] Vidocq might blow his own trumpet but he is quick to credit the brigade and indeed the bureaucratic support he has received from Henry, the prefect of police, Bertaux, a cross-examiner 'of great merit', and Parisot, the governor of prisons.[88] Additionally it is the formal codes for detectives and spies established under Vidocq—which regulate their practice and inculcate them into the police force as an institution—that are responsible, according to Vidocq, for creating a safer environment. Still, we shouldn't take Vidocq at his word. For one thing, the nature of the organization described in *Memoirs* falls a long way short of the principles established by Bentham's projected civil service reforms (paid full-time officials, meritocratic promotions according to pre-established criteria, etc.). And while Vidocq may be complimentary about the 'frankness, unanimity and...cordiality' that existed among the heads of the police during his early years, his portrait of factionalism, incompetence, and bureaucratic dysfunction during his final years as head of the Brigade de Sûreté is damning:

> In the present day, chiefs or subalterns mistrust each other; they reciprocally fear and hate each other; a continual state of hostilities is kept up; each dread in his comrade a foe who will denounce him; there is no longer a sympathy of action in the different departments of the administration: and from where does this proceed? Because each man's post and duties are not sufficiently definite. Nothing is distinctly defined; and no person, even those in the highest office, is placed in the department for which he is best fitted. Most usually the préfet himself, on being elected to fill that important situation, is wholly ignorant of his duties or the police, and yet he ascends at once to the highest rank in it, than to pass through apprenticeship.[89]

What we have here is not the uniform, efficient organization of reformist fantasy but a snakepit of rivalry, nepotism, and inadequacy and in this context Vidocq's political machinations—forming alliances, supporting whoever will shore up his own position, regardless of consequences—place one strain of Machiavellian thought, e.g. the art of holding onto power, at odds with another, e.g. governing according to utilitarian principles.

There is a sense, of course, of this as *realpolitik*, Vidocq showing us things as they are, not as he wants them to be, but on top of this, there remains the strong suspicion that Vidocq is less interested in securing the city than in exercising his own power and extending his fiefdom. The violence he and his officers mete out—the fact that 'we broke legs and arms unsparingly' and 'I was invulnerable; and some asserted I was enveloped in armour from head to toe'[90]—suggests both a will to power, where ends do not justify means, and a desire to flaunt practices whose legitimacy is thrown into doubt precisely because he seems to enjoy them; and because they arise from his criminal apprenticeship. In other words, more so even than in *The Prince*, *Memoirs* subject the distinction between legal and illegal to careful scrutiny and while it's certainly true that Machiavelli doesn't necessarily

---

[87] Vidocq, *Memoirs of Vidocq*, Vol. 2, p. 255.
[88] Vidocq, *Memoirs of Vidocq*, Vol. 2, p. 167.
[89] Vidocq, *Memoirs of Vidocq*, Vol. 2, p. 167.
[90] Vidocq, *Memoirs of Vidocq*, Vol. 2, p. 246.

condemn immoral acts, presumably including theft and murder, because they may lead to 'virtuous' ends, the sense that Vidocq, as law enforcer, is in fact no different from the men who have stolen and killed raises profoundly difficult questions about the role of the law. Indeed if this role, according to Machiavelli in *The Discourses*, is to 'restrain human appetites and to deprive them of all hope of doing wrong with impunity',[91] Vidocq lives and operates outside its jurisdiction, a problem for someone whose job it is to enforce the law.

The notion that Vidocq-as-criminal is no different from Vidocq-as-policeman, and that his successes as the latter depend on the skills and capacities of the former, and indeed that his actions are only ever self-directed, i.e. intended only to secure his own position, again raises the troubling question of legitimacy. In the context of the emerging crime story, we cannot say with any certainty what Vidocq's motives are, nor can we dismiss his reformist ambitions as hollow, nor indeed can we unproblematically position him either as thief, bully, or as committed utilitarian and empiricist keen to define justice according to end results, i.e. whatever brings about order. Throughout *Memoirs* we get hints about the chaos, immorality, and violence of the law—the use of informers or secret agents, nearly all of whom 'were caught in the very act of committing crime'; the reliance on such figures for ensuring 'the entire safety of the capital'; and the potential bias of the justice system itself and the prospect of 'political policing' or what Vidocq describes as 'an institution created and maintained by a desire of enriching certain persons at the expense of a government whose alarm it perpetually excites'.[92] There are also countless references to Vidocq's propensity for violence and cruelty in his pursuit of malefactors, his 'working' of suspects during interviews, and his proximity to the criminals he is charged with apprehending.[93] But there are also many references to what can be, and indeed is, achieved via the application of reformist ideas to the effective functioning of the police and justice system as a whole; to the reduction of crime as a result of the implementation of new police practices; to regularize police activities according to a clearly delineated and therefore transparent code (for example 'to put in execution, annually, from four to five hundred warrants... to procure information, to undertake searches, and obtain particularities of every description; to make nightly rounds... to assist the commissaries of the police in their searches, or the execution of search warrants'[94]); to reform the penal codes so that punishments should be 'graduated by necessity, in proportion to the greater or inferior understanding of the delinquent' and to introduce a new code of practice for the use of secret agents.[95] To put this another way, what distinguishes Vidocq's *Memoirs* is their willingness to fold this ambivalence into a thoroughgoing investigation into the affairs of the state; and in so doing to shine a light, consciously or otherwise, on an important tension in our understanding of

---

[91] Machiavelli, *The Discourses of Niccolo Machiavelli Vol. One*, ed. William Stark (London: Routledge and Kegan Paul, 1950), p. 311.
[92] Vidocq, *Memoirs of Vidocq*, Vol. 2, pp. 205, 165, 261.
[93] Vidocq, *Memoirs of Vidocq*, Vol. 2, p. 211.   [94] Vidocq, *Memoirs of Vidocq*, Vol. 2, p. 254.
[95] Vidocq, *Memoirs of Vidocq*, Vol. 4, p. 5; for the code for the use of secret agents see Vol. 3, pp. 26–7.

the law, one that finds its first and most acute articulation in Machiavelli: that that rule of law, as Femia puts it, is 'a necessary component of justice, as an absolute value, to be preserved at all costs' and that legal procedure should be followed but that this wouldn't 'necessarily coincide with justice'.[96]

POSTSCRIPT: BALZAC AND VAUTRIN

Vidocq's politics, as manifest in *Memoirs*, are messy and confused. A pragmatist, with no discernible political loyalties or affiliations, he at times casts himself as unambiguous defender of private property and the rule of law. At other times, he makes a distinction between his non-partisan actions as the scourge of criminals and the political police who, as we have seen, are described as 'an institution created and maintained by a desire of enriching certain persons'. Still at other times, he demonstrates quasi-socialist sympathies by allowing for a link between crime and property or at least acknowledging that 'misery will engender crime' and that 'misery in a society...is not a scourge from which we can shield ourselves'.[97] As a policeman just trying to do his job, i.e. apprehend criminals, his claim of political neutrality would become familiar to readers of police procedural novels later in the nineteenth and in the twentieth century but Vidocq's slipperiness or his disingenuousness is interesting here because it points, wittingly or otherwise, to a link between policing and class politics and the wider structures of power in society—and an acute awareness of both the coercive and ethical elements of police practice, e.g. the need to break legs and also to win consent through the practical demonstration of effective procedure.

This duality would become an important feature of the emerging genre and though it is Poe who is often credited with inventing the Bi-Part Soul—the detective who also bears the traces of the criminal—Vidocq's legacy, unsurprisingly would be felt most keenly in France by writers like Emile Gaboriau, Victor Hugo, and Honoré de Balzac. Gaboriau's Inspector Lecoq (see Chapter 3) and Hugo's Jean Valjean are loosely based on Vidocq[98] as is Balzac's Vautrin who first appeared in his 1834 novel *Père Goriot* and again in *Illusions Perdues* (1843) and *Splendeurs et Misères des Courtisanes* (1847). Whereas Gaboriau's detective follows Vidocq's path from criminal to police inspector, Balzac's Vautrin is a criminal spy, a largely unreformed thief, and a much venerated (at least by other convicts) prison escapee. It is instructive that Balzac has chosen to emphasize this aspect of Vidocq for his own character but the fact that Vautrin is not, at the same time, an agent of the law doesn't mean that the novel has nothing to say about the way in which Paris is policed or the extent to which the police, as representative of the state, end up buttressing existing class relations and arrangements of power. What Balzac's novel does so well is identify a tension in Vidocq's *Memoirs* relating to the efficacy of the

---

[96] Femia, *Machiavelli Revisited*, p. 81. [97] Vidocq, *Memoirs of Vidocq*, Vol. 2, p. 257.
[98] See Victor Bromert, *Victor Hugo and the Visionary Novel* (Cambridge, MA and London: Harvard University Press, 1984), p. 27.

law and the complicity of the police in enforcing that law and then exacerbate it in ways that would be instructive for subsequent practioners of the emerging crime fiction genre.

On the face of it, *Père Goriot* would seem to be a straightforward morality tale in which Vautrin's scheme to ensnare the gullible, capricious Eugène de Rastignac in his plans to profit from the murky world of family fortunes and romantic entanglements must not be allowed to succeed. Vautrin's scheme involves coupling the poor but socially ambitious Rastignac with Victorine, a wealthy, plain-looking, morally unsullied heiress for whom Rastignac has no feelings, and in doing so undermining his burgeoning attachment to the already married Delphine de Nucingen. Pursued by the Minister of the Police and his agent Monsieur Gondureau who declares Vautrin to be a dangerous man with 'certain qualities which put him in a class of his own' and whose arrest 'has become a matter of the highest importance to the State',[99] Vautrin is eventually arrested when the chief of the Sûreté receives a tip-off and ambushes him with pistols at his Parisian boarding house. But this reading of the novel—which pits Vautrin's criminality against the state—misses many of the novel's complexities, for Balzac suggests that there is little to separate the legitimate violence of the police and the illegitimate violence of Vautrin's army of villains. 'We are counting on some physical violence tomorrow morning so that we can kill [Vautrin]', Gondereau comments, displaying no concerns about the morality of his actions. 'That way we can avoid a trial, the expense of food and custody, and society is rid of him' (p. 173). On top of this, Vautrin is not only the most impressive figure in the novel: he is also the most insightful and maybe even the most honest. Drawing on some of Vidocq's hard-nosed pragmatism, Vautrin condemns the state and the law as corrupt or rather argues that in so far as both are reflections of man's innate self-interest, they cannot but help serve the needs of the rich and powerful:

> Why two months in prison for a dandy who robs a boy of half his fortune in one night, and hard labour in the galleys for a poor devil who steals a thousand-franc note with 'aggravating circumstances'? That's the law for you. There's not one article that does not lead to absurdity... Despise mankind then, and look at how many ways there are of slipping through the net of the law. (p. 103)

In one sense this is a long way from Vidocq's admiration for his own reforms and the ability of the police to bring security to lawless parts of the city. In another sense, it is seizing upon an anti-establishment impulse in *Memoirs* and indeed a sentiment that the law, at bottom, serves those in power, and developing it to its logical conclusion. Vautrin's assertion that the existing socio-political order is 'a monstrous betrayal of the Social Contract' gives his criminality a politicized inflection which is lacking in the first volume of Vidocq's *Memoirs*, but it needs to be treated with caution, especially in light of Vautrin's obvious self-interest. Ultimately the law must triumph, as it does in Vidocq's *Memoirs*, and Vautrin's arrest and

---

[99] Honoré de Balzac, *Père Goriot*, trans. A.J. Krailsheimer (Oxford: Oxford University Press, 1999), pp. 152, 153–4.

therefore his removal from the novel indicates that his perspective has been rejected. But in so far as Vautrin's bleak pronouncements about human nature and the extent of social and political corruption come to pass, it is his voice that lingers longest. For Rastignac, as for 'père' Goriot who is abandoned by his two daughters, Vautrin's claim that human relations and sentiments have been defiled by greed and the logic of the marketplace is inescapable. Balzac's novel may not show off its status as a tale of crime and punishment and its expansive social canvas and urban portraiture would seem to place it first and foremost alongside other nineteenth-century realist texts, but it would bequeath the nascent crime genre two important lessons. First, the law must always triumph even as it—and the state—is exposed as biased and protective of vested interests; and second, the resulting tension would not be easy to resolve—either for a criminal like Vautrin or a policeman like Vidocq.

Vidocq's narrative plays out this tension in slightly different ways but the fundamental dynamic remains the same: what we see, on the one hand, is the emergence of a truly modern police force and bureaucratic state, enabling and enabled by new regulatory codes and new structures of organization, and on the other hand, the recidivist traces of an earlier era at once associated with the aberrant and criminal. It is not the case that Vidocq is a significant figure in the genre because his transformation from thief to policeman prefigures a similar shift in crime writing as a genre. Such analysis tends to overstate the differences between the criminal biographies of the early eighteenth century and the 'new' crime stories, like *Memoirs*, that would come to prominence in the nineteenth century. Rather Vidocq's significance derives from the careful fusion, in his narrative and persona, of the tropes of legalism and criminality, rationality and deviance, and proceduralism and individual cunning. What marks *Memoirs* out in the final analysis is not that Vidocq rejects his criminal past and embraces the rule of law but that he embraces a reformist agenda *and* the impulses that served him as criminal in order to promote the rule of law. As with Godwin's *Caleb Williams*, Vidocq's *Memoirs* hold up a dark mirror to the logic and culture of penal reform, appropriating some of its language and aspirations and yet at the same time alluding to its shortcomings, the inadequacies or limitations of utopian sentiment and procedural efficiency as ways of addressing the problem of crime.

3

'A Mysterious Power Whose Hand is Everywhere'

Imagining the State and Codifying the Law in the Mid-nineteenth Century

The apartment was in the wildest disorder—the furniture broken and thrown about in all directions. There was only one bedstead; and from this the bed had been removed, and thrown into the middle of the floor. On a chair lay a razor, besmirched with blood. On the hearth were two or three long and thick tresses of gray human hair, also daubed in blood, and seeming to have been pulled out by the roots.[1]

(Edgar Allan Poe, 'The Murders in the Rue Morgue')

A philosopher produces ideas, a poet poems, a clergyman sermons, a professor compendia and so on. A criminal produces crime. If we look a little closer at the connection between this latter branch of production and society as whole, we shall rid ourselves of many prejudices. The criminal not only produces crime but also the criminal law... The criminal moreover produces the whole apparatus of the police and of criminal justice, constables, judges, executioners, juries, etc.; and all these different lines of business, which form equally many of categories of the social division of labour.[2]

(Karl Marx, *Theories of Surplus-Value Part 1*)

There is obvious ironic intent in Marx's claim that criminals produce not just crime but also an entire apparatus of legal codes and crime controls, and indeed a whole body of textbooks about the law and also of 'art, literature and novels' about crime. Marx uses this analogy to refute another claim—that service industries should be considered 'productive' because people pay for the services provided—but beneath the careful ironies (e.g. 'many honorable craftsmen' are employed in the production of instruments of torture) there is a serious point: not perhaps that crime per se has produced the *raison d'être* for the rise of the bureaucratic state but that efforts to quell criminal activity have, in turn, required ever more sophisticated crime control mechanisms and the organization of detectives, judges, lawyers, and executioners into institutional structures theoretically capable of interpreting and

---

[1] Edgar Allan Poe, 'The Murders in the Rue Morgue', *Selected Tales* (Oxford: Oxford University Press, 1991), p. 112.
[2] Karl Marx, *Theories of Surplus-Value Part I*, trans. Emile Burns, ed. S. Ryazanskaya (London: Lawrence & Wishart, 1969), p. 387.

imposing law within jurisdictional limits. To extend this analogy further, it is the crime scene—the physical imprint of the crime or what remains after the crime for the investigator to collate and scrutinize—that enables the detective to set in motion the entire investigative and judicial process. As Dominique Kalifa rightly notes, ' "scenes" play an essential role in the construction of crime realities'.[3] This is what Edgar Allan Poe's 'The Murders in the Rue Morgue' (1841) shows us so ably: what Poe gives us is not just a vivid description of Madame L'Espanaye's apartment immediately following a frenzied attack which has left mother and daughter mutilated almost beyond recognition but more particularly a 'scene' in which the physical traces of the murders, notably on the corpses themselves—to invert the formulation from Poe's proto- or anti-detective story 'The Man of the Crowd' (1840)—*do* permit themselves to be read.[4]

It is a truism hardly worth repeating that Poe gave the emerging genre both the first really memorable crime scene and the first brilliant detective capable of reading the scene in such a way as to accurately recover what took place there. But whether this makes Poe the 'father' of the emerging genre is another matter altogether.[5] Certainly the now discredited notion that Poe invented the crime story and that the genre was miraculously conceived with the publication of 'The Murders in the Rue Morgue' can be easily dealt with, not least because it ignores the trailblazing work of Defoe, Godwin, Vidocq, and others and for that matter the foundational claim of this book: that the emergence of the crime story is directly linked to the consolidation of the modern state. More to the point, as Martin Kayman argues, it isn't exactly clear what Poe 'invented' from such a slight body of work: two short stories ('Rue Morgue' and 'The Purloined Letter' (1845)) and the slightly lengthier 'The Mystery of Marie Rogêt' (1842–3):

> In the first place, it is no wonder that the Dupin stories did not generate a genre, in that... they present no framework of regularity which would permit such a development, beyond their idiosyncratic hero, who has... little interest in crime as such... In short, it would not be easy to make a detective-story out of a socially unconcerned recluse with no real interest in crime as such and no professional or institutional relationship with the police.[6]

If we return to Marx's formulation for a moment, we might say, with an eye on Poe's detective stories, that the criminal produces crime and in turn the investigator

---

[3] Dominique Kalifa, 'Crime Scenes: Criminal Topography and Social Imaginary in Nineteenth-Century Paris', *French Historical Studies*, 27:1 (Winter 2004), p. 175.

[4] Walter Benjamin famously described 'The Man of the Crowd' as 'something like the X-ray picture of a detective story' thereby alluding to the way in which the tale refuses to provide answers about the old man that observation and rational inquiry promise; hence Poe's description, at the start of the tale, of a German book, and by implication the man himself as something 'that does not permit itself to be read' (Poe, *Selected Tales*, p. 97). See Benjamin, *Charles Baudelaire: A Lyrical Poet in the Era of High Capitalism*, trans. Harry Zohn (London: Verso, 1983), p. 48.

[5] Maurizio Ascari, for example, argues that the foundational myth 'identifying Poe as the father of detection was created to support a normative account of the genre'. See *A Counter-History of Crime Fiction: Supernatural, Gothic, Sensational* (Basingstoke: Palgrave Macmillan, 2007), p. 10.

[6] Martin A. Kayman, *From Bow Street to Baker Street: Mystery, Detection and Narrative* (Basingstoke: Macmillan, 1992), p. 137.

who must read the crime scene in order to determine what has taken place, but not what Marx identifies as 'the whole apparatus of the police and criminal justice' and in turn the entire edifice of the state system. For this, readers would have to wait until the 1860s and 1870s and lengthier works like Charles Warren Adams's *The Notting Hill Mystery* (1865), Emile Gaboriau's *Monsieur Lecoq* (1868), and Anna Katharine Green's *The Leavenworth Case* (1878) which constitute the major case studies for this chapter. Poe's tales of ratiocination may undercut the division between self and other in daring ways and, in the solutions they offer, they may disquiet more than they reassure.[7] That said, they give us little sense of how the genre's preoccupation with the law and the impartiality or otherwise of the state might be understood in light of changing social, economic, and political circumstances.

In this sense, Poe's focus on the instability of the self, while radical in one sense (because it questions our belief in ourselves as autonomous, rational creatures), is also potentially depoliticizing because it runs the risk of privileging the individual at the expense of the social totality and hence obscuring how crime and the investigation of crime are beholden to, and perhaps even determined by, their social context. By privileging the aristocratic amateur over the professional policeman, Poe's tales would establish a general tendency or pattern, more prevalent among English as opposed to French writers, whereby private operatives 'and not the official representatives of law enforcement, were the principal bulwark against law breaking and social, moral and political deviance'.[8] As we will see later in the chapter, this preference for gentleman amateurs over waged policemen would have significant consequences for the kind of detective story that would come to dominate in England and its capacities to see crime and the policing of crime as rooted in a set of particular socio-economic contexts.

A brief look at 'The Purloined Letter' gives us a better sense of what Poe does *not* examine and therefore what the limitations of his story might be. The tale features a battle of wits between Dupin and a government minister, D—, who has purloined a letter from the Queen which he has hidden in his apartment and is using to blackmail the authorities. We are told nothing, for example, about the wider political context informing the Queen's struggle with D—(e.g. is he a Republican?) and how he and Dupin might be implicated in a wider conflict between conservatives and reformers. Nor are we given any real insight into the nature of policing and bureaucratic organization: whether figures in the Parisian police, beyond

---

[7] Peter Thoms writes: 'Just as Poe's stories seem to construct the detective as a figure of order, they also critique that figure, subverting the opposition between criminal and detective and challenging the investigator's innocent or objective viewpoint of the world.' See 'Poe's Dupin and the Power of Detection', in Kevin J. Hayes (ed.) *The Cambridge Companion to Edgar Allan Poe* (Cambridge and New York, NY: Cambridge University Press, 2002), p. 133.

[8] Haia Shpayer-Makov, 'Revisiting the Detective Figure in Late Victorian and Edwardian Fiction: A View from the Perspective of Police History', *Law, Crime and History*, 2 (2011), p. 165. Shpayer-Makov notes that this fictional tendency runs counter to the impression that the modern police force, 'which spread out over the entire country during the second quarter of the nineteenth century, financed by public funds, were the primary apparatus for tackling crime, and were increasingly perceived as such' (p. 166).

Monsieur G——, support D——'s action, whether D——'s challenge has legitimate political cause, and whether any split loyalties on the part of the police and judiciary in turn unsettles the state's larger claim to neutrality. Poe is most definitely *not* interested in this kind of contextualizing, and taken on their own terms, his tales do not necessarily suffer from its absence, but as examples of the emerging genre—examples that have assumed elevated or canonical status—their status as political or politicized writing seems less assured. If crime fiction derives much of its richness from its ambivalent treatment of the criminal justice system, and if, because of this treatment, crime fiction is uniquely positioned to move beyond the novel's, and indeed bourgeois culture's, fascination with the individual, Poe's tales end up reaffirming, rather than unsettling, Moretti's claim that 'bourgeois culture is fundamentally a culture of private life, which is reluctant to identify and resolve itself entirely in great collective institutions'.[9] By the same logic, writing that, by its nature, *is* immersed in the affairs of state, i.e. these great collective institutions, might be able to illuminate, better than the novel in general (and Poe's tales in particular), the operations and effects of power beyond a fascination with interiority and the self—and hence oppose the individualizing tendencies of bourgeois culture more generally.

For Moretti and other critics, notably Dennis Porter and Ernest Mandel, the crime novel is exemplary of the individualizing tendencies of bourgeois culture, precisely because it 'creates a problem, a "concrete effect"—the crime—and declares a sole cause relevant: the criminal' and in doing so 'slights other causes (why is the criminal such?) and dispels the choice that every choice is partial or subjective'.[10] Or as Mandel puts it, in so far as the crime novel is centered on the conflict between individual and evil, 'it is simply the ultimate rationalization of the competition between private commodity-owners on the market-place'.[11] But what if this account of the crime story—as focused on the struggle between individual detective and criminal—is both partial and limited? Moretti bases his claims about the crime story's recuperative tendencies primarily on his reading of Conan Doyle's Sherlock Holmes stories; but the centrality of Doyle or indeed Poe to the emergence of the crime story is itself part of a troublesome critical consensus that has grown up around the genre and that has been surprisingly difficult to dislodge. Indeed, the aim of this book is not simply to trace the story of this emergence further back into the eighteenth century but rather, in so doing, to demonstrate how proto-crime stories like *The Beggar's Opera* and *Caleb Williams* self-consciously situate their accounts of crime and policing (and of individual criminals and police) in the context of larger questions about the nature of socio-political organization. If this is where the claims of a particular kind of politically motivated crime fiction and of what David F. Greenberg calls 'Marxist

---

[9] Franco Moretti, *Signs Taken for Wonder: Essays in the Sociology of Literary Form*, trans. Susan Fischer, David Forgacs, and David Miller (London and New York, NY: Verso, 1983), p. 127.
[10] Moretti, *Signs*, p. 144.
[11] Ernest Mandel, *Delightful Murder: A Social History of the Crime Story* (London: Pluto, 1984), p. 124. Also see Dennis Porter, *The Pursuit of Crime: Art and Ideology in Detective Fiction* (New Haven, CT: Yale University Press, 1981).

criminology' coincide; i.e. the idea that crime and policing don't exist 'in isolation' and 'must be analysed in the context of [their] relationship to the character of society as a whole',[12] this is not to characterize those crime stories—like Emile Gaboriau's *Monsieur Lecoq*—which move outwards from the initial crime scene and the single detective to construct an entire state imaginary as necessarily Marxist.

As this chapter makes clear, writers like Gaboriau, Green, and Adams are best understood as ambiguous commentators on what we might call nineteenth-century liberalism—that's to say, as novelists ostensibly committed to a particular account of the impartial state and the sanctity of individual freedom whose work subtly questions what this impartiality and freedom mean. Hence while Ronald Thomas links the emergence of the crime story with the 'development of the modern police force and the creation of the modern bureaucratic state', the idea that the work performed by the crime story is only orientated towards 'bringing under control the potentially anarchic forces unleashed by revolutionary movements, democratic reform, urban growth, national expansion and imperial engagements'[13] needs amending. The focus is also on the capabilities of the institutions set up to do this, and by moving the crimes themselves, and the attendant investigations, from the private into the public realm, these stories would put pressure on the rigidity of the public/private dichotomy—a dichotomy, not uncoincidentally, at the heart of a bourgeois, masculinist world view. Novels like Mary Elizabeth Braddon's *Lady Audley's Secret* (1861–2) and Green's *The Leavenworth Case* also require us to think about the gendered implications of the public/private dichotomy and the extent to which, against liberalism's emphasis on individual freedom, the reality for most female subjects—in literature and life—was subordination to the 'norms' of patriarchal culture.

PUBLIC VERSUS PRIVATE: LIBERAL, MARXIST, FEMINIST DEFINITIONS

In his excellent account of American hard-boiled fiction *Gumshoe America* (2000), Sean McCann maintains that the 'detective story has always been a liberal genre, centrally concerned with the fundamental premise of liberal theory—the rule of law—and with the tensions fundamental to democratic societies that constantly threw that principle into doubt'.[14] If classic liberal theories, as McCann comments, 'presume that political society is formed by the consent forged among free

---

[12] See 'Introduction', David F. Greenberg (ed.), *Crime and Capitalism: Readings in Marxist Criminology* (Palo Alto, CA: Mayfield Publishing Company, 1981), p. 17.

[13] Ronald R. Thomas, 'Detection in the Victorian Novel', in Deirdre David (ed.) *The Cambridge Companion to the Victorian Novel* (Cambridge: Cambridge University Press, 2001), p. 170. Also see Thomas, *Detective Fiction and the Rise of Forensic Science* (Cambridge: Cambridge University Press, 1999), p. 4.

[14] Sean McCann, *Gumshoe America: Hard-Boiled Crime Fiction and the Rise and Fall of New Deal Liberalism* (Durham, NC and London: Duke University Press, 2000), p. 6.

individuals', the law becomes a codified expression of this process, a set of statutes established to formalize these guiding principles of individual freedom and rational self-interest. As such the function of the law is to serve 'neutrally to protect the independent workings of society' and to analogize an account of the state as 'a mere night watchman'.[15] McCann shows us how the basic premise of this view—that self-interest would and could manifest itself as general order—is challenged by the *raison d'être* of the crime story; the rupturing of social harmony occasioned by the intrusion of crime. In other words, the eruption of 'uncontrolled passions, unchecked desires and unconstrained power' threatened the idea of self-interest as a regulating harmonizing force and threw into doubt the entire premise of liberal society. In doing so, McCann maintains, the detective story might point 'to the thinness and fragility of the classical liberal vision by raising the prospect of its nightmarish inversion'; but by resolving the problem (i.e. by catching the criminal and restoring the status quo) it also demonstrated faith in the capabilities of liberal society to police itself, without the imposition from above, especially if these interventions were handled by free-thinking amateurs and other members of civil society rather than by agents or auxiliaries of the state. If the problem lay with defective individuals, rather than with the system itself, everything could be resolved simply by scapegoating those who embodied 'the worst of its evils'.[16]

McCann compares this type of crime story with the hard-boiled variation that would emerge in the United States from the 1920s and that would place this version of liberalism under even greater strain following 'the rise of organized capitalism and the evident failure of the unfettered market to deliver a just society'.[17] Still, his account misses not just the extent to which the socio-political criticisms ascribed to hard-boiled crime fiction are also present in earlier crime stories but also how these criticisms mirror what we might call Marxist retorts to liberalism (for example about the false separation of public and private spheres, the partiality of the law, and the failure of the market to deliver social justice). It is difficult to see what an explicitly Marxist crime story might look like, especially in a nineteenth-century context, but as Philip Howell argues, the distance 'between Marxist urban science and detective fiction is not as great as might be supposed'.[18] Intriguingly Howell suggests that 'Marxian political economy is itself generically a nineteenth-century "mystery of the city," driven as it is by "a narrative and rhetoric of exposure"'[19] and if Marx himself was dismissive of Eugène Sue's *Mysteries of Paris* for its melodramatic capitulations, Howell points out that Marx's desire to 'transcend the problems associated with literary treatments of urban problems' was compromised 'by his reliance on Engels' accomplished urban reportage'.[20] The

---

[15] McCann, *Gumshoe America*, p. 7.
[16] McCann, *Gumshoe America*, p. 8.
[17] McCann, *Gumshoe America*, p. 6.
[18] Philip Howell, 'Crime and the City Solution: Crime Fiction, Urban Knowledge and Radical Geography', *Antipode*, 30:4 (1998), p. 362.
[19] Howell, 'Crime and the City Solution', p. 363.
[20] Howell, 'Crime and the City Solution', p. 362.

reference to Engels's *The Condition of the Working Class in England* (1843) is instructive because in seeking to link its grim account of working-class life in Manchester to questions of crime and culpability, the contours of an argument about the social causes of crime and of the state's complicity in upholding and perpetuating 'criminal' practices starts to take shape. The following passage mirrors the kind of move from an individualistic account of crime to one that emphasizes its social and political circumstances that we also find in some crime fiction of the era, and of earlier eras:

> When one individual inflicts bodily injury upon another, such injury that death results, we call the deed manslaughter; when the assailant knew in advance that the injury would be fatal, we call his deed murder. But when society places hundreds of proletarians in such a position that they inevitably meet a too early and an unnatural death, one which is quite as much a death by violence as that by sword or bullet; when it deprives thousands of the necessaries of life, places them under conditions in which they *cannot* live—forces them, through the strong arm of the law, to remain in such conditions until that death ensues which is the inevitable consequence—knows that these thousands of victims must perish, and yet permits these conditions to remain, its deed is murder just as surely as the deed of the single individual.[21]

Engels makes an explicit connection between individual acts of manslaughter and murder as these are codified in the law which, of course, are the starting points of many crime stories, and the 'unnatural' deaths of workers in the factories, which are not usually the stuff of crime fiction but that, for him, should be seen as murder 'just as surely' as if a man has with malice aforethought shot and killed another man. Engels also widens his account of illegality to include the conditions of existence suffered by all of the working class and which, as he clarifies, make their rebellion, via collective protest *and* petty criminality, all but inevitable.[22] At stake is the question of how far petty criminality (e.g. theft) should be seen as a legitimate form of political protest. If Engels is quicker than Marx to see crime, potentially as least, as a politicized act,[23] both would want to see individual actions, even if they occur in the private setting of the home, as the effects or consequences of social organization. The same could be said of the police who may claim to stand above or apart from society but who, in *Condition*, act to safeguard the productive forces and in doing so turn a blind eye to the 'unnatural' deaths of workers in factories and society in general.

The crime story in the mid-nineteenth century, either in France or Britain, would not adopt such an overly political stance but nor should we see these early

---

[21] Friedrich Engels, *The Condition of the Working Class in England*, ed. Victor Kiernan (London: Penguin, 1987), p. 127.
[22] Engels writes: 'The contempt for the existing social order is most conspicuous in its extreme form—that of offences against the law', a notion which explains why 'crime has increased in England, and the British nation has become the most criminal in the world.' See *Condition*, p. 127.
[23] In *The Condition of the Working Class in England*, Engels asks 'what inducement has the proletarian not to steal?' (p. 143) while Marx viewed the criminal classes or *lumpenproletariat* with suspicion, even going as far as to call them 'social scum'—see Karl Marx, *Essential Writings of Karl Marx: Economic and Philosophic Manuscripts, Communist Manifesto, Wage Labor and Capital, Critique of the Gotha Program* (St Petersburg, FL: Red and Black Publishers, 2010), p. 171.

examples of the genre as endorsing the kind of rigid separation of public and private spheres that in turn underpins a bourgeois/capitalist world view. In terms of the emerging genre, it may be tempting to see the conditions of existence described by Engels (whereby a war of all against all 'is only the logical sequel of the principle involved in free competition'[24]) as raw material for a type of hard-boiled writing—exemplified by Dashiell Hammett—that would flourish in the US from the 1920s.

But just as Chapter 5 warns against reading Hammett's work as the straightforward manifestation of leftist politics, we should also be careful about positioning all mid-nineteenth-century crime and detective stories as articulations about the liberal separation of public and private spheres—even if there are leftist elements in Hammett's work and liberal sentiments in novels by Gaboriau and Green. Both positions miss the extent to which the genre, from its earliest incarnations, has always existed in the push and pull of what Gramsci would later call hegemonic and counter-hegemonic impulses. To McCann's otherwise excellent account—where nineteenth-century detective fiction raises questions about the 'legitimacy of a liberal society' but always finds ways of recuperating a liberal vision of society and the law[25]—we might reasonably ask whether this vision, and the distinction between public and private worlds it depends on, is always recuperated.

To Engels's claims about the links between social organization and policing, meanwhile, we might ask whether the reforms to the justice system carried out in the first half of the nineteenth century and the bureaucratization of policing set up a body of waged professionals capable of acting with relative autonomy in relation to the productive forces—and whether this found its way into the era's crime stories. And to both, we might think about whether nineteenth-century liberalism and Marxism, and their influence on the politically unconscious of the exemplary crime stories of the era, pay sufficient attention to the particular challenges of being a woman in a deeply patriarchal culture. In theory at least, as Carole Pateman concedes, liberalism and feminism enjoy a close relationship, insofar as their roots lie in the emergence of individualism and the emancipation of 'free, equal beings' from 'hierarchical bonds'.[26] But what a novel like *Lady Audley's Secret* shows us is that while the liberal distinction between private and public may give male characters like Robert Audley the freedom to make decisions and exercise their authority, this same freedom operates to silence and limit female subjectivity. In doing so, such works help us to see, or not to see, the extent to which a liberal social contract involves what Lisa Adkins calls 'a double move of freedom and subjection',[27] and therefore to the ways in which feminist and Marxist objections to liberal theory find real affinity with one another.

---

[24] Engels, *Condition*, p. 156.   [25] McCann, *Gumshoe America*, p. 11.
[26] Carole Pateman, *The Disorder of Women: Democracy, Feminism and Political Thought* (Cambridge: Cambridge University Press, 1989), p. 118.
[27] Lisa Adkins, 'The New Economy, Property and Personhood', *Theory, Culture & Society*, 22:1 (2005), p. 116.

IMAGINING THE STATE

> With few exceptions, crime is an incomprehensible event: an opaque fact whose motives or circumstances are never transparent, a type of blind spot, and an often unspeakable story. Hence the endless stream of representations it engenders. For it all unfolds as if understanding crime...hinges upon its various representations, starting from the initial witness statements or the initial topographic surveys performed by the detective and proceeding on to countless legal, journalistic and literary reconstructions.[28]
>
> (Dominique Kalifa)

Crime, as Kalifa postulates, is an 'opaque fact' or 'unspeakable story' that, in turn, requires a 'stream of representations' to give it tangible form. We might say the same thing about the state. We think we know what the state is and does, but, beyond the spectacle of public executions, its authority is often exercised out of public sight via what can seem to be arcane legal codes and unexceptional bureaucratic dictates. In its multiple institutional forms and spanning its judicial, policing, administrative, and executive capacities, the state is not easily personified and typically remains an opaque presence in much fiction. Nonetheless, the characteristic movement inherent in much crime writing from criminal act to crime scene to investigator and eventually to an entire apparatus of crime control in turn gives some shape or form to the state or at least allows us to see it as a tangible entity and appreciate its labyrinthine operations. This would seem to be what Emile Gaboriau has in mind by structuring the first volume of *Monsieur Lecoq* in the manner he has: from the dinginess of Mother Chupin's salon on the periphery of Paris where three men have been assassinated by an unknown assailant, the first part of Gaboriau's novel unfolds to detail both the investigative process, with its forensic assessment of the available evidence and the various people involved, and the attendant policing and judicial procedures and administrative structures. In so doing, Gaboriau constructs what we might call a state imaginary: not an objective account of the entire edifice of the state but an insight, largely though not exclusively from the point of view of an individual figure, into the minutiae of its policing function.

Gaboriau's state imaginary is not a totalizing vision. It doesn't project the state as a perfect, gleaming monolith, transcendent and disinterested, standing above or apart from society in a manner evocative of Hobbes's *Leviathan*. Yet too often the critical reception of Gaboriau's novels, following Michel Foucault's assessment in *Discipline and Punish* and D.A. Miller's *The Novel and the Police*, has made this kind of a claim. Miller certainly is guilty of taking Lecoq's admiration for 'that mysterious power whose hand was everywhere, which one could not see nor hear, but which heard and saw everything'[29] at face value. It is true that this description of the police neatly summarizes the panoptic capacities of 'disciplinary power' as imagined by Foucault and reinterpreted by Miller: 'an ideal of unseen but all-seeing

---

[28] Dominique Kalifa and Margaret Jean Flynn, 'Criminal Investigators at the Fin-de-siècle', *Yale French Studies*, 108 (2005), p. 36.

[29] Emile Gaboriau, *Monsieur Lecoq* (New York, NY: Charles Scribner's Sons, 1904), p. 19.

surveillance, which, though partly realized in several, often interconnected institutions, is identified with none.'[30] But this notion of an unseen, all-seeing 'gaze'— what Gunning calls 'a mastering, objectifying surveillance embodied in the alignment of knowledge and vision in the scientific gaze and the panoptic vision of social control'[31]—seems a long way from the messy and imperfect 'realities' of police work and judicial compromises that Gaboriau describes in *Monsieur Lecoq* and *The Widow Lerouge* (1866). Take, for example, the final sentences of the latter which would appear to refute the idea of the police as an all-seeing asymmetrical power produced by the perfect confluence of bureaucratic rationale and scientific positivism:

> After having believed in the infallibility of justice, [Père Tabaret]...saw no errors as great as judicial ones. The old amateur detective doubted the existence of crime, and believed that the evidence of one's senses proved nothing. He circulated a petition for the abolishment of capital punishment, and organized a society for aiding the poor and innocent accused.[32]

The implications of Gaboriau's concluding remarks are far-reaching, especially in so far as the inadequacy of the criminal justice system is used to cast doubt on the very definition of crime—i.e. the fact that the poor typically are the subject of police enquires and often innocent suggests that crime cannot be seen merely as the breaking of state-sanctioned legal codes. Nonetheless we need to be careful about taking them *too* seriously, for in *The Widow Lerouge* and *Monsieur Lecoq* the aberrant activities of individual criminals *are* exposed by the committed actions of a small group of state agents and auxiliaries. *The Widow Lerouge* may, then, raise doubts against the justice system but it also operates, in one sense, according to the individualizing logic of the emerging genre, identified by Moretti—'to dispel the doubt that guilt might be impersonal, and therefore collective and social'.[33]

In other words, by drawing attention to what can be achieved via the careful application of rational thought and due process, Gaboriau celebrates the successes of his detectives (public and private) as much as he laments the inadequacies of the system they serve—and by doing so obscures, perhaps deliberately, any social or political critique he may want to gesture towards. Like his detectives, Gaboriau is no political radical but the critical tendency to use his work, following Foucault, as characteristic of the panoptic tendencies in the genre, seems equally to miss the

---

[30] D.A. Miller, *The Novel and the Police* (Berkeley and Los Angeles, CA: University of California Press, 1988), p. viii.
[31] Tom Gunning, 'Lynx-Eyed Detectives and Shadow Bandits: Visuality and Eclipse in French Detective Stories and Films before WW1', *Yale French Studies*, 108 (2005), p. 74.
[32] Gaboriau, *The Widow Lerouge* (New York, NY: Charles Scribner's Sons, 1903), p. 436.
[33] Moretti, *Signs*, p. 136. David Schmid argues that this logic typically takes two forms: 'either the source of the crime is presented as a single individual, in the form of the criminal; or the solution to the crime is presented as a single individual, in the form of the detective.' But crucially Schmid argues that if this individualist focus is pushed or extended, crime fiction is more than capable of providing 'politically-engaged critiques of capitalist, racist and patriarchal spatializations of power'. See 'Imagining Safe Urban Space: The Contribution of Detective Fiction to Radical Geography', *Antipode*, 27:3 (1995), p. 243.

mark.[34] Gaboriau is a pivotal figure in the emerging landscape of mid-nineteenth-century crime fiction not because Lecoq ever achieves a kind of cartographic mastery of his milieu. Rather it is because he is the first to develop Vidocq's interest in procedure into a fully realized and distinctively modern account of bureaucratic organization that shows what can be achieved through the application of rational norms to the realm of policing, without turning a blind eye to the detrimental effects of institutional rivalry, vested interests, and failure.[35]

Let us return to the initial crime scene and examine in more detail how Gaboriau uses the evidence left behind as a point of departure for the larger task of imagining the state. For a start, it should be made clear that Lecoq's ability to read and make sense of evidence is not the gift of his superior intellect. Rather he is successful because he is more diligent than others (i.e. his superior, Gevrol) at following guidelines already laid down by statutes and custom. Hence, while Gevrol's explanation (i.e. that the treble shooting is the product of a squabble between 'former jail-birds', p. 67) is a product of guesswork and prejudice, Lecoq's interest in the case's peculiar qualities emerges from his careful inspection of the physical evidence: women's footsteps leading away from Mother Chupin's salon and the presence of an expensive diamond. This interest is heightened by the manner and conduct of the suspect who is apprehended at the salon and who 'must belong to the highest ranks of society' (p. 96). Lecoq's careful gathering of the evidence allows him to set up different lines of inquiry (for example by following the footprints from the crime scene to the road he deduces that two women were picked up by a coachman heading into Paris; by finding the diamond he initiates a search of the city's jewellers, etc.). More specifically, this gathering of evidence is necessary to ensure 'due process'; casts of the footprints are taken to aid Lecoq's investigation and so they can be brought before a judge and 'used in evidence' (p. 56). Therefore when the suspect, who calls himself May, questions the state's case against him, he does so by evaluating the 'quality' of the available evidence. The parry and counter-parry that constitute Lecoq's exchanges with May are not to be understood, first and foremost, as a contest between the super-detective and the super-criminal, but as subjects in procedural drama: policeman and suspect whose subjectivities derive from the respective roles they perform. In this sense, their actions need to be understood in the context of the wider, bureaucratic framework that Gaboriau constructs: Lecoq's authority, for example, is conferred on him by the 'judge of instruction' who, we are told, 'is charged with collecting proofs and testimony and in preparing the case for presentation in court' (p. 83). As such, the careful reports

---

[34] See Michel Foucault, *Discipline and Punish: The Birth of the Prison*, trans. Alan Sheridan (London: Penguin, 1991), pp. 67–9.

[35] In making these claims about *Monsieur Lecoq*, I am referring predominantly though not exclusively to the first volume, subtitled 'L'Enquête', because this focuses on the investigation. The second volume, subtitled 'L'Honneur du Nom', is essentially an historical novel in its own right providing an account of aristocratic rivalry in the Napoleonic and post-Napoleonic era; an account which in the end explains what the Duc de Sairmeuse did to Madame Chupin's salon in the first place and exonerates his subsequent actions. In fact, while it may go against Gaboriau's authorial intentions, there is some profit in reading the first volume as a novel in its own right because it both retains an overall sense of structural integrity and provides enough answers to the questions it raises.

that Lecoq scribes ('that would be admitted under the title of an inquiry', p. 63) and the novel's detailed descriptions of particular legal statutes (e.g. Article 613 which allows the judge, prior to trial, 'to adopt such measures concerning them as he may deem necessary for the interests of the prosecution', p. 187) are part of an attempt to convince readers about the robustness and transparency of the justice system.

At stake is the efficiency of the state as a whole but we should not necessarily assume that Gaboriau wants us to see the system itself as efficient. For alongside this desire to defend existing statutes and procedures (and a whole slew of legal reforms instituted since the turn of the century) Gaboriau also raises some troubling questions about the nature of hierarchical organization and by implication the wider authority of the state. He does this by drawing attention to the extent of inter- and intra-departmental conflict and by hinting at the ways in which latent class privilege prevents even those as dedicated and fair-minded as Lecoq from arriving at the right conclusions. In doing so, Gaboriau raises, consciously or otherwise, important questions about what John Stuart Mill called 'the free development of individuality' and 'the nature and limits of the power which can be legitimately exercised by society over the individual'[36] and, in turn, about whether the circumscription of this 'free development of individuality' by the institutional structures set up to enforce the law and police society is a good thing. By all accounts Gaboriau was a liberal thinker, i.e. someone committed to a more egalitarian society and open to ideas of reform but without espousing sympathy either for the monarchy or revolution. Bearing this out, his work demonstrates a bourgeois distrust of privilege and the machinations of the aristocracy and repugnance for the squalor of the criminal classes and for extreme poverty in general. The jurist in him meant that he believed in the capacities of the justice system to tackle social ills, even if he could see well enough its imperfections. But this account of Gaboriau as a committed liberal is challenged by a more careful reading of his work, in this instance, the first volume of *Monsieur Lecoq*, and particularly the central struggle between May and Lecoq.

On the face of it, Gaboriau would seem to have written a detective novel that conforms in every way to the disparaging account of the genre offered by Moretti—one where the central struggle positions individuals (detective and criminal) against one another and where the society as a whole is 'innocent, and thus free to carry on'.[37] But to make this claim is to ignore Lecoq's position within the justice system—of which he, Inspector Gevrol (a rival), Father Absinthe (an auxiliary), and the judge in overall charge of inquiry, Segmuller, are all a part. If Mill privileges private over public and argues that the state should only intervene in the private affairs of 'free individuals' in cases where their security is threatened, *Monsieur Lecoq* refutes the notion that the individual should be prized over the collective. Just as Marx famously declared that 'man is no abstract being squatting

---

[36] John Stuart Mill, *On Liberty*, ed. Gertrude Himmelfarb (London: Penguin, 1987), p. 59.
[37] Moretti, *Signs*, p. 139.

outside the world',[38] Gaboriau's novel locates Lecoq in a highly differentiated hierarchical environment where his actions only make sense as expressions of his role as a waged policeman. This is not to suggest that Gaboriau goes as far as endorsing a Marxist move to implicate all articulations of individuality as markers of class status and to see human relations in straightforwardly deterministic terms. But equally the idea that the state, as characterized by its bureaucratic structures and processes, is either the expression of the consent forged by free individuals or a politically neutral body, standing apart from society, impartially adjudicating between competing interests, would not seem to describe the inner logic of *Monsieur Lecoq*.

If Gaboriau's portrait of the state's crime control apparatus emphasizes its efficiency and fairness, he is also keen to foreground the damaging effects of departmental squabbles and petty rivalries; between, for example, Gevrol whose 'powers of penetration were not, perhaps, very great' but who, we are informed, 'thoroughly understood his business' (p. 3), and Lecoq who has a different idea of what took place at Mother Chupin's saloon. Gaboriau handles their fractious relationship with admirable deftness. Just as Lecoq has to tread carefully because even the faintest whiff of 'unduly taking advantage of a comrade' would carry grave consequences 'in a profession where competition and rivalry are...potent' (p. 20), he cannot wholly ignore his suspicions regarding Gevrol who 'enjoys too much liberty in the depot' (p. 288). That said, even though Lecoq does not believe that Gevrol is openly corrupt ('If a hundred thousand francs were counted out upon the table and offered to him' (p. 289) by May in return for his freedom, Gevrol, we are told, would not accept it), Lecoq is at a loss to explain how May is always able to keep one step ahead of their investigation; the implication being that he is being aided by an insider; a suspicion which in turn points to divisions in the ranks and which raises hard questions about the professed neutrality of the police and/or the judiciary. These suspicions are confirmed, later in the first volume, when it is revealed that the first judge assigned to the case, Monsieur D'Escorval, absented himself because he knew May (and didn't want his family's links to the suspect to be made public) but not before he'd been coerced into passing information to May.

Taken on its own terms, this revelation and this entanglement require us to pose some far-reaching questions against the impartiality of the state's bureaucracy, a move that is not uncoincidentally attempted by Marx and in some ways brings their respective positions into alignment. Gaboriau's depiction of the judiciary and due process as destabilized by conflicts between members of the bureaucratic class is tempered by his defence of the criminal justice system as a whole. But nor should we see Marx's account of state bureaucracy in purely functionalist terms, i.e. that economic decisions alone determine what the state does and who it supports. Marx maintains that '[t]he mode of production of material life conditions the general

---

[38] Marx, *Critique of Hegel's Philosophy of Right*, trans. Annette Jolin and Joseph O'Malley, ed. Joseph O'Malley (Cambridge: Cambridge University Press, 1970), p. 131.

process of social, political and intellectual life'[39] but elsewhere in his work, notably *The Eighteenth Brumaire of Louis Bonaparte* (1852), which deals with the events leading up to the Bonapartist coup of December 1851, this *general* principle is modified. Here, especially, we are given a view of the state and its bureaucratic officialdom as relatively autonomous. Marx's thoughts on this subject take him in competing directions and it's the issue of how Marx handles the tensions implicit in his own thinking I'd like to use in order to bring Gaboriau's depiction of state power into sharper focus. Looking ahead to Gramsci's account of the state as fractious and comprising competing power blocs, and of state rule as a mixture of armed coercion and constitutional arrangements aimed at soliciting the support of the general population,[40] Marx's account of the run-up to the coup and its aftermath delineates the state's multiple institutional forms and the establishment of a 'professional' class, ostensibly committed to administering 'general' law, as opposed to protecting the interests of the economically powerful.[41] As Engels later pointed out in a letter to Conrad Schmid, this new profession, buoyed by financial independence and codes of practice enshrined under law, greatly valued 'the relative independence once transferred to it and gradually further developed', although he qualifies this remark with the claim that any 'new independent power' must in the end 'follow the movement of production'.[42] In his *Critique of Hegel's Philosophy of Right*, Marx attempts a similar manoeuvre. While he cedes that the bureaucracy could be independent (of the productive forces) *to a degree*, and that a salaried, professional body could claim to represent the general interest better than members of the aristocracy, Marx also makes it clear that the bureaucracy must, in the final reckoning, be understood as 'the state's consciousness, the state's will, the state's power, as a Corporation'.[43]

What is so fascinating about *Monsieur Lecoq* is how closely it would seem to mirror the logic of this move: this sanctioning of the 'relative' independence of the criminal justice system while underscoring the extent to which law enforcement professionals like Lecoq and Segmuller must, in the end, defend the status quo because it is their job to do so. Marx is angered by this partiality (and agitates for revolutionary change) while Gaboriau seems more accepting of it and like the crime story in general ends up buttressing, willingly or otherwise, the authority of the state. But even here *Monsieur Lecoq* is less accommodating than it might

---

[39] Marx, *A Contribution to the Critique Political Economy*, trans. S.W. Ryazanskaya, ed. Maurice Dobb (Moscow: Progress Publishers, 1977), pp. 20–1.
[40] I offer a fuller version of Gramsci's account of the state in Chapter 5.
[41] See Marx, *The Eighteenth Brumaire of Louis Bonaparte* (Moscow: Progress Publishers, 1972): Marx traces the growth of 'executive power with its enormous bureaucratic and military organisation' (p. 104) through the French Revolution, the restoration under Louis Philippe and the second Bonaparte and makes the claim that while in the first two instances bureaucracy 'was the instrument of the ruling class, however much it strove for power on its own' (p. 105), only in the latter case 'does the state seem to have made itself completely independent' (p. 105)—though quite what he means here by the term 'completely' remains a matter for further deliberation and debate.
[42] Engels qtd in Drew Humphreys and David F. Greenberg, 'The Dialectic of Crime Control', in Greenberg (ed.) *Crime and Capitalism*, pp. 217–18.
[43] Marx, *Critique*, p. 46.

initially appear. To develop this point, it is worth recalling Moretti's claim that the genre is dedicated to the principle of full disclosure. He writes:

> Holmes is not a policeman, but a private detective: in him, detection is disengaged from the purpose of the law. His is a purely cultural aim. It is preferable for a criminal to escape... and the detection to be complete—rather than for him to be captured and the logical re-construction to be pre-empted.[44]

This may be true of Doyle's stories but if we take the first volume of *Monsieur Lecoq* on its own terms, much is left unexplained.[45] Exactly why this is the case will help us, I think, to better identify the move between liberal and not-so-liberal positions staked out in the novel. In the second volume Gaboriau provides a more extensive account of the familial rivalry between the Sairmeuses and D'Escorvals which explains what took May (who is in fact the Duc de Sairmeuse) to Mother Chupin's salon and why he shot the three men. But it is instructive that, at the end of the first volume, Lecoq seeks to resolve the unanswered questions not through his own initiative but by turning to the renowned amateur detective Monsieur Tabaret (who also appears in *The Widow Lerouge* and who, we're told, 'worked as much and far better than the two inspectors of the police', p. 343). Taberet listens to the younger man's description of the case and points out the mistakes that Lecoq has made—mistakes that have been seized upon by Lecoq's critics as evidence of his limitations as a detective. (Sherlock Holmes dismissed him as 'miserable bungler'.[46]) There is something potentially disruptive about the idea of failure, especially in light of what Moretti describes as the genre's push towards full disclosure—I'll develop this point in the next paragraph. But it's also the case that Lecoq's inability to see what is right in front of him is the product not just of his shortcomings as a detective, but rather of his class position. Lecoq is the archetypal petty bourgeoisie; the son of 'a rich and respectable family' from Normandy who received 'a good solid education' before falling on hard times following his father's ruination and death (p. 17). As such the man's scepticism is sufficiently developed to see the failings of his immediate superior, Gevrol, but not someone as powerful as a judge of inquiry; hence he doesn't think to look into the mysterious accident that absents D'Escorval from the investigation. It is true Lecoq realizes that something might be amiss, perhaps the glimmer of a nascent political consciousness. 'Could it be,' he thinks, when D'Escorval rushes from the interrogation of May, 'that he holds the key to the mystery?' (p. 105). Likewise, towards the end of the

---

[44] Moretti, *Signs*, p. 143.

[45] Treating the first volume of *Monsieur Lecoq* on its own terms is a potentially problematic move as the questions which are left partially unresolved here are indeed fully explained in the second volume. But the two volumes are very different in their tone and content and while the first volume qualifies as a crime novel because of its exclusive focus on the investigation (and on the relationship between investigator and perpetrator), the second volume is closer in form and theme to the historical novel. There are also precedents for treating the first volume on its own terms; as Stephen Knight notes in *Crime Fiction 1800–2000*, the English translation published by Hodder in 1920 offered no sense that a second part was forthcoming. 'Customers', he remarks, 'must have been puzzled why Lecoq had become so famous for his brilliant conclusions, faced with this indecisive ending' (p. 50).

[46] Arthur Conan Doyle, *Study in Scarlet* in *The Adventures of Sherlock Holmes* (Ware, Hertfordshire: Wordsworth, 1992), p. 18.

novel and having pursued May as far as the Hôtel de Sairmeuse, Lecoq idly speculates that their suspect might be the Duc de Sairmeuse but, because of his own class position and the deference he must show to those above him, he 'dismissed this idea, and despised himself for entertaining it' (p. 338).

This dismissal, and Lecoq's self-remonstration, is revealing on a number of levels. First, it shows how crimes and misdemeanors committed by the country's social and political elites go undetected, because those tasked with enforcing the law are either so beholden to the idea of social hierarchy or do not possess the necessary authority to confront the higher-ups. This is still a long way from Marx's insinuation that the state's bureaucracy is an instrument of class domination but perhaps not as far as we might think. The Duc de Sairmeuse and M. D'Escorval may be scions of old families (rather than the new captains of industry) and hence their hold over their social inferiors is the product of long-held custom. But Lecoq's blindness is symptomatic of a meekness in the face of privilege, something which in turn points to a lack of equanimity and fairness in the system as a whole, since he and others exhibit no such meekness when faced with the criminal acts perpetrated by the poor. Even when Lecoq is emboldened by the 'truth' to expose the Duc, he is warned by Tabaret about the futility of such action. 'Free, this man is almost omnipotent,' Tabaret says of the Duc, 'and you, an infinitesimal agent of police, will be broken like glass' (p. 365). Second, and perhaps paradoxically, the lesson of Gaboriau's novel is precisely the opposite: what this revelation teaches Lecoq is the importance of pursuing his investigation in *every* direction, even if this means unearthing duplicity and corruption at the heart of the state. This takes us some way towards another of Marx's claims about bureaucracy (that it *is*, also, an independent body whose agents, as Held puts it, 'do not simply coordinate political life in the interests of the dominant class of civil society'[47]). What is most revealing about *Monsieur Lecoq*, however, is the way it seeks to bring together these competing and to some extent *irreconcilable* positions—and in doing so, how it thematizes the emerging genre's dilemma vis-à-vis the state.

To put this another way, Gaboriau's novel wants to stress the vigour and impartiality of figures like Lecoq and hence the reach and authority of the newly emerging bureaucratic state. While Lecoq acknowledges that the Duc is 'far beyond my reach' he expresses a determination to bring the aristocrat under his 'power' (p. 365). It is true that Gaboriau meant *Monsieur Lecoq* to be a two-volume novel and the second volume offers us a full explanation of the Duc's motives, something that defuses Lecoq's indignation and opens the way for further compromises. But if we take the first volume on its own terms, what it demonstrates so well is the ways in which the detective moves in and out of subject-positions that buttress *and* undermine the state's authority, drawing attention to (without ever quite resolving) the structuring tension of the emerging crime story: namely that the relative autonomy of policemen like Lecoq and the effectiveness of bureaucratic procedures are

---

[47] David Held, 'Central Perspectives on the Modern State', in Gregor McLennan, David Held and Stuart Hall (eds) *The Idea of the Modern State* (Milton Keynes and Philadelphia, PA: Open University Press, 1984), p. 54.

central to a particular vision of the state and equally that these same figures and procedures cannot, despite their best intentions, create an institution and society where class and other vested interests no longer matter and don't impede the pursuit of justice.

THE PUBLIC/PRIVATE DICHOTOMY

There is some debate as to whether Gaboriau's novels belong more comfortably in the tradition of *le roman judiciare* (with its focus on the vagaries of justice and the justice system and its impact on ordinary lives) than *le roman policier* (with its more self-evident association with the police and police procedure); and regarding *Monsieur Lecoq* we might say that the first volume is best understood as the latter type and the second volume as the former.[48] Still this distinction offers a useful way of thinking about the corresponding development of crime fiction in Britain and the United States where what we might call the *roman judiciare* came to dominate and where, as Shpayer-Makov argues, novelists exhibited a marked preference for private as opposed to public detectives even though 'official representatives of law enforcement were the principal bulwark against law breaking and social, moral and political deviance'.[49] There are numerous reasons why this might have been so; why English and to some extent American writers were a good deal more reticent than their French counterparts to embrace the *roman policier* and the perspective of the waged cop.[50] For a start, an organized police presence had existed in France since the sixteenth century and by the middle of the nineteenth century, following Vidocq's overhaul of the Sûreté, this force, as Heather Worthington puts it, 'had a clear detective function'.[51]

Hence readers in France, at least compared to their counterparts in England, may not have been as bothered by the notion of the police being the main focus of a novel. Many English commentators in the early years of the nineteenth century, with one eye on the perceived militarization of policing in post-Revolutionary France, regarded the idea of a centralized police force 'an anathema to the English ruling elite's perception of English liberty and constitutionalism'.[52] In the aftermath of the Napoleonic wars, successive parliamentary select committees rejected proposals to establish a police force in London on the grounds that 'it was difficult

---

[48] See David Platten, 'Origins and Beginnings: The Emergence of Detective Fiction in France', in Claire Gorrara (ed.) *French Crime Fiction* (Cardiff: University of Wales Press, 2009), p. 19.
[49] Shpayer-Makov, 'Revisiting the Detective Figure', p. 165.
[50] Heather Worthington makes the point that despite the relative anonymity of the police in fiction of the era, 'the detective made his appearance in factual literature and in reality' and this 'was not the private detective so beloved of later crime fiction; rather, it was the police detective'. See *The Rise of the Detective in Early Nineteenth-Century Popular Fiction* (Basingstoke: Palgrave Macmillan, 2005), p. 4.
[51] Worthington, 'From The Newgate Calendar to Sherlock Holmes', in Charles J. Rzepka and Lee Horsley (eds) *A Companion to Crime Fiction* (Malden, MA and Oxford: Blackwell, 2010), p. 18.
[52] See Clive Emsley, 'The Origins and Development of the Police', in Eugene McLaughlin and John Muncie (eds) *Controlling Crime* (Milton Keynes and Philadelphia, PA: Open University Press, 2002), p. 17.

to reconcile an effective system of police with that perfect freedom of action and exemption from interference which are the great privileges and blessings of society in this country'.[53] Such attitudes, of course, reveal more about English prejudices and anxieties about social or political organization in France than about the realities of policing on the Continent,[54] but their ability to shape public discourses about policing would prove to be extremely durable in the English popular imaginary for the remainder of the nineteenth century.

It is not true that England had no centralized police force prior to the establishment of the Metropolitan Police in early 1829: the Bow Street Runners had patrolled the streets of the capital since the 1750s and the Middlesex Justices Act of 1792 constituted what Reynolds calls the first proper move towards 'the centralization of law enforcement under direct government control'.[55] Nor is it true that policing in England was orientated towards a purely preventative function; the creation of a small detective branch in the Metropolitan Police Force in 1842 formally recognized the importance of detection (i.e. the gathering of evidence) as a necessary function of policing. And it is certainly wrong to suggest the policing in England was ever a politically neutral activity or one that could be reconciled with the rights of the individual and the claims of liberty. The brutal suppression by armed soldiers of working-class protests at Peterloo in 1817 and in Newport in 1839 attested to the militaristic, class-inflected nature of policing (especially at times of social unrest). As Briggs notes, charged 'with the maintenance of public order and the control of society in the widest sense', the police 'embarked upon an unceasing surveillance of all aspects of working-class life'.[56] Where the mid-nineteenth-century English novel did address the issue of policing and where the police were represented, the anxiety was not a working-class fear of state intervention but exactly the opposite: since most of the real-life police detectives, as Shpayer-Makov maintains, came from the working class and lower middle classes,[57] the fear that expressed itself most readily in the fiction of the period was, in fact, a middle- and upper-class one about working-class detectives snooping about in their private affairs. Here at least D.A. Miller is right to claim that the relentless privileging of private over public in the exemplary novels of the era meant that self-policing was often a more pertinent issue for characters and indeed novelists than the imposition of order from outside, e.g. by the police.[58]

---

[53] Qtd in Peter Hitchens, *A Brief History of Crime: The Decline of Order, Justice and Liberty in England* (London: Atlantic Books, 2003), p. 102.

[54] Linda Colley makes the point that the French army under Napoleon was actually a good deal more meritocratic than its equivalent in England: 'Consequently, the prolonged success of French arms in Continental Europe did more than threaten British territorial ambition. It was also politically subversive, casting doubt on the belief that men of land and birth were inherently more suited to the exercise of authority than any other social group.' See *Britons: Forging the Nation 1707–1837* (London: Pimlico, 2003), p. 159.

[55] Elaine A Reynolds, *Before the Bobbies: The Night Watch and Police Reform in Metropolitan London, 1720–1830* (Basingstoke: Macmillan, 1998), p. 85.

[56] John Briggs, Christopher Harrison, Angus McInnes, and David Vincent, *Crime and Punishment in England: An Introductory History* (London: UCL Press, 1996), p. 150.

[57] Shpayer-Makov, 'Revisiting the Detective Figure', p. 185.

[58] Miller, *The Novel and the Police*, p. xii.

This point is well illustrated by Kate Summerscale's recent 'true crime' account *The Suspicions of Mr Whicher* (2008) which traces the influence of the Road Hill House murder in July 1860 and the subsequent police investigation led by Inspector Whicher of Scotland Yard's Detective Branch on Wilkie Collins's sensation novels, particularly *The Woman in White* (1860) and *The Moonstone* (1868). 'The Road Hill case turned everyone detective. It helped shape the fiction of the 1860s and beyond, most obviously Wilkie Collins's *The Moonstone*. Whicher was the inspiration for that story's cryptic Sergeant Cuff who has influenced nearly every detective hero since.'[59] Summerscale provides compelling evidence for the first part of this claim; that the public's interest in the Road Hill case helped to promote what Collins, in *The Moonstone*, called 'detective-fever'.[60] But Summercale doesn't dwell upon significant differences between the case and Collins' fictionalization of it. While her account focuses on the institutional framework that impinges on Whicher's investigation and explores Whicher's fraught relationship with senior figures at Scotland Yard and the Home Office, such contexts are entirely absent in *The Moonstone*. Nor do we really see evidence in Collins's work of the class anxieties alluded to above; the fact, as Summerscale remarks, the police detective was a 'member of the working classes whose pernicious imaginings could sully a middle-class home'.[61] Though officially part of the 'Detective Police'[62] Cuff is presented as an enigmatic and thoroughly individualistic sort; a hatchet-faced figure with a formidable reputation for 'unraveling a mystery' (p. 132); a lover of roses; an amiable, melancholic man who answers to his own code of conduct rather than to the demands of the police and whose investigation doesn't intrude *too much* into the private lives of the Verinder household and their guests (perhaps one reason why it fails). Cuff authors only one (a small one at that) of eight narratives that comprise the novel and is careful to avoid direct references to his institutional role or the pressure of having to answer to those higher up in the police organization (later in the novel we learn that he has 'retired from business' and doesn't 'care a straw' about his reputation which suffered as a result of his initial failure to find the diamond, p. 491).

It is difficult to disregard the discrepancy between the increasingly dominant role played by real-life police detectives in combatting serious crimes, especially as the century progressed, and the preference exhibited by writers of English fiction, and also crime fiction, for private detectives. But the more interesting issue is how or whether this preference affects the political complexion of the novels themselves or at least their capacity to trace and illuminate the workings of public power. This is not to suggest that writers in the 1850s and 1860s like Collins, or Mary Elizabeth Braddon, or indeed Charles Dickens ignored the role and place of the police and by extension the state. It is just they did not permit their police detectives to intrude too much, thereby exhibiting a concern, conscious or otherwise, about

---

[59] Kate Summerscale, *The Suspicions of Mr Whicher or The Murder at Road Hill House* (London: Bloomsbury, 2008), p. xi.
[60] Wilkie Collins, *The Moonstone* (London: Penguin, 1986), p. 160.
[61] Summerscale, *The Suspicions of Mr Whicher*, p. 146.
[62] Collins, *The Moonstone*, p. 138.

ceding too much visibility and authority to working-class characters or indeed about laying bare the inner workings of the justice system. Hence Cuff plays second fiddle to Franklin Blake in *The Moonstone* and Inspector Bucket is a relatively minor figure in the much larger social panorama of *Bleak House* (1850). There is a self-evident political imperative at work in the marginalizing of working-class voices, but the preference for tackling crime in a private rather than public setting, and by private individuals rather than by employees of the state, would have far-reaching consequences for the capacities of such novels and novelists to properly tackle and lay bare the stubborn persistence of inherited privilege in English life.

Two 'sensation' novels are indicative: Braddon's *Lady Audley's Secret* (1861–2) and *The Leavenworth Case* (1878) by the US writer Katharine Anna Green. Novels about 'sensational' subjects like murder were meant to stir and shock middle-class readers and, as Stephen Knight notes, they drew upon a Gothic dissidence and the energy of popular theatre to suggest 'that strange and terrible events could occur right within the respectable home, the shrine of Victorian values'.[63] Still, while it is not hard to see how the intrusion of murder, theft, blackmail, rape, and madness into the lives of the well-to-do might have unsettled and even scandalized middle-class readers, the working out of the plots typically involved cover-ups and denials relating to any wrongdoing on the part of the wealthy and an unwillingness to submit the private lives of the well-off to the public scrutiny of the justice system.

Lady Audley's Secret makes a clear point of underlining what might trouble its middle-class readers: not merely that 'brutal and treacherous murders; slow, protracted agonies from poisons administered by some kindred hand [and] sudden and violent deaths by cruel blows' might be commonplace but rather that such an act, in this particular story, is perpetrated by an outwardly reputable woman. 'No crime has ever been committed in the worst rookeries about Seven Dials that has not been also done in the face of sweet rustic calm.'[64] Here that face belongs to Lady Audley, née Lucy Graham, a 'fragile creature' (p. 76) with a 'wax-doll beauty' (p. 263) who, it is eventually revealed, murdered (or tried to murder) her first husband George Talboys. Her secret, what she tries and fails to keep from her second husband Sir Michael Audley (who doesn't even know about her first marriage) is not just the attempted murder but also that she suffers from a strain of madness which means that at times of stress her mind 'utterly lost its balance' (p. 346). There is something daring about depicting an outwardly respectable woman as sexually attractive, ruthless, and manipulative, someone willing to kill to protect her secret (especially if this means ensuring never having to return to her 'hard, cruel, wretched life—the life of poverty, and humiliation, and vexation, and discontent', p. 316). Braddon's well-meaning efforts to render Lady Audley as sympathetic or at least as someone whose ambitions—e.g. to escape a life of poverty—might not have been different from the majority of her readers, are further reminders that

---

[63] Stephen Knight, *Crime Fiction, 1800–2000: Detection, Death, Diversity* (Basingstoke: Palgrave Macmillan, 2004), p. 39.
[64] Mary Elizabeth Braddon, *Lady Audley's Secret* (Oxford: Oxford University Press, 1998), p. 54.

criminality should be understood as a social rather than individual phenomenon; i.e. that Lady Audley's violence has its roots in her own subordinate gender and class position.

But the subversive impulses of Braddon's novel need to be assessed in the context of the role of Robert Audley as the novel's surrogate detective. Robert 'was supposed to be a barrister' (p. 32) and therefore thinks with the mindset of a lawyer, someone well aware of the significance of small details or circumstantial evidence, 'infinitesimal trifles' which may in the end reveal 'the whole secret of some wicked mystery' (p. 119). Part of his role is to try and piece together 'the fatal chain of circumstantial evidence' (p. 220) that would seem to implicate his aunt. And herein lies the problem for him, and for the novel as a whole. While Gaboriau's Lecoq may have been compromised by his class position and aspirations, Robert's investigation directly threatens his family and hence his (secure) position in the world. As a trainee barrister, he is aware more than most of the devastating effect on his family and status should his aunt's crimes ever come to public light; hence it is understandable that he wouldn't want her to face criminal proceedings, however much he may claim to want 'justice' for 'the dead first' (p. 158). There are doubts about whether the system could provide justice because in a regimented, hierarchical society where class position determines how you are treated under the law the idea of impartiality is put under strain. But rather than force Robert to choose between justice and punishing the guilty, and protecting his own position, Braddon engineers a suitable compromise: Lady Audley is privately banished to an asylum in France and everything can go back to the way it was. Certainly difficult questions about how the justice system might cope with the airing of the dirty secrets of the great and the good in public, and the implications for the representations of the state, are conveniently circumvented.

This underwriting of the public/private dichotomy affords Robert the freedom to pursue the truth, whatever this is, and justice, as he sees it, in a private rather than public context and hence sanctions one of the cornerstones of nineteenth-century liberal theory: the rights of free individuals to manage their own affairs, assuming, to use Mill's qualification, that no harm is done to others. In this instance of course Lady Audley's actions have resulted in very severe harm to others but this right to liberty is still, rather problematically from an ethical perspective, privileged over the demands of the law. Braddon's relentless privileging of private over public causes her other problems too, specifically related to what Mill tries to untangle in his essay 'The Subjection of Women' (1869): namely that liberalism, despite its professed egalitarianism, might be complicit in perpetrating the patriarchy in the domestic or private realm.[65] In Braddon's novel, Robert's freedom to act in a private capacity obscures the extent to which this freedom is founded on and comes at the expense of his aunt's incarceration—and obscures how the professed individualism and egalitarianism of a particular strain of liberal thought in fact supports the 'patriarchal reality of a social structure of inequality'.[66]

---

[65] Mill, *The Subjection of Women*, ed. Edward Alexander (New Brunswick, NJ: Transaction, 2001).
[66] Pateman, *The Disorder of Women*, p. 120.

Anna Katharine Green's *The Leavenworth Case* is far more willing to expose the private lives of a wealthy New York family to the rigours of the law, and therefore probe the character and limits of the justice system, but the freedom of its male protagonists, both in their private and public capacities, is once again premised on the silencing and subjugation of the two main female characters. The victim is billionaire philanthropist Horatio Leavenworth and the chief suspects are his two surviving nieces, Eleanore and especially Mary, due to inherit his fortune. The official police investigation, led by Ebenezer Gryce, a detective from the police department, is sensitive to the complicating issues of class but not to the extent that it would overlook the guilt of the well-to-do, if proven, thereby establishing the professed neutrality of the justice system. 'Eleanore has laid herself open to the suspicion of the police and must take the consequences', Gryce says. 'I am sorry; she is a noble creature, I admire her; but justice is justice, and though I think her innocent I shall be forced to put her under arrest.'[67] But Gryce also needs the narrator and protagonist, Everett Raymond, operating in a private capacity as partner in a New York law firm, to insinuate himself into the social circle of the two nieces in order 'ferret out the real criminal from a score of doubtful characters' (p. 74). Reflecting his own class biases, and out of his admiration for Eleanore in particular, Raymond is keener than Gryce to exonerate the two nieces. On one level then Mary and Eleanore become objects of the scrutinizing male gaze, with Raymond's freedom to pursue his own investigation, at times in tandem with the official one and sometimes at odds with it, working, whether he realizes it or not, to silence and contain the two nieces. But on another level, the complex interplay between public and private, between the official investigation led by Gryce and the private one led by Raymond, allows Green more scope than Braddon to interrogate the extent to which the imposition of law and the working out of justice are compatible with institutional forms established to address the 'problem' of crime.

Overlaying this is Green's willingness to depict the wealthy classes as venal and self-interested, at least in the persona of Mary who, unlike Lady Audley, does not have a mental illness to excuse her behaviour. Raymond's private enquiry then focuses on unravelling Mary's clandestine affairs; her secret marriage to an Englishman and the subsequent disapproval of her uncle, resulting in her disinheritance, a move of course which gives her a very strong motive for wanting the uncle dead. The likelihood of Mary's guilt is strengthened by her admission of her greed and love of money (p. 243) and through the death by self-administered poison of a loyal servant once she comes to suspect Mary. In this sense, the society is a decidedly uncivil one; a base, ugly world where someone of Mary's class is willing to kill to protect her claims on Leavenworth's millions and let her cousin Eleanore, who also suspects that Mary is guilty, go to prison, rather than admit what she's done. No wonder that Raymond prevaricates at the prospect of unmasking her as the murderer, particularly as it threatens his own world view of the wealthy as civilized and enlightened. Unlike in Braddon's novel, there is no chance of carting Mary off

---

[67] Anna Katharine Green, *The Leavenworth Case* (London and New York, NY: Penguin, 2010), p. 193.

to an asylum either, because of Gryce's involvement and the public clamour that justice is seen to be done. Green sustains this tension right up to the final chapter where her own class sympathies and the need to produce a surprise ending get the better of her. Leavenworth's secretary confesses to the murder and the tension, built up over the course of the entire narrative, between competing versions of procedure and justice evaporate. Not only is the ending trite and unnecessary; it also means that the great and good can close ranks around the nieces and Gryce can be seen to exercise the law in a way that doesn't threaten social hierarchies and class privilege.

UNCIVIL SOCIETY

Beginning with the crime scene, Gaboriau, in *Monsieur Lecoq*, creates a police detective capable of deciphering its clues and reading its hidden secrets, and from there, an entire state imaginary; an account of police practices and judicial processes that gives shape to the state's labyrinthine operations and its multiple institutional forms. Much of the richness of the novel derives from the intricate portrait of this emerging formation, from the practical difficulties associated with conducting an effective investigation to the complexities implicit in the fraught relationship between individual and institution. The 'crime scene' in *The Notting Hill Mystery* is gestured at rather being than a physical fact but its implications are just as far-reaching.

The novel opens with an official letter written by Ralph Henderson, a private enquiry agent, to the—Life Assurance Association laying out his grave suspicions regarding the actions of Baron R—who has made a claim against five separate life policies taken out in Manchester, Liverpool, Edinburgh, Dublin, and London for a total of twenty-five thousand pounds, after the death, in highly suspicion circumstances, of his wife Madame R—. It is not the state per se that is being imagined here but the entire apparatus of the law because the letter itself is just a prelude to what follows: Henderson is acting not just as private enquiry agent but also as surrogate legal counsel, laying out the case against Baron R—, gathering legally binding depositions from witnesses and reports from accredited professionals and carefully tying the circumstantial evidence together, not to prove Baron R—'s guilt but to alert various insurers and perhaps the police about his likely guilt. As Henderson puts it, 'These I have arranged, as far as possible, in the form in which they would be laid before counsel, should it ultimately be deemed advisable to bring the affair into Court.'[68]

First published in extract form in *Once a Week* magazine starting on 29 November 1862, its authorship when it appeared as a book in 1865 was credited to Charles Felix, though Felix was acknowledged to be a pseudonym. The novel never received the acclaim, public or critical, feted on *The Moonstone* or

---

[68] Charles Warren Adams, *The Notting Hill Mystery* (London: The British Library, 2012), p. 7. All subsequent citations refer to this edition.

Lady Audley's Secret and quickly disappeared from view. Its reputation was briefly revived by Julian Symons in 1975 when he found the novel languishing in the vaults of the British Library; and again in 2012 when it was reissued as a British Library edition to more widespread critical praise. This followed an instructive piece of detective work by Paul Collins who, in a *New York Times* article a year earlier, identified the author as Charles Warren Adams, sole representative of the novel's original publisher, Messrs. Saunders, Otley & Co.[69] *The Notting Hill Mystery* is an extraordinarily inventive piece of writing—and not just because it incorporates such a wealth of para-textual materials into its structure (e.g. witness statements, letters, diary extracts, forensic reports, magazine articles, and police reports). Indeed its originality and the fact that it fell out of favour with the public weaned on the kind of sensation novels written by Collins and Braddon might be related. At first glance the narrative bricolage is strongly reminiscent of Collins's use of multiple narrators in *The Moonstone* and *The Woman in White* but the overall effect is actually quite different. For while Henderson, like Franklin Blake and Walter Hartright, remains in overall control of the narrative, orchestrating the arrangement of the letters, journal entries, and reports, his task is not to establish the truth, but rather to put together a legally sound case for the prosecution. This prevailing sense of uncertainty (i.e. what can and more importantly cannot be proven) and the fragmented, non-linear structure mean that we never get the reassurances provided by the explanation of events characteristic of detective and sensation fiction. Nor do we get a sudden moment of reversal or surprise (as in *The Woman in White* where Godfrey Ablewhite is revealed to be the murderer): Baron R— is identified as a suspect in the first few pages and nothing changes in this respect. The chain of circumstantial evidence may, as Henderson maintains, be 'so complete and close fitting in every aspect, as seems almost impossible to disregard' (p. 7) but elsewhere some doubts creep in, not because Henderson believes Baron R— is really innocent but because he knows that his guilt will not easily be proven in court. 'I confess that after this minute and laborious investigation,' he remarks in his letter to the secretary of the—Life Assurance Association, 'I could still have wished a more satisfactory result' (p. 2). At the end of the novel Henderson's grounds for suspecting Baron R—of having poisoned his wife (and having caused by other means the deaths of her twin sister and her sister's husband) in order to collect their inheritance and cash in their life policies, have been laid out, but we do not *know* any more at the end than we do at the beginning. The concluding paragraph is not a neat summation of what happened but, fittingly, a series of open-ended questions. 'Is that chain one of purely accidental coincidences or does it point to a series of crimes, in their nature and execution almost too horrible to contemplate?' And then, even more disturbingly, Henderson asks: 'Supposing the latter to be the case—are crimes thus committed susceptible of

---

[69] Paul Collins, 'The Case of the First Mystery Novelist', *New York Times*, 7 January 2011; http://www.nytimes.com/2011/01/09/books/review/Collins-t.html?pagewanted=all, accessed 24 August 2012.

proof, or even if proved, are they of a kind for which the criminal can be brought to punishment?' (p. 284).

The notion that Baron R—— may escape justice, or even exposure, for his crimes, or rather the crimes he might have committed, is troublesome enough for contemporary readers. One can only guess how Victorian readers would have reacted. Either way, the novel, directly or indirectly, implicates the ability of the state to safeguard its citizens. Baron R——, after all, remains a free man at the end of the novel and the resulting social vision is disturbing: the police, it would seem, aren't even aware that a crime has been committed and that Baron R——should be considered a suspect, something that fosters a troubling vision of society as dangerously anarchic where greed and murder are rewarded, rather than punished. In turn, this raises the issue of whether Baron R——'s actions should be dealt with by the police or within civil society, which of course is where Henderson, as a freelance contractor working for an insurance company, operates. It also requires us to think about the precise nature of the relationship between the state and civil society in the first place. In *The German Ideology*, Marx and Engels make the point that civil society 'develops with the bourgeoisie' and evolves 'out of production and commerce', which, in turn, 'forms the basis of the State' thereby linking the state *and* civil society to the consolidation of capitalism; but in the same paragraph they also argue that insofar as civil society 'embraces the whole commercial and industrial life of a given stage' it 'transcends the State' even though it must at the same time 'inwardly...organize itself as State'.[70] In Adams's novel, the state apparatus is almost entirely absent, and in its place we are privy to the inner logic of civil society—not merely the rituals and routines of people's day-to-day-lives but more pointedly the commercial drives that compel them to do what they do. The most impressive figure, in this sense, is undoubtedly Baron R——, not a born and bred aristocrat but a self-made man, whose entrepreneurial zeal is directed towards capital accumulation, even though this is achieved via murder, theft, and blackmail. In the eyes of the law, his crimes may be heinous and punishable by death, but in the realm of civil society, where Henderson conducts his affairs, the issue of what differentiates the Baron's criminality from the energetic commercialism of capitalism is troublingly brought to the fore.

More intriguingly, the novel asks us to think about the equally thorny issue of the state's relationship with or to the law (and vice versa), described by Fryer et al. as 'the central and at the same time the most difficult question confronting the sociology of the law'.[71] On the evidence of *The Notting Hill Mystery*, it is not sufficient to claim that the state and the law are synonymous and that the law expresses or refers to the legal practices and systems of the state. If we take Henderson to be an advocate of the law or rather his actions to be analogous of the work undertaken by prosecution counsel in preparation for a trial, should we assume that he also

---

[70] Karl Marx and Friedrich Engels, *The German Ideology*, trans. & ed. S. Ryazanskaya (London: Lawrence & Wishart, 1965), pp. 48–9.
[71] 'Introduction', in Bob Fryer, Alan Hunt, Doreen McBarnett, and Bert Moorhouse (eds) *Law, State and Society* (London: Croom Helm, 1981), p. 15.

personifies or speaks for the state? Not necessarily. After all, Henderson is a claims adjuster hired by the—Life Assurance Association to look into the claims made by Baron R—. In other words, he is acting for himself in the first instance and then for the—Life Assurance Association whose goal is to maximize returns for its proprietors and its stockholders (and is thus part of civil society as defined by Marx and Engels: 'the commercial and industrial life of a given stage'). Whether to pay the Baron's claim or not, therefore, is first and foremost an economic decision; at this juncture it has little to do with the law, or indeed with the state. Legal prosecution may follow but equally it may not, and in any case we can't presume that the weight of evidence required by the state to gain a guilty verdict and the insurance company to turn down the claim are the same. What is significant is that the insurance company has taken the lead here and hence any subsequent effort to bring Baron R—to trial under the law will be influenced by the prior efforts of Henderson acting to defend the commercial interests of his paymasters. In this way, Adams's novel analogizes, whether it intends to or not, civil society, as Marx and Engels would have it, organizing itself as the state; not, that is, superseding the state but acting as the determining force, whereby the commercial imperatives of the insurance industry are shown to come before, and to carry more narrative weight than, the claims of the law.

Later in the twentieth century, the US crime novelist James M. Cain would, in bleak, doom-laden tales like *The Postman Always Rings Twice* (1934) and *Double Indemnity* (1936), depict a closed milieu where the inadequate legal system is wholly beholden to the demands of the insurance industry.[72] Adams's novel is not willing to sanction such a radical view: in one sense the insurance companies have done nothing wrong and their investigation, via Henderson, into Baron R—'s affairs, is effectively handled and likewise there is nothing to indicate that the prosecution, if and when the Baron is tried, will not conduct itself with due process. Still, the fact that the police have no inkling that Baron R—may have poisoned his wife attests, if nothing else, to the flaws or inadequacies of the justice system as a whole. Furthermore, the idea that it takes the interventions of a private enquiry agent, acting for a commercial organization, to do what the police have been unable to do, at least muddies the water in terms of the relationship between business and law, and hence between the intertwined realms of the state and civil society. If the police are oblivious to the machinations of individuals like Baron R—what does this say about the state's capacity to protect its citizens? If the action of a commercial outfit pre-empts the law does this suggest that the business of keeping an eye on the bottom line produces a more vigilant system of control than the state is able to oversee? And where does this leave claims about the normalizing power of self-interest, which as McCann points out, forms the basis for liberalism's view of social harmony? These are awkward questions and if Adams's novel provides no real

---

[72] In *The Postman Always Rings Twice* (1934), for example, the issue of whether or not Frank Chambers and Cora Papadakis are tried for murder is determined not by their guilt under the law but by an arrangement between rival insurance firms in order to minimize their financial exposure.

answers (why should it?), it demonstrates how the crime story can peer into the dark recesses of the justice system and tease out its flaws and its ambiguities.

There are limits to the subversive potential of a novel like *The Notting Hill Mystery*, not least because it suggests, in the final analysis, that the needs of private enterprise, of the affairs of the insurance company, are not at odds with the demands of the law and that both are equally keen to punish wrongdoing—to see that someone like Baron R—does not get away with murder, even if, by the end of the novel, this remains only a possibility. Likewise, in its treatment of gender and power, it may highlight the harm perpetrated against wives by their husbands in private but it is never quite able to move beyond an account of its female characters as victims and only affords them a voice retrospectively via diary extracts. Still, just as *Monsieur Lecoq* constructs an entire state imaginary from its crime scene, thereby proving Marx's maxim that criminals do not just produce crime but also 'the whole apparatus of the police and criminal justice', *The Notting Hill Mystery*, anticipating Michel Foucault more than Marx, suggests that crime control's productive function has an even wider application. Here crime doesn't simply produce the police and justice system but a slew of new subjectivities in the realm of civil society—criminologists, psychologists, crime reporters, forensic scientists, and as *The Notting Hill Mystery* shows us, insurance brokers and claims adjusters—new subjectivities whose job is both to punish wrongdoing and to scrutinize criminality, to seek knowledge and impose this knowledge, to produce new forms of knowledge in order to create a safer society.

This, in turn, draws attention to the tangled links between public power and private enterprise and the extent to which private initiatives, such as Baron R—'s machinations, should be seen as a reflection on the ostensibly legitimate operations of the free market; and how the work of a private agent like Henderson analogizes the fairness and effectiveness of the justice system as a whole. Looking ahead to the direction in which the crime story in France, Britain, and the US would move at the end of the nineteenth century and start of the twentieth century (and which forms the basis of Chapter 4), it may be too schematic to claim that a split or division occurs in the crime story of this earlier epoch. Nonetheless it is instructive to reflect on the differences between novels like *Lady Audley's Secret* and *The Leavenworth Case* which find ways of resolving their issues outside the law or smoothing over tensions between the claims of the law and the interests of the wealthy, and works like *The Notting Hill Mystery* and *Monsieur Lecoq* where, consciously or otherwise, pressure is put on the foundational principles of liberalism's account of the state and society: the rights of free individuals to pursue their self-interest unchecked by state power; the separation of public and private; the neutrality of the state and by implication the justice system; and the compatibility of the demands of the law and the needs of the wealthy and powerful. It is a schism that would become more pronounced by the turn of the century and, as we will see, would have profound implications for the development of the genre in the twentieth century.

4

Crime, Business, and Liberty at the Turn of the Century
The Individual, the State, and the Emergence of Modern Capitalism

One of the more interesting dissections of the problem of the relationship between public and private in the nineteenth century is offered by Michael Faber's *The Crimson Petal and the White* (2002), a contemporary reworking of the Victorian 'sensation' novel, featuring Sugar, a game prostitute, alternatively figured as self-fashioning subject and sexualized object, worker, and kept woman. The contested nature of the public/private dichotomy is thematized most obviously in the space of the brothel, at once 'inside' or private, not just in the sense it is enclosed but also in that it permits or even demands the reproduction of a masculinist ideology (based on who is paying and hence is in charge); and yet also 'outside' or public, in the sense that individuals like Sugar are allowed to exchange their labour for financial remuneration and, in theory at least, better themselves in the process. In a clever and highly knowing way, Faber gradually exposes the limits of the latter position—the liberal, bourgeois fantasy—in favour of a more avowedly Marxist and feminist stance whereby Sugar's labour-power never acquires an external relationship to her,[1] so that her subjection to capitalist and patriarchal power necessarily limits any freedom she might otherwise claim. This double move, of freedom and subjection, brings into focus the relationship between labour, money, and production, which Faber, unusually for a crime novelist, wants us to see rather than not see. It is unusual because, as Franco Moretti argues, while '[m]oney is always the motive of crime in detective fiction' the genre is typically 'silent about production' or what he calls 'that unequal exchange between labour-power and wages which is the true source of wealth'.[2] Faber is very much interested in money and production precisely because he wants to show that the domains of the brothel, factory, and home are linked and that the question of what counts as crime has a

---

[1] Labour here is a form of employment involving what Lisa Adkins, drawing on Marx, calls 'the contracting out of property in the person...in exchange for a wage' which can only be a 'free exchange' if we assume an individual owns their labour power as a commodity and 'that this relation to labour power is the same relation enacted in regard to any other form of material property' which is not typically the case. See 'The New Economy, Property and Personhood', *Theory, Culture & Society*, 22:1 (2005), p. 116.

[2] Franco Moretti, *Signs Taken for Wonder: Essays in the Sociology of Literary Form*, trans. Susan Fisher, David Forgacs, and David Miller (London and New York, NY: Verso, 1983), p. 139.

wider socio-political context and is never simply a private matter between individuals.

It is perhaps unfair to compare Faber's contemporary reworking of the Victorian crime novel with Arthur Conan Doyle's Sherlock Holmes stories which Moretti uses to develop his critique, not least because Faber's treatment of the subject reflects both his own liberal–left politics (i.e. those of his own epoch) and an acute awareness of how far the genre has developed in the intervening period. But it is revealing how closely Faber's deft handling of the brothel as inside/outside space evokes Walter Benjamin's assessment of the turn-of-the-century arcades: the street brought inside or the exterior spaces interiorized. As Tom Gunning explains:

> The exterior as interior becomes a crucial emblem for Benjamin's analysis of the nineteenth century, because this ambiguous spatial interpenetration responds to an essential division on which the experience of bourgeois society is founded, the creation of the interior as a radical separation from the exterior, as a home in which the bourgeois can dwell and dream undisturbed by the noise, activity, and threats of the street, the space of the masses and of production, a private individual divorced from the community.[3]

The dilemma I want to address in this chapter is whether, or to what extent, crime stories of this period in Britain and France, notably works by Doyle, Arthur Morrison, Gaston Leroux, and Marcel Allain and Pierre Souvestre, are able or willing to unpick or unravel this same distinction; in other words, how much they want to insist on the kind of radical separation of inside/private and outside/public that a bourgeois view of the world depends on. Based almost exclusively on an appraisal of the Sherlock Holmes stories, Moretti is insistent on the emerging genre's recuperative agenda—'a hymn to culture's coercive abilities'[4]—but while I don't disagree with his account of the Holmes stories, what I want to argue here is that a wider, deeper look at the genre on both sides of the Channel reveals a group of texts committed, in different ways, to questioning the assumptions behind this radical separation of public and private; and as a consequence to extending what Gunning calls 'this ambiguous spatial interpenetration' to the categories of state and civil society which map, not always neatly or unproblematically, back onto notions of public and private. The political ramifications of such a move, and of the genre's ability to interrogate the material conditions of modernity (e.g. the bureaucratization of policing, the emergence of new technologies to map criminality, the rise of modern capitalism) will form the basis of this chapter's critical outlook.

The notion of nineteenth-century fiction—crime or otherwise—as enforcing an interior/exterior split and in doing so privileging the interior over the exterior (i.e. the sanctified realm of middle-class subjectivity, a space of refuge from the maw of the city, the marketplace, and the forces of production) finds its most persuasive articulation in D.A. Miller's 1988 book *The Novel and the Police*. Miller's thesis is Foucauldian insofar as he is less interested in the activities of the police and the

---

[3] Tom Gunning, 'The Exterior as Interieur: Benjamin's Optical Detective', *boundary 2*, 30:1 (2003), p. 106.
[4] Moretti, *Signs Taken for Wonder*, p. 143.

exercise of public power than in the micro-politics of the domestic realm and the way in which self-regulating subjects internalize 'normalizing perceptions, prescriptions, and sanctions [that] are diffused in discourses and practices throughout the social fabric'.[5] As others have argued, and as I noted in Chapter 3, the police operate at the periphery of the Victorian novel, that is to say the nineteenth-century English novel (the same could not be said about the French novel), even in the case of particular detective stories, such as those of Sherlock Holmes, where the subject matter—e.g. the investigation of crime—would seem to necessitate or even presuppose their dominating presence.[6] For Miller, then, the police refers not to a body of men or an institution of the state but to a general condition whereby individuals' adherence to the normal practices of everyday life is sufficient to ensure the smooth running of society. From Foucault's expansive definition of the police as 'the set of means by which the state's forces can be increased while preserving the state in good order',[7] the station-house, for Miller, is not confined to a specific locale but is dispersed across society as a whole; and instead of inquiring how the police 'function as a topic in the world of the novel' we should ask how the novel participates 'in a general economy of policing power'.[8]

If we take Doyle's Holmes stories as our point of departure, it is hard to wholly disagree with Miller's claim, not least because the police are at best marginal to the investigation. Perhaps as a result, Miller's book has spawned numerous Foucauldian readings of crime fiction in general and the Holmes tales in particular; readings that attest to their disciplinary capacities. Rosemary Jann, for example, points to the ways in which Doyle's work participates in the disciplinary modes of regulation and surveillance which maintain order beyond the activities of the state, while Moretti likens Holmes's all-seeing gaze to the panopticon.[9] Still it is instructive that Miller's subject is the novel per se, rather than the crime story, and that he writes about the police in Dickens and Trollope rather than about the police or the absence of the police in Doyle, thereby sanctioning, implicitly or otherwise, a distinction between the detective formula which is 'set in bounded space... and passes off its investigative technique as extraordinary' and the 'ordinary' novel which leads us to think that no intervention by 'special policing power' is required.[10] As such

---

[5] D.A. Miller, *The Novel and the Police* (Berkeley, CA and London: University of California Press, 1988), p. viii.

[6] Haia Shpayer-Makov points out that the dominance of private detectives in Victorian fiction is not borne out by the 'reality' in which most serious crimes would have been investigated by the police. See 'Revisiting the Detective Figure in Late Victorian and Edwardian Fiction: A View from the Perspective of Police History', *Law, Crime and History*, 2 (2011b), pp. 165–93. Also see Shpayer-Makov, *The Ascent of the Detective: Police Sleuths in Victorian and Edwardian England* (Oxford: Oxford University Press, 2011).

[7] Michel Foucault, *Security, Territory, Population: Lectures at the Collège de France, 1977–78*, trans. Michel Senellart (Basingstoke: Palgrave Macmillan, 2007), p. 313.

[8] Miller, *The Novel and the Police*, pp. xii, 2.

[9] Rosemary Jann, 'Sherlock Holmes Codes the Social Body', *ELH*, 57:3 (1990), pp. 685–708; Moretti, *Signs Taken for Wonder*, p. 143. It should be noted that Moretti's claims here predate Miller's book.

[10] This is Joan Copjec's reading of Miller's work. See Copjec, 'The Phenomenal Nonphenomenon: Private Space in Film Noir', in Copjec (ed.) *Shades of Noir: A Reader* (London and New York, NY: Verso, 1998), p. 171.

we need to think a lot more carefully about the usefulness of Miller's insights for assessing the merits and limits of the crime story where the police (and this is even true of the Sherlock Holmes stories) cannot be wholly absent and where the state must perform a role, even if this role is obscured or circumscribed by the presence of a more gifted, effective private operative.

One of the key preoccupations of this chapter is the issue of whether particular writers end up sanctioning a split between public and private realms (and hence ignoring the extent to which private enterprise and public power have always been deeply intertwined and that most crimes have a political as well as a private explanation). That said, it should be noted that even in examples where the interior and exterior do appear to belong to separate realms (or where the bourgeois fantasy of the quiet, ordered domestic realm and of the freedom of the unfettered individual to act is most keenly felt), this division is never absolute. As Gunning, following Benjamin, argues, the interior may 'constitute itself as a space cut off from the world' but this process of private appropriation relies 'not only on separation and insulation but also on disguise and illusion' as the distinction between interior and exterior, and between the 'private dreaming self and the public space of production and history' collapses under the weight of its own contradictions.[11] This is especially true of the crime story where the materiality of the crime scene, when scrutinized by the investigator, necessarily bears the imprint of the crime itself, and where even the most ordered domestic spaces must bear traces of the intrusion of violence from within or without. Benjamin and Carlo Ginzburg have both located the origins of the genre in this idea of the trace: 'the infinitesimal trace' which permits 'the comprehension of a deeper, otherwise unattainable reality' via the application of observation and deductive logic or what Ginzburg calls the evidential or conjectural paradigm.[12] Ginzburg offers a long history of this paradigm but ties its increasingly dominant presence in the Western cultural and political imaginary to the emergence of capitalist methods of production and consolidation of the modern state—and not uncoincidentally to the rise of the detective novel. The gathering and processing of evidence, Ginzburg suggests, finds its most comprehensive articulation in the post-1870 drive to quantify criminal activity and name and identify individual deviants, e.g. via fingerprinting and anthropometric methods, notably developed by Alphonse Bertillon, based on recording bodily measurements. As Ginzburg concludes, this 'prodigious extension of the concept of the individual [i.e. by isolating and capturing distinctive or unique features of individuals] was in fact occurring by means of the State, its bureaucracy and police'.[13]

The crime story, of course, is implicated in this double manoeuvre—both the recovery or attempted recovery of what happened from the objects left behind and which bear the crime's trace, and the move from the investigation to the construction of the entire justice system—'starting from the initial witness statements or the initial topographic surveys performed by the detective and proceeding onto

[11] Gunning, 'The Exterior as Interieur', pp. 107, 112.
[12] Carlo Ginzburg, *Clues, Myths and the Historical Method*, trans. John and Anne C. Tedeschi (Baltimore, MD and London: The Johns Hopkins University Press, 1989), pp. 101, 106.
[13] Ginzburg, *Clues*, p. 123.

countless legal journalistic and literary reconstructions.'[14] In both instances, any absolutist distinction between interior and exterior, or public and private, dissolves, as the apparently inconsequential is imbricated in the construction or reconstruction of an entire socio-political world. That said, not every crime story explores, or wants to explore, the complex interpenetration of public and private because there are considerable political consequences of doing so; for a start, such a strategy risks unravelling the bourgeois dream of the sanctity of the home. It also requires us to give up the notion that the private realm, the realm of civil society, constitutes an arena where free individuals can freely pursue their self-interest and where fairness is achieved largely through the regulatory effects of the marketplace itself rather than via the intervention of the state. In other words, to develop an appropriately complicated account of the interpenetration of public and private requires the crime writer to focus on, for example, how the institutions of state collude in the unequal distribution of wealth (i.e. how certain powerful individuals exploit their influence to pursue their own self-interest) or to explore the inadequacies of the criminal justice system or to suggest that individual acts of criminality have larger systematic causes or explanations; or indeed to depict civil society not as a self-regulating domain where fairness or morality, as Adam Smith would argue, is ensured by free individuals freely pursuing their self-interest but rather as a vicious, unstable, amoral universe where the strong devour the weak.

In the first part of this chapter, my focus is on Doyle's Sherlock Holmes stories, particularly those from *The Return of Sherlock Holmes*, published as a collected edition in 1905, and Gaston Leroux's almost contemporaneous *The Mystery of the Yellow Room*, first published in France in 1907 as *Le mystère de la chambre jaune*. On the face of it there is much to link Holmes's conjectural method—that 'allowed one to move inductively from what one sees to what one knows'[15]—to the rapidly expanding practices and ambitions of the modern, bureaucratic state (despite Holmes's apparent disdain for those who do the state's bidding). Still, Doyle's support, conscious or otherwise, for an individualist or laissez-faire ethos, derived in part from J.S. Mill, means he is unable or unwilling to pursue this connection in any meaningful way. Rather, as we'll see, Doyle, following Mill, becomes an advocate for the shrunken state and for individual liberty, a move that has far-reaching political implications for a consideration of the emerging shape and character of the crime story. As such, my reason for looking at the Holmes stories is not to reaffirm their perceived centrality to our collective understanding of the genre's development but to suggest they constitute a significant point of departure—in their refusal or their unwillingness to address, let alone dissect, the deeply intertwined relationship between private enterprise and state power. Given Doyle's enormous influence and popularity, then and now, this would have profound consequences for the way in which the genre would develop in Britain, at least in the twentieth century. Conversely while Gaston Leroux's investigator, the redoubtable

[14] Dominique Kalifa, 'Criminal Investigators at the Fin-de-siècle', trans. Jean Flynn, *Yale French Studies*, 108 (2005), p. 36.
[15] Andrea Goulet, 'The Yellow Spot: Ocular Pathology and Empirical Method in Gaston Leroux's *Le mystere de la chambre jaune*', *SubStance*, 34:2 (2005), p. 40.

journalist Joseph Rouletabille, would appear to favour a method based on abstract reason—a method that Goulet, via Ginzburg, describes as Galilean (one 'characterized by physic-mathematical methods that emphasize abstract thought over the material data accessible to the senses'[16])—that in turn distances him from state praxis, Leroux's willingness to locate Rouletabille's investigation in a public context means he puts more pressure, than Doyle at least, on the related precepts of the 'free' market, individual liberty, the night-watchman state, and the sanctity of the home.

In the second part of the chapter, the focus switches to Arthur Morrison's *The Dorrington Deed-Box* (1897), and Marcel Allain and Pierre Souvestre's *Fantômas*, the first instalment of which was published in 1911. Morrison is more famous for his Martin Hewitt series, a conventional reworking of the Sherlock Holmes format, and for his naturalistic accounts of slum life in London's East End, but as Clare Clarke's pioneering work has shown, his lesser-known stories featuring rogue private investigator Horace Dorrington, like the popular and critically celebrated *Fantômas* stories, offer a compelling insight into 'the formal, political and ideological complexity of a genre that is more conventionally concerned with the upholding of law and order'.[17] In both examples, the erosion of the distinction between detective and criminal thematizes an entire world view where the withdrawal of the state doesn't leave in its place a society, as envisaged by Doyle, where well-meaning individuals need only intervene minimally in the realm of civil society to restore it to good health. Rather we're given a series of disjointed insights into a violent, unstable, absurd universe where the pursuit of self-interest leads not to social stability but its opposite, i.e. social breakdown, and where the affinity of the crime story with particular bureaucratic, entrepreneurial, and scientific protocols does *not*, as Gunning puts it, 'yield an identification of the genre with the abstract vision and processes of rationality'.[18]

THE STATE SHRINKS, DISSOCIATES, AND RETURNS: DOYLE AND LEROUX

On the surface the similarities between Doyle's Sherlock Holmes and Leroux's Joseph Rouletabille are self-evident. Both are young (Rouletabille, at eighteen, is a good deal younger than Holmes), brilliant, determined, and arrogant; both set themselves up in opposition to the official police force (Holmes as a private detective, Rouletabille as a journalist); both are highly skilled at eliciting important information from physical evidence; both demonstrate an encyclopaedic knowledge

---

[16] Goulet, 'The Yellow Spot', p. 40.
[17] Clare Clarke, 'Horace Dorrington, Criminal-Detective: Investigating the Re-Emergence of the Rogue in Arthur Morrison's *The Dorrington Deed-Box*', *Clues: A Journal of Detection*, 28:2 (2010), pp. 7–18. Also see Clarke, *Late Victorian Crime Fiction in the Shadows of Sherlock* (Basingstoke: Palgrave Macmillan, 2014), pp. 128–54.
[18] Gunning, 'Lynx-Eyed Detectives and Shadow Bandits: Visuality and Eclipse in French Detective Stories and Films before World War I', *Yale French Studies*, 108 (2005), p. 79.

of arcane facts and are not unfamiliar with 'new' scientific developments; and both, though not quite infallible, are unerringly adept at arriving at the right answers, even if their respective methods, as we'll see, differ quite considerably. This capacity for discerning the truth and exposing, if not actually punishing, criminal actions has led most critics to characterize the stories in recuperative terms; i.e. as demonstrating a conservative rather than questioning social and political ethos. 'Holmes's culture will reach you anywhere', Moretti maintains, underlining the detective's pantoptic or regulatory capacities. 'This culture knows, orders, and defines all the significant data of individual existence as part of social existence.'[19] Jann concurs, arguing that Holmes's ability to organize 'even the most bizarre details to their proper place' in what she calls pseudoscientific topographies 'helps enforce the fixity and naturalness of the social ordering that rests upon them'[20] and hence the status quo more generally; a claim that also builds upon Stephen Knight's interpretation of the stories as assuaging 'the anxieties of a respectable, London-based, middle-class audience' (even if his ideological critique places it at odds with Jann's Foucauldian approach).[21] David Platten, meanwhile, finds the same kind of reassuring impulse in figures like Rouletabille 'whose mastery of logic and reason is such that they are apparently able to explain the inexplicable'.[22]

My claims in the chapter so far might suggest an affinity with a counter-argument put forward by Mark Knight, Stephen Joyce, Clare Clarke, and Ronald Thomas. Thomas, for example, warns against seeing the crime story as 'too singular and monolithic' as 'an ideological force' and claims that it retains its 'capacities for exposure, resistance and transgression';[23] and Joyce argues that 'representations of the police and private detectives are far less triumphant, and far more conflicted, than Foucault and his followers would allow'.[24] Clarke, meanwhile, shows very well how Doyle's ambivalent attitude towards work and the profession of authorship can be read into Holmes's character and how the stories as a whole 'dissect' rather than 'shore up' dominant attitudes about 'work, professionalism and morality'.[25] Still, the idea that the Holmes stories or *The Mystery of the Yellow Room* should be read, critically, as texts that set out to expose the degree to which crime is rooted in social inequalities or question the fairness and competence of the justice system will not do, either. My point is neither to dispute Stephen Knight's perfectly reasonable claim that the Holmes stories are ideologically aligned with those of his

---

[19] Moretti, *Signs Taken for Wonder*, p. 143.

[20] Jann, 'Sherlock Holmes Codes the Social Body', p. 686.

[21] Stephen Knight, *Form and Ideology in Crime Fiction* (Basingstoke: Macmillan, 1980), p. 67. Knight places his emphasis on the ideological function of crime fiction, putting class at the centre of his analysis, while Jann's claims about the regulatory aspects of the Sherlock Holmes stories draw from Foucault's understanding of disciplinary power which does not recognize class as the only or main determining factor in the exercising of a more totalizing, panoptical power.

[22] David Platten, *The Pleasures of Crime: Reading Modern French Crime Fiction* (Amsterdam: Rodopi, 2011), p. 16.

[23] Ronald Thomas, *Detective Fiction and the Rise of Forensic Science* (Cambridge: Cambridge University Press, 1999), p. 14.

[24] Simon Joyce qtd in Mark Knight, 'Figuring out the Fascination: Recent Trends in Criticism on Victorian Sensation and Crime Fiction', *Victorian Literature and Culture*, 37 (2009), p. 328. Also see Joyce's *Capital Offences: Geographies of Class and Crime in Victorian London* (Charlottesville, VA and London: University of Virginia Press, 2003), p. 229; Clarke, *Late Victorian Crime Fiction*, pp. 5–9.

[25] Clarke, *Late Victorian Crime Fiction*, p. 103.

predominantly middle-class readership, notably those who bought *The Strand* (a magazine 'orientated towards the family and respectable success in life'[26]), nor is it to dismiss Clare Clarke's notion that many of the Holmes stories demonstrate far greater moral, formal, and ideological complexity than Jann and others are willing to allow.[27] Rather, in line with the central focus of my book on the relationship between the emerging genre and the consolidation of the modern state, my aim is to explore how far the particular approaches to the problem of crime, demonstrated by Holmes and Rouletabille, and by the stories they're part of, reflect the larger ambitions and inner logic of the consolidating state form and capitalist methods of production. In other words, it is only by scrutinizing this relationship, and the ways in which the Holmes tales and *The Mystery of the Yellow Room* treat the complex intersections between the state and civil society (and the police and the free market) in their depiction of crime control practices, that we can begin to discern the exact nature of their socio-political allegiances.

At first glance, and despite Holmes's desire, at least in the early stories (e.g. those collected in *The Adventures of Sherlock Holmes*, first published in 1892), to differentiate himself from Scotland Yard plodders like Inspector Lestrade or play up their antagonistic relationship—in 'The Speckled Band', for example, he remarks on Dr Roylott's 'insolence' for confounding him with 'the official detective force'[28]—there is some scope for identifying him as surrogate policeman or state auxiliary. This tendency is brought to the fore in the later stories, notably those collected in *The Return of Sherlock Holmes*, published in 1905. In the second story, 'The Norwood Builder', Holmes is once again in competition with Lestrade to find the guilty party (and of course triumphs in the end) but in subsequent stories the relationship between Holmes and the official police is much less hostile. In 'The Dancing Men', Inspector Norton of the Norfolk Constabulary tells Holmes he 'is proud to feel we were acting together'[29] and while this pretence of togetherness conceals (of course barely so) a deeply asymmetrical relationship (e.g. the master–pupil dynamic we see in 'Black Peter'), in 'The Six Napoleons' Holmes is quite happy to be described as 'the well-known consulting expert' and even Lestrade has to admit that 'we are very proud of you' and that 'there is not a man, from the oldest inspector to the youngest constable, who wouldn't be glad to shake you by the hand' (p. 202). It is true that Holmes's successes in some respects reflect poorly on the investigative abilities of the official police force, and on the criminal justice system as a whole, but if we see Holmes in some kind of quasi-official capacity, it allows us to develop profitable links between his method and the logic of bureaucratic organization or what Ginzburg calls 'the silent emergence of the epistemological model...towards the end of the nineteenth century'.[30]

Ginzburg's move to link the emergence of this model (i.e. the gathering, processing, storage, and interpretation of information—evidence, facts, marginalia, traces, data—and the use of the senses to reconstruct the truth using an inductive

---

[26] Knight, *Form and Ideology in Crime Fiction*, p. 70.
[27] Clarke, *Late Victorian Crime Fiction*, p. 77.
[28] Arthur Conan Doyle, *The Adventures of Sherlock Holmes* (London: Penguin, 2007), p. 223.
[29] Doyle, *The Return of Sherlock Holmes* (London: Penguin, 1981), p. 68.
[30] Ginzburg, *Clues*, p. 96.

method) to the advent of a new bureaucratic logic, founded on a need to identify and record criminal recidivists, has obvious resonances with the Holmes stories. Ginzburg's references to the creation of police files and photographic archives and to the quantification of the individual via anthropometric methods developed by Bertillon (e.g. body measurements) and, following Galton's 1888 breakthrough, fingerprinting, find their obvious equivalents in the Holmes stories. In 'A Scandal in Bohemia' we learn that for 'many years he had adopted a system of docketing all paragraphs concerning men and things, so that it was difficult to name a subject or a person on which he could not at once furnish information' (*Adventures*, p. 10), while in 'The Empty House' Watson describes 'the chemical corner' and the rows of 'formidable scrapbooks and books of reference' that 'many of our fellow citizens would have been glad to burn' (*Return*, p. 25). We are told about Holmes's intimate knowledge of fingerprinting—the fact that 'no two thumb-marks are alike' (*Return*, p. 47), a fact that in 'The Norwood Builder' leads to the exposure of the guilty party—and in 'The Priory School' Holmes demonstrates an arcane knowledge of the marks left by bicycle tyres (*Return*, p. 119) something that is informed by this move to classify, categorize, quantify, and hence to achieve control over his domain of study. Likewise, Ginzburg's account of the conjectural paradigm is, in part, exemplified by Holmes's evidence-based method whereby he has been able to deduce from observing minute but concrete details, imperceptible to most people, the mundane truths of existence.

But it is important to remember that Ginzburg directly ties this newly emerging logic to the state, i.e. the bureaucracy and police, and the consolidation of capitalist means of production. As such we need to ask whether the Doyle stories are prepared to sanction this position, not least because Holmes himself, despite inclinations at times to identify himself with the official police, is also keen to emphasize his autonomy. Of course, as Ginzburg notes, the 'prodigious extension of the concept of the individual' (i.e. through techniques like fingerprinting which could establish an individual's uniqueness) was 'occurring by means of the State' and as such there is perhaps not as great a contradiction here as might first seem. But just as it is difficult, I would argue, to ascribe any great radical or oppositional charge to the stories, i.e. to see them as exhibiting views outwardly or in any way critical of the dominant social order and its attendant norms, we should be careful about seeing Holmes as some kind of cheerleader for the state and/or capitalism, at least in a straightforward sense. To get locked into this particular either/or debate is to reproduce the terms of a critical argument that cannot quite get at the particular dynamic of the Holmes stories. These should not be described either as conservative or radical (which may mean something in terms of generic innovation but are empty signifiers, politically speaking) but rather as liberal, in the manner of J.S. Mill's *On Liberty* (1859) which constitutes an important touchstone for Doyle.[31]

[31] Josef Hoffman notes that in his memoirs 'Doyle mentions not only Huxley's philosophy but also that of John Stuart Mill, which influenced his day and age... What Mill and Holmes share is a scientific basis of logic that relies on the gaining of new insights about reality, be they scientific or pragmatic investigations.' *Philosophies of Crime Fiction*, trans. Carolyn Kelly, Nadia Majid, and Johanna da Rocha Abreu (Harpenden: No Exit Press, 2013), pp. 75–6.

Holmes's status as *private* detective is crucial because it means his actions can't be unproblematically equated with the state. Likewise the fact the state only plays a marginal role in most stories, leaving Holmes as private citizen to intervene in the private affairs of individuals, means that Doyle can hold on to a view of the state, derived from Mill and before him from Smith, as potentially at odds with individual liberty and where, except in cases where an individual has knowingly inflicted harm on another individual (and needs official censure/punishment), the claims of the individual should always be privileged over the claims of the state.

Contra to Sherlock Holmes, Gaston Leroux's detective prodigy Joseph Rouletabille makes much of his preference for abstract thought (i.e. as opposed to Holmes's dogged reliance on the interpretation of physical evidence). There is even a Holmesian detective, an official policeman called Frédéric Larsan, who, in opposition to Rouletabille, seeks to find a solution to the apparently impossible problem of the story—the attack on Mademoiselle Stangerson by an assailant who, immediately afterwards, disappears into thin air or at least vanishes from a room from which, we are told, there is no means of egress—through the 'pitiless' application of logic and the recovery of clues, like footprints and bicycle tracks from the periphery of the Stangerson's rural estate.[32] But Rouletabille only trusts 'proof, in my eyes' (*Yellow Room*, p. 76) or proof that he can see and touch, up to a point; i.e. only if it accords with what he calls 'pure reason' (p. 158):

> If I am taking cognisance of what is offered me by my senses I do so but to bring the results within my circle of reason. That circle may be the most circumscribed, but if it is, it has this advantage—it holds nothing but *the truth!* Yes, I swear I have never used the evidence of the senses but as servants to my reason. I have never permitted them to become my master. (p. 112)

Platten tries to distinguish between the 'abstract realm' of Rouletabille's 'Cartesian reasoning' and Larsan's empirical, evidence-based method according to the 'different philosophical traditions of Britain and France'[33] (in effect, the French Leroux versus the British Doyle, with Larsan as a Holmes proxy), as though such complex, highly differentiated traditions can be shoehorned into this kind of schematic national imaginary. Much better is Andrea Goulet's imaginative reading of this distinction in terms of an *esprit logique* and an *esprit observateur* or, following Ginzburg, a tension between two epistemological models that came to the fore in the nineteenth century: a Galilean one characterized 'by physic-mathematical methods' and an 'evidential' model 'based on the observation and the reconstruction of truth based on material traces, symptoms and clue'.[34] Goulet cleverly links Rouletabille's fascination with the yellow room itself, a locked room which may or may not be as hermetically sealed as everyone seems to think, both to the 'yellow spot' of the eye

---

[32] Gaston Leroux, *The Mystery of the Yellow Room* (Mineola, NY: Dover, 2006), pp. 75, 50. (All subsequent citations refer to this edition, which is an unabridged republication of the 1908 English translation originally published by Brentano's of New York.)
[33] Platten, *The Pleasures of Crime*, pp. 23, 22. [34] Goulet, 'The Yellow Spot', p. 40.

which, though described as an opening or hole in the retina, 'does not correspond to any loss of matter'[35] and the Stangersons's scientific experiments.

Based upon a theory called 'the Dissociation of Matter' (Leroux, p. 2) these experiments explore the transformation of 'ponderable matter' into 'imponderable ether' (Leroux, p. 139). My point is not simply that Leroux has found an ingenious way of using one of the central themes of the novel—the investigation into the dissociation of matter—to reflect on an important aspect of the investigation, i.e. whether individuals can really disappear into thin air. Rather it is to argue that Rouletabille's preference for abstraction, and his hostility to what Goulet calls the 'flexible rigour of the conjectural paradigm',[36] which in turn is implicated in the consolidation of state power, capitalist methods of production, and bureaucratic norms, requires us to think about the implications vis-à-vis the foundational question of my book: the nature of the relationship between the emerging genre and the consolidation of the state. For if dissociating matter and abstract thought are being privileged over the conjectural model and its links to the state and capitalism, might we also ask whether Leroux, as novelist, is making some kind of political point? Is he in some way objecting to what Ginzburg calls 'the silent emergence of an epistemological model…towards the end of the nineteenth century', since this model is implicated in the expansion and consolidation of a 'new' form of centralized, bureaucratic power? Rouletabille makes it clear he has no interest in serving the interests of the state and law ('I am not a policeman, I am a journalist; and my business is not to arrest people', p. 156) but Goulet describes his outlook as 'conservative' at least in a philosophical sense, since it looks back to Galileo and the privileging of pure reason or abstraction over the more typical modus operandi of the detective. Whether or not we figure Rouletabille as conservative in this sense or 'radical' insofar as his outlook poses a challenge to the emerging disciplinary norms of a bureaucratic, capitalist order, one could argue that Leroux's fascination with dissociating matter has profound implications not just for the realm of scientific investigation: for what if the evidentiary basis of the justice system itself is being questioned?

Ultimately Leroux pulls back from this kind of far-reaching questioning of the conjectural or epistemological model, not least because Rouletabille's method, as Goulet points out, is also dependent on gathering and interpreting physical evidence (rather than being the manifestation of pure abstraction). 'Rouletabille is not quite as pure in method as "the Galilean physicist"' who pays no attention to the empirical, Goulet argues, and 'beyond the inevitable contamination of deductive by inductive methods, the very sensationalistic nature of *Mystery of the Yellow Room* as narration dilutes the purity of its avowed rationality'.[37] Goulet explains this dilution in terms of the courtroom melodrama at the end of the novel where Rouletabille uncovers the murderer and at the same time appeals to a modern taste for the sensational, i.e. what we can see, touch, and hear. More importantly, I want to argue that, despite Rouletabille's assertion about being a journalist and not a

---

[35] Goulet, 'The Yellow Spot', p. 30.   [36] Goulet, 'The Yellow Spot', p. 43.
[37] Goulet, 'The Yellow Spot', p. 43.

policeman, his performance in the courtroom ties him back into calculus of the state, the private citizen acting in the public interest and in doing so blurring the distinction between the realms. As the narrator tells us right at the beginning the case, described as a 'police story' (p. 1), shows off Rouletabille's capacities as detective *and* reporter, and hence the extent to which the realm of policing and writing about crime, i.e. public dissemination, should be seen as interdependent.

> It should not surprise us to find in one man the perfection of two such lines of activity if we remember that the daily press was already beginning to transform itself and to become what it is today—the gazette of crime... We can never have too many arms, public or private, against the criminal. (p. 10)

Here, then, the state doesn't disappear—dissociate—only to return at the end of the narrative; Rouletabille's investigation proceeds alongside that of police detective Frédéric Larsan (who is revealed to be the murderer or attempted murderer, a master-criminal posing as a police detective) and of the examining magistrate Monsieur de Marquet. Rather, in contrast to Doyle's Sherlock Holmes stories (to which I'll return in the next section, 'Crime, Business, and Liberty') where the state shrinks and even dissociates, in order to accommodate Holmes's interventions as Mill-inspired articulations of liberty and the free market, *The Mystery of the Yellow Room* offers a more complex, intertwined account of the relationship between public power and private initiatives. Rouletabille's preference for abstraction exposes the limits of an evidentiary model based on the collating and ordering of data and where the irresistible logic of this same model, in the end, is impossible to suppress. Rouletabille may not care whether Larsan is punished under the law but the fact that the trial is a public event speaks about the testing of the criminal justice system and the evidentiary model upon which it is founded.

CRIME, BUSINESS, AND LIBERTY IN DOYLE AND MORRISON

Rouletabille's disdain for empiricism (with its links to bureaucracy) ameliorates in the end to such an extent that his investigative efforts, hewn from an antithetical philosophical tradition, cannot be distinguished from the affairs of state. Doyle, meanwhile, manoeuvres his Sherlock Holmes stories in almost exactly the opposite direction. That's to say, he entertains the notion of Holmes as surrogate policeman and draws parallels between Holmes's investigative method and the expansion of state bureaucracy, with its need to order, collate, and quantify, only to reiterate Holmes's autonomy and to underscore Holmes's libertarianism or his willingness to defend the principle of individual liberty against the encroachment of the state—the very body that he, on one level, would seem to serve. This leads to a defence, conscious or otherwise, of the self-regulatory aspect of the free market, which draws from J.S. Mill and Adam Smith, where the pursuit of self-interest is, in most instances, sufficient to ensure social stability and where state intervention is necessary only in the rare cases where individuals seek to knowingly inflict harm on others. Here, Holmes becomes not the personification of what Moretti calls 'culture's coercive abilities' but rather cheerleader for a Mill-derived liberalism, so that his interventions do not stand in for the actions of the police but, quite the opposite, ensure that the presence of the police, and by implication the state, isn't necessary to bring the realm of private enterprise into harmonious equilibrium. There is a clear political position being staked out here, one that is directly challenged by Arthur Morrison's Dorrington stories, where the relative absence of the police creates a similar environment for Morrison's private enquiry agent to operate in but where a culture of acute self-interest, as epitomized by Dorrington himself, leads not to social harmony but the opposite: divisiveness, disunity, murder, violent competition, and speculative greed, all essential features, Morrison appears to be suggesting, of modern capitalism.

On the face of it, Holmes and Dorrington would, in their actions and personalities, both seem to corroborate Mill's three main objections to government interference and hence embody a preference for individual liberty, in the sense Mill uses the term. It is worth paying close attention to these objections, in order to see where the main points of tension actually lie. The first objection, Mill remarks in *On Liberty*, is 'when the thing to be done is likely to be better done by individuals than by the government'.[38] The 'thing' in the Holmes and Dorrington stories is detection and it is undoubtedly true that both men are a good deal more competent than their public counterparts at ferreting out information and exposing the truth. In the case of Sherlock Holmes, this is perhaps so beyond dispute that it hardly needs to be stated, as part of Holmes's appeal is tied to his unerring ability to better the official police, even or especially in stories like 'The Norwood Builder' where the hapless Lestrade is convinced, misguidedly of course, that his theories will this time win out.[39] Dorrington's moral compass may be a little askew, meanwhile, but as Clarke has convincingly demonstrated, in the absence of a visible police force, his ability to induce the truth from scraps of physical evidence—a barely visible bottle label in 'The Case of the "Mirror of Portugal"' or a simple plaster in 'The Case of Janissary', both of which lead him directly to the culprits—is exemplary and on a par with Holmes.[40]

Mill's second point is that individuals should pursue their own initiatives rather than rely on agents of government 'as a means of their own mental education' and as a method of 'strengthening their active faculties'.[41] Again the connections with Holmes are self-evident—when not working, Holmes is the 'introspective and pallid dreamer of Baker Street' but when on a case he becomes the epitome of Mill's ideal subject: 'this active, alert man...alive with nervous energy', we are told in 'The Priory School' (*Return*, p. 119). But Dorrington, too, is no slouch when it comes to pursuing his initiatives and strengthening his mental faculties. Even when dealing with ruthless, potentially dangerous figures, his ability to get his own way and to emerge both unscathed and handsomely remunerated is a feature of the

---

[38] John Stuart Mill, *On Liberty*, ed. Gertrude Himmelfarb (London: Penguin, 1987), p. 180.
[39] See Doyle, *The Return of Sherlock Holmes*, p. 46.
[40] Clarke, 'Horace Dorrington, Criminal-Detective', pp. 7–18.
[41] Mill, *On Liberty*, p. 180.

tales. In 'Old Cater's Money' he successfully inserts himself into a complex exchange between two potential heirs to a large inheritance and a servant who has squirrelled away his master's will and codicil, and coerces one of the parties into paying him a thousand pounds, under threat of making public a document that would seem to discount the man's inheritance claims.

But it is the third of Mill's objections to government interference that I want to focus on—that government intervention 'unnecessarily adds to its power'[42]— because it draws attention to important differences in the character and ambition of both writers. To quote Mill: 'Every function superadded to those already exercised by the government causes its influence over hopes and fears to be widely diffused, and converts, more and more, the active and ambitious part of the public into hangers-on of the government.'[43]

The anxiety is of the state expanding its reach, thereby inducing a state of mindless conformity. The implication is that the individual is better able, than the state, to know what is good for him or her. In this reading, the state is too cumbersome and unwieldy, and already exercises too much influence over individual lives. Still, even in Mill's terms, the state must intervene in certain circumstances: 'the only purpose for which power can be rightfully exercised over any member of a civilized community, against his will, is to prevent harm to others'.[44] Crime control, then, if it is aimed at preventing individuals or groups of individuals from inflicting harm on others, is a legitimate activity of government. But notwithstanding the idea it might be better carried out by free-thinking individuals, rather than slow-witted agents of the state, there remains the issue of what constitutes harm in the first place; and whether individual innovation—fighting against custom and tradition—especially in the context of business might be a valuable practice, even where or when laws have been infringed (and assuming that the harm done to others is 'tolerable'). In his Holmes stories, Doyle suggests that the private individual, discreetly looking into the affairs of others in order to determine whether punishment is appropriate, is better able to make restitution and bring about social utility than the official police, precisely because someone like Holmes can use his judgement (in a way the rule-bound police cannot) to determine how certain infractions should be treated, and hence is less likely to upset the cut and thrust of everyday existence—a euphemism for the functioning of the free market. Put another way, as Ronald Thomas argues, this person is then free to replace 'a political explanation of a crime with a personal one' and thereby refute 'the possibility that private matters may have political determinants'.[45]

An exchange between Holmes and Dr Leslie Armstrong in 'The Missing Three-Quarter' is indicative:

> So far as your efforts are directed towards the suppression of crime, sir, they must have the support of every reasonable member of the community, though I cannot doubt

---

[42] Mill, *On Liberty*, p. 181.   [43] Mill, *On Liberty*, pp. 181–2.
[44] Mill, *On Liberty*, p. 68.
[45] Ronald Thomas, *Detective Fiction and the Rise of Forensic Science* (Cambridge: Cambridge University Press, 1999), p. 224.

that the official machinery is amply sufficient for the purpose. Where your calling is more open to criticism is when you pry into the secrets of private individuals, when you rake up family matters which are better left hidden...

No doubt, doctor; and yet the conversation may prove more important than the treatise. Incidentally I may tell you that we are doing the reverse of what you very justly blame, and that we are endeavouring to prevent anything like public exposure of private matters which must necessarily follow when once the case is fairly in the hands of the official police.   (*Return*, p. 260)

The exchange is revealing, for a number of reasons. First, as Armstrong makes clear in his initial comments, he accepts the need for a robust police presence to act in the face of genuine criminality but he also draws attention to a common complaint regarding the police, i.e. that they meddle, unnecessarily, in the lives of ordinary people especially when their problems are personal and not punishable under the law. Holmes cedes this point but argues that he should not be regarded as a state auxiliary and underlines his commitment to ensuring that what he calls 'private matters' are not needlessly exposed to public scrutiny. Here, then, Doyle seems to be making a distinction between what Watson, at the start of 'The Blue Carbuncle', calls 'legal crime' (*Adventures*, p. 180), which is the business of the official police, and 'private matters' which can be handled more discreetly by a figure such as Holmes. As Watson remarks in 'The Blue Carbuncle', it is notable that 'of the last six cases which I have added to my notes, three have been entirely free of legal crime'—i.e. those cases 'which may be striking and bizarre without being criminal' (*Adventures*, p. 180).

A brief look at the stories in *Adventures* and *Return* confirm this preference. 'A Case of Identity' features a rogue father-in-law who disguises himself as suitor for his stepdaughter and jilts her at the altar to preserve his control over her inheritance (but whose actions are deemed not to be a police matter, even if they deserve moral censure). Likewise Holmes turns a blind eye to the actions of Mr Turner in 'The Boscombe Valley Mystery' whose accidental murder of a neighbour wrongly implicates the victim's son, especially when the perpetrator reveals he is dying and is contrite for what he has done. No further steps are taken when Holmes solves the case of 'The Man with the Twisted Lip' by revealing that a man who has gone missing, Neville St Clair, has in fact been posing as a beggar in London. Nor does Holmes call on the police when he locates the bride of 'The Noble Bachelor' who had disappeared just after their wedding, nor when he unearths a counterfeiting ring in 'The Engineer's Thumb'. Even when he exposes Dr Roylott in 'The Speckled Band' for knowingly poisoning his stepdaughter, Holmes does not bring the matter to the police (because Roylott is poisoned by one of his snakes). In *Return*, Jonas Oldacre, Abe Slaney, Peter Carey, and Messers Woodley and Williamson all are punished for their crimes by the law (in 'The Norwood Builder', 'The Dancing Men', 'Black Peter', and 'The Solitary Cyclist') but just as often Holmes hushes up the affairs he has been called upon to look into or unilaterally decides that they do not require the attentions of the police (in 'The Priory School', 'The Six Napoleons', 'The Three Students', 'The Golden Pince-Nez', 'The Missing Three-Quarter', 'The Abbey Grange', and 'The Second Stain').

In order to distinguish between those cases where Holmes feels it is necessary to call on the police and those where he decides the actions of others do not merit official punishment, we need to turn back to Mill. Throughout *On Liberty*, as already noted, Mill is keen to emphasize individual responsibility and the limits on government intervention. But if custom or conduct dictates that one shouldn't injure or harm the interests of others, i.e. each person should bear his or her fair share 'of the labours and sacrifices incurred for defending society... from injury or molestation',[46] Mill also argues that damage or the prospect of damage to others doesn't always justify the interference of rest of society. In these situations, as Vincenzo Ruggiero points out, some acts 'may be hurtful to others or wanting in due consideration to their welfare'; but if these acts don't directly bring about harm or violate a person's constitutional rights, they may be 'punishable by opinion not law'.[47]

The story 'Charles Augustus Milverton' exemplifies this logic. Lady Eva Brackwell, Holmes learns, has written some 'imprudent' letters which have fallen into Milverton's hand and that threaten her imminent marriage to the Earl of Dovercourt. To use Mill's distinction, Milverton's actions may cause harm to Brackwell but this prospect alone is not sufficient to warrant government intervention. By proposing to burgle Milverton's home and take 'no articles save those which are used for an illegal purpose' (*Return*, p. 169), Holmes implies that Milverton has committed a crime but it is not an illegality that the official police can punish since Milverton hasn't broken the law by merely insinuating it would be in Brackwell's interest to pay for the safe return of her letters. Rather than open up this issue and explore the incipient tension between liberty and crime, Doyle resolves the matter via recourse to melodrama. During the burglary, Holmes and Watson are interrupted by one of Milverton's victims who shoots the blackmailer dead, allowing them to retrieve the imprudent letters for Lady Brackwell before the police are called. The committing of a 'real' crime, i.e. murder, means that Holmes doesn't have to determine whether Milverton's actions have injured his client or simply affected her 'moral and spiritual welfare' and hence whether interference by the government is warranted or not.[48]

Part of the problem, for Doyle as well as Holmes, is that Milverton's activities—bringing together suppliers, such as potentially compromising information, and customers, e.g. those willing to pay money for the safe return of said information—closely mirror, or perhaps are no different from, those of a legitimate businessman. 'It is purely a matter of business', Milverton remarks (*Return*, p. 165). Using Mill as a touchstone, Ruggiero argues that liberty and crime can 'almost collide' because there is often little to distinguish between 'business crime' (i.e. causing financial harm to others through actions that may not be morally questionable but do not break the law) and Mill's vital and self-actualizing individual 'swimming against the flow of conformity and economic stagnation'.[49]

---

[46] Mill, *On Liberty*, p. 141.
[47] Vincenzo Ruggiero, 'On Liberty and Crime: Adam Smith and John Stuart Mill', *Crime, Law, Social Change*, 51:3–4 (2009), p. 447.
[48] Ruggiero, 'On Liberty and Crime', p. 445.
[49] In fact, here Ruggiero is specifically referring to Schumpeter rather than Mill. See 'On Liberty and Crime', pp. 446–7.

This, in turn, means that, for Doyle as well as Mill, intervention must not impair the ability of individuals to freely pursue their self-interest in the marketplace, even where their actions cause some degree of harm to others (unless of course physical injury has occurred, a debatable issue in 'Charles Augustus Milverton'). The extent to which this translates into a defence of the free market, and of capitalism in general, can be seen if we look at 'The Blue Carbuncle'. The story opens with an important rider that establishes its 'scene': the cut and thrust of city life where bizarre rather than openly criminal occurrences are the norm. 'Amid the action and reaction of so dense a swarm of humanity, every possible combination of events may be expected to take place, and many a little problem will be presented which may be striking and bizarre without being criminal' (*Adventures*, p. 180). This, then, is the embodiment of the free market: 'four million human beings all jostling each other within the space of a few square miles' and where the activities of most, as Watson remarks about their most recent cases, are 'entirely free of legal crime' (*Adventures*, p. 180).

The matter is brought to Holmes's attention by Peterson, the commissionaire, who sees a man carrying a goose under his arm being attacked 'by a little knot of roughs' and dropping the goose before making his escape into 'the labyrinth of small streets that lie at the back of Tottenham Court Road' (*Adventures*, p. 181). Peterson recovered the man's hat and the goose. The hat, we are told, bore the initials 'H.B.' while attached to the leg of the goose was a card bearing the note 'For Mrs Henry Baker' (p. 181). Holmes's mission, then, would seem to be a simple one: to find Henry Baker and reunite the goose with its owner. A little later, Peterson returns to inform Holmes that his wife has discovered a large gemstone inside the goose, which Holmes deduces is the same one that was stolen from the Hotel Cosmopolitan: a theft for which a plumber called John Horner has been charged.

The story juxtaposes a legal crime—the theft of the gemstone—with a 'striking and bizarre' incident which is merely of 'interest' to Holmes because it poses a challenge: to trace the ownership of the goose. To do this requires looking into, without actually interfering in, the operation of the 'free' market. Baker, he discovers, purchased the goose from Mr Windgate, landlord of the Alpha pub, who picked up two dozen geese from Breckinridge, a Covent Garden salesman, who in turn bought the birds from Mrs Oakshott, an egg and poultry supplier in Brixton. The cases converge when Holmes confronts another man who has been pestering Breckinridge about the whereabouts of the missing goose and unmasks him as James Ryder, head attendant at the Cosmopolitan and the man who in fact purloined the missing gemstone. Ryder's sister, we discover, married Mr Oakshott and while visiting the farm hid the stone inside one of the geese. Confronted by Holmes, Ryder has no choice but to confess and is contrite for what he's done; but Holmes's decision to let him off with a warning is less to do with his contrition or the fact he is deemed not to be a threat to others (though, in Mill's terms, this is an important factor). Rather it is because Ryder's illicit actions are too closely intertwined with the operations of the licit economy and any intervention by the official police runs the risk of upsetting these operations. 'When I pay good money for a good article there should be an end of the business,' an irate Breckinridge tells Holmes, 'but it's "Where are the geese?" and "Who did you sell the geese to?" and "What will you take for the geese?"' (*Adventures*, p. 195).

His irritation is an indication of the sensitivity of Holmes's task: not to undermine the right of free individuals to freely undergo their daily business. The passing of the jewel into the goose, which becomes a symbol of this free exchange of money and goods, is symptomatic of the proximity of liberty and crime. If, as Mill contends, letting people find their own way is always preferable to imposing ideas and values onto them via custom or law,[50] Holmes's decision to quietly reset the equilibrium so men like Breckinridge can go back to their business underscores a preference for self-regulation over state regulation. Holmes should not be seen either as surrogate policeman or, as Moretti argues, the embodiment of culture's will to power 'beyond simple institutional repression'[51] but as advocate of laissez-faire economics and the small state. Significantly, this light touch is only possible in the context of a vision of society where the rational pursuit of self-interest produces social stability rather than division and where antisocial behaviour, and crime in general, is an aberration rather than the norm. Doyle's preference for having Holmes investigate incidents 'free of legal crime' or permitting him to quietly intervene outside of the law speaks about exactly such a liberal vision.

Superficially, Morrison's tales featuring private enquiry agent Horace Dorrington would seem to tread on similar territory. In the absence of the police, who play only a minimal role, the stories focus on the schemes and machinations of individuals seeking to secure their financial advantage, by underhand, nakedly criminal methods. In 'The Case of Janissary' a bookmaker is trying to nobble a racehorse in order to profit from fluctuations in the betting odds; in 'The Case of the "Mirror of Portugal"' a diamond trader conspires to rob a rival of a precious gemstone acquired through family inheritance; and in 'The Affair of the "Avalanche Bicycle and Tyre Co., Limited"' a dishonest bicycle manufacture is trying to deceive speculators into investing their money in a shell company. In one sense, then, there is little to distinguish these crimes from those attempted in some of the Sherlock Holmes stories: John Clay's elaborate plans to rob a bank in 'The Red-Headed League' or Dr Roylott's scheme to kill off his stepdaughter in 'The Speckled Band' in order to keep control over her inheritance.

But there are significant differences that point to an entirely antithetical political orientation and perspective on the part of Morrison. Doyle seems to want to distinguish between legal crime and the 'striking and bizarre' or that which does not require official punishment and presents a generally reassuring view of the economy where self-interest doesn't necessarily lead to social breakdown and where self-regulation, if facilitated by Holmes, can make the necessary correction. Morrison's vision is altogether bleaker and more terrifying. In his Dorrington stories, not only is everyone out to injure everyone else, by stealth, violence, or whatever means at their disposal, in order to further their self-interest, but there is also no distinction between crime and liberty or crime and business. Rather, the exploits

---

[50] See Mill, *On Liberty*, pp. 136–40.   [51] Moretti, *Signs Taken for Wonder*, p. 143.

of individuals in the stories, usually revolving around the trope of speculation, e.g. turning money into more money, are *direct symptoms* of the same free market that Doyle seeks to defend. Morrison's political sympathies may have been socialist rather than Marxist, concerned with the plight of the poor instead of seeking revolutionary upheaval; but his account of modern capitalism, where human decency is absent and where the logic of financial gain shapes and overwhelms every other impulse, and where no other impulses exist apart from the desire to speculate and accumulate, whatever the cost and injury to others, has distinctively Marxist overtones.

Just as significantly, while Holmes functions as a safety net, someone who can quietly intervene in the private affairs of individuals when self-regulation isn't quite sufficient to ensure the smooth-running of society, Dorrington is wholly implicated in the grubbiness of the world he inhabits. Rather than acting out of some generalized notion of the good, his first impulse is always to sniff out his own advantage. As he says in 'Old Cater's Money', 'Here is the case in a nutshell. It is my business, just as it is yours, to get as much as I can for nothing';[52] or as he makes clear in 'The Case of Janissary', 'I may as well tell you that I'm a bit of a scoundrel myself, by way of profession' (p. 96). The fact that the police are only mentioned by Dorrington to frighten others into parting with their money adds to the sense of a world where sanctimonious homilies about the morality of the marketplace, or the goodness of individuals, or the state acting to protect the vulnerable from harm are exposed as hollow and where the impulse to cheat and murder reflect the supposedly legitimate imperatives of a modern capitalist economy.

Early in the first story of *The Dorrington Deed-Box*, 'The Narrative of Mr. James Rigby', a distinction is made between the Neapolitan mafia gang, the Camorra, likened to a 'gigantic club for the commission of crime and the extortion of money' and 'the lawful government of the country' (p. 7). But this ironclad distinction between licit and illicit realms is undermined by describing the Camorra's operational efficiency in terms of 'a railway company' contracting 'for the carriage of merchandise' (p. 8). Government, business, and organized crime are brought into the same equation, a move that would become more commonplace later in the twentieth century but that also reflects back on early or proto-crime stories like those featuring Wild and Cartouche where organized gangs led by individuals versed in the basics of statecraft filled the policing vacuum to pursue their financial advantage.

In the stories of *The Dorrington Deed-Box*, Dorrington is always at pains to stress his credentials as a businessman even when his schemes involve little more than blackmail or extortion. When Jacques Bouvier shows up in his office in 'The Case of the "Mirror of Portugal"' requesting help to recover a stolen diamond, and refuses to pay an advanced fee of twenty guineas, Dorrington makes much of his failure to meet particular contractual standards ('You have no money, and you offer no fee as a guarantee of your *bonâ fides*', p. 113) and later, he makes the same point to Jacques's cousin Léon: 'You wish to be a client, and you wish me to recover your

---

[52] Arthur Morrison, *The Dorrington Deed-Box* (Rockville, MD: James A. Rock & Company, 2003), p. 295.

lost diamond. Very well, that is business. The first thing is the usual fee in advance—twenty guineas' (p. 121). Given Dorrington's intention is to steal the diamond for himself, it may seem misguided to debate his credentials as a businessman or to question his sincerity in terms of meeting his contractual obligations, but we need to be just as careful not to dismiss this account of himself. For what, Morrison seems to be asking, distinguishes Dorrington from a legitimate diamond trader? This question becomes even more pertinent when the thief is revealed to be Ludwig Hamer, a Hatton Garden diamond merchant whom Dorrington describes as 'a man of business, with a head on your shoulders—the sort of man I like doing business with' (p. 137), even if later, Dorrington makes it clear that Hamer's status vis-à-vis the law is more precarious than his own. 'You are liable to an instant criminal prosecution. I have simply come, authorized by a client, who bears all the responsibility, to demand a piece of property which you have stolen' (p. 140).

Morrison's intent is not to see crime and business as proxies or to use crime as a metaphor for business and vice versa but rather to collapse any distinction between the categories and to see business itself—especially regarding finance capital and speculation—as crime; in other words, to see the entrepreneurial impulse, implicitly celebrated by Doyle, as criminal or at least as founded upon a set of principles that could be construed as criminal, in that the primary intentions of those identified as capitalist are to exploit and defraud. This claim is best exemplified in 'The Affair of the "Avalanche Bicycle and Tyre Co., Limited"' and it is worth examining this, the best story in the collection, in light of Marx's insights into accumulation and fictitious capital. On the face of it, the subject of the 'Avalanche Bicycle' is a criminal scam. Its 'scene' is the speculative frenzy surrounding the manufacture and sale of bicycles:

> Cycle companies were in the market everywhere. Immense fortunes were being made in a few days and sometimes little fortunes were being lost to build them up. Mining shares were dull for a season, and any company with the word 'cycle' or 'tyre' in its title was certain to attract capital, no matter what its prospects were like in the eyes of the expert. (p. 153)

The scam in question, as Dorrington discovers and tries to exploit for his own ends, is the brainchild of Paul Mallows, the managing director of the 'well-known establishment of the "Indestructible Bicycle Company"' (p. 158). Unbeknown to potential investors, he is also head of the newly established 'Avalanche Bicycle and Tyre Company' which, at the start of the story, has just issued a prospectus with its 'promises of tremendous dividends, backed up and proved beyond dispute by such ingenious piles of business-like figures, every line of figures referring to some other line for testimonials to its perfect genuineness and accuracy' (p. 157). Rather than manufacture new bicycles in factories in Birmingham and Exeter, as the prospectus states (the factories listed are in fact 'shells' where no work is taking place), cycles 'of the "trade" description are bought' in bulk and the new, upmarket name is put on them.

> They come cheap, and they sell at a good price—the profit pays all expenses and a bit over; and by the time they all break down the company will be successfully floated, the money—the capital—will be divided, the moving spirit and his

confederates will have disappeared, and the guinea-pigs will be left to stand the racket—if there is a racket. (p. 189)

Seemingly a throwaway remark, the rider here—'if there is a racket'—is crucial because it questions whether a crime has been committed. The idea that 'innocent' investors are being willfully misled and that the 'moving spirits' intend to take their investment and disappear suggests malpractice but Morrison wants us to think about what is at stake here: buying cheap and selling dear, accumulating surplus profits, investing real money in shares whereby the expected yield or return is only tangentially connected to what is being produced. Here the veil of crime slips away to reveal two important rudiments of modern capitalism: accumulation and speculation. Ernest Mandel defines capital as 'value looking for accretion, for surplus-value' and asserts the 'basic drive of the capitalist mode of production is the drive to accumulate capital'.[53] Capital accumulation, as Mandel shows, presupposes 'production for profit' and has 'profit maximization as its very rationale' so that 'constant reorganizations of the production process' are geared towards 'reducing costs'.[54]

As such, the Avalanche Bicycle and Tyre Company's strategy of buying cheap and selling dear—i.e. reducing costs—could easily be construed as profit maximization pure and simple, even if it doesn't entail reorganizing the production process (since there is no production). The real issue is what happens to the profits accrued, especially vis-à-vis the 'long established' Indestructible Bicycle Company (p. 154) since, as Marx puts it, the 'first condition of accumulation is that the capitalist must have contrived to sell his commodities, and to reconvert into capital the greater part of the money received from their sale'.[55] Accumulation is linked to speculation, at least in the context of the story, because Mallows has 'reconverted' a proportion of the surplus value generated from the sale of bicycles (e.g. via Indestructible) into capital which he is then seeking to sell in the form of shares in his new venture (Avalanche), even if he is not upfront about his own involvement in or with a direct competitor. The urge to accumulate—or 'reconvert the greatest possible portion of surplus-value... into capital'[56]—is not so much criminal as one of the cornerstones of modern capitalism; this need to reinvest being forced upon capitalists like Mallows by what David Harvey calls 'the coercive laws of competition'[57]—i.e. if you don't, you'll be swallowed up by the competition.

If there is nothing necessarily criminal about producing bikes as cheaply as possible and charging a lot for them, Morrison's reference to a 'racket' refers to Mallows's intention of selling stock in his new venture, via new promotional methods, and then winding the company up just as the first bicycles begin to break down (and making off with all the capital). But again Morrison's rider—*if there was*

---

[53] Ernest Mandel, 'Introduction', in Karl Marx, *Capital: A Critique of Political Economy. Vol. 1*, trans. Ben Fowkes (London: Penguin, 1990), p. 60.
[54] Mandel, 'Introduction', p. 65.
[55] Marx, *Capital: A Critique of Political Economy. Vol. 1*, p. 709.
[56] Marx, *Capital: A Critique of Political Economy. Vol. 1*, p. 742.
[57] David Harvey, *A Companion to Marx's Capital* (London and New York, NY: Verso, 2010), p. 257.

a racket—seems to advise caution. To clarify this issue, we need to look more closely at the nature of the speculation and what if anything it yields. In *Capital Vol. 3*, Marx distinguishes between old-fashioned usury—which 'does not change the mode of production, but clings on to it like a parasite and impoverishes it'[58]— and finance capital, which mobilizes credit to real production and hence enables the expansion, rather than withering away, of the productive forces. If we turn our thoughts back to Morrison's story, we remember that nothing is actually produced by the mobilization of credit towards the new venture, e.g. the factories are merely 'shells'. So what are the implications? One point might be that there is little to choose between Mallows's so-called racket (and the speculative frenzy surrounding the desire to buy stock in the Avalanche Bicycle company) and what Marx calls 'fictitious capital'[59] in so far as both are premised on a disjuncture between real production and bills of exchange which are pieces of paper and have no immediate or direct connection to what is being produced. As such, Mallows's scam—if it is a scam—and the scene of the story in general come close to replicating what occurs 'when capitalists hurl money at new and untried projects... without any certainty that their investments will be recovered'.[60] This plunge into the future may be 'a great lever for productive advancement' (as even Marx is happy to concede) but 'it puts capital and credit on speculative foundation, in the form of fictitious capital, which cannot always be sustained'.[61] One possible conclusion to draw, in terms of 'The Affair of the Avalanche Bicycle Company', is that Morrison wants us to see the 'racket' as a direct comment on fictitious capital: not in its positive manifestation as an enabler of production but in its parasitic formulation—parasitic on production (e.g. taking away surplus value from production) and also on labour. Here, Morrison is perhaps suggesting, the inherently short-termist desire to maximize profits speaks about a more general tendency in capitalism—one Morrison want us to see as destructive rather than productive, hence the hollow nature of the Avalanche venture and Mallows's violence, once threatened with exposure.

The idea of crime as capitalism and capitalism as crime, even if this manoeuvre is never explicitly articulated in *The Dorrington Deed-Box*, would have been hugely disconcerting to most readers of Doyle's Sherlock Holmes stories. Certainly Morrison's portrait of everyday existence as an arena of cutthroat competition where the strong devour the weak, and where no safety net exists in the form of the police or a private citizen capable of acting to further the general good, would not have sat well with readers more used to Doyle's rather more reassuring stories. McCann argues that 'the classic detective story celebrated the victory of public knowledge and civic solidarity over the dangers of private desire' and that the ethical drama of this kind of writing 'is a drama of the commitment to civil society'[62]—

---

[58] Marx, *Capital: A Critique of Political Economy. Vol. 3*, intro. Ernest Mandel, trans. David Fernbach (London: Penguin, 1981), p. 731.
[59] Marx, *Capital: A Critique of Political Economy. Vol. 3*, p. 525.
[60] Richard Walker, 'The Spectre of Marxism: The Return of *The Limits to Capital*', *Antipode*, 36:3 (2004), p. 435.
[61] Walker, 'The Spectre of Marxism', p. 435.
[62] Sean McCann, *Gumshoe America: Hard-Boiled Crime Fiction and the Rise and Fall of New Deal Liberalism* (Durham, NC and London: Duke University Press, 2000), pp. 4, 15.

and it is perhaps not hard to see why the Holmes stories are used as exemplary texts. They may show a society struggling to come to terms with crime in all of its guises, and the merely 'striking and bizarre', but their account of everyday existence, the realm of civil society, underscores the extent to which private initiatives, even where characterized as 'legal crime', are not ascribed public or political motivations. Rather than scrutinizing and putting pressure on the public/private dichotomy (for example, by asking whether the market is capable of producing a fair society without the intervention of the state), the Holmes stories secure the division between public and private by figuring Holmes himself as private citizen rather than surrogate policeman and by indicating that his quiet interventions are sufficient to restore the balance between individual interests and the general good. In doing so, concerns about the legitimacy and adequacy of the criminal justice system itself are rendered moot, the domestic is privileged as a sanctified space, and the world of capitalism and business, while potentially unruly or even dangerous can, with Holmes's assistance, be made to enhance rather than threaten individual liberty.

Morrison's *Dorrington Deed-Box* shatters this liberal vision and exposes its attendant ideology as at best illusory, and at worst dangerous. To start with, there is no faith in the notion either that the individual's pursuit of his or her self-interest will result in a stable, ordered society or that the free market can, in effect, regulate itself. Rather, people are venal, grubby, and greedy (even though some are better at hiding this than others) and their self-interest leads them into violent, often deadly, competition with others. Morrison never explicitly states whether this is a natural state (e.g. Hobbes's individuals in a state of nature) or whether this disposition is a product of certain historical circumstances, e.g. capitalism, but Dorrington's tendency to mask his violent, acquisitive nature via near-constant references to 'business' would seem to suggest the latter. Certainly Morrison's vision of crime as capitalism and capitalism as crime, where the two cannot be separated and where it becomes futile to talk about crime as legal infraction since the law is absent and to enforce the law would mean going up against the logic of business, places it a long way from Smith's benevolent view of the market's invisible hand. Morrison's account is further spiked by his refusal to have his private detective act to restore society to good health and by the absence of a Watson-like narrator who can reassure and contextualize the issues for the reader. Instead the stories are narrated by James Rigby, one of Dorrington's victims who subsequently pieces together the narratives that make up the collection from snippets of information found in Dorrington's abandoned office. Rigby's naivety—witnessed in the first story 'The Narrative of Mr James Rigby'—is held up as a warning to readers not to take anyone at their word and to view everyone they come across with suspicion.

There is an obvious affinity between the Dorrington stories and Marx's theories of capital, even if Morrison has no faith or interest in the revolutionary potential of the ordinary person. But in their refusal to sanction a role for the state or the individual, in a public or private capacity, to confront social breakdown and the problem of crime, the stories run the risk of extinguishing the emerging genre's structuring tension (e.g. that the state and the law are both necessary for tackling social problems and implicated in the reproduction of trenchant social inequalities). Conversely but mirroring this logic, Doyle's refusal to cede that the violence induced by the competitive logic of capitalism mightn't be brought under control even by the bureaucratic and scientific protocols at the state's disposal, or that the split between public and private might not be as clear-cut as he wants to imagine, risks extinguishing this same tension, though from a diametrically opposed point of view. In other words, if the problem with Morrison's stories, at least in so far as trying to place them into an emerging genealogy of the genre (going back to Gay, Godwin, and Vidocq) might be formulated as 'too much Marx, not enough liberalism', and if the problem with Doyle's Holmes stories is 'too much liberalism, not enough Marx', then it's to another turn-of-the-century writer, or to other writers, we need to turn, in order to show how this tension might be brought into more effective equilibrium and to offer a sharper sense of where the genre might go in the new century, in order to demonstrate its subversive potential. While Morrison's vision, as Clarke concedes, was too bleak and too deterministic to carry large numbers of readers with him,[63] a necessity for any popular writer, Doyle's is too reassuring and too beholden to a Mill-derived liberalism to give it sufficient critical purchase vis-à-vis the (bureaucratic) difficulties of trying to control crime and on the many social problems created by capitalism. Both elements would be necessary, as Marcel Allain and Pierre Souvestre's *Fantômas* amply demonstrates, if the genre was going not merely to survive but also thrive in the new century.

FANTÔMAS AND THE RADICAL AMBIVALENCE OF MODERNITY

The original *Fantômas* novel, first published in February 1911 and spawning thirty-one sequels, sets in place the series' structures and power dynamics: its paradigmatic struggle between master-criminal and archetypal police detective. This may seem to be a familiar set-up, and no different from the Holmes–Moriarty conflict of Doyle's stories; however, Allain and Souvestre steer their creation into darker, less comfortable territory in a number of ways. First, beyond the fact that Fantômas himself is established as a criminal force of nature, a singular 'genius' or 'devil' or both—someone whose 'daring is boundless' and 'power immeasurable'[64]—it is hard to discern what his criminality represents because it is so amorphous and without obvious motivation. The much-discussed opening where Fantômas is designated as 'nothing' and 'everything' and 'nobody' and 'somebody' prefigures a more generalized description of his modus operandi and *raison d'être*—spreading terror (p. 1). Meanwhile, Juve, his arch rival and 'the famous detective of the Criminal Investigation Division' (p. 5) may be committed to bringing Fantômas to justice and in so doing might exhibit not merely extraordinary powers of observation and

---

[63] Clarke, *Late Victorian Crime Fiction*, p. 153.
[64] Marcel Allain and Pierre Souvestre, *Fantômas*, intro. John Ashbery (London: Penguin, 2006), p. 65.

deduction but also a firm grasp of newly emerging scientific techniques for measuring and controlling criminality. But his efforts, impressive as they may be, are unable to apprehend and punish Fantômas, who successfully engineers his escape in the final chapter, and throughout the thirty-two novels of the series. In doing so, and in exceeding the genre's typical demands for 'moral restitution'[65] and challenging 'representational strategies of numerical classification of criminals as a means of social and "scientific" control',[66] Allain and Souvestre unpick the reassuring logic of the detective narrative (whereby the trajectory is towards revelation and closure). And in so doing, they enact, consciously or otherwise, what Marshall Berman calls the radical ambivalence of modernity, whereby the possibility of 'adventure, power, joy, growth transformation' enabled by new modes of thought and technological and scientific advances is countered by the threat of 'perpetual disintegration' and bewilderment in the face of 'immense bureaucratic organizations' and relentless upheaval.[67]

Emma Bielecki is right to claim that Fantômas is no monster or devil, the symptom of an earlier epoch where his grotesque excesses are a marker of what sets him apart from civilization, but rather is 'a briskly efficient, practical man, albeit one lacking a moral conscience' who can 'infiltrate bourgeois milieus as easily as he can the criminal underworld'.[68] The issue of classification, of the need exhibited by an increasingly bureaucratic culture to measure and quantify (driven by new technological developments), is occasioned by the facelessness of crowds and the allure of anonymity offered by the city. Hence Fantômas's exceptional qualities and his ubiquity—his similarities to everyone else—become another marker of modernity's ambivalence: Poe's man of the crowd *and* Nietzsche's superman.[69]

Fantômas's protean, shape-shifting qualities have been much commented on, his 'countless plastic identities',[70] to quote Robin Walz, standing in for an essentialized self, itself a twentieth-century preoccupation that looks ahead to Hammett's Sam Spade and Patricia Highsmith's Tom Ripley. Fantômas is an unstable marker of selfhood—someone who is nothing and everything, a cipher who 'sometimes... assumes the forms of two human beings at the same time' and who works alone and 'with accomplices' (p. 3), flesh and blood and yet a spectral presence who 'hovers above the strangest mysteries' (p. 4). In the first novel he inhabits and discards

[65] Robin Walz, *Pulp Surrealism: Insolent Popular Culture in Early Twentieth-Century Paris* (Berkeley, CA and London: University of California Press, 2000), p. 43.
[66] Nanette Fornabai, '"Fantômas", Anthropometrics, and the Numerical Fictions of Modern Criminal Identity', *Yale French Studies*, 108 (2005), p. 61.
[67] Marshall Berman, *All That is Solid Melts into Air: The Experience of Modernity* (London and New York, NY: Verso, 2010), pp. 15, 14.
[68] Emma Bielecki, 'Fantômas's Shifting Identities: From Books to Screen', *Studies in French Cinema*, 13:1 (2013), p. 9.
[69] Nietzsche's figure of the superman is introduced in *Thus Spake Zarathustra* ['I teach you the superman. Man is a thing to be surmounted']. See Friedrich W. Nietzsche, *Thus Spake Zarathustra*, trans. A. Tille (London: Dent & Sons, 1958), p. 5. I am not suggesting a direct link between Fantômas and Nietzsche's superman but one could argue for an affinity between Allain and Souvestre's and Nietzsche's accounts of modernity, i.e. a rejection of tradition as represented by church, state, and nation, the emergence of new discourses of science and the debasement of culture by financial interests. The relentless overcoming of the old by the new becomes an essential feature of the modern.
[70] Walz, *Pulp Surrealism*, p. 57.

(among others) the personae of Etienne Rambert, a sixty-year-old industrialist, and Gurn, a forty-something former soldier. Indeed the story abounds with doubles and disguises, as Juve too assumes multiple identities in his hunt for Fantômas, to the point where Juve is mistaken for the master-criminal. The unmooring of selfhood finds another articulation in the unmotivated violence, so that Fantômas's bloodlust is only loosely connected to the inner logic of personality (e.g. he kills Lord Bertram because he, or Gurn, is having an affair with Beltham's wife, but no real explanation is offered for his decapitation of Mme de Langrune and we are led to assume he deliberately sunk a boat killing one hundred and fifty passengers only to create the assumption that one of his identities also died in the wreckage).

If there is something distinctively modern about this use of unmotivated violence to invoke generalized terror, and about the notion of identity itself as fluid and essentially blank (e.g. the idea, as Walz puts it, that 'there is no real "someone else" behind the mask'[71]), Fantômas, though not motivated by any one cause or grievance, might be best understood in terms of an unspecified assault against tradition—and the attendant claims of family, church, state, and nation. As Federico Pagello puts it, 'it would be hard to find in the field of popular culture a more "internationalist" subtext than the systematic aggression to the bourgeois state carried out by Fantômas in his adventures'.[72]

But exactly what kind of vision of the state do we get in the Fantômas stories? And would it be fair to say that Allain and Souvestre ultimately privilege their master-criminal over the forces of the state that pursue him, notably Inspector Juve? By allowing him to escape capture, are they making a point about the limits of the justice system? Certainly Juve is no inadequate, blundering Lestrade-type figure and his brilliant scientific deductions (e.g. discovering 'that a sulphate of zinc had been injected into the [Lord Beltham's] corpse to prevent it from smelling' p. 119), and his observational prowess, such that one character claims he 'hasn't got eyes in his head but telescopes, magnifying glasses' (p. 203), are symptomatic of the technological and bureaucratic developments of the era: especially concerning the measuring and classification of criminality. Juve puts faith in 'Dr. Bertillon's effraction dynamometer' (p. 176) and, by using it to measure the strength of a potential suspect, is able to rule out his involvement in one of the crimes under investigation.

Fornabai is right to question Juve's reliance on Bertillon's machine: that is, his insistence 'on anthropometrics' ability to identity the one, true criminal, only to face the multiplicity of numerical simulacra that can stand in for that singularity', but not that Juve, and hence the state, is 'impotent' in the face of Fantômas's dissembling.[73] The expanding scope and reach of the justice system, and indeed its successes at bringing criminals to justice, is acknowledged in the first novel's opening

---

[71] Walz, *Pulp Surrealism*, p. 59.
[72] Federico Pagello, 'Transnational Fantômas: The Influence of Feuillade's Series on International Cinema during the 1910s', *Belphégor*, 11:1 (2013), http://belphegor.revues.org/125, accessed 15 August 2015.
[73] Fornabai, '"Fantômas", Anthropometrics', p. 67.

chapter: 'The police do their work better in our time than ever before,' we are told, aided by 'science' which 'has done much for modern progress'. It is just that scientific developments have also aided criminals like Fantômas: 'the hosts of evil have the telegraph and motorcar at their disposal, just as the authority has' (p. 3).

It is not necessarily that the state is impotent then; rather as Bielecki puts it, that the Fantômas books reveal the limits of anthropometrics, in that no essential difference between criminals and non-criminals could be inhered through scientific measurement.[74] In one sense, then, Allain and Souvestre's creation may look backwards at the famous bandit–criminals of earlier epochs and extend the lineage of Wild, Macheath, Cartouche, and Vidocq into the modern era, even if their challenge to the state's monopoly and legitimacy ends on the scaffold while Fantômas always remains at large and unpunished. But what marks Fantômas as modern is not just that the stories resist the urge towards 'moral restitution' or operate 'outside logic and deduction'[75] and indeed narrative closure, but that behind the positivist claims of scientific rationality, technological development, and bureaucratic organization resides an alternative view of modernity-as-imprisonment and where individuality in the face of the growing impersonality of organized life would increasingly be expressed through inchoate violence and an impulse to destroy, and an attendant notion of the absurd. The lesson would not be lost on the key figures of twentieth century crime fiction, from Hammett to Himes and from Sciascia to Sjöwall and Wahlöö.

[74] Bielecki, 'Fantômas's Shifting Identities', p. 8.
[75] Walz, *Pulp Surrealism*, pp. 43, 45.

5

'No Good for Business'
States of Crime in the 1920s and 1930s

A brief exchange in Dashiell Hammett's *The Glass Key* (1931) is revealing as much for what is disavowed as for what is actually said. Ned Beaumont is a political fixer for mayor Paul Madvig but suspects that his boss is implicated in the murder of the son of one of his key political allies. 'I'm after Paul's scalp', Beaumont tells a private eye called Jack Rumsen before asking, 'Want to work on it for me?'[1] Rumsen refuses—he tells Beaumont that he can't afford to alienate 'the man that runs the city' (p. 751). But the exchange is revealing because it sheds light on Beaumont's unarticulated motivations: not to exact justice for the murdered man or even to discover the truth about what happened but rather to untangle himself from his long-standing links with Madvig and the politics of City Hall. If he can pin this murder on his boss, then perhaps he can become a free agent. The dilemma is the allure of autonomy: like other tough guy figures, Beaumont might want to see himself as unco-opted but the very fact that he feels compelled to go after his boss's 'scalp' points to a generalized anxiety that his actions and indeed his very existence cannot be disentangled from the machinery of City Hall which he tries, in vain, to define himself against.

Hammett, though, pushes this issue into more uncomfortable territory. Not only does Ned Beaumont fail to convince us that his motives are other than what they are (i.e. he is just chasing a debt owed to him or that he wants to see Madvig behind bars), but his long-standing association with Madvig whereby friendship is reimagined by Hammett as a strategic arrangement through which both men can prosper professionally and financially[2] indicates the extent to which his actions shore up the political establishment. The ties that bind Beaumont to the affairs of state run too deep for him to fashion himself as a genuinely private detective. This, in turn, goes some way to explaining the mystery of the novel's ending: why he elopes with a woman he has no interest in or affection for. It is not uncoincidental that Madvig declares himself to be madly in love with the same woman. For Beaumont this act is the only means he can imagine of destroying his relationship with Madvig. But in doing so, he makes it clear that there is no space, no private realm, where the

---

[1] Dashiell Hammett, *The Glass Key* in *The Four Great Novels* (London: Picador, 1982), pp. 750–1.
[2] This idea is developed from Leonard Cassuto's claim about *The Maltese Falcon* whereby 'business practices' in the novel 'govern the family relationships and other intimate ties'. See *Hard-Boiled Sentimentality: The Secret History of American Crime Stories* (New York, NY: Colombia University Press, 2008), p. 52.

tentacles of the state, of public life, and of marketplace, cannot reach. *The Glass Key* and hard-boiled crime fiction in general might seem to be founded on a fantasy of radical individualism, as critics like Porter and McCann contend,[3] but its inner logic points to exactly the opposite scenario: the loss of individual autonomy in the face of the state's growing power and its interpenetration with capital—what Chris Breu calls hard-boiled fiction's 'adaptation to, as well as reaction against, the workings of corporate capitalism'.[4]

There is typically a temptation when assessing the work of a writer like Hammett and the entire pantheon of hard-boiled American crime fiction, to emphasize his/its exceptional qualities. Such is the literary ambition, the perceived political radicalism, and the realism or verisimilitude of a novel like *The Glass Key* that it constitutes a new type of writing—as Chandler put it 'never to have been written before'[5]—and hence a moment of rupture in the development of the genre.[6] Part of my aim is to put such an account to the sword; to argue, in effect, that Hammett's willingness to problematize the individuality of his protagonists and to locate them uneasily within the orbit of the state means that we can make profitable connections between his work and that of other crime novelists of the period, notably the prolific Belgium-born writer Georges Simenon. This is not to downplay Hammett's considerable achievements as crime novelist or deny the originality of his bloody, whiskey-soaked vision. Nor even is it to suggest that in responding to the particular conditions of US life in the early 1920s and 1930s—an era marked by the consolidation and transformation of industrial capitalism—his novels don't set out in unusual and provocative ways to depict the ills of a society beholden to and debased by the marketplace. But there are dangers in overplaying Hammett's political commitment (i.e. his Marxist or left-wing sympathies and hence the extent of his anti-capitalist critique) and the uniqueness of the novels he wrote (i.e. whether he did write scenes no one had ever written before). Part of Hammett's skill as a crime novelist lies in the daring manner in which he brings seemingly disparate, perhaps even contradictory, views and political outlooks into violent conflagration. In *Red Harvest* (1929), for example, the Continental Op embodies the authority of the law and is not necessarily dismissive of the law's normative and utilitarian ambitions—to promote social justice or to serve some idealized notion of the 'greater good'—and yet he is also painfully aware of the ways in which the law is

---

[3] Dennis Porter claims that private eyes 'are recognizable champions of ordinary Americans because they are embodiments of an idealised average Americanness, both in their self-reliance and in the assertion of an egalitarianism of the gun'. See *The Pursuit of Crime: Art and Ideology in Detective Fiction* (New Haven, CT: Yale University Press) p. 171. Sean McCann, meanwhile, refers to the genre's 'alternative commitment to radical individualism and moral neutrality'. See *Gumshoe America: Hard-Boiled Crime Fiction and the Rise and Fall of New Deal Liberalism* (Durham, NC and London: Duke University Press, 2000), p. 78.

[4] Christopher Breu, *Hard-Boiled Masculinities* (Minneapolis, MN: University of Minnesota Press, 2005), p. 5.

[5] Raymond Chandler, *Later Novels and Other Writings*, ed. Frank McShane (New York, NY: Library of America, 1995), p. 978.

[6] For examples of this tendency to characterize hard-boiled crime fiction as qualitatively different from earlier forms of crime writing, see McCann, *Gumshoe America*, pp. 1–15 and Breu, *Hard-Boiled Masculinities*, pp. 1–2.

skewed towards particular class interests and hence helps to entrench class-based inequality.

But rather than establishing Hammett's uniqueness, this pulls him into the slipstream of other crime stories examined in my book to date. There are two points worth underlining here. First, in line with my intention to situate Hammett's *private* operatives (Beaumont, Spade, the Continental Op) very much in the public realm and to push a reading which examines their links to, and complicity with, big business and political elites, one of the central arguments of this book has been that a particular kind of crime writing (exemplified, say, by Gay's *The Beggar's Opera*, Vidocq's *Memoirs*, or Gaboriau's *Monsieur Lecoq*) moves well beyond a focus on the struggle between individual detective and criminal to root crime in the social and economic conditions of its time. And second, by thinking about Hammett alongside Simenon and also the German playwright and novelist Bertolt Brecht, I want to challenge scholarly narratives about national particularity and exceptionalism and argue that the genre's capacity for mapping and at times confronting state power can only be understood if its development is grasped in terms of an expanded trans-Atlantic circuit connecting the US and continental Europe, notably—in this chapter at least—France or rather France and Belgium.

It is worth saying something here about the state of English crime fiction and about the post-Doyle development of the genre in the first half of the twentieth century. While my critical brushstrokes in this respect are admittedly crude and generalizing, my shift of interest to a US–continental European axis is intended to reflect on the way in which a tradition initiated by Doyle and consolidated by 'golden age' writers like Agatha Christie (with their emphasis on the intricacies and nuances of domestic life as opposed to the workings of public power) for the most part led the genre, in Britain, away from its roots in expansive social portraiture and explicit political critique.[7] There are of course notable exceptions: the urban noir of Gerald Kersh offered a British interpretation of a form or style of 'noir' writing more readily associated with the US and infused with a similar doomed poetry and social critique, and a series of novels and short stories by Edgar Wallace including *Room 13* (1924), *The Mind of Mr R.G. Reeder* (1925), and *Terror Keep* (1927) introduced the fascinating character of R.G. Reeder, a man who holds 'an appointment in the office of the Public Prosecutor, which is analogous to, but

---

[7] I am not suggesting that this type of crime fiction is incapable of offering political reflection and I am aware of the potentially worrying gendered implications of the argument I am proposing, i.e. that crime fiction focusing primarily on the household rather than the institutions of the justice system, in which female characters are more likely to play a major role and which may be a more attractive proposition to female writers, are less able than works such as *The Glass Key* to map and interrogate the interpenetration of the state and the marketplace. Works by Christie and other Golden Age writers may be formally innovative and speak about how a 'profound' interest or investment 'in dynamics of power inevitably incorporates discourses of gender and sexuality' (Gill Plain, *Twentieth-Century Crime Fiction: Gender, Sexuality and the Body* (Edinburgh: Edinburgh University Press, 2001), p. 8). But it is also true that such works, precisely because they pay little attention to the operations of the justice system and its complex relationship to capital, have less to say about crime fiction's ambivalent thematization of the state which, after all, is the subject of this book.

distinct from, a position in the Metropolitan Police'.[8] Wallace enjoyed a prolific career as a thriller writer dating back to the turn of the century and while some aspects of these later stories, at least from a contemporary perspective, seem hackneyed—the sub-Edgar Allan Poe references to the burden of Reeder's criminal mind or a Holmesian struggle between master-detective and master-criminal—what endures is their careful, nuanced portrait of bureaucratic life (e.g. the ticking clock of the office, the importance of good record keeping, and the lack of personal attachment to departmental successes and failures) and the sense of interdepartmental tension between the Public Prosecutor's office, the Metropolitan and City Police force, and indeed the links between these public institutions and organizations like the Bank of England. If these links are not developed as fully as they are in Hammett's *Red Harvest* or Simenon's *Tropic Moon*, the Reeder stories hint at the ubiquity of bribery and low-level police corruption and the worlds they occupy (e.g. private clubs, corporate HQs, offices of state, police stations, organized crime haunts, factories) are suggestive of the interpenetration of business and politics and are as far removed from the discreet drawing rooms and private spaces of a Christie novel as it is possible to imagine.

Looking beyond Britain's shores, to France and the US in the first instance, there are dangers in making crude connections between crime fictions written by authors with different political and aesthetic ambitions and responding to particular local and national circumstances, often in highly distinctive ways. While Hammett's leftist sympathies are never far from his creative work and while his four great detective novels—*Red Harvest*, *The Maltese Falcon* (1930), *The Dain Curse* (1930), and *The Glass Key*—are imbued with a strong sense of period detail and social context, Simenon is typically regarded as a social conservative whose work exhibits the petty bourgeois preoccupations of his parents and has no clear 'historical markers or indications of any larger political circumstances'.[9] Still, as Lee Horsley notes, precisely because Hammett 'was involved in leftist politics in the mid-thirties' there has been a 'critical tendency to read back into his novels...a Marxist political agenda'—a move Horsley sees as problematic because the world Hammett created 'is characterized not by remediable political-economic ills but by deep-seated moral disorder'.[10] Meanwhile, the apparently socially conservative Simenon is often quite far-reaching in his critique of bourgeois complacency and hypocrisy. Moreover, the genre is more than able to accommodate different social and political outlooks, not least because its thematization of state power is so ambivalent.

---

[8] Edgar Wallace, *The Casefiles of Mr J. G. Reeder* (Ware, Hertfordshire: Wordsworth Editions, 2010), p. 179.

[9] Page Dubois, 'Oedipus as Detective: Sophocles, Simenon, Robbe-Grillet', *Yale French Studies*, 108 (2005), p. 109. For further accounts of Simenon's perceived social and political conservatism and his downplaying of context, see Lucille Becker, *Georges Simenon Revisited* (New York, NY: Twayne, 1999), p. 4 and Christopher Shorley, 'Georges Simenon and Crime Fiction between the Wars', in Claire Gorrara (ed.) *French Crime Fiction* (Cardiff: University of Wales Press, 2009), p. 44.

[10] Lee Horsley, *Twentieth-Century Crime Fiction* (Oxford: Oxford University Press, 2005), pp. 166–7.

This last point requires careful consideration. One of the reasons for bringing Hammett, Simenon, and Brecht together is because their work can be said to speak about the consolidation and expansion of the state that took place in the aftermath of the First World War, the Russian Revolution, and the economic crises that followed the Wall Street Crash. This consolidation and expansion took different forms in different countries. Arguably efforts by state agencies and institutions in the US, fearful about the growing influence of trade unions and the spread of Communism, to coerce or pacify potentially unruly working-class communities was that much more pointed than, say, in France, even if similar trends could be noted there too.[11] By the same token, the physical scars of the First World War are felt more acutely in Simenon's early novels, even if this manifests itself only obliquely, in a generalized sense of anxiety or dislocation. Hammett's ambivalence to the state always assumed a highly explosive and overtly politicized form; the Continental Op is painfully aware of the state's partiality (i.e. how beholden it is to a corrupt business oligarchy) but he is so tied to its socio-political logic that he can't envisage an alternative, a situation that threatens to split him straight down the middle. By contrast, Simenon's Maigret novels may depict the growing influence of state institutions, especially in terms of the development of communications technology and techniques of forensic analysis, but Maigret himself adopts a more accommodating position vis-à-vis the institutions he serves. That said, he is by no means blind to the inadequacies and biases of the law and if we see Simenon's *romans durs* (hard or serious novels) and Maigret novels as more alike than different (i.e. as part of the same artistic endeavour) then the author's socio-political critique, irrespective of his perceived conservatism, comes into sharper focus.

At stake here is the extent to which the state should be seen as both separate from and autonomous to the rest of society, itself a fundamental premise of nineteenth-century liberalism. Here, the role or function of the state was important but limited—to provide the security and the general administrative framework for individuals to freely and equally participate in the marketplace, intervening only when a threshold of harm was reached or when the smooth running of the market (e.g. the free exchange of goods and labour) was threatened. This view was challenged by Marx and Engels who maintained that the state could not be separated from civil society because by defending private property rights and the separation of classes, it had already taken a side and was responsible for entrenching deeply unfair patterns of domination and subordination. The issue of the state's relationship to civil society is a contentious one, especially for Marxist critics who argue about Marx's characterization of civil society in his early and mature writing and question whether civil society should be equated with the economic realm of labour, production, and exchange.[12]

---

[11] Thomas Heise does not compare the situations in the US and France but his article provides an important way of reading Hammett's *Red Harvest* vis-à-vis the US state's incursions into working-class communities. See '"Going Blood-Simple Like the Natives": Contagious Urban Spaces and Modern Power in Dashiell Hammett's *Red Harvest*', *Modern Fiction Studies*, 51:3 (Fall 2005), pp. 485–512.

[12] In *The German Ideology* Marx and Engels tie the establishment of civil society to the rise of the bourgeoisie and the consolidation of property relations and in doing so underscore the extent to which

Rather than rehearse these debates I'd like to turn to the claims of the Italian Marxist Antonio Gramsci, and not simply because he was writing at the same time and in response to the same political and economic conditions as Hammett, Simenon, and Brecht. Gramsci's reversal of the assumed primacy of the economic base over the superstructure both collapses the division between the state and civil society and allows us to develop an account of this relationship which, in turn, reveals their interpenetration (as he famously put it, 'the state = political society + civil society'[13]) and both the ethical and coercive capacities of this expanded state form. These moves help bring into sharper focus what is implicit in the crime fiction of this period, even if writers such as Simenon and even Hammett are by no means as committed as Gramsci to class warfare and revolutionary goals—or indeed exhibit little interest in these goals.

HAMMETT, GRAMSCI, BRECHT—AND SIMENON

Part of my argument is that the crime fiction of Hammett, Brecht, and Simenon should be understood in the context of the massive structural realignment between states and capitalism in Europe and the United States following the end of the First World War and the Russian Revolution. However, this argument will only work if the symmetries and disjunctions between these writers, vis-à-vis the implicit and explicit political ambitions of their work, are carefully laid out. Hammett's *Red Harvest* is the most useful starting point because more than any other novel it thematizes the shift from one form of capitalism to another (the so-called robber baron era and the consolidation of monopoly capitalism, as personified by the novel's ageing mine owner and megalomaniac Elihu Wilsson, to the development of newer, more efficient methods of production in the first three decades of the twentieth century) and the deepening links between big business and government. The opening pages of *Red Harvest*, which describe the deployment of the national guardsmen to beat up striking miners, lay bare any lingering pretensions about the state's neutrality but intriguingly this move has taken place prior to the start of the novel, and during the narrative itself we see very little of the state's coercive arsenal. Rather, in the guise of the Continental Op, we are encouraged to reflect on the state's attempts to consolidate capitalism and also ameliorate its worst excesses.

To understand how these moves are connected we need to turn back to Gramsci. For Gramsci, the resilience of the state depends not just upon its ability to coerce

---

the political and socio-economic realms are both facets of productive relations. 'Civil society embraces the whole material intercourse of individuals within a definite stage of development of productive forces' (Karl Marx and Friedrich Engels, *The German Ideology*, trans. & ed. S. Ryazanskaya (London: Lawrence & Wishart, 1965), pp. 48–9). In later works and especially after his *The Eighteenth Brumaire of Louis Bonaparte* (Moscow: Progress Publishers, 1852) Marx raises the issue of the relative autonomy of the political classes and thereby indicates that the relationship between the base and superstructure, and between the productive forces and political and civil society, might not be a wholly deterministic one.

[13] Antonio Gramsci, *Selections from the Prison Notebooks of Antonio Gramsci*, ed. Quintin Hoare and Geoffrey Nowell-Smith (London: Lawrence & Wishart, 1971), p. 263.

its subjects through monopolistic control over the means of violence. Rather this resilience is also explained by its success in winning consent through the workings of hegemony and the increasing interpenetration of civil, political, and economic realms—making it harder, if not impossible, to find positions wholly outside of power to oppose its operations.[14] A brief look at Hammett's second novel, *The Maltese Falcon* (1930), confirms that he was mining a similar vein of thought; how greed and self-interest function as a code for the way in which control is exercised as much through activities in the marketplace as via the institutions of the state. The novel deals with the avaricious yearnings of a motley collection of latter-day gold diggers but the threat to civil society posed by Casper Gutman, Joel Cairo, and Brigid O'Shaughnessy can be accommodated because it is not at odds with the logic of capitalism. Hammett positions his erstwhile private eye Sam Spade as pivot between the forces of capital accumulation and the demands of the law and makes it clear that the two are not in the end to be viewed as antagonistic. Spade is not immune to the get-rich-quick ambitions of the other characters and in the end acts decisively in favour of the law, but arguably not because the law says he must, or because he is frightened of the repercussions, but because it is in the long-term interests of his detective business to give up those who have lied, cheated, and killed in order to secure their own financial self-advantage, even if the moral character of their actions is irrelevant in the face of the relentless march of self-interest.

It is perhaps not difficult to see how and why we might be able to bring figures like Hammett, Gramsci, and Brecht into profitable dialogue, given that *Red Harvest*, *The Prison Notebooks*, and *The Threepenny Opera* (1928) were all written within a few years of one another, in response to similar social, political, and economic circumstances: state-sponsored crackdowns against the working classes and trade unions following the Russian Revolution and the rise of international Communism, and the consolidation of monopoly capitalism in the same period. (Simenon is a less easy 'fit' with this group and I'll explain his place in the chapter presently). Hammett, Gramsci, Brecht: this is not an arbitrary grouping, even if one needs to be careful about drawing them into too close an alliance and ignoring their particular political and aesthetic views. It isn't straightforward to ascertain their political views, despite their shared sympathies for leftist politics. While Gramsci—the foremost Italian Communist of his generation—was imprisoned near Bari in southern Italy in 1928 for his part in the fight against fascism, Brecht never actually joined the Communist Party despite a commitment to Marxism as a political project, and Hammett only joined the Communist Party in the 1930s, after his four major crime novels had been published, having previously served as a Pinkerton agent on the side of mine owners and against striking workers. Both Hammett and Brecht were called to testify before the House of Un-American

---

[14] For Gramsci, the state's hegemony is always supported by 'the armour of coercion' (p. 263) and while periodically there are crises 'in the ruling class's hegemony' which occur 'because the ruling class has failed in some major political undertaking' the use of physical force to hold onto power must be accompanied by attempts to secure the consent of the populace (*Selections from the Prison Notebooks*, pp. 211, 263–7).

Activities in the late 1940s to explain their political allegiances. In terms of their aesthetic preoccupations, there are interesting points of connection and incongruity too. For example, while Brecht always identified himself as an avant-garde playwright, and eschewed what he saw as the 'comforting illusion'[15] perpetuated by much popular drama, Hammett worked almost exclusively within a readily identifiable popular genre, even if he shared Brecht's distaste for the baseness of much popular culture and famously declared that he wanted to turn detective fiction into serious literature. 'I'm one of the few...people moderately literate,' he wrote in a letter to Blanche Knopf in 1928, 'who take the detective story seriously. I don't mean that I necessarily take my own or anybody else's seriously—but the detective story as a form. Some day some body's going to make "literature" of it, and I'm selfish enough to have my hopes, however slight the evident justification may be.'[16]

What links Brecht and Hammett is their desire to write about crime and criminal worlds in order to reflect upon the nature of contemporary existence, and write about such worlds in ways intended to unsettle and provoke complacent bourgeois readers and deal seriously with the overdetermined relationship between capitalism and state power. Brecht wrote about the crime novel and seemed more enamoured of British rather than American examples which, he thought, 'have far weaker formulas and are guilty of hankering for originality'[17] and as such defended the 'clue–puzzle' element of the genre for the intellectual challenge it posed to readers. Brecht, then, is less interested in crime fiction's claims to what he calls 'Verism' than in the possible disjuncture it throws up between its own world where 'people act' and the world of 'the literary novel and real life' where 'the life of the atomized masses and the collectivized individual passes without trace'.[18] Brecht may have approved of the Continental Op's or Sam Spade's modus operandi—and perhaps also Hammett's politics or at least his latent critique of capitalism—but as he pointed out (quite problematically) the crime novel should not aspire to become anything more than itself. It is ironic and revealing then that his own ambitions as playwright should so closely mirror Hammett's as crime novelist. If Hammett wanted to turn a popular genre into not just art but also political allegory, perhaps not to directly politicize his readers but certainly to show them the ugliness of American capitalism, Brecht set out to write plays that would force audiences to see the miseries inflicted on them in the name of 'business' and 'progress'—as precursors to transforming their political affiliations. Both, then, used their work to expose the familiar bourgeois world of work and commerce not as a site of individual expression and self-fulfilment but rather as predatory and exploitative. By doing so, and by showing how the individual was complicit in the pursuit and

---

[15] Non and Nick Worrall, 'Commentary' in Bertolt Brecht, *The Threepenny Opera*, trans. Ralph Manheim and John Willett (London: Methuen, 2005), p. xxx.
[16] Hammett qtd in Mark McGurl, 'Making "Literature" of it: Hammett and High Culture', *American Literary History*, 9:4 (Winter 1997), p. 706.
[17] Brecht, 'On the Popularity of Crime Novels', in Aaron Kelly, *The Thriller and Northern Ireland since 1969* (Aldershot: Ashgate, 2005), pp. 167–9. This is Kelly's translation of Brecht's essay.
[18] Brecht, 'On the Popularity of Crime Novels', p. 168.

production of power, Brecht and Hammett, though committed to varying degrees to left politics, offered a more complex understanding of the committed writer: not someone, to quote Francis Mulhern, whose work was embedded in left party politics in order to 'pre-figure the unalienated order of socialism'[19] but rather someone whose political loyalties were tangled up with the exigencies of their role as the state's unwilling executioner and muddied by their embeddedness in the market.

If it is easy to see how a novel like *Red Harvest* and play like *The Threepenny Opera* might find common ground with a Gramscian reading of hegemony and exploitation, it is perhaps worth pointing out that Gramsci himself wrote—albeit briefly—about detective stories and theatre and, as a critic, posed the kind of questions that also shape my own preoccupations. For example, how the emergence of new cultural forms needs to be understood as a response to political and economic conditions; and whether these new forms can be harnessed for politically progressive ends. There are clear parallels between Gramsci's criticism of popular theatre—whereby 'talking puppets move about variously, without ever drawing out a psychological truth [and] without ever managing to impose on the listener's creative imagination a character or passions that are truly felt or adequately expressed'[20]—and Brecht's charge against the complacency and falseness of what he calls dramatic as opposed to epic theatre.[21] Gramsci may not have known or known about Brecht as playwright but in light of their shared Marxist affinities, they both exhibit a belief—or perhaps a hope—that cultural formations do not simply reflect political and/or economic realities but agitate for change by forcing audiences to think critically about what they are watching.

Vis-à-vis the artistic and political status of detective fiction, it is perhaps harder to find much common ground between Gramsci and Hammett, especially given Gramsci's suspicion that the vigilante-heroes of Alexander Dumas's novels (and perhaps by extension a figure like the Continental Op?) and the fascist militiamen of 1920s Italy are both products of petit-bourgeois yearnings. Gramsci wrote briefly about the detective story in Europe (he didn't seem to be aware of Hammett or American Black Mask writers) but his analysis is instructive for a number of reasons. Rejecting the claim that the English detective or judiciary story represents a 'defence of the law' while the French equivalent exalts the criminal, he identifies 'a cultural passage' in the detective story from the latter to the former and, in turn, links this to the rationalization of existence under capitalism. The crucial question, for him, is whether the adventure promised by the detective story speaks about, or indeed is a response to, what is predictable in a world increasingly dominated by the forces of 'coercive rationalization'.[22] The fact that the actions of Hammett's Continental Op are wildly unpredictable and violent and yet also part of a publicly

---

[19] Francis Mulhern, *The Present Lasts a Long Time* (Cork: Cork University Press, 1998), p. 91.
[20] Gramsci, *Selections from Cultural Writings*, ed. David Forgas and Geoffrey Nowell-Smith (London: Lawrence & Wishart, 1985), p. 55.
[21] For Brecht's account of the differences between dramatic and epic theatre, see 'Commentary' in Bertolt Brecht, *The Threepenny Opera*, p. xxxiii.
[22] Gramsci, *Selections from Cultural Writings*, pp. 369, 374.

sanctioned campaign to pacify the excessiveness of Personville means that Hammett's novel covers similar territory. Gramsci's musings on the detective story are too brief to draw definitive conclusions but insofar as he distinguishes between the 'beautiful' adventure which is the product of an individual's 'free initiative' and the 'ugly and revolting' adventure which is the product of 'conditions imposed by others', he implicitly offers us a way of distinguishing the Continental Op and Hammett's protagonists more generally from accusations of bourgeois wish-fulfilment and crypto-fascism: the Continental Op may appear to be free and unco-opted but his actions end up revealing his complicity in the political and economic system that he, willingly and unwillingly, serves. We might also reflect on whether Hammett's desire to give us an unvarnished vision of American life as it is organized under capitalism is a political act—since in Brechtian terms, the idea of tearing off the veil constitutes a crucial move towards mobilization and political enlightenment.

Georges Simenon may seem, at first glance, like a fairly anomalous addition to this group; someone who never expressed any sympathies for Marxism or believed that fiction should agitate for revolutionary change. His creations, such as Inspector Jules Maigret and the blank, put-upon characters of his *romans durs*, would seem to speak more powerfully about the benefits of quietly going about one's business or indeed quietly swimming against the tide, in ways that reflect individual rather than collective bewilderment at the nature and meaninglessness of modern life. Still, just like Hammett, Simenon sought to push against the perceived limitations of the crime fiction genre and, by doing so, steer his novels into the terrain occupied by the so-called 'greats' of modern European fiction. Chris Shorley explains how correspondence between Gide and Simenon sheds light on this ambition: for example how Simenon told Gide, following the first cycle of Maigret novels, that he'd 'explicitly abandoned his detective' and 'aimed to write a whole new strain of *romans durs*... in which crime and investigation could give place to the closer scrutiny of the essential... human self... and explore wider issues such as colonialism'.[23] (By 1939 Gide was openly proclaiming Simenon as 'perhaps our greatest novelist'.[24])

Hammett himself was a great admirer of Simenon's work, declaring him, in 1950, to be 'the best mystery writer today' because of his 'intelligence'[25] and it is inconceivable that Simenon wasn't acutely aware of Hammett's significance, given the similarities between aspects of his *romans durs* and Hammett's work (see the next section, entitled Hammett and Simenon 1). The standard response to Simenon's output as a novelist is to distinguish between his Maigret novels and *romans durs*; to argue that the latter 'rely on comforting tropes' and exhibit no obvious 'historical markers or indications of any larger political circumstances'[26] while the former unsettle and provoke, and cut right to the heart of what Balzac

---

[23] Shorley, 'Georges Simenon and Crime Fiction', p. 41.
[24] Shorley, 'Georges Simenon and Crime Fiction', p. 41.
[25] Hammett qtd in Matthew J. Bruccoli and Richard Layman, *Hardboiled Mystery Writers: Raymond Chandler, Dashiell Hammett, Ross Macdonald* (New York, NY: Caroll & Graf, 2002), p. 205.
[26] Dubois, 'Oedipus as Detective', pp. 108–9.

called 'la condition humane'. By contrast—and in line with Lucille Becker's assertion that 'even in his detective novels...Simenon recreated the genre and transformed it into a viable literary genre'[27]—my aim is to situate both outputs on the same continuum. The implications of this are twofold. First, in so far as there are many points of connection between Hammett's novels and Simenon's *romans durs* in particular (i.e. regarding a shared philosophical outlook, one characterized by an air of disaffection and bewilderment), it is misguided at best to identify Simenon as an advocate of the status quo, even if his political sympathies, as far as these can be ascertained, were aligned to his petit bourgeois roots. Second, if we see the concerns of Simenon's *romans durs* as bleeding into his detective novels, this in turn has important consequences for his thematization of the state and the efficacy of the law. Later in this chapter (the section Simenon and Hammett 2), I'll consider a selection from the early cycle of Maigret novels in more detail—*Lock 14* (first published in 1931 as *Le Charretier de 'La Providence'*), *The Yellow Dog* (first published in 1931 as *Le Chien Jaune*), and *The Bar on the Seine* (first published in 1932 as *Le Guinguette à deux sous*)[28]—and ask whether the political disquiet of Simenon's *romans durs* poses questions against the fairness of the crime control apparatus described in these novels. As the reassuring surfaces of Simenon's Maigret novels give way to reveal darker undercurrents, I will return to one of his early *romans durs*—*Tropic Moon* (first published in 1933 as *Coup de Lune*)—which provides a blistering critique of colonialism, the bias of the law, and the privileging of economic over judicial concerns, one that in turn suggests Simenon and Gramsci do not belong to entirely different realms.

HAMMETT AND SIMENON 1: A PHILOSOPHY OF DISQUIET

There is a story in Hammett's *The Maltese Falcon* that seems to encapsulate an entire way of seeing and interpreting the world and that is perfectly in tune with the prevailing mood of bleakness and quiescence struck by the novel as a whole. The story, told by Sam Spade to Brigid O'Shaughnessy, is about an outwardly prosperous real estate agent, Flitcraft, who lived in the Tacoma suburbs with his wife and child and who disappeared one afternoon following a golf match, never to return to his family. Years later, after someone resembling the missing man is seen in Spokane, Spade is called upon to investigate and discovers that Flitcraft has started a new business and set up another home in the suburbs with a new wife and child. When Spade confronts him, he is unapologetic and claims to feel no guilt for leaving his first wife and child, having left them well provided for. During their conversation it emerges that one day Flitcraft was walking past a building site and

---

[27] Becker, *Georges Simenon Revisited*, pp. vii–viii.
[28] These novels constitute the second, sixth, and eleventh Maigret novels published in France, according to http://www.trussel.com/maig/maibib.htm, accessed 12 May 2015.

a beam 'fell eight or ten stories down and smacked the sidewalk alongside him'.[29] Up to this point, Spade notes, Flitcraft had been a model citizen and father but this incident forced him to see the arbitrariness of his existence. 'He knew then that men died at haphazard like that, and lived only while blind chance spared them' (p. 64). Spade explains that it wasn't the sense of injustice or even the arbitrariness that shocked Flitcraft; the fact he had almost been killed by a random falling beam. It was the notion that by trying to 'sensibly' order his affairs, he 'had got out of step, and not in step with life' and that he wouldn't find peace until he had adjusted himself to the meaninglessness of existence. 'He adjusted himself to beams falling, and then no more fell,' Spade summarizes, 'and he adjusted himself to them not falling' (p. 64).

Flitcraft's story is not necessarily a bleak one. The first wife agrees to a quiet divorce and everything quickly returns to 'normal'. She has been well provided for and Flitcraft as Charles Pierce, as he now calls himself, returns to his new life in Spokane. But insofar as it points to the essential randomness and meaninglessness of life (i.e. none of the usual coordinates such as work or marriage seem to ground Flitcraft's existence) and proposes quiescence as solution (i.e. all we can do is adjust ourselves to the fact that beams may fall and not fall), it leaves little room even for a charismatic figure like Spade to fashion his own identity or intervene in the world. This, of course, has important ramifications for our consideration of the politics of Hammett's work but it also provides us with a means of bringing Simenon into proximity with Hammett, especially as these same preoccupations are articulated in two *romans durs* produced at about the same time as *The Maltese Falcon*: *The Engagement* (first published in 1933 as *Les Fiançailles de M. Hire*) and *The Man who Watched the Trains Go By* (first published in 1938 as *L'Homme qui regardait passer les trains*) as well as a much later novel *Monsieur Monde Vanishes* (first published in 1952 as *La Fuite de Monsieur Monde*).

There is no single falling beam incident in either *The Man who Watched the Trains* or *Monsieur Monde Vanishes*, just a cumulative dissatisfaction on the part of Kees Popinga and Monde with the sterile conformity of their comfortable bourgeois existences. Popinga has been a hard-working and loyal employee at a Groningen shipping firm but when he is told by the boss about the firm's bankruptcy and his own potential ruin (his savings and mortgage are both tied to the company) he sees it as an opportunity to escape; not just from his job and the 'highly moral' town he has lived in all his life but also from his wife and children.[30] He travels first to Amsterdam to try and woo his boss's mistress and when she spurns him and the scene (which we as readers never actually witness) turns violent and results in her murder, Popinga flees on the night train to Paris where he tries to keep one step ahead of the police. Monde's flight, this time from Paris to Marseilles and finally Nice, is precipitated not by a particular event but rather by a subtle change in perspective; 'instead of automatically checking the time on the

---

[29] Hammett, *The Maltese Falcon* (New York, NY: Vintage, 1992), p. 63.
[30] Georges Simenon, *The Man Who Watched the Trains Go By*, trans. Stuart Gilbert, rev. David Watson (London: Penguin, 2006).

electric clock as he usually did, he raised his eyes and noticed the pink chimney pots outlined against a pale blue sky' which in turn 'brought a breath of Mediterranean air to his mind'.[31] In itself this act of perception is meaningless but at work, after he has learnt of an illicit affair involving his son and a young warehouseman, he takes three hundred thousand francs from the safe and heads to the station, with both a clear and unclear sense of why he is doing so.

> What was happening... was so much more essential! He could not possibly have explained it, or even thought about it in a logical way. When, a short while before, he had decided... But he hadn't decided anything. He had had nothing to decide... He felt no surprise. He had been expecting this for a long time, all his life long.   (p. 26)

At their heart, both novels set themselves up as meditations on what it means to be free and whether freedom can be willed into existence but ask other related questions, such as what men like Popinga and Monde are meant to do with their energies, their desires, and whether it is possible to reconcile the need for restraint and their yearning to unshackle themselves from social orthodoxies. Certainly it would be wrong to dismiss the freedom yearned for and to some extent realized by Popinga and Monde as illusory, a fleeting interlude between a monotonous past and a still-to-be-decided future. Whether this freedom is the product of individual intent or not, its realization comes close to articulating the existential mantra of Jean-Paul Sartre who in his 1946 book *Existentialism and Humanism* famously declared, 'Man is nothing else but that which he makes himself'[32] or as Popinga concludes, '[s]ince the past was dead and done with, the only thing to do was to make the most of his new freedom' (p. 27). In both novels, Simenon is careful not to romanticize the new existences of his protagonists or the bleak, precarious worlds they inhabit. Equally he is keen to show that there is a richness, vitality, and texture to their actions and environments, at least in comparison to the sterile rigidity of their former lives. Just as Monde discovers, in Nice, an alternative community of artists and bohemians who mix freely with petty criminals and drug addicts (so much so that he changes his name to Désiré Clouet in order to reflect his new environment and identity), Popinga finds stimulation and excitement in Paris where not only does he discover the city itself but rather is given the chance to prove himself to be 'cleverer' and 'more resourceful' than the police who are pursuing him, not least because unlike them, he is 'tied to nothing, to no one, to no set idea' (p. 89).

More so than *Monsieur Monde*, *The Man Who Watched* asks pressing questions about the contingent nature of identity, or the extent to which the new role (of murderer, fleeing criminal) inhabited by Popinga mirrors his former role as father, boss, and husband. In a sense both are roles he performs rather than manifestations of an essential self, a situation that affords him some notion of freedom but also leaves him dangerously prone to the whims of fate. Popinga's description of what

---

[31] Simenon, *Monsieur Monde Vanishes*, trans. Jean Stewart (New York, NY: New York Review of Books, 2004), p. 18.
[32] Jean-Paul Sartre, *Existentialism and Humanism* (London: Methuen, 2007), p. 30.

led him to abandon his former life is also remarkably similar to Flitcraft's. Indeed his sense of having 'settled into a groove... of a trusted employee, of a conventional married man and father' simply because 'others had decided it should be thus' and then deciding 'for myself, for a change' (p. 135) almost exactly echoes Spade's framing of Flitcraft's predicament; that 'in sensibly ordering his affairs he had got out of step, and not in step with his life' (p. 64).

So what does this tell us about both novels and indeed both authors, vis-à-vis the political thrust of their work? It is highly likely that Simenon knew and admired *The Maltese Falcon*, especially given his own move to the US after the Second World War and given André Gide, a great admirer of Simenon's novels, was also a powerful advocate of Hammett's. Still, while emphasizing their similarities (of tone, idiom, description) one should not get too carried away. Hammett wrote *The Maltese Falcon* in the shadow of the Wall Street Crash (he had probably completed the novel in some form by October 1929) and as such the novel can profitably be read as a critique of unchecked capitalist greed or even, as Charles Rzepka argues, of Marx's commodity fetishism: 'the false attribution of an inherent value to material objects that possess it only by virtue of what can be obtained in exchange for them'[33] whereby the ultimately worthless statuette exposes and speaks to the illusory nature of value or at least the vast gap between use and exchange value in the context of a culture of greed and speculation. Hammett's left politics have been the subject of much scrutiny, and as Horsley has already noted, while *The Maltese Falcon* shows 'the greed and exploitation of unrestrained capitalism',[34] it offers no palliatives, no cures, no potential solutions, and certainly not the revolutionary ones envisaged by Marx. If Hammett exhibits Marxist sympathies but falls a long way short of embracing Marx's political views *en masse*, what about Simenon? Clearly it would be wrong to needlessly politicize Simenon—in many ways the archetypal apolitical petit bourgeois who once declared, '[y]ou would look in vain through my two hundred and twenty novels to find any traces of ideology'.[35] Still, we shouldn't forget that just as Flitcraft's realization (of being out of step with his life), and his resultant anxiety, isn't expressed in explicitly political terms, neither is Popinga's in *The Man who Watched*. In other words, his revolt is a personal one and doesn't ask questions of, and demand answers about, the nature of society as it is organized by the state under capitalism.

So what conclusions can we draw? First and most obviously, given the account Spade offers about Flitcraft in *The Maltese Falcon* and Popinga's realization in *The Man who Watched* of the dreadful consequences of adhering to social norms, there is an element of social critique in both novels. It is Spade's hope that he has assimilated the lessons of Flitcraft's explanation; i.e. that he has adjusted himself to beams falling and not falling, and hence to the absurdity and meaninglessness of the universe. But of course the universe is not simply absurd and without meaning: it

---

[33] Charles Rzepka, *Detective Fiction* (Cambridge: Polity, 2005), p. 194.
[34] Horsley, *Twentieth-Century Crime Fiction*, p. 166.
[35] Simenon qtd in Bill Alder, 'Maigret, Simenon, France: Social Class and Social Change in the 1930s Maigret Narratives of Georges Simenon', *Clues: A Journal of Detection*, 29:2 (Fall 2011), p. 54.

is also in thrall to the political and economic logic of a system that rewards greed and skews the law towards the interests of the wealthy. In this sense, the political quiescence implied by Flitcraft's 'adjustments' (and by Spade's appropriation of the apparent message of Flitcraft's account) requires closer scrutiny. At the start of the novel, Spade is all cocksure swagger; a man who will not be dictated to and who believes in nothing and no one but himself. Subsequently his neutrality is tested first by the allure of financial remuneration and then by the prospect of emotional attachment (to Brigid who eventually, he decides, is not worth 'playing the sap' for). Given Spade has apparently heeded the lessons of Flitcraft's actions and adjusted himself to the meaninglessness of the universe, he might hope, appropriating Sartre's maxim, to be able to make himself and find some kind of freedom in the process. But just as there are strings attached to Sartre's formulation (if there is nothing, no 'values or commands', to direct our behaviour, 'we are left alone, without excuses' and are 'condemned to be free'[36]) so Spade finds only an extremely limited or thin version of the freedom that Flitcraft's reincarnation as Charles Pierce has promised him.

To find out why, we need to turn our attention back to the detective story that frames Flitcraft's story, and also to detective fiction's foundational relationship to the state. Spade may well want to parade his autonomy, his detachment from everything and everyone, but inevitably this need runs up against his function as detective, and by implication the links between detection and the law. In so doing, Hammett allegorizes the claims of political commitment—in the end Spade has to take a side, e.g. he cannot simply do nothing—but, contra Sartre, by choosing a side he does not become a free agent somehow living an authentic life. Rather the choices he faces, and by implication the choices available to the politically committed writer, are severely limited by his role or function as a detective and hence his proximity to exactly the structures of power that leftist politics would want to oppose. It is worth quoting Rzepka at length because his reading of *The Maltese Falcon* draws attention to these limitations and hence explains what is so bleak about the novel's ending:

> The detective's only way out of this futile, empty cycle of desire, story and value-in-exchange lies in his professional commitment to the work at hand, the labour of detecting pursued for its own end, not for what it can get you, and least of all for pleasure. In this last respect, Spade evinces a much bleaker, existential version of detection than his predecessor, the Continental Op... In fact, Spade carries out his professional duty precisely because 'all of [him] wants' to do the opposite.[37]

At first glance there is little to connect Sam Spade, a figure described by his creator as 'a dream man in the sense that he is what most private detectives I worked with would like to have been',[38] and Kees Popinga, the awkward, slightly deluded protagonist of Simenon's *The Man who Watched*. For despite Popinga's belief in his own abilities, his capacity to outwit his pursuers and to move around Paris almost

---

[36] Sartre, *Existentialism and Humanism*, p. 38.
[37] Rzepka, *Detective Fiction*, p. 194.
[38] Hammett qtd in Bruccoli and Layman, *Hardboiled Mystery Writers*, p. 117.

at will, his demise is as inevitable as it is pathetic; as soon as he realizes a thief has lifted his wallet his world falls apart and it is but a short step to capture and capitulation. As he contemplates his fate in the immediate aftermath of the theft, he notices his reflection in the mirror of the bar and sees 'a face expressing nothing, neither anguish nor despair, hope nor fear'. Its blankness 'reminded him of a face he had seen ten years before... of a man who had just been run over by a tram and had both legs cut off' (p. 182). But this conjunction of nothingness and immobilization is not as far from Spade as we might think, at least as Rzepka has described him. In order to draw out the implications of seeing Spade and Popinga as doubles, it is sensible to first pay attention to Simenon's *The Engagement*, because it is in here that the proximity between the world of the detective (who acts, who watches, who is potent) and of the social misfit/outsider/criminal (who doesn't act, who peeps, who is impotent) finds its most complex and satisfying articulation.

The novel centres on Monsieur Hire, 'a short man, on the fat side, with a curled moustache',[39] who is both pornographer and peeping tom and, following the discovery of a bloody towel in his apartment, becomes the chief suspect in the case of a murdered call girl whose body is found on a building site near Hire's apartment in Villejuf on the outskirts of Paris. Initially a scratch mark on Hire's face is taken as further proof of his guilt (fragments of skin were discovered under the dead woman's fingernails indicating she'd gouged her attacker) but even when this is revealed to be a harmless shaving cut, suspicion mounts and two police detectives are drafted in to keep Hire under constant surveillance. The distinction between criminal and detective and deviancy and the law would seem to be clearly drawn, not least because the idea of asking readers to identify with a pornographer and peeping tom would seem to be an unpromising one. Still, Simenon takes this unlikely scenario and, in a series of brilliant manoeuvres begins to mould it into something entirely new. It soon becomes clear that the object of his voyeuristic yearning, a voluptuous red-headed women called Alice who lives in the apartment opposite him, is aware of his interest in her and actively courts it by appearing at her window caressing her nipples and later 'proudly revealing her exuberant breasts' (p. 46). When Alice initiates contact by inviting herself into his apartment, his terrified, monosyllabic answers conceal a real concern or affection for her, and the scene ends up being touching (with the two of them holding hands on his bed), despite our suspicion that she is merely toying with him (something that in turn reinforces a readerly identification with him). It is Hire's dream of escape, and his plans to run away with Alice to Switzerland on a train leaving from the Gare de Lyon that links him most forcefully with Popinga, Monde, Flitcraft, and by implication Sam Spade. For Hire, Popinga, Monde, and Flitcraft, flight constitutes an instinctive response to the deadening, routinized nature of existence—though while Hammett's account of this existence underscores what has been debased by financial speculation and greed, Simenon is happier, as John Gray puts it, to focus on a generalized 'absence of meaning' and the resulting 'inconsequence of human

---

[39] Simenon, *The Engagement*, trans. Anna Moschovakis (New York, NY: New York Review of Books, 2007), p. 5.

life'.[40] That said, the way that Simenon handles this material in *The Engagement* suggests there are profitable links to be made with Hammett's *The Maltese Falcon*.

A typical reading of Hire's voyeurism would want to characterize it in exploitative terms; in other words, that it analogizes the male gaze, the ways in which this gaze reduces Alice to the status of object, and hence constitutes an entire way of seeing the world, based on male potency and female impotency. But even a cursory look at Simenon's text shows us how inadequate this reading is. Hire's voyeurism, like the pornographic materials he peddles, may be exploitative in one sense, but in keeping an eye on her, he is also watching out for her, a point made by Alice when she scolds Hire for looking and doing nothing when her boyfriend Émile violently assaults her in her apartment. The notion that Hire's voyeurism might be beneficial to Alice is augmented by the presence of the police detectives whose job is also to keep an eye on her and make sure nothing bad happens. Here, though, the police and Hire are not treated as antagonists but rather as doubles—Hire's voyeurism mimics the detectives' surveillance. Pushing this point further, Simenon proposes that Hire's impotency, i.e. his unwillingness or inability to intervene, is replicated by the detectives who can do nothing about any of the attacks (against women) that have taken place in Villejuf. The connection between Hire and the detectives, and between voyeurism and surveillance, is underscored by the sexualized content of their respective gazes; Hire's peeping tom antics are reflected in or by the clumsy, arguably more misogynistic attempts by one of the detectives to 'sweet-talk' her. In comparison Hire's conduct is respectful and gentle and the irony of this, and of the complex doubling that Simenon's subtle control of the narrative makes possible, is reinforced by the fact that Hire is misrecognized at a bowling club where he is the star performer as a policeman. When one of the detectives questions a member of the club about Hire, the man answers, 'Since you're with the police, you should know who he is, because he's with the police too—and he must be in a pretty powerful position' (p. 67). But what is Simenon's point? Are the comparisons between a pornographer and the police derogatory to the latter or complimentary to the former?

This connection raises troubling issues for the police and the law, for not only is the detective's attitude a threat to Alice's safety but rather his casual indifference to the issue of male (sexual) violence means he, and the police more generally, are not really interested in addressing the problem. Rather they just want to make an arrest and Hire is the ideal fall guy. Beholden to the logic of the 'quick fix' they have no interest in the larger claims of truth and justice—a point that Hammett also makes in *The Maltese Falcon*. Not only are the police shown to be ineffectual, at least in comparison to the action-oriented Spade; their indifference to the truth also means that expediency trumps ethics. As Spade tells Gutman, if 'we give them a fall-guy...they'll stop right there' (p. 177); an almost identical scenario to the one that plays out in *The Engagement* where Hire is selected for this sacrificial role. Reflecting on Simenon's interest in looking and both power and powerlessness we should remember that Spade's 'camera eye', as it is described by Peter Humm

[40] John Gray, 'Afterword' in Simenon, *The Engagement*, pp. 134, 135.

(a seemingly objective way of looking that under careful scrutiny reveals the limitations rather than the omnipotence of the subject[41]) is by no means the guarantor of order. Spade's abilities to see round corners and make the necessary adjustments may be more developed than, for example, those of Hire who isn't able to foresee his demise at the hands of a baying mob. But Hire is not necessarily myopic and his failure, in the end, speaks less about a failure of vision than an inability to act, to think, to rise above one's circumstances.

In a world devoid of meaning (Simenon) or rendered meaningless by the ills of modern capitalism (Hammett), Spade's hubris allows him to entertain the illusion of being in control but his preoccupation with Flitcraft and the lessons of Flitcraft's brush with falling beams suggests otherwise. As such, Gray's careful ruminations on *The Engagement*—i.e. that we can expect no justice in the world because the police 'do not care about the facts and simply want to close the case' and that injustices come 'not from malice but indifference'[42]—applies just as well to *The Man Who Watched* or indeed *The Maltese Falcon*. The lesson of Flitcraft's insights, and what unsettles Spade so much, is that he is but a step from a similar fate and the only thing standing between him and the abyss are the codes of his office; codes that, as McCann says of the law in *Red Harvest*, have been 'stripped of ethical content'.[43] In all of this, Simenon and Hammett ask what freedom and by implication commitment mean in a context where one's ability to act, in any kind of manner, political or otherwise, is severely curtailed by the institutional and circumstantial contexts in which one finds oneself. If for Sartre, as Adorno put it, the task of committed art was 'to awaken the free choice of the agent which makes authentic existence possible',[44] Hammett and Simenon suggest that free choice and authentic existence are at best illusions created by the very socio-economic order that their characters strive in vain to define themselves against.

HAMMETT AND BRECHT: THE LONG ARM OF THE STATE

If there are some compelling philosophical and formal affinities between Hammett and Simenon, the links between Hammett and Bertolt Brecht are of a more self-evident political nature; and are not confined to their efforts to expose capitalist greed and bourgeois complacency using forms (i.e. the crime novel and popular theatre) that readers and audiences would have been instantly familiar with. Both were fascinated and repulsed by the shiny veneer of American capitalism and conversely by its rotten underbelly figured in terms of cops and gangsters and by scenes of dimly lit back alleys, smoky jazz clubs, and packed boxing rings. Both too

---

[41] See Peter Humm, 'Camera Eye/Private Eye' in Brian Docherty (ed.) *American Crime Fiction* (Basingstoke: Macmillan, 1988), pp. 23–38.
[42] Gray, 'Afterword', pp. 132–3.
[43] McCann, *Gumshoe America*, p. 114.
[44] Sartre qtd in Christopher Pawling, *Critical Theory and Political Engagement: From May '68 to the Arab Spring* (Basingstoke: Palgrave Macmillan, 2013), p. 18.

demonstrated little faith in the ability of progressive politics to initiate meaningful social change, notwithstanding Brecht's faith in the transformative potential of epic or non-naturalistic/non-dramatic theatre. It is no coincidence that Brecht started to read Marx while in America—as Parmalee says, '[h]is politics change because he reads Marx; and he reads Marx because of his interest in America'[45]— and while Hammett underwent no such 'road to Damascus' conversion, both men smuggled anti-capitalist perspectives into their work, darkly exciting tales of crime and punishment, without draining these of human drama or boring their readers and audiences with sterile treatises on the evils of surplus value. If this comes closer to explaining their similarities as writers, it is worth thinking about the ways in which Brecht's *The Threepenny Opera* (first performed in 1928) and the later novelization *The Threepenny Novel* (1934) and Dashiell Hammett's *Red Harvest* strip away the populist veneer surrounding the outlaw figure and co-opt the individual into a system of authority where the imperatives of the state and civil society, and of the law and capitalism, are brought together into a fraught and combustible relationship.

If *The Maltese Falcon* focuses primarily on the dog-eat-dog milieu of private enterprise where bonds of family and community have long been sacrificed to the debased logic of competitive individualism, *Red Harvest* reverses this focus to demonstrate the ways in which the state assimilates willing and unwilling participants into its domain, in order to rule by consent and coercion. It is significant that the major disturbance in *Red Harvest* takes place before the novel has started and before the Continental Op has arrived in the western US town of Personville. As the Op learns from Bill Quint of the International Workers of the World, a strike at the mine has been violently curtailed by a motley collection of 'hired gunmen, strike-breakers, national guardsmen, and even parts of the regular army'.[46] In other words the miners have been defeated by Elihu Willsson, the boss of the mining company, only because he has been able to call in private gunmen and, crucially, the repressive apparatuses of the state (e.g. national guard and parts of the regular army). The dispute between Willsson and the miners is reflective of a broader struggle in the first three decades of the twentieth century between the owning and working classes and is broadly equivalent to Gramsci's account of a *genuine* crisis of authority: what happens when the masses 'have passed suddenly from a State of political passivity to a certain activity, and put forward demands which taken together, albeit not organically formulated, add up to a revolution'?[47] The viciousness of Willsson's response, in consort with the forces of the state that have been loaned to him, attests to the coercive character of the state in the novel and, by implication, in the US more generally. Indeed, Gramsci's description of the US state in the late nineteenth and early twentieth centuries in terms of a passage from economic individualism to 'regime of industrial concentration and monopoly'[48]

---

[45] Patty Lee Parmalee, *Brecht's America* (Columbus, OH: Ohio State University Press, 1981), p. 134.
[46] Hammett, *Red Harvest* in *The Four Great Novels*, p. 13.
[47] Gramsci, *Selections from the Prison Notebooks*, p. 210.
[48] Gramsci, *Selections from the Prison Notebooks*, p. 293.

nicely describes the process by which Willsson—the embodiment of monopoly capitalism—has come to preside over Personville.

In Gramscian terms, the phase of economic–corporate primitivism—whereby the state apparatus is solely geared towards safeguarding the forces of production—has to be superseded by an 'ethical' turn whereby state power is exercised not just through physical coercion but as a result of the perceived attractiveness of the ideas it stands for.[49] Gramsci acknowledges that the situation in the United States cannot be directly compared to that in Italy and much of continental Europe and points out that, by the early 1930s, the US had 'yet to emerge from the economic-corporate phase'.[50] Elsewhere, though, he suggests that Americanization (characterized primarily in terms of Fordism) presupposes the expansion of the state into all realms of socio-political life: indeed, what he calls 'passive revolution'—a feature of this Fordist turn—is based on the rationalization of the productive forces via 'a skilful combination of force (destruction of working class trade unionism on a territorial basis) and persuasion (high wages, various social benefits...subtle ideological and political propaganda)'.[51]

Turning our attention back to *Red Harvest*, the violent suppression of the miners prior to the start of the novel and Willsson's pre-eminence suggests that the town, and by extension the US, has yet to emerge from its 'robber baron' period. That said, the fact that Willsson's pre-eminent status seems to have been usurped by the private gunmen he brought in to break the strike and that the vanquished miners, and all traces of working-class dissent, are essentially non-presences throughout the novel does suggest some kind of transition in the way Personville is governed. The extent of the violence unleashed by the arrival of the gangs and the general rowdiness of the poolrooms, bars, and boxing halls suggest that state-sponsored efforts to pacify the spaces of working class life will only ever be partial.[52] Nonetheless it is significant that the blood-letting that follows the Continental Op's arrival in the city is not the product of a political dispute between Willsson and the miners but rather an economic dispute between rival business factions, or what I am calling elements of the capitalist or proto-capitalist classes.

In this sense the gang warfare that breaks out following the retreat of the soldiers at the start of the novel, in actuality, constitutes a relatively minor realignment within the ranks of the already-rich and wannabe-rich. Gunmen and bootleggers like Pete the Finn, Lew Yard, and Max Thaler are not representative working-class figures or proto-social bandits whose violence can be understood as a form of primitive rebellion against an unjust, all-powerful state. Rather they are proto-capitalists every bit as eager as Willsson to exploit working-class thirst for liquor and gambling. In other words what *Red Harvest* illustrates is not what Gramsci calls a genuine crisis of the state's authority but a nasty, asymmetrical dispute among rival capitalists—on terms which inevitably favour the incumbent kingpin.

---

[49] Gramsci, *Selections from the Prison Notebooks*, pp. 262–3.
[50] Gramsci, *Selections from the Prison Notebooks*, p. 272.
[51] Gramsci, *Selections from the Prison Notebooks*, p. 285.
[52] For a much fuller reading of this incursion, see Heise, 'Going Blood-Simple Like the Natives'.

At first glance there would seem to be little that separates Willsson's legitimate enterprises (e.g. banking, mining, newspapers) from the illegitimate enterprises of Pete the Finn and Lew Yard (e.g. bootlegging, bail bonding, loan sharking, and gambling). Just as Willsson is not shy of using violence to get his own way, the gang leaders see the value of adopting a business-minded approach to their activities; as Pete the Finn says, 'That damned gunwork is out... This busting the town open is no good for business' (p. 136). This point is underlined by Dinah Brand who is unable to distinguish between 'Max, Lew, Pete... and Willsson' (p. 38). In part, then, the fighting that takes place can be interpreted as disagreements among the capitalist classes—or between different factions of capital. But my point is that these factions are not competing on equal terms. From the very start, the circumstances favour Willsson who has moved beyond the 'economic individualism' that Gramsci describes. It is the gunmen, not Willsson, who collectively pursue what Freedman and Kendrick call a 'radically individualist' agenda and must therefore operate 'without the formal sanction of the State'[53]—a situation that leaves them vulnerable and open to challenge. Willsson, on the other hand, though threatened by the dog-eat-dog competition unleashed by the arrival of the gangs, is ultimately much less vulnerable to external threat precisely because of his privileged position within the existing state system. As Freedman and Kendrick conclude:

> Whereas the position of the Personville Mining Corporation could be assaulted—and unsuccessfully at that—only by the collective action of the militantly organized working class, the actual defeat of the gangsters is triggered by the lone, chubby figure of the Continental Op (who is officially employed, not accidentally, by Elihu Willsson).[54]

As the seemingly distinctive domains of politics and business, of public power and private enterprise, bleed into each other and it becomes increasingly hard to differentiate the private gunmen from Willsson and the larger forces of the state, it is worth turning our attention back to the problem inherent in Gramsci's writing of distinguishing between the state and civil society. Hoare and Nowell-Smith, for example, make the point that Gramsci did not 'succeed in finding a single, wholly satisfactory conception of "civil society" and the State' and that the state is both defined as political society + civil society and elsewhere as a 'balance between civil society and political society'.[55] But insofar as *Red Harvest* is more than simply an account of brute force wielded by the police and army against the working class and insofar as it suggests the interpenetration of political and civil society, it alludes to the same transition in the state formation that Gramsci is seeking to map. If the state = political society + civil society, it also becomes what Buci-Glucksmann calls 'the site of class compromises, the place where a power bloc is articulated and organized, a bloc that can become "contradictory and disarticulated" in a war of

---

[53] Carl Freedman and Christopher Kendrick, 'Forms of Labor in Dashiell Hammett's *Red Harvest*', *PMLA*, 106:2 (Mar. 1991), p. 211.
[54] Freedman and Kendrick, 'Forms of Labor', p. 211.
[55] Quintin Hoare and Geoffrey Nowell-Smith (eds), *Selections from the Prison Notebooks of Antonio Gramsci*, p. 207.

position'.[56] What we see in *Red Harvest*, then, is akin to a violent Gramscian war of position as competing politicians-cum-gangsters and gangsters-cum-politicians vie for control of the city. Hammett, of course, is not a political theorist offering us a sustained and coherent account of power and his grasp of the multiple institutions of the state and its frequently contradictory operations is more instinctive than Gramsci's. But as with Gramsci, Hammett's novel—by siding with Willsson and sanctioning a return to the status quo and the strengthening of both the state and the capitalist economy—affirms what Lloyd and Thomas describe as 'the ultimate unity of the state formation as an instrument of class rule'.[57] Hence at the end of the novel it is the 'white collar soldiers' (p. 181), acting on Willsson's authority, who profit from the disorganization to seize back control of Personville and what we see here and throughout is not the Hobbesian 'state of nature' described by critics like Stephen Marcus[58] but rather what Gramsci describes as the incorporation of hegemony and its apparatus into the state.[59]

Like Hammett's novel and indeed Brecht's *ur*-text, Gay's *The Beggar's Opera* (which I looked at in Chapter 1), *The Threepenny Opera* explores markedly similar terrain. If Gay's play traces the relationship between crime, business, and policing and suggests both the bias of the law (as an instrument of class domination) and the gradual co-option of the bandit figure by the system he ostensibly opposes, Brecht's play builds upon this idea and develops it to its logical conclusion. Peachum's cottage industry in Gay's original becomes a fully-fledged corporate enterprise in Brecht's version, whereby Peachum, as sole owner and proprietor of The Beggar's Field Ltd, licences plots of land for his workers to practise their 'trade', even providing costumes to elicit public sympathy and hence increase profits. As Vincenzo Ruggiero points out, Brecht's play shows us the parasitic element of organized crime which in turn analogizes the practices of the licit economy and hence of capitalism in general. In other words, Brecht compares 'the rules that govern criminal enterprise with those guiding conventional economic enterprise' so that '[a]ll layers of society are said to embrace such rules, which Brecht associates with greed and exploitation'.[60] What Brecht also does is take a notion that was implied in Gay's original—Macheath's co-option in this same system—and make it explicit. Macheath here is no social bandit or anywhere near it. Rather he is the mirror image of Jeremiah Peachum: a gangster-turned-businessman who has rationalized his criminal enterprise according to the logic of hierarchical organization and the pursuit of profit. As such, he has no qualms about getting rid of unproductive assets such as Dreary Walter who, he suspects, is selling 'stuff on the

---

[56] Christine Buci-Glucksmann, *Gramsci and the State*, trans. David Fernbach (London: Lawrence & Wishart, 1980), p. xi.
[57] David Lloyd and Paul Thomas, *Culture and the State* (London and New York, NY: Routledge, 1998), p. 21.
[58] Stephen Marcus, *Representations: Essays on Literature and Society* (New York, NY: Random House, 1975), p. 326.
[59] Gramsci, *Selections from the Prison Notebooks*, pp. 262–3.
[60] Vincenzo Ruggiero, *Crime in Literature: Sociology of Deviance and Fiction* (London and New York, NY: Verso, 2003), p. 47.

side'[61] and hence can be turned over to Tiger Brown, High Sheriff of London and the play's sole representative of the law. Moreover, as he is in the process of moving his assets into banking 'altogether', Macheath is happy to sacrifice his gang members in order to bolster his standing with Brown. 'Within four weeks,' he tells Polly Peachum, 'all that human scum will be safely in the cells at the Old Bailey' (p. 37). Polly is appalled by his unapologetic hypocrisy but her outrage, justified as it is, also misses the point: if they are figured by Macheath as unproductive assets in a ledger book then, according to the rules of business, to 'write them off' is a prudent act.

To underline this point, Brecht declared that the 'bandit Macheath must be played as a bourgeois phenomenon' and offered the following qualifications. 'The bourgeoisie's fascination with bandits rests on a misconception: that a bandit is not a bourgeois. This misconception is the child of another misconception: that a bourgeois is not a bandit.'[62] Rejecting Hobsbawm's 'social bandit' thesis,[63] Brecht's desire to yoke together banditry and capital accumulation suggests that, as in *Red Harvest*, the resulting struggle between Macheath and Peachum should not be seen as one-sided and unequal, with our sympathies 'naturally' flowing to the underdog, but as squalid conflict between like-minded capitalist adversaries. The state, as personified by Brown, is not necessarily neutral in all this and, irrespective of personal relations, intervenes to ensure what Brecht calls the 'reduction of bloodshed to a minimum' as a 'business principle'.[64] Hammett's detective performs a similar role in *Red Harvest*, despite his self-evident dislike of Willsson and notwithstanding the fact that his initial efforts to bring the city to order result in an even greater orgy of bloodletting. As is implied by Gramsci's formulation, the state's encroachment into the private affairs of individuals is necessary to smooth out any disagreements between competitive individuals and ensure that the right conditions for business prevail. If it is true that the gangs in *Red Harvest* and *The Threepenny Opera* are to be seen primarily as bourgeois phenomena (and not manifestations of working-class unruliness), we might also conclude that the state is 'neutral' only insofar as it is happy to arbitrate between disputes amongst rival factions of capital. The absence of genuine working-class representation, meanwhile, is indicative merely of the manner in which class unrest has already been purged from existence.

In a critical appraisal of Brecht's *Threepenny Novel* which was published in 1936, eight years after the first production of *The Threepenny Opera*, Walter Benjamin described Brecht's text as a detective novel or an inversion or indeed an 'x-ray' of detective fiction:[65]

---

[61] Brecht, *The Threepenny Opera*, p. 36.
[62] Brecht, 'Notes by Brecht', *The Threepenny Opera*, pp. 82–3.
[63] For a fuller account of this argument about social banditry as a legitimate form of primitive rebellion, see Eric Hobsbawm, *Bandits* (London: Abacus, 2003).
[64] Brecht, 'Notes', *The Threepenny Opera*, p. 83.
[65] Benjamin first used this phrase 'something like the X-ray picture of a detective story' to describe Poe's 'The Man of the Crowd': see Walter Benjamin, *Charles Baudelaire: A Lyrical Poet in the Era of High Capitalism* (London: Verso, 1983), p. 48.

According to the rules of the detective novel, bourgeois legality and crime are two opposites. Brecht's procedure consists in retaining the highly developed technique of the detective novel but abandoning its rules. *This* detective novel depicts the objective truth about the relationship between bourgeois legality and crime, the latter being shown as a special case of exploitation sanctioned by the former.

Benjamin concludes:

> It is quite natural that in this borderline case of a detective novel there is no place for a detective. The role of agent of the law allotted to the detective under the rules of the game is here taken over by Competition. What takes place between Macheath and Peachum is a struggle between rival gangs, and the happy ending is a gentleman's agreement which formally apportions to each his share of the booty.[66]

Vis-à-vis Brecht's work, Benjamin's analysis cannot be faulted but it is not quite true that the originality of Brecht's novel lies in its inversion of the genre's separation of legality and crime or its insistence on collapsing this distinction. For a start, this account could just as easily be directed at *Red Harvest*, and not just because Hammett's novel also demonstrates how Willsson's willingness to flout the law to shore up his own interests are sanctioned because he 'was president and majority stockholder of the Personville Mining corporation, ditto the First National Bank, owner of the *Morning Herald* and *Evening Herald*, the city's only newspapers, and... part owner of nearly every other enterprise of any importance' (p. 12). We also see a struggle between rival gangs resolved in Willson's favour because he has the fuller resources of the state at his disposal. As I have also argued, Hammett's novel doesn't so much constitute a generic aberration (in the way Benjamin argues that Brecht's *Threepenny Novel* is) as a development or reworking of the genre's structuring tension between different versions or visions of the law, albeit one skewed in the final analysis towards the interests of capital. What distinguishes *Red Harvest* from Brecht's novel and play is, as Benjamin indicates, the presence of his detective, the Continental Op, but far from representing a neutral or even individualistic perspective, Hammett insists that his detective, whatever his misgivings and in spite of his desire to 'clean up' Personville, does the work that Benjamin allots to Competition; namely the re-inscription of the status quo.

Crucially, though, the Continental Op's complicity with and in a system he can see is not simply flawed but rather utterly vile produces within him such unease that it threatens to split him down the middle. The Op's self-division (and hence what we might see as his alienation) disrupts the smooth surface of Hammett's novel and produces in readers the same kind of 'jolt' that Brecht maintains is forged by 'epic' theatre's desire to reveal rather than reproduce existing 'conditions' and force its audience to think critically about what they are watching.[67] In doing so, Hammett's novel comes close to mirroring Benjamin's claims about the author–producer who does not stand outside of capitalism but interrogates its ills and shortcomings from an inside position and disseminates these interrogations widely,

---

[66] Benjamin, *Understanding Brecht*, trans. Anna Bostock (London: Verso, 1998), pp. 82–3.
[67] See Worrall, 'Commentary', in Brecht, *The Threepenny Opera*, pp. xxxii–xxxiii.

e.g. as Brecht does, as a precondition to further politicization.[68] More surprisingly, perhaps, some of the same tensions and undercurrents are latent in the Jules Maigret novels of Georges Simenon, despite Simenon's often-mentioned social conservatism. In this sense the advantage of seeing Simenon's Maigret novels and *romans durs* not as distinct but as part of the same social and political project lies in allowing us to clearly identify the operation of hegemony; not the smooth working out of power but characters coming to terms with the complexities of their own desires and the unstable effects of authority, figured by Simenon in terms that are more jagged and critical than some accounts of his work are prepared to allow for.

SIMENON AND HAMMETT 2: PAPERING OVER THE CRACKS

There is a brief scene in an early Maigret novel *Lock 14* where Simenon's erstwhile police inspector likens the pose adopted by his colleague during a car chase to 'a detective in pursuit of a criminal in an American film'.[69] If this indicates an awareness on Simenon's part of the influence of American crime fiction (and especially of Hollywood crime movies) on his own writing, this relationship, and the broader one linking France and the United States is more specifically thematized by the denouement of *The Yellow Dog*. Here, it is revealed that the chief suspect in an ongoing murder investigation, Léon Le Glérec, has spent time in New York's notorious Sing-Sing prison following his arrest and trial for cocaine smuggling. On its own, the affair is a minor footnote, a plot point that explains Le Glérec's antipathy towards the bourgeois hypocrites of the Breton town where the novel is set; men like Michoux and Le Pommeret who regard Concarneau as their own fiefdom and its inhabitants as subjects to exploit and discard. But it does, I think, underscore two significant preoccupations both for Simenon himself and for my book as a whole. First, it draws attention to the presence and influence of exactly the kind of trans-Atlantic circuits that my account of crime fiction has been seeking to explore. In this case, Le Glérec has been persuaded to abandon the typical trading practices of Breton's boaters—carrying 'early vegetables to England'[70]—in favour of the more lucrative, but illegal, trade in cocaine from France to the United States.

Just as Maigret is sufficiently cognizant of US movies to know that in *Lock 14* his colleague is driving like a cop, so the trans-Atlantic connections are deepened here by the presence of trading routes linking Breton port towns like Concarneau and Quimper with the eastern seaboard of the US and Canada. But the significance of Le Glérec's trading practices goes deeper than this. For a start we're told that he has been forced to abandon his bread-and-butter trade (i.e. vegetables to England) because of the worsening economic situation. As he says to Maigret, 'It

---

[68] Benjamin, *Understanding Brecht*, p. 98.
[69] Simenon, *Lock 14*, trans. Robert Baldick (New York, NY: Penguin, 2006), p. 87.
[70] Simenon, *The Yellow Dog*, trans. Linda Asher (London: Penguin, 2006), p. 112.

was a bad year. The franc was rising. England was buying less produce. I was worried about paying the interest' (p. 113). In other words, as Bill Alder argues, the 'crimes that Maigret investigates have social causes rather than being the outcomes of actions of aberrant individuals'.[71] While some critics are keen to disavow the socio-historical context of Simenon's Maigret novels (i.e. Dubois claims that they exhibit very few 'historical markers or indications of any larger political circumstances'[72] and Shorley suggests the novels, though imbued with a clear sense of class politics, downplay 'the importance of the history and politics of interwar France'[73]) Alder, rightly I think, argues otherwise. In *The Yellow Dog*, the same 1920s economic boom that has advantaged only men like Michoux and Le Pommeret and not the ordinary workers at the fish-canning factory is similarly exploited by Elihu Willsson in *Red Harvest*, at the expense of the miners who see little benefit. Likewise the depression that hits Europe and America at the end of the 1920s affects workers in Concarneau and Personville hardest and in turn precipitates both Le Glérec's turn to riskier practices and (to some extent) the miners' strike prior to the start of *Red Harvest*. Simenon may not parade his social and historical markers from the rooftops and his Maigret novels may not be as explicitly political as Hammett's, but as Alder concludes, because 'they are inherently a social project, the interwar Maigret texts have much in common with the style of crime fiction pioneered by Dashiell Hammett, in which crime is given a context that is recognizably that of contemporary capitalist America'.[74]

At stake here is the larger issue of how the detective, private operator, or employee of the state negotiates these social contexts; how or to what extent figures like Maigret and the Continental Op, as state agents or auxiliaries, negotiate a path between different, potentially antagonistic class factions, their superiors, and the demands of their respective offices, in order to do what they have been paid to do. Certainly it would be a mistake to see their actions as representative of an individualistic sensibility, i.e. that they act outside of or in opposition to the jurisdictional limits of the state. For McCann, *Red Harvest*'s seeming preference for the Op's violence as a means of bringing the city to order (as opposed to trade unionism, political reform, and progressive journalism which all fail to tackle the problem) sanctions radical individualism as the 'de facto philosophy' of the hard-boiled school.[75] Such an account, however, ignores the extent to which the Op's political credentials as unco-opted come under severe scrutiny. At first glance, and in the narrowest politico-juridical sense (i.e. thinking of the state solely as policeman—or what Gramsci calls 'Stato-carabiniere'[76]) one may well question whether the Op's first loyalty is to the state. After all, having been hired by Elihu Willsson's son Donald, a crusading newspaperman, to investigate political corruption, and then by Willsson to empty the city of 'its crooks and grafters' (p. 42), the Op loses the

---

[71] Alder, 'Maigret, Simenon, France', p. 55.
[72] Dubois, 'Oedipus as Detective', p. 109.
[73] Shorley, 'Georges Simenon and Crime Fiction', p. 44.
[74] Alder, 'Maigret, Simenon, France', p. 56.
[75] McCann, *Gumshoe America*, p. 78.
[76] Gramsci, *Selections from the Prison Notebooks*, p. 261.

semi-official status bestowed on him, particularly after his investigation threatens to expose Willsson's complicity in the mire of corruption. His near-assassination by the police chief, Noonan, seems to affirm his status as unwanted outsider and indeed the extent to which he is personally affronted by the city. 'I don't like the way Poisonville has treated me', he tells Thaler. 'I've got my chance now, and I'm going to even up... Poisonville is ripe for the harvest. It's a job I like and I'm going to do it' (p. 64). The Op is by no means ideologically co-opted, in the narrowest sense of the term, and his autonomy from Willsson in particular is evidenced by his linguistic prowess (i.e. when set against Willsson's flaccid blusterings) and by his refusal to play 'politics' for Willsson (p. 43). Later in the novel, he seems even more unsure which side he is on, telling his associates from the Continental Detective Agency about his conflicting plans for Willsson: 'Maybe ruin him, maybe club him into backing us. I don't care which' (pp. 108–9).

The apparent autonomy of the detective, private or public, has led many critics to characterize him (or her) not simply as an avatar of modernity but more specifically as a figure capable of bringing order to the city and representing the human face of the crime control apparatus. It is perhaps no coincidence that the proliferation of crime fiction in the 1920s and 1930s accompanied the expansion and penetration of the state into all spheres of life, and whereas Hammett viewed this intrusion with scepticism, Simenon, on the face of it, embraced the new technological innovations at the police's disposal and could see benefits to the expanded reach of the state. In *The Bar on the Seine* the main suspect in a murder enquiry is apprehended when forensic analyses have pinpointed his whereabouts to a particular geographical locale and the circulation of information to local police officers has led to a sighting of him. If this all seems too panoptic or instrumental, Maigret's modus operandi mixes psychology and humanism, and calls upon an ability to read people and scenes and to see 'everything at once with an almost unreal clarity'.[77]

Benjamin wrote briefly about the 'kriminalromane' in an essay entitled 'Crime Novels, on Travel' and according to Salzani considered writing a series of crime novels, possibly in collaboration with Brecht.[78] For Benjamin, crime fiction offered its readers the chance to momentarily escape from the boredom and anxieties of modern life and to forensically explore its dark textures and nuances via the figure of the detective cast as modern day flâneur.[79] Benjamin worked and corresponded with Siegfried Kracauer who produced a book-length study of the detective novel *Der Detektiv-Roman* (1925), a philosophically dense, highly instructive analysis which distinguishes between the figure of the detective who exhibits a rationality and ethical code linked to nameless higher sphere (with obvious Messianic connotations) and the forces of the law which the detective can call upon (and with

---

[77] Simenon, *The Bar on the Seine*, trans. David Watson (London: Penguin, 2006), p. 31.
[78] See Carlo Salzani, 'The City as Crime Scene: Walter Benjamin and the Traces of the Detective', *New German Critique*, 34:1 (Winter 2007), pp. 165–87.
[79] See Benjamin, 'Travelling with Crime Novels', trans. Aaron Kelly, in Aaron Kelly (ed.) *The Thriller and Northern Ireland since 1969* (Aldershot: Ashgate, 2005), pp. 165–6.

whom he maintains an ironic distance) but which are founded upon a legalism stripped bare of any real ethical content.[80]

Benjamin and indeed Brecht were both aware of Simenon and had read his early Maigret novels. While there are obvious points of contact between Benjamin's account of the modern flâneur and Maigret's apparently infallible gaze ('it saw everything at once, with an almost unreal clarity'), Kracauer's analysis is more instructive because it sheds light on an important tension in detective fiction generally and Simenon's Maigret novels in particular: namely between the rational, ironic voice of the detective and the legalism he or she at times unwillingly personifies. This tension is evidenced most clearly in *The Bar on the Seine* in which it is Maigret's job to find out who killed Marcel Feinstein, a Parisian tailor and shop owner, and an unidentified man whose body was thrown, six years earlier, into the Seine near a bar where Feinstein and others regularly socialize. According to the dictates of the genre, it is imperative that Maigret find the killer or killers and subject them to the due process of the law. But Maigret's gradual immersion in the group who socialize at the bar and his growing interest in James, an accountant who we're told was everyone's favourite and 'the person who bound them together' (p. 25), complicates proceedings and poses questions against his legal/judicial responsibilities. Indeed it is James who points to the absurdity or asymmetry of a situation where a squalid, personal dispute results in the 'whole machinery of the law swing[ing] into action' (p. 74), an insight that leaves Maigret 'with a sense of unease, which took him a long time to shake off' (p. 76). The law, of course, cannot accommodate unease or the ironic register that the detective must strike to signal this unease, which is exactly Kracauer's point. In the end the detective must restore order, and in the case of *The Bar on the Seine* (where James's culpability for one of the murders is revealed), this results, for Maigret at least, not in any sense of achievement but produces 'a dull, grey despair. A despair with no words of lament, no grimaces of pain' (p. 124).

Simenon's Maigret novels are more often regarded for their 'comforting tropes'[81] and while it is true they do move towards explanation, order, and closure, Simenon is not necessarily interested in papering over the cracks, or drawing our attention away from the kind of tension described above. By the same logic, Hammett, who is typically regarded as a more 'radical' crime novelist (whatever this term means—perhaps that his critique of capitalism is somehow more developed and central to his project as writer) wants us to see the Continental Op, first and foremost, as a state-sanctioned auxiliary, even if it is true that, as Freedman and Kendrick claim, his labour is 'bohemian' and 'non-alienated' at least when set against the 'economic' labour of the miners and the 'political' labour of the hired gunmen.[82] From these different points of departure, Simenon's and Hammett's respective positions begin to converge. Let us return for a moment to *Red Harvest*

---

[80] See Gertrud Koch, *Siegfried Kracauer: An Introduction*, trans. Jeremy Gaines (Princeton, NJ: Princeton University Press, 2000), pp. 11–25.
[81] Dubois, 'Oedipus as Detective', p. 108.
[82] Freedman and Kendrick, 'Forms of Labor', p. 210.

and the issue of the Op's unco-opted status. Aimed at ridding Personville of its crooks and grafters, the Op's labour is police work in all but name and he is being paid (by Willsson) to do so. Hence he treats the city's ageing patriarch in a qualitatively different manner than he does the other gang leaders or the other factions of capital. 'Thaler, Pete the Finn, Lew Yard and Noonan are the men who've made Poisonville the sweet-smelling mess it is,' he tells Dinah. 'Old Elihu comes in for his share of the blame, too, but it's not his fault, maybe. Beside, he's my client, even if he doesn't want to be, so I'd like to go easy on him' (p. 79).

My point is twofold. First, the Op constitutes a liminal figure in the novel, moving in and out of positions of authority and in turn suggesting that hegemony is not *always* successful in soliciting consent. And second we need to think about the Op's labour in the context of Gramsci's expanded notion of the state—by which he means not only 'the apparatus of government, but also the "private" apparatus of "hegemony" or civil society'.[83] As such, it would be wrong to see the Op *simply* as a state-sponsored vigilante intent on purging the enemies of the industrial–capitalist state, just as it would be equally wrong to see him as a pro-working-class sympathizer committed to furthering the struggle for rights and equality. Rather, he is best understood as someone whose private initiatives fall, though not always neatly, into the realm of the expanded or 'ethical' state. Gramsci's idea of the state here incorporates the apparatus of government with 'elite' organizations like the Church, schools, and, I'd argue in the case of *Red Harvest*, the Continental Detective Agency. Given the novel's linguistic slippages between the unnamed Old Man who runs the agency and old Elihu, who is also referred to as the 'old man', one could argue that both men personify a related logic of statecraft and power. As such, the Op's carefully expressed loyalties—to his job, the Old Man, and his role as detective—underscore not his autonomy but rather his uneasy place in this expanded conception of the state.

We need to be careful about making this point too unequivocally, just as we need to be careful about overstating the instrumentalist power of the state. To understand the state, via Gramsci and latterly David Harvey, is to think about a system of rule in dynamic, relational, and unstable terms.[84] So it is with *Red Harvest* which characterizes a world where corrupt lawyers, capitalists, and police officers are locked in a vicious struggle for power and control; in other words, a milieu of warring power blocs, shifting allegiances, and constant struggle. More particularly, we should not think that Gramsci's conception of hegemony—'the hegemony of one social group over the entire nation'[85]—requires a general wilting in the face of power. Rather, the operation of hegemony always presupposes the possibility or likelihood of opposition or struggle. Seen in this light, the Op isn't simply the lackey of a narrowly conceived politico-juridical state. Rather he moves in and out of subject positions that buttress the authority of the state and undermine

---

[83] Gramsci, *Selections from the Prison Notebooks*, p. 261.
[84] See David Harvey, *Spaces of Capital: Towards a Critical Geography* (Edinburgh: Edinburgh University Press, 2001). Developing this point, Harvey argues that 'The state should in fact be viewed, like capital, as a relation' (p. 280).
[85] Gramsci, *Selections from the Prison Notebooks*, p. 204.

it from within. As such, his desire to bring order to Personville (and to do so on his own terms) constitutes not only the practice of hegemony but also the struggle against hegemony.

Part of my broader argument about crime writing as a genre is that it performs a similar function; that, as a genre which has developed in different ways, under different historical conditions, crime writing is best understood as an ongoing series of negotiations with the proliferating state formation underscoring its ethical and coercive potentialities. Turning our attention back to Simenon, the Maigret novels, at first glance, may not appear to lend themselves easily to such a reading, particularly if one sees them as 'comforting' or smoothing over rather than opening up social divisions. My reading, expanding on an essay and book about Simenon's Maigret novel by Bill Alder,[86] takes exactly the opposite tack. That's to say, it sees these novels as riven by class antagonisms which replicate in some form or another the warring factions of Hammett's novel (though in a far less bloody and explicit manner) and in which Maigret is barely able to keep a lid on the resulting tensions and is himself sequestered, like the Op, into positions of authority that he is not entirely comfortable with. Alder's work instructively draws distinctions between different social strata as they're portrayed in the early Maigret novels, notably *The Yellow Dog*; between, say, the *notables* or 'members of the professions who, through their economic standing... lived apart from the rest of populace and governed as if by right', the haute-bourgeoisie as personified by the mayor who've risen to positions of authority through a mixture of hard work and duplicity, and modestly aspiring petit-bourgeois figures like Emma, a waitress, and Le Glérec who are victims of the *notables* and representative of the popular classes.[87] As with *Red Harvest*, the working class in *The Yellow Dog*, who work in the fish-processing factory, are invisible. The key tensions, then, relate not to a (Marxian) struggle between the owning and working classes but revolve around disputes among the bourgeoisie; between the establishment, if you like, and what Alder calls the *petites gens*, a group or class from which Simenon himself hailed. (As he said of his own background, '[w]e were poor. But not really poor, not right at the bottom of the social ladder.'[88]) Alder is right to point out that Maigret's sympathies are instinctively with the latter and that, in part, the Maigret novels exhibit '[p]etit bourgeois ideology in an age of monopoly capitalism'; a way of seeing the world that both desires stability and therefore supports the existing order and is anxious about a loss of status and position vis-à-vis the growing dominance of 'the most modern monopoly capitalism'.[89]

Nonetheless the question of how or how far Maigret himself offers what Alder calls 'a defensive shield for the petit-bourgeoisie as a whole'[90] is much less clear. This is not to disregard Simenon's social conservatism and his reticence to speak

---

[86] Alder, *Maigret, Simenon and France: Social Dimensions of the Novels and Stories* (Jefferson NC: McFarland, 2012).
[87] Alder, 'Maigret, Simenon, France', pp. 48–50.
[88] Simenon qtd Alder, 'Maigret, Simenon, France', p. 54.
[89] Alder, 'Maigret, Simenon, France', p. 54.
[90] Alder, 'Maigret, Simenon, France', p. 55.

about his work in explicitly political terms. Rather it's to put some pressure on an account of Maigret as a kind of mediator whose role is to balance competing interests and bring about a fair outcome. Both *Lock 14* and *The Yellow Dog* feature plots in which the dissolute rich are set against the ordinary man or woman: if not the working poor then, as Alder would have it, the *petit bourgeois* or *petites gens*. In the latter, the murder of Mary Lampson, a seemingly well-to-do socialite travelling through Paris on a barge with her aristocratic husband and a group of drunken hangers-on, finally implicates not her husband, Sir Walter, as Maigret, one suspects, would want it, but a broken down carter, Jean, who was once Mary's fiancé before being transported and who, after being reunited with her by chance, kills her in a fit of jealous rage for abandoning him. The result is a complex, messy situation best summed up by Maigret's caustic assessment of the wealthy. '[F]ull of good intentions. The trouble is that life, with its acts of cowardice, its compromises, its insistent needs, is stronger' (p. 148). Here Maigret is positioned, problematically for him, as defender of the establishment. In *The Yellow Dog*, meanwhile, though Maigret's intervention does, in the end, exonerate the hard-working and modestly ambitious Emma and Le Glérec and implicate the wealthy but cowardly Dr Michoux, there is no sense that it will bring any lasting sense of order and stability to the town, especially since the causes of social unrest and class tension remain wholly intact.

The complex tapestry of social affiliations and loyalties, and Maigret's not always easily discernible or comfortable position in the social stratum, finds its richest articulation in *The Bar on the Seine*. Maigret's gradual immersion into the social affairs at the bar, the *guinguette à deux sous*, allows him to witness at first hand the tangled relationships of the various players; relatively well-off people 'who owned their own cars' and who 'all owned boats—either motor boats or small dinghies'—'tradesmen, owners of small companies, an engineer, two doctors' (p. 25). One might expect Maigret, reflecting Simenon's wariness of the attitudes and affairs of the well-to-do, to take against their casual familiarity with each other and him and their leisured, inebriated lifestyle. But to our, and perhaps his, surprise Maigret finds himself drawn into their affairs, intrigued especially by James without quite being able to determine why. 'Maigret was part of the group,' we are told, 'without really belonging' (p. 25), emphasizing his liminality and of course echoing Hammett's positioning of the Op. Maigret's disdain, also expressed as self-disdain, comes across at times but it is tempered by an acknowledgement of his own complicity. 'It was a formless world', he says of James's Pernod-soaked self-contained existence, 'a teeming ant-hill of flitting shadows where nothing mattered, nothing had any purpose... A world into which James... with his apathetic way of talking, had sucked Maigret without seeming to do so' (p. 77). This sense of apathy, of nothing mattering, and Maigret's essentially sympathetic treatment of James's quasi-existentialist outlook (and perhaps his recognition of its value, on some level) runs up against the cut-and-dried dictates of the law where transgressions like murder matter very much. Here the self-divisions within Maigret are most pronounced and while, in the end, he will do as we expect him to do and uphold the law, actually doing this and arresting James for his part in one of the murders produces a sense of despair so strong that it threatens to unravel him as a person.

There are echoes of the Op's divided loyalties in *Red Harvest*. Indeed, if we see the actions of the Op and Maigret as simultaneously exercising hegemony and opposing hegemony (cast in terms of the unfairness and also the dry instrumentalism of the law), the distance between both men, and their creators, suddenly doesn't seem all that great, one of degree rather than substance. For Maigret's dull grey despair, read the Op's confused rage at what Personville is turning him into. 'It's this damn berg. You can't go straight here' (p. 139). Maigret, of course, reins in his despair in a quiet, dignified way, whereas the Op unravels further, only partially aware of the consequences, for him, of having to toe the line and uphold an order he can see perfectly well to be rotten. (This process reaches its zenith when he wakes up from a laudanum-induced slumber to find his hand touching an ice pick that's been thrust into Dinah Brand's chest and he isn't sure whether he had something to do with her murder or not.) In the end, just as Simenon doesn't make a big deal of Maigret's self-divisions and lets his anxiety dissolve into the ether, Hammett pulls back from the precipice and the Op's innocence is confirmed, allowing him to play his part in restoring order to the city. The irony of this is more pronounced in *Red Harvest* than it is in *The Bar on the Seine* or *The Yellow Dog*—in other words, the Op's role in returning Personville to its 'white collar soldiers' is set against his disgust at having to do so, hence his comment about restoring order only for Willsson to let it 'go to the dogs again' (p. 181). But if we turn to one of Simenon's earliest *romans durs*, *Tropic Moon*, what would seem to be a damning assault on the ills of colonialism in Africa grows into something darker and more ambitious and it is here, finally, that the affinities between the two novelists, especially regarding their ambivalent attitudes towards the state, come into sharpest focus.

The novel centres on a young man with good connections and prospects, Joseph Timar, aptly described by Norman Rush as ethically blank and a 'cloud of unknowing'[91] who arrives in Libreville in Gabon at the start of the novel 'flushed with enthusiasm'[92] and keen to make something of himself. In the context of colonialism, this is a euphemism for a willingness to exploit the native population and natural resources for personal gain, even if Timar himself is unable to reflect on his own complicity. Once there, he becomes entangled first sexually and then financially with Adèle Renaud, a woman who possesses a good deal more cunning and insight than Timar and whom he suspects of shooting dead a black man called Thomas. This is a crime that the white authorities are compelled to investigate, if only to keep a lid on simmering racial tensions and to be seen to be exercising the law. As soon as Adèle sniffs out Timar's connections, she persuades him to arrange, via his uncle in France, for them to be granted a three year concession to log a prime piece of land in the interior, in return for putting up the capital to finance

---

[91] Norman Rush, 'Introduction', in Georges Simenon, *Tropic Moon*, trans. Marc Romano (New York, NY: New York Review of Books, 2005), p. x.
[92] Simenon, *Tropic Moon*, p. 3.

the plantation. Simenon cleverly uses the ostensible crime in the novel, the murder of Thomas, to reflect on the larger crime of colonialism, even though no one in the novel, black or white, is able to see what we, as the readers, can see: the sexual degeneracy, callousness, and rapacious greed of the colonialists and the resulting loss of any ethical perspective.

In this sense, Timar is no Continental Op, at least not at first glance, someone who arrives in a new place, a new town, with the character and 'chops' to determine the course of events and perhaps effect change. Rather he is a limited, myopic man, subject to the kind of feverish sexual desire and jealousy that allows him to turn a blind eye to Adèle's crime, even though he professes a need to know about it, a need that is effectively neutered when she admits what she has done. His passivity finds physical form when, following a trip upriver to their plantation, Timar falls victim to dengue fever and is immobilized. Timar may see himself as a 'good' man but there is little to distinguish him from the other colonials, a point reinforced to us when, replicating Adèle's promiscuity, he has sex with a young black woman in a village hut. His pursuit of Adèle from the plantation back to Libreville, meanwhile, is not motivated by a desire to see that justice is done but rather is driven by jealous rage, the notion that Adèle may be having an affair with another white colonist.

By contrast, the Op arrives in Personville with both the pedigree and mandate to tackle the problem of political corruption, and his determination to effect change is bolstered when an attempt is made on his own life. 'I've got my chance now, and I'm going to even up... Poisonville is ripe for the harvest. It's a job I like, and I'm going to do it' (p. 64). The Op's initial efforts to determine who has done what to who and hence to bring about some kind of justice are partly successful (i.e. he deduces quite quickly that it was a bank clerk called Albury who shot and killed Donald Willsson, the novel's first murder, and later he proves it was MacSwain, a washed-up former cop, and not Max Thaler, who killed the police chief's brother). However by the time the seventeenth murder has been committed, even the Op who in any case has been instrumental in stoking the violence has lost track of who has killed who and why. His decision, then, to force Elihu Willsson's hand and compel him to call in reinforcements to bring the city to order ('You're going to tell the governor that your city police have got out of hand... You're going to ask him for help—the national guard would be best', p. 180) is not the rational act of a man in control of himself and the situation but an admission of failure and a sticking plaster intended to restore only the semblance or pretence of order—'all nice and clean and ready to go to the dogs again' (p. 181). But what is the larger point being made? Here we might look again at the end of *Tropic Moon* and the sham trial taking place in Libreville where a native man (who Adèle has effectively bought from a tribal leader to play the role of guilty party) is being prosecuted for Thomas's murder. The murder itself, up to this point in the novel, has opened up cracks in the ranks of the white colonials; between the ordinary ex-pats who are wholly unconcerned by the death of a black man and the representative authority figures (e.g. the police chief and governor) who see it as 'a very nasty business' (p. 16) because it has the potential to stoke the unrest of the natives and upset business (e.g. a little later we're told 'the blacks are furious' about it). Still, the fact that the governor is, in the end, willing to overlook compelling physical evidence attesting to Adèle's guilt ('it was the woman who killed Thomas—we have proof of it', p. 37) and sanction the sham trial of a nameless black man tells us all we need to know about the entangled relationship between the state, the law, and commerce, especially in a colonial setting.

One reading of Timar's dramatic last-minute intervention in the trial—he interrupts proceedings and shouts out, 'He didn't kill him! [...] It was her! And you know it' (p. 123)—would be to see it as an act of conscience, a desire to do the right thing before it is too late. But such a claim is undermined by Timar's febrile state of mind, the notion that he is in the grips of sexual jealousy so intense that he sees conspiracy everywhere. Unwittingly Timar stumbles upon an important truth: they are all in on it but it is not a conspiracy against him. Rather the conspiracy is one aimed at perpetuating the status quo; a quick, painless trial in which a local man is convicted and then the white settlers can return to the profitable business of exploiting the natives. Here the forces of the state (personified by the governor and police chief) and the interests of the loggers (notably Adèle) are conjoined and as with *Red Harvest* the status quo reinforces the legitimacy of an order founded upon the logic of exploitation and financial gain, i.e. capitalism and/or colonialism. In such an environment, the ethical claims of individuals like Timar and the Op (such as they are ethical) and of the exploited (the black natives in *Tropic Moon* and the miners in *Red Harvest*) are wholly ignored. In both novels, too, the capacities of the protagonists to effect meaningful change are severely limited and in the end little separates Timar who falls apart following his courtroom outburst and is instructed to leave Gabon and the Op who, but for the codes and strictures of his office, may well suffer a similar fate. 'It's right enough for the Agency to have rules and regulations', the Op says, prophetically. But 'anybody that brings ethics to Poisonville is going to get them all rusty' (p. 107).

If it's the rules that ultimately save the Op, we might reflect on what this suggests about the state and the Op's relationship to it; and perhaps think about extending our conclusions beyond *Red Harvest* and *Tropic Moon* to Maigret who by no means functions, in any straightforward way, as what Rush calls the embodiment of justice and 'the bringer of order'.[93] In Gramsci's terms, the need for and indeed *raison d'être* of the modern state arises out of the kind of competitive pressures and antagonistic class interests we see not just in *Red Harvest* and *Tropic Moon* (government elites vs loggers) but also in the Maigret novels (e.g. the *notables* or bourgeoisie set against petit bourgeoisie).[94] In all this, the state does not play a neutral role, adjudicating between the private claims of equal citizens but, as we see in *Tropic Moon*, intervenes to safeguard the smooth running of the economy. Perhaps Simenon would not want to characterize a novel like *Tropic Moon* as Marxist but the affinities are too self-evident for us to wholly ignore: despite what

---

[93] Rush, 'Introduction', p. ix.
[94] In this respect, Gramsci's work constitutes an important touchstone for later Marxist theories of the state, notably Nicos Poulantzas's *State, Power, Socialism* (London: NLB, 1978).

Harvey describes as 'the complexities, accidental events, fluid and unstable interactions, which surround political, legal, administrative and bureaucratic life' (and these might include the murders in both novels), the state has to 'perform its basic functions' and find a way of organizing and maintaining the capitalist economy.[95] But Timar's disintegration and the Op's anger at the iniquities of the moribund regime he ends up having to prop up could be construed as a kind of passive protest; an awareness of the problem without offering a solution. The Maigret novels and *Red Harvest* may paper over the cracks, but *Tropic Moon* tears off the veil and lets us see the situation for what it really is. And while the tone of the Maigret novels is less confrontational, we can see the Op's anger, Maigret's despair, and Timar's collapse as kernels of a more thoroughgoing political critique; crucially, though, it is a critique borne of despair and resignation, one that yields nothing and goes nowhere.

[95] Harvey, *Spaces of Capital*, p. 283.

6

'On the Barricades'
Crime Fiction and Commitment in an Era of Radical Politics

The year 1968 is often regarded as the high point of radical politics in Europe and the United States, not least in France which saw in May an 'unprecedented' popular revolt against the institutions of the state.[1] After 1968, the political energies of the myriad radical movements that briefly coalesced to threaten the status quo fractured and dissipated; prior to 1968 these same movements took their fights to the authorities and their capitalist partners, sporadically, in discrete, piecemeal situations. If this is a hopelessly reductive narrative, one that overlooks the extent and coordination of political agitation across American and European cities from the late 1950s and early 1960s and fails to fully acknowledge the volatile potential of revolutionary protest well into the 1970s, it serves as a useful structuring device for this chapter. The primary purpose is to consider the effects and implications of trying to incorporate the dissident energies and anger of radical politics into a form or genre historically orientated as much towards buttressing as questioning the authority of the state and legitimacy of the law. The chapter's historical bookends, which extend from the mid-1950s when Chester Himes relocated from the United States to Paris and penned his first detective novel, to 1981 with the publication of Jean-Patrick Manchette's final, completed crime novel *La Position du Tireur Couché* (translated from the French by James Brook as *The Prone Gunman*), are admittedly broad but significantly tilt the focus of critical enquiry away from Britain and to a lesser extent the United States and towards the European continent, notably France and Sweden.[2] If this offers implied support for Robert Polito's provocative claim that 'European writers have often proved savvier than their stateside counterparts at folding crime inside a radical social critique',[3] this also requires further qualifications.

---

[1] See Margaret Atack, *May 68 in French Fiction and Film: Rethinking Society, Rethinking Representation* (Oxford: Oxford University Press, 1999), p. 1.

[2] My shift of interest away from Britain and British crime fiction in Chapter 5 and this one is not intended to be read as a critical judgment against this body of work but rather to suggest that, following the influence of Doyle and Christie, British crime fiction in the first half of the twentieth century, with some notable exceptions, was less interested in interrogating the intricacies of the state system and its links with capital, and drawing out the political implications of these complex relations, than corresponding crime fiction traditions in either the United States or continental Europe. This is not, however, to suggest that British crime fiction of the era was not political in other ways.

[3] Robert Polito, 'The Real Cool Killers', *Bookforum*, http://www.bookforum.com/inprint/018_01/7312, accessed 26 August 2015.

First, as Polito cedes, there are always anomalies, notably for this chapter, the American Himes. There is also the question of what is meant by 'radical social critique' and whether writing can ever directly serve political causes and certainly writing as compromised by its affinities with power as the crime novel. Finally the idea that writers can be unproblematically straightjacketed into discrete national traditions or that it is possible to disentangle discrete strands of European and American crime fiction, given the nature and extent of transatlantic cross-pollination from the late nineteenth century onwards, is one that needs to be resisted.

If this last claim has been better acknowledged and serviced by scholars in French studies than their American or indeed their English counterparts,[4] there remains a tendency even here to claim French writers for their own—that, for example, Manchette's works offer a 'radical evolution in French crime writing' or a '[s]pecifically French reworking of the genre',[5] despite the acknowledged debt Manchette owes to his American hard-boiled antecedents and the numerous references in his novels to the curios of US popular culture. Likewise Sjöwall and Wahlöö's 'Report of a Crime' series, featuring police detective Martin Beck, is nearly always discussed in terms of the ways in which it intervenes in debates about the efficacy and failure of the *Swedish* welfare state;[6] and Himes's 'Harlem domestic' series is typically assessed, especially by his American critics, for its capacities to lay bare and confront the related problems caused by US racism and capitalism and in doing so to offer critical reflection on the larger failures of post-war American society.[7]

This chapter, and the book it is part of, is by no means an attempt to argue against such works: McCann's *Gumshoe America*, for instance, with its perceptive and far-reaching analysis of the limits of New Deal liberalism, is one of the sharpest and best accounts of Himes's fiction published. And yet, as critics such as Higginson and Eburne suggest, if there are other stories to tell about Himes and his work and influences, other connections to make, particularly ones linking the United States, Africa, and Europe in what Higginson terms a 'trans-Atlantic circuit',[8] we could surely make similar claims for the crime novels of Sjöwall and Wahlöö,

---

[4] See Claire Gorrara, 'Introduction' in Gorrara (ed.), *French Crime Fiction* (Cardiff: University of Wales Press, 2009); Gorrara, 'Cultural Intersections: The American Hard-Boiled Detective Novel and Early French Roman Noir', *Modern Humanities Research Association*, 98:3 (July 2003), pp. 590–601; Pim Higginson, *The Noir Atlantic: Chester Himes and the Birth of the Francophile Crime Novel* (Liverpool: Liverpool University Press, 2011); Alasdair Rolls and Deborah Walker, *French and American Noir: Dark Crossings* (Basingstoke: Palgrave Macmillan, 2009).

[5] Susanna Lee, 'May 1968, Radical Politics and the *Néo-Polar*' in Gorrara (ed.) *French Crime Fiction*, p. 71; Gorrara, 'Narratives of Protest and the *Roman Noir* in Post-1968 France', *French Studies*, 54:3 (2000), p. 313.

[6] See Andrew Nestingen and Paula Arvas, 'Introduction', in Nestingen and Arvas (eds) *Scandinavian Crime Fiction* (Cardiff: University of Wales Press, 2011), pp. 1–17; Michael Tapper, 'Dirty Harry in the Swedish Welfare State', in *Scandinavian Crime Fiction*, pp. 21–33.

[7] See Sean McCann, *Gumshoe America: Hard-Boiled Fiction and the Rise and Fall of New Deal Liberalism* (Durham, NC and London: Duke University Press, 2000), pp. 251–305; Thomas Heise, 'Harlem is Burning: Urban Rioting and the "Black Underclass" in Chester Himes's *Blind Man with a Pistol*', *African-American Review*, 41:3 (Fall 2007), pp. 487–506.

[8] Higginson, 'Mayhem at the Crossroads: Francophone African Fiction and the Rise of the Crime Novel', *Yale French Studies*, 108 (2005), p. 162.

and Manchette. We could claim, for example, that the former do not simply aim their 'political critique' at the 'Swedish welfare state'[9] but at the exigencies and contradictions of state power and its affinities with contemporary capitalism; or that Manchette's late work moves beyond its national frames to explore the incipient tensions in Western capitalist societies between the rights and freedoms that define modern political subjectivity and a creeping sense of powerlessness and despair in the face of an increasingly limitless power that knows no borders. By bringing these writers, and the politics informing their work, into productive dialogue, the hope is to create new ways of understanding the crime novel's capacities for imaginatively intervening in the world—and the limits of these interventions. The prevailing tendency to treat the genre's development in individual countries in separate terms, with some notable exceptions, mitigates against this approach.[10]

Crime fiction, as I've argued throughout the book, has always been a resolutely transnational phenomenon—from the numerous connections between Wild's London and Cartouche's Paris to the pan-European context of penal reform informing both Godwin's *Caleb Williams* and Vidocq's *Memoirs*. This transnationalism took off in the 1930s and 1940s, following the passage of writers between new and old worlds and the corresponding exchange of ideas—Simenon's brief sojourn in the US in the aftermath of the Second World War and Brecht's move there during the war, for example. But this movement and exchange of ideas, of influences, reached its first high point in the 1950s and 1960s and could be detected not just in the presence of American crime writers like Himes in Paris, and his interactions with French crime writers like Manchette, or in the extent of influence travelling in both directions across the Atlantic. More importantly it could be found in the developing political consciousness of a group of crime writers with nominal leftist inclinations (and not necessarily in explicit consort with one another) around the issue of the genre's complicated engagement with political protest.

These were not straightforwardly 'engagée' writers, in the manner imagined by Sartre in his seminal 1947 essay 'What is Literature?';[11] but if Sartre's emphasis on the writer as committed has led some to wrongly characterize him as politically naive (i.e. promoting the idea of writing as a form of political advocacy), we should remind ourselves that Sartre's uneasiness with what he saw as the left's centralizing tendencies finds its corollary in crime fiction's complex relationship with the structures of power that produce it. Certainly there is little evidence of what Pawling calls Sartre's 'philosophy and politics of hope, progress and human action'[12] in these crime novels but nor is there a turning away from political engagement either. These were nonconformists, ill at ease with the establishment and informed

---

[9] Nestingen and Arvas, *Scandinavian Crime Fiction*, p. 3.
[10] These notable exceptions, in addition to Higginson's *The Noir Atlantic*, include Charles Rzepka, *Detective Fiction* (Cambridge: Polity, 2005) and Stewart King, 'Crime Fiction as World Literature', *Clues: A Journal of Detection*, 32: 2 (Fall 2014), pp. 8–19.
[11] In fact '*littérature engagée*' for Sartre means socially responsible as much as politically committed literature with the writer taking responsibility for the political implications of his or her work. See Jean-Paul Sartre, *What is Literature?* trans. Bernard Frechtman (London: Methuen, 1967).
[12] Christopher Pawling, *Critical Theory and Political Engagement: From May '68 to the Arab Spring* (Basingstoke: Palgrave Macmillan, 2013), p. 17.

by the legacy of Marxism, keen to expose, through exaggeration and recourse to the absurd, the limits of the kind of rationalist epistemology that had typically been the genre's lynchpin, and to shine a light on abuses of power and the many failures of the justice system.[13] But they were also realists to an extent, whose characters, by virtue of their proximity to the centres of power, unwillingly found themselves forced into positions at odds with their professed faith in anti-establishment politics. Sciascia in Italy; Dürrenmatt in Switzerland; Himes in the United States; Himes and Manchette in France; Sjöwall and Wahlöö in Sweden—crime writers, all with their own distinctive voices and agendas, nonetheless committed to examining, in different ways, the effects of social breakdown, and all influenced, in various degrees, by the ever quickening circulation of radical ideas, and radical politics, of Marxism (in all of its hues and incarnations), Situationalism, Black Power, and a residual Surrealism, across national borders and continents.

There are two distinct phases in this unfolding story. The first focuses on two early novels by Leonardo Sciascia, *Il giorno della civetta* (1961, translated as *The Day of the Owl*) and *A ciascuno il suo* (1966, translated as *To Each His Own*); and an early novel by Friedrich Dürrenmatt called *Das Versprechen* (1958, translated as *The Pledge*). Broadly speaking, these novels, published between the late 1950s and the mid-1960s, mark the first wave of this more explicit politicization of the crime fiction genre. The structure of the novels remains essentially realist, in so far as a crime takes place and an investigation ensues, but the shared ambition here is to question the rationalist underpinnings of the crime story and in doing so to reveal not the neat confluence of justice, reason, and the law but rather the extent of the justice system's irrationality and its surrender to the interests of organized crime and capital (which are often figured as interchangeable). This prevailing sense of the irrational leaks into the narrative at the level of form, e.g. it produces a correlative articulation of the absurd which in turn unsettles, though not wholly so, the realist veneer of the narrative.

The second wave, though to some extent overlapping chronologically with the first, focuses on the period from the mid-1960s to the late 1970s. Some of the early novels of Himes's Harlem domestic series, such as *The Real Cool Killers* (1959) and *The Heat's On* (1961), perhaps fit better in this earlier group but in Himes's case the focus here is mainly on the later Harlem novels, especially *Blind Man with a Pistol* (1969) and the unfinished *Plan B*, started in 1967 but not published in French until 1983. Maj Sjöwall and Per Wahlöö's 'Report of a Crime' (Roman om ett brott) series, beginning with *Roseanna* (1965) and culminating with *The Terrorists* (1975), and the three late novels of Jean-Patrick Manchette, *Le petit bleu de la côte ouest* (1976, translated as *3 to Kill*), *Fatale* (1977), and *The Prone Gunman* (1981) make up my crime corpus. In these novels, the desire to confront the ills of modern social, economic, and political organization (e.g. racism, capitalism, the

[13] David Peace in a revealing foreword to Jean-Patrick Manchette's *Fatale* describes Manchette and Hammett as 'Great RED Writers' and includes other figures I'll explore in this chapter as part of this group, notably Dürrenmatt, Sciascia, and Sjöwall and Wahlöö. 'Foreword' by David Peace, in Jean-Patrick Manchette, *Fatale* (London: Serpent's Tail, 2015), pp. vi, vii–viii. Peace credits the translation to Manchette's son Doug Headline.

surrender of public life to private interests), is more pronounced, and produces both a heightened sense of the absurd (which in turn pushes even harder against the realist conventions of the genre) and produces a corresponding sense of defeat and failure, the realization that writing can change very little and that the power of the state and capitalism is too entrenched and too pervasive to get a grip on, let alone dislodge. The result of this tension—pitting the radical anger of the day, its reformist energies and revolutionary zeal, against the crushing realization of the state's immovability and of capitalism's permanence as a mode of a social and political organization—would be the realization of some of the most violent, angry, demented, unsettling, despairing, innovative crime novels ever published.

THE ABSURDITY OF REASON: SCIASCIA AND DÜRRENMATT

Captain Bellodi, Sciascia's police investigator in *The Day of the Owl*, is a committed jurist and Republican, 'a man who has played his part in a revolution and has seen law created by it'—as Sciascia so eloquently puts it, 'the law of the Republic, which safeguarded liberty and justice, he served and enforced'.[14] Bellodi's absolute faith in the law of the Republic, of the state, underpinned by reason and principles of fairness and equality (e.g. the law as 'definitely codified and the same for all', p. 29) runs up against the closed, violent, and partisan milieu of Sicilian existence. Hence, the law, as perceived by those embroiled in this milieu, is 'utterly irrational, created on the spot by those in command, the municipal guard, the sergeant, the chief of police, the magistrate, whoever happened to be administering it' (p. 29). At stake here, then, are two competing versions or visions of the state: one, Bellodi's, the virtuous Republican first envisaged in Machiavelli's *Discourses on Livy* and developed by Voltaire, where law, borne of reason and impartially administered, holds everyone, rich and poor, to account; and the other, that of Calogero Dibella, the informer who likens the law to 'a barbed wire entanglement' (p. 29) and which extends from Dibella to local Mafioso Don Mariano Arena and right up to the highest echelons of government, where deals are struck behind closed doors and where outcomes are rigged to benefit those with money who already wield power and influence. In the context of Sciascia's novel these two visions produce what Joseph Farrell calls a 'bilinear' structure where the official enquiry, led by Bellodi, into the murder of local businessman, Salvatore Colasberna, by party or parties unknown is 'paralleled by a counter enquiry whose principal aim is to frustrate the enquiry itself' and which 'proceeds from the heart of state'.[15] That is to say, it extends from those directly or indirectly implicated by the investigation, including Arena (a man beyond 'the pale of morality and law', p. 102, who could not persuade Colasberna to 'seek protection', p. 79) as far as shadowy figures at the highest

---

[14] Leonardo Sciascia, *The Day of the Owl*, trans. Archibald Colquhoun and Arthur Oliver (London: Granta, 2013), p. 30.
[15] Joseph Farrell, *Leonardo Sciascia* (Edinburgh: Edinburgh University Press, 1995) p. 70.

levels of Italian politics, for whom the law can 'be damned' (p. 92). These two visions confront one another most pointedly following Arena's arrest, during his interrogation by Bellodi, the Captain's jurisprudence and investigative savvy in the end no match for the mafioso's native cunning, amoral pragmatism, and ruthlessness—even if Bellodi correctly directs his questions towards Arena's business concerns, rather than the murder itself, and surmises, 'It's no good trying to catch a man like this with the penal code' (p. 100) and '[t]here should be a swoop made on the banks' (p. 101), not only for 'people like Mariano Arena' and revealingly 'not only in Sicily' (p. 101).

There has been a tendency among critics to identify *The Day of the Owl* first and foremost as a novel about the mafia,[16] despite Sciascia's irritation 'to see it read as a source of folklore' and at his status as 'expert on the mafia'.[17] However, Bellodi's passing reference to elsewhere ('not only in Sicily') and his interest in Arena's complex business arrangements—and indeed the fact that Colasberna is not killed, as some try to claim, 'out of jealousy' (p. 17) but because of his refusal to yield to 'the protection offered by the association...on a much vaster scale' (p. 19)—encourage us to see the specific problem of the mafia in western Sicily as speaking about or to the ills of modern capitalism. This in turn reminds us of Robert Saviano's claim that 'it is not the mafia that has transformed itself into a modern capitalist enterprise, it is capitalism that has transformed itself into a mafia'.[18]

In other words, it may be Sciascia's intent to show us 'what the mafia was in its shift from country to city'[19] and to underscore the extent to which the mafia's organization mirrored the workings of the licit economy. But his further qualification that 'capitalism is a mafia that produces' and 'the mafia is a non-productive capitalism'[20] allow us to see the descriptions of corruption and graft, of the steering of public work contracts to approved contractors, of the skewing of the law towards the interests of the powerful, and of Arena's relentless accumulation of capital through legal and illegal means as the product of, and comment on, a mode of socio-economic organization that extends far beyond Sicily. Hence Bellodi realizes that 'the whole of Italy is a sort of Sicily' (p. 117) and perhaps one could add the whole of Europe. Here, Claude Ambroise's argument that '[n]o matter how it appeared at the time of its publication, [*The Day of the Owl*] now seems less a novel on the mafia, and more a novel on the state'[21] or at least a novel on the state's imbrication in and with modern capitalism and vice versa is particularly insightful. In this novel we learn who murdered Colasberna about half way through: hence the real denouement, as Farrell points out, is the 'unmasking of the body politic'[22]— and what we find is not Bellodi's flawed, hopelessly idealized and, one should point out, resolutely liberal vision of the virtuous Republic underpinned by the sweet reason of the law, but, to quote Michael J. Shapiro, 'an alternative political ontology' where 'the

---

[16] JoAnn Cannon claims the novel is 'a riveting story of mafia intrigue'—see 'The Detective Fiction of Leonardo Sciascia', *Modern Fiction Studies*, 29:3 (Autumn 1983), p. 525; Barbara Pezzotti, citing Farrell, states it is 'difficult not to consider' it 'a mafia story'—see *Politics and Society in Italian Crime Fiction: An Historical Overview* (Jefferson, NC: McFarland, 2014), p. 77.

[17] Sciascia qtd in Farrell, *Leonardo Sciascia*, pp. 67, 11.

[18] Robert Saviano, 'Foreword', trans. Paolo Mossetti in Anabel Hernández, *Narcoland: The Mexican Drug Lords and Their Godfathers*, trans. Iain Bruce (London: Verso, 2013), p. viii.

[19] See Farrell, *Leonardo Sciascia*, p. 67.   [20] Sciascia qtd in Farrell, *Leonardo Sciascia*, p. 19.

[21] Ambroise qtd in Farrell, *Leonardo Sciascia*, p. 70.   [22] Farrell, *Leonardo Sciascia*, p. 75.

political' is located 'not within institutions and orientations towards these institutions' but rather is founded 'on the centrality of the encounter', e.g. between different accounts of the law.[23]

In this novel, Bellodi escapes unscathed, relatively speaking, despite his 'impotent rage' (p. 116) and, following a brief exile in his hometown of Parma, plans to return to Sicily—'Even if it is the end of me' (p. 120). This impotence is carried forward to Sciascia's *To Each His Own* where another good man—this time a civilian, Professor Laurana—unlike the hypothetical detective novels which the unnamed narrator reflects on, is not able to assemble a 'sure solution' from the rubble of facts surrounding him.[24] The critical consensus on Sciascia's crime novels would seem to emphasize their innovations rather than their continuity with tradition: Cannon, for example, talks about their 'departure from the norms of detective fiction as a reflection on the author's decreasing faith in the power of reason in an irrational world'.[25] But the novel that *To Each His Own* most recalls, intended or otherwise, is Godwin's *Caleb Williams*, where a seemingly well-intentioned, curious figure, without the sanction or protection of public office, intuitively discerns the truth about a murder that has been wrongly diagnosed by others, including those charged with implementing the law, but is unable to name and exact punishment on the guilty because they are protected by their elevated status and rank. In both cases, intentions, good or otherwise, matter little and their 'human, intellectual curiosity' is a character defect, a combination of hubris and naivety.

Caught between a realization that the sanction of the state is necessary to enforce the law and bring about a justice and an awareness, even an instinctive one, that the wealthy and powerful can do as they please, Laurana quickly begins to flounder. Therefore, when he is killed at the end—his corpse buried 'under a heavy pile of lime in an abandoned sulphur mine' (p. 138)—the inevitability limits its tragic potential. The verdict of Don Luigi, spokesman for the town, is both dismissive and damning. 'He was an ass' (p. 146). Sciascia, the writer and Voltairean, may extol his faith in reason and law—in an interview with Marcelle Padovani in 1979 he declared, 'Yes, I believe. In reason, in liberty and in justice which together are reason.'[26] By putting a book of Voltaire's love letters in Laurana's hand while he waits in the Café Romeris towards the end of the novel, Sciascia is perhaps making a point: in Farrell's words, that reason 'is the basis of civil and ethical value systems' and 'not the modus operandi of the investigator'.[27]

Reason, for Sciascia, is not or not yet absurd—it remains, for him, the basis of ethical claims and social justice—but the maniacal laughter of Don Benito when Laurana expresses interest in the man who may or may not have killed two men at the start of the novel is the product not of craziness, as Laurana initially surmises, but of fear (i.e. fear that the same men may come after him if he talks to Laurana).

---

[23] Michael J Shapiro, *The Time of the City: Politics, Philosophy and Genre* (London and New York, NY: Routledge, 2010), p. 6.
[24] Sciascia, *To Each His Own*, trans. Adrienne Foulke (Manchester: Carcanet, 1992), p. 53.
[25] Cannon, 'The Detective Fiction', p. 525.
[26] Sciascia qtd in Farrell, *Leonardo Sciascia*, p. 22.   [27] Farrell, *Leonardo Sciascia*, p. 79.

More to the point, reason, on its own, without being incorporated into the lifeblood of the judicial system, can do nothing to confront entrenched power: power that in this novel moves beyond the mafia to implicate the whole of society or at least the confluence of organized religion, money, and politics. Laurana's failure is borne of not heeding the lessons of words—by Camus—he reads. '"Only the action that affects the organization of a system exposes men to the harsh light of the law"' (p. 72). With Sciascia swapping Voltaire for Marx, insofar as the famous opening lines of *The Eighteenth Brumaire of Louis Napoleon* are echoed in Don Benito's claim that the vulnerability of the legal system to influence is initially tragic and then farcical (p. 96), the novel, as Shapiro says about *The Day of the Owl*, 'refashions force relations' by showcasing 'the micropolitics of daily survival' and the multitude of threats to individual citizens over and above 'the participatory "civic engagement" associated with orientations towards official political institutions'.[28]

If Laurana's failure to find a 'sure solution' reflects back upon an entire tradition of detective fiction, in which this failure is either corroborated (e.g. *Caleb Williams*) or refuted (e.g. the Sherlock Holmes stories), Dürrenmatt's *The Pledge* uses an even more self-conscious meta-fictional device to explore the limits of the crime story's typical dependence upon rationality and a rationalist epistemology. The events of the novel are related to an unnamed writer of detective stories by a retired chief of police, Dr H—, after Dr H— has attended a lecture given by the writer, which gives the former policeman the chance to rail against the falseness and artificiality of the form:

> No, what really bothers me about your novels is the story line, the plot. There the lying just takes over, it's shameless. You set up your stories logically, like a chess game: here's the criminal, there's the victim, here's an accomplice, there's a beneficiary; and all the detective needs to know is the rules, he replays the moves of the game, and checkmate, the criminal is caught and justice has triumphed. This fantasy drives me crazy. You can't come to grips with reality by logic alone... success in our business very often amounts to more than professional luck and pure chance working in our favour.[29]

Here the 'fantasy' of the detective story is set against both the 'reality' of police work and Dr H—'s account of a particular investigation, involving a close colleague, Matthäi, who pledges to the mother of a murdered girl that he will find and bring the murderer to justice. Dürrenmatt's unusual narrative structure—employing the same device used by Conrad's *Heart of Darkness*, a story within a story—is not simply an innovation for its own sake: rather as with Conrad's Marlow, it shields Matthäi from us and means we have no unmediated access to his thoughts and motivations. During Dr H—'s telling of his tale, in a car on a journey through Switzerland, they stop at a petrol station where he points out the pump attendant—'unshaven and unwashed' with eyes that were 'staring, stupefied' (p. 5), a man who has been 'obliterated' (p. 6)—who we quickly find out is Matthäi, in the present time of the novel. The genre's move towards unmasking or uncovering,

[28] Shapiro, *The Time of the City*, p. 5.
[29] Friedrich Dürrenmatt, *The Pledge*, trans. Joel Agee (New York, NY: Berkley Boulevard, 2000), p. 8.

then, relates both to the search for the killer and the explanation for Matthäi's descent into the abyss. In both instances the problem of rationality is implicated but Dürrenmatt pushes his account of this problem further than Sciascia, in that the rationality so prized by the detective novel and the criminal judicial system becomes, in the face of chance and the absurd, a form of madness. As Kenneth Whitton puts it, 'Dürrenmatt wants to show us that the ordinary detective story's belief in rationality is itself irrational. Human planning is futile because reality is unfathomable and defies calculation.'[30]

In his narrative, Dr H—describes the official investigation which identifies an itinerant pedlar as the murderer (the pedlar confesses, under duress, and then takes his own life) and Matthäi's decision to postpone his retirement in order to track down the real killer who he believes is still at large. With nothing more to detect, and no more evidence to gather and process, Matthäi is transformed from a reserved, diligent policeman, an organization man who 'used the police apparatus like a slide rule' (p. 10), into an obsessive, a drinker, someone on the verge of a 'nervous breakdown' (p. 84). In this new persona he turns to methods that are 'unusual' and even 'magnificent' (p. 120) but that are also arbitrary and ethically dubious. Earlier we've been told that 'laws are based only on probability, on statistics, not causality' (p. 9) and as such Matthäi's decision to purchase a gas station on a route that he believes the murderer might travel (based on assumptions about his domicile), and his hiring of a woman and more particularly her seven-year-old daughter Annemarie, who, unbeknownst to either of them, he intends to use as 'bait', has a certain twisted logic. His method, based on inaction and patience—on waiting, 'Relentlessly, obstinately, passionately' (p. 123)—has its roots in inductive logic but reason yields to something darker, obsession certainly but perhaps even madness, so that in the end the situation, we're told, becomes 'absurd' (p. 145). In other words, reality, so prized by Dr H—at the start of the novel, in opposition to the safe fantasy of the detective story, metamorphoses into an altered state where Matthäi is either mad or brilliant or both and where this madness is given official sanction, after Dr H—has thrown the resources of the police department behind Matthäi's scheme. Indeed, just as it seems he might be right, and the killer is about to take the bait, nothing happens, the trail goes cold, and Matthäi quite literally falls apart (p. 148). This permits Dr H—to castigate the tendency of the detective story to bring its constitutive parts into neat resolution—'hope is rewarded, faith triumphs, and the story becomes acceptable for the Christian world' (p. 150).

In his account, the ending of most detective stories is 'ridiculous, stupid and trivial' (p. 152) and the statistical model based on the logic of risk assessment which underpins the entire edifice of policing and justice is made to seem, at best, outmoded, and at worst irrelevant. The logic of police work, based upon the idea that patterns of behaviour can be discerned, is undone precisely because reality itself doesn't 'conform to [Matthäi's] calculations' and hence 'the worst possible thing *does* take place' (p. 152). Of course Dürrenmatt cannot leave it there and in

---

[30] Kenneth S. Whitton, *Dürrenmatt: Reinterpretation in Retrospect* (Providence, RI and Oxford: Berg, 1990), p. xix.

the end we get an explanation about the child killer from a very old, wealthy woman who married her chauffeur, a mentally ill man many years her junior, who she comes to realize has butchered a number of young girls. But her death-bed confession has no cathartic value; rather it feels, we're told, 'like a mockery' (p. 168): a ludicrous near-corpse explaining, without a shred of remorse, that she didn't bring her suspicions to the police at an earlier point, thereby saving the lives of at least two girls, because she feared embarrassment. Reality is made absurd and in so doing Dürrenmatt unravels, though not completely so, the shape and contours of the crime story. If there is a critique here of instrumental reason, as it is wielded in the name of the law, the attendant politicization is not imposed on the genre from outside but rather emerges from the struggles of the police characters, Matthäi and H—, to reconcile what they do, e.g. the everyday absurdities produced by police work, with the claims of justice. In doing so the commitment of the left writer is not evidenced by his or her taking sides in a class war but by self-reflexively assimilating the anxieties and problems of policing into the form of the novel and by problematizing the instrumentalization of rationality. Hence Dürrenmatt's claims that while protest remains a decidedly tricky proposition for the writer, not least because 'causes and effects are so entangled that we are unable to determine precisely what it is we have accomplished', there is, at the same time, 'a sort of duty to be a Marxist; but it is not a duty to parrot Marxist phrases, but to think Marxism through anew'.[31]

DE-MYSTIFYING THE CAPITALIST STATE: SJÖWALL AND WAHLÖÖ, HIMES, MANCHETTE 1

Sciascia wrote two further crime novels in the 1960s but, following Dürrenmatt's lead, turned his attention to other media and other literary forms in his middle and later years. Both became better known as playwrights than as authors of crime stories. Sciascia's work, especially *The Day of the Owl*, best delineates the hidden contours and fault lines of a shadow state—not the consummation of 'democratic proclivity and institutional success'[32]—but a complex nexus of personal relations in which civic norms are hocked to private interests. Still, his protagonist, Bellodi, is, as Farrell puts it 'too heavily idealised'[33] and too unaffected and individualistic in outlook to allow Sciascia to fully explore the implications for the whole criminal justice system of the web of affiliations he begins to sketch out. Dürrenmatt uses *The Pledge* to challenge the rationalist epistemology that, in part, underwrites the crime story and the judicial system but the insights we get of this system are too fleeting to properly service a contrary political agenda. In any case, the extent of what Galbraith called *The Industrial State* (1967) or Miliband called *The State in Capitalist Society* (1973)—following 'the extraordinary growth' of the bureaucratic

---

[31] Dürrenmatt, *Friedrich Dürrenmatt: Plays and Essays*, ed. Volkmar Sander (New York, NY: Continuum, 1982), pp. 304, 308.
[32] Shapiro, *The Time of the City*, p. 5.   [33] Farrell, *Leonardo Sciascia*, p. 22.

and administrative systems and the interpenetration of the 'state system' and capitalist enterprises[34]—would not have been fully apparent in the early 1960s. Hence it is to other writers, with leftist or anti-establishment inclinations (e.g. Sjöwall and Wahlöö, Himes, and Manchette, who wrote on into the late 1960s and 1970s) that we will have to turn to, in order to get a better sense of how the extraordinary tensions between the revolutionary impulses of the era, the coercive capacities of the state's institutions, and the expansionary ambitions of capital are negotiated in the era's exemplary crime fiction.

Maj Sjöwall and Per Wahlöö's police novels are less genre-bending than those by Himes and Manchette but they are no less significant as explorations into the nature and limits of state power. Rather than using the form of the police procedure, to quote John Scaggs, as a 'powerful weapon in the reassurance of the dominant social order',[35] Sjöwall and Wahlöö seek to forensically dissect the state apparatus not just through their intricate, painstaking depiction of police work *as work* but also through their efforts to use the strengths of the procedural form (i.e. its focus on a collective rather than on a representative exceptional individual) to lay bare an entire system. Here, following Leroy Panek and Peter Messent, the term 'police novel' is preferred to 'police procedural' because it draws attention to the ways in which the messy, banal, routinized nature of police work or procedure in turn allows us to see 'the *institutional and systemic* framework in which the police (and other law enforcers) work'—so that taken as a whole the police novel, as Messent puts it, becomes 'an ongoing (serial) enquiry into the state of the nation, its power structures and its social concerns'.[36] By using a popular form and anchoring the work in a recognizable social reality, where the effects of capitalism as a mode of social organization are readily apparent, Sjöwall and Wahlöö demonstrate a form of political commitment but avoid accusations of propagandizing by subsuming these articulations into the everyday realm of work and the workplace.

In the hands of less engaged writers, this approach—focusing on the mundane nature of police work and on a group of dedicated, if unexceptional, detectives simply doing their jobs—could be a formula for obscuring the larger political questions of the age (how is society organized, by whom, and for what ends?). But Sjöwall and Wahlöö's skill is to situate the investigative process in the context of the institutional and judicial systems in which it operates and to remind us that law enforcement in the procedural mode, as Eddy Von Mueller rightly points out, is 'an industrialized process': i.e. 'there is a complex division of labor, marked by professional hierarchies and specialized training...and like many industrial labourers, police officers are often alienated, both from their constituency (the public they are expected to "serve and protect") and their ostensible masters'.[37] To deal

---

[34] Ralph Miliband, *The State in Capitalist Society* (London: Quartet Books, 1973), pp. 47, 50.
[35] John Scaggs, *Crime Fiction* (London: Routledge, 2005), pp. 91, 98.
[36] Peter Messent, 'The Police Novel', in Charles J. Rzepka and Lee Horsley (eds) *A Companion to Crime Fiction* (Oxford and Malden, MA: Wiley-Blackwell, 2010), pp. 177, 178. Also see Leroy Panek, *The Police Novel: A History* (Jefferson, NC: McFarland, 2003).
[37] Eddy Von Mueller, 'The Police Procedural in Literature and on Television', in Catherine Ross Nickerson (ed.) *The Cambridge Companion to American Crime Fiction* (Cambridge: Cambridge University Press, 2010), p. 97.

with the first part of this formulation, i.e. police work as an industrial process marked by a complex division of labour, one only need look at Sjöwall and Wahlöö's decision to carve up the investigations so that each member performs a differentiated role and crucially to recognize this through rapid switches in the narrative point of view. *The Fire Engine That Disappeared* (1969) is exemplary: in the space of five chapters (i.e. Chapters 6–10), the third person omniscient viewpoint shifts from Beck to Skacke to Beck to Larsson Rönn to Melander and then back to Beck. This move away from what David Schmid calls the 'individualist emphasis' of much detective fiction, an approach which for Schmid 'limits the genre's ability to provide politically engaged critiques of capitalist...spatializations of power',[38] allows for a more complex account of the investigative process and lets us see how the individual activities of the group are part of the operation of the judicial system as a whole—which for Sjöwall and Wahlöö is not a politically neutral body.

The work undertaken by Beck and others may not be industrialized, in the sense that they are part of an automated production line, but the procedural method is certainly one that eschews romanticized notions of individual brilliance (e.g. the Holmesian detective with his leaps of intuitive logic) in favour of routine, legwork, and system. 'Police work is built on realism, routine, stubbornness, and system... And experience and industry play a larger role there than brilliant inspiration'.[39] Certainly there is great skill in the investigative methods demonstrated by Beck and others, as evidenced by Murder Squad's extremely high clear-up rate.

The Locked Room (1972) is a good example of the distinction between sloppy and 'good' police work. Beck, who has been convalescing after being shot and wounded at the end of *The Abominable Man* (1971), is assigned to an ongoing enquiry, initially designated as suicide by gunshot where the victim was found in a locked room but where, as Beck soon discovers, no weapon was found. Contra to the inadequacies of the initial enquiry, Beck sets about his task with customary dedication, digging into the victim's employment as a warehouseman and working out through forensically sifting through the warehouse records that the dead man had come upon evidence of drug smuggling and had used the information to blackmail the man who killed him. In itself, Beck's investigation is not necessarily revealing of the novel's political unconscious, to use Jameson's term.[40] Recalling Dürrenmatt, it is chance and not procedural rigour which intervenes to deliver the killer: forensics link the murder weapon to a gun used during a bank robbery seemingly carried out by a thief called Mauritzon (but in fact, as we discover at the end, perpetrated by his girlfriend). Mauritzon, by his own admission, shot and killed the warehouseman but he is not punished for this act because the evidence, despite Beck's investigation, is purely circumstantial. Meanwhile he is tried and found guilty of committing a crime for which he is innocent: robbing a bank and shooting

---

[38] David Schmid, 'Imagining Safe Urban Space: The Contribution of Detective Fiction to Radical Geography', *Antipode*, 27:3 (July 1995), p. 243.
[39] Maj Sjöwall and Per Wahlöö, *The Abominable Man*, trans. Thomas Teal (London: Harper Perennial, 2007), pp. 31–2.
[40] Fredric Jameson, *The Political Unconscious: Narrative as Socially Symbolic Act* (London: Routledge, 2002).

a security guard. Here it is not simply that the judicial system is unable to correctly apportion legal culpability; rather what rankles with Beck, and by extension the reader, is that his superiors openly dismiss his brilliant, painstaking investigation as 'scandalous' and the product of 'sheer fantasy'.[41]

The alienation felt by Beck and the other detectives, then, is not quite akin to the factory worker, the transformation of flesh and blood into an inanimate commodity, but they are undoubtedly estranged both from the general population they purportedly serve, especially the young, and from their immediate superiors. Both problems have been exacerbated by the nationalization of the police force in 1965 after which 'it had begun to develop into a state within a state',[42] an increasingly centralized and indeed politicized body where executive decisions are taken without any consultation with the rank and file.

If this politicization is partly evident in the early novels, e.g. in *The Laughing Policeman* (1968) where a decision is made to protect the US ambassador from anti-Vietnam protestors to the neglect of 'the regular duties of the police'[43] and where the police's handling of the demonstration—'clumsy and inept or…brutal and provocative' (p. 15)—induces a backlash among the citizenry, its consequences are that much more pronounced in a later novel like *Cop Killer* (1975). Here, a throwaway remark by a teenage girl, following a shoot-out in which a policeman has been killed—'we all hate cops' (p. 224)—seems to confirm, for Kollberg at least, the unbridgeable gap between police and policed and explain his own dwindling 'solidarity' with the body he ostensibly serves (p. 13).

Kollberg's decision to leave the police at the end of *Cop Killer* brings into focus this tension between ordinary police work and the political context for this work that has been gathering pace throughout the series as a whole. Beck himself may be politically underdeveloped at least in so far as he 'detested everything even remotely related to politics and that he promptly retreated into a shell every time there was any mention of…political involvement'.[44] But just as his post-marriage relationship with the leftist Rhea Nielsen provokes an uncharacteristic outburst against the police ('climbers or obsessed by a sense of their own importance or just idiots', *Locked*, p. 173), Sjöwall and Wahlöö let their own Marxist sympathies infiltrate the works (sparingly it has to be said) and give discernible shape to what we might call the emerging capitalist state only when it is justified by what's been revealed by a specific investigation.[45] Before their imminent or insider critique of this particular

[41] Sjöwall andWahlöö, *The Locked Room*, trans. Paul Britten Austin (London: Fourth Estate, 2011), p. 301.
[42] Sjöwall andWahlöö, *Cop Killer*, trans. Thomas Teal (London: Fourth Estate, 2011), p. 118.
[43] Sjöwall and Wahlöö, *The Laughing Policeman*, trans. Alan Blair (London: Orion, 2002), p. 5.
[44] Sjöwall andWahlöö, *Murder at the Savoy*, trans. Joan Tate (London: Fourth Estate, 2011), p. 121; all subsequent citations refer to this edition.
[45] Andrew Nestingen offers this persuasive account of the series' Marxist affinities: 'the novels increasingly suggest that the alliance between the Social Democratic Party and the capitalist elite works through the actions of often ham-handed welfare state officials who act in the interests of the capitalists, with whom they are aligned as members of a national elite.' See 'Scandinavian Crime Fiction and the Facts: Social Criticism, Epistemology, and Globalization', in Andrew Pepper and David Schmid (eds), *Globalization and the State in Contemporary Crime Fiction* (Basingstoke: Palgrave Macmillan, 2016).

socio-political/economic formation is unpacked further, I want to turn to Himes's Harlem domestic series because Himes offers us a complementary sense of 'the problem' (though of course inflected by the peculiar dynamics of race and racism); i.e. of being a 'good' cop and yet having to serve a body that seeks only to protect the social, political, and economic status quo.

Sjöwall and Wahlöö begin with their 'rounded and ultimately sympathetic' police detectives and tread cautiously and with all kinds of caveats towards something more political—what Nestingen and Arvas call 'ideological and political critique' and 'criticism of the police institution and associated bureaucracies'[46] and what I'm calling a move to demystify the contours of the capitalist state. Himes, meanwhile, the gung-ho maverick, unconcerned about causing offence, flips this dynamic on its head and gives us Harlem first of all, a vile, base, violent, predatory, exploitative milieu into which his two 'ace' detectives must fit and to which they are, in narrative and political terms, subservient. Himes's domestic stories—domestic because as he explains 'they generally concern themselves with the domestic life of Harlem' and show people 'eating, sleeping, carousing, wounding and killing one another'[47]—peel back the layers to reveal the foundations of racism and capitalist exploitation upon which the neighbourhood and city are constructed. It is typically stiflingly hot, as in *The Heat's On* (1961) where 'the flat lowland of Harlem east of Seventh Avenue was like the frying pan of hell'[48] and where the boiling pot analogy—what Fred Pfeil calls 'a volcano in constant eruption' or 'a sordid Walpurgisnacht'[49]—conjures up the spectre of black people quite literally 'cooking in their overcrowded, overpriced tenements' (p. 23), not as victims but as flesh and blood turned into objects by the dehumanizing logic of racism and capitalism.[50]

Across the series as a whole, Himes gives us brief glimpses of what a black community *could* look like—the Dew Drop Inn at the start of *The Real Cool Killers* (1959) where the 'colored patrons' were 'having the time of their lives';[51] or the impromptu barbecue at the start of *Cotton Comes to Harlem* (1965) where 'nothing troubled the jubilance of these dark people filled with hope'.[52] But almost immediately this veneer is stripped away to reveal the baser practices of exploitation which inevitably set black people against one another in what Manthia Diawara calls 'a perverse mimicry of the status quo'.[53] The Dew Drop Inn is the scene of

[46] Nestingen and Arvas, 'Introduction', p. 3.
[47] Chester Himes qtd in Oliver Belas, 'Chester Himes's The End of a Primitive: Exile, Exhaustion, Dissolution', *Journal of American Studies*, 44:2 (May 2010), p. 382.
[48] Himes, *The Heat's On* (London: Allison & Busby, 1992), p. 23.
[49] Fred Pfeil, *Another Tale to Tell: Politics and Narrative in Postmodern Culture* (London: Verso, 1990), p. 66.
[50] 'Seen by others solely as instruments for realising their own ends', McCann comments, citing Michael Denning, 'the people in Himes's world are rapidly reduced, as Himes puts it elsewhere, to "meat".' See McCann, *Gumshoe America*, p. 291.
[51] Himes, *The Real Cool Killers*, in Robert Polito (ed.), *Crime Novels: American Noir of the 1950s* (New York, NY: Library of America, 1997), p. 733.
[52] Himes, *Cotton Comes to Harlem* (London: Allison & Busby, 1988), p. 6.
[53] Manthia Diawara, 'Noir by Noirs: Towards a New Realism in Black Cinema', *African-American Review*, 27:4 (Winter 1993), p. 528.

two mutually reinforcing 'scenes' of exploitation—it is where white businessman Ulysses Galen hawks his overpriced King Cola products and where he rents space from Big Smiley, the black owner, to whip young black girls for money. The barbecue, meanwhile, is merely a pretext or ruse dreamt up by Deke O'Malley, a black conman, for tricking poor black people out of their life savings.

If Harlem, for Himes, is a milieu inhabited by thieves, conmen, addicts, prostitutes, and gamblers, precisely because these are the only subjectivities that can survive in a world debased by capitalism, his plots, essentially thinly disguised reworkings of Dashiell Hammett's *The Maltese Falcon*, typically revolve around to-the-death struggles to locate objects of perceived value, conceived, by Himes, as reversals of the logic of commodity fetishism. That is, the hunt presupposes the true (base) economic character of the participants (and of the scene itself) rather than analogizing the operation of the market as neutral and disinterested, only to then uncover its exploitative tendencies. In *The Heat's On*, a gallery of black grotesques including Sister Heavenly, a small-time heroin dealer who conceals her produce in the rectums of rabbits, Uncle Saint, her put-upon lackey, Gus and his wife, and an African from Ghana vie with the syndicate to locate a missing shipment of heroin, all turning on and in some instances killing each other or themselves. As a witness to violence says in *Blind Man with a Pistol* (1969), 'Suddenly they were savaging one another like wild beats'.[54] The literal manifestation of canine-eating-canine comes when Sister Heavenly methodically disembowels a dog—wrongly, as it turns out, believing heroin has been stashed in its stomach because there 'wasn't anything she wouldn't do for money' (p. 135). As Cassuto aptly puts it, 'Himes has no confidence in the binding ability of social contracts: the ideal of rational self-interest never establishes itself, so crowds lead to conflagration.'[55]

If a liberal account of the market emphasizes freedom and mobility (social, geographical, and economic), Himes's Harlem, despite its thriving black economy (no pun intended) is no borderless domain of free exchange and movement, even in its apparently unregulated chaos. Distorted by the politics of race and by subsequent efforts to corral the black population into segregated and heavily policed ghettoes, whites are permitted to enter Harlem to do business, typically to buy sex, but blacks are encouraged, and at times compelled by force, to remain in their ghetto, their illegalities tolerated so long as they don't spill out beyond the ghetto borders. The role of the police, as agents of the state, is both a straightforward and complex one: to enforce this racial segregation and to facilitate white movement in and out of Harlem, and to manage the subsequent and at times combustible interracial exchanges. As Grave Diggers tells a white man, who has come to a Harlem brothel for sex, 'If you white people insist on coming up to Harlem where you force colored people to live in vice-and-crime-ridden slums, it's my job to see that you are safe' (*Real Cool Killers*, p. 788).

Here, then, the contours of the capitalist state or the state in capitalism begin to assume particular form, vis-à-vis the imperatives of race and racism: what Manning

---

[54] Himes, *Blind Man with a Pistol* (London: Allison & Busby, 1986), p. 69.
[55] Leonard Cassuto, *Hard-Boiled Sentimentality: The Secret History of American Crime Stories* (New York, NY: Columbia University Press, 2009), p. 228.

Marable describes as an ever more 'authoritarian mode of race and class control'.[56] Marable's account is so useful for dissecting Himes's depiction of Harlem because by arguing that racial oppression has its roots in the economic realm or at least that racism and economic exploitation cannot be disentangled, he is drawing attention, as is Himes, to the difficulties, if not the impossibility, of black people ever achieving genuine freedom 'within the political economy of capitalism' whereby the actions of the state must and do reinforce the 'essentially oppressive' character of a system of rule 'grounded in the continuing dynamics of capital accumulation and the exploitation of labor power'.[57] These conditions, where oppression is systematized and made inevitable, and where despair must prevail, despite what Himes describes in a later novel as the complexity of black poetry and dreams ('enough to throw a Harvard intellectual', *Blind Man*, p. 173) make Harlem virtually unpoliceable. 'We got the highest crime rate on earth', Grave Digger tells his white boss, before outlining the root causes, both political and economic. 'And there ain't but three things to do about it. Make the criminals pay for it—you don't have to do that; pay the people enough to live decently—you ain't going to do that; so all that's left is let 'em eat one another up' (*Cotton*, p. 14).

To claim that Himes's novels lay bare the contours of the capitalist state—or what Marable calls the increasingly authoritarian mode of racial and class control—is fine up to a point but exactly what this thing is and how Himes's portrait of the interlocking axes of state power and capitalism moves on or troubles the terms of debate about the state's not necessarily clear-cut relationship with capital requires further elucidation. It was Marx who famously argued, in *The Communist Manifesto*, that the 'executive of the modern state is but a committee for managing the common affairs of the whole bourgeoisie',[58] and from this comes David Harvey's claim that the state has always been 'a central pivot to the functioning of capitalist societies'. Harvey's qualification—that the state's 'forms and mode of functioning have changed as capitalism has matured'[59]—allows us to move beyond a functionalist account of the relationship between economic and political realms.

This position is developed most fruitfully by Nicos Poulantzas in his claim about the 'relative autonomy' of the state and his subsequent account, following Gramsci, of the state not as a weapon or instrument of domination but as series of structural relationships or networks and of capital as volatile, divided, and fractious.[60] In the end, this account is marked by an intensification of the state's reach and authority, albeit one that recognizes, as Bob Jessop puts it, that any changes in the form of the state must in turn problematize its 'functions for capital'.[61] On a personal level, Himes had little time for Marx and his acolytes, arguing as Wright had done before

---

[56] Manning Marable, *How Capitalism Underdeveloped Black America: Problems in Race, Political Economy, and Society* (London: Pluto Press, 2000), p. xviii.
[57] Marable, *How Capitalism Underdeveloped Black America*, p. xxxviii.
[58] Karl Marx, *The Essential Writing of Karl Marx* (St Petersburg, FL: Red and Black, 2010), p. 163.
[59] David Harvey, *Spaces of Capital* (Edinburgh: Edinburgh University Press, 2001), p. 269.
[60] Nicos Poulantzas, *State, Power, Socialism* (London: New Left Books, 1978).
[61] Bob Jessop qtd in Peter Bratsis, 'Unthinking the State: Reification, Ideology and the State as a Social Fact', in Stanley Aronowitz and Peter Bratsis, *Paradigm Lost: State Theory Reconsidered* (Minneapolis, MN: University of Minnesota Press, 2002), p. 248.

him that the Communists had never 'really worked toward any solution to the Negro problem in the United States'.[62] And even if his depiction of Harlem wants to claim racial and economic oppression as inseparable, his account of the state, and indeed the capitalist state, admits to none of these nuances and complexities. In all of this, his two detectives Coffin Ed Johnson and Grave Digger Jones are parachuted into the novels, sometimes not until the third or fourth chapters, by which time it is too late to halt the escalating violence, and are presented with the unenviable and in fact impossible task, as black men, of enforcing a set of laws, to quote Heise, 'that secure a racist society that victimizes them' or at least perpetuate their own subordination.[63] In other words, what we are presented with in Himes's Harlem novels is an account of the capitalist state not as fractious and volatile but rather as monolith (i.e. law = white power).

Under the weight of Himes's unrelenting efforts to flatten any distinctions between capital, whiteness, and the justice system (where the significance of race in the perpetuation of institutional and class power cannot be underestimated), the idea that the crime novel can intervene as a politically progressive force to expose injustice and speak truth to power comes under severe pressure. In all of this, one should not lose sight of the many successes of Himes's two 'ace' detectives, right the way up until the penultimate (completed) novel of the series, *Cotton Comes to Harlem*, in bringing the narratives to uneasy resolution (e.g. providing explanations, negotiating the institutional racism, and identifying if not actually bringing the perpetrators to justice). As Coffin Ed says, in *The Heat's On*, to reiterate his centrist views and to restate the importance of law to these views: 'Folks just don't want to believe that what we're trying to do is make a decent, peaceful city for people to live in, and we're going about it the best way we know how' (p. 174). The problem for Himes and his two detectives is that their room for manoeuvre is so limited. The resulting frustration (whereby the lumpen black population are condemned to 'eat one another up' and where the law can do next to nothing to prevent this from happening) manifests itself in an absurdist, politically inflected vision of comic incongruity and grotesquery. This surreal amalgam would only do so much work for Himes, however, and as the series progressed and the frustrations (of the author and detectives) grew, this absurdist vision would succumb to the call for organized political violence and with this came the realization, for Himes especially, of the limits of the crime novel as a vehicle for radical protest.

It harder to see the protagonist of Jean-Patrick Manchette's *Fatale* (1977), the professional killer and avenging angel, Aimée Joubert, as heir to Coffin Ed and Grave Digger—the capitalist state's unwilling executioner, a person caught between competing visions of society and justice but who in the end must serve the interests of the authorities. For a start, Aimée is, ostensibly at least, a free agent, someone who finds her own victims (rather than working for a third party) and has no need for the state's resources. Additionally, her targets would seem to be plucked from the bosom of the class, the *haute bourgeoisie*, that have most benefited from the

---

[62] See Michel Fabre and Robert E. Skinner (eds), *Conversations with Chester Himes* (Jackson, MS: University Press of Mississippi, 1995), p. 28.
[63] Heise, 'Harlem is Burning', p. 499.

cosy arrangement between the state and capitalism. Potentially at least this establishes Aimée as a protest figure whose actions—setting the town's great and good at one another's throats and presiding over the resultant destruction—end up furthering a progressive, even an anti-capitalist/anti-statist agenda. If we interpret Manchette's work straightforwardly through the lens of protest—as Platten puts it, 'a site of resistance to the perceived violence of the State' or attack 'on the ravages of trans-national capitalism and its deleterious effects on the individual and community',[64] or to use Margaret Atack's phrase 'a renewal of the genre directly related to 1968 and the themes of protest: the power of the state, police brutality and the need for social and political change'[65]—this type of reading is hard to dislodge, even if Platten is right that the novels lay bare the destructive tendencies of capital.

Manchette's own musings on the subject are maddeningly elliptical and even contradictory: on the one hand he dismisses the connection between his use of 'Marxist categories, Situationist categories' and the notion that his novels 'have a revolutionary function'; on the other hand he talks about the 'carefully crafted "Marxist" architecture' of *Fatale* and the 'affinity between a downgraded nihilist and an offshoot of the former ruling class, both at odds with the current ruling class'. He also claims that the novel is structured around three political quotes:

> Baron Jules' speech... on the transient character of bourgeois rule, which comes from an Engels' article... [the Baron's] last words, extracted from Hegel's *Phenomenology of the Spirit*... about individual criminal revolt... [and] the last sentence, which is by de Sade... [on] the need to move away from the bourgeois moment in order to rebuild a Unitarian world.[66]

But what exactly does this add up to? If by Manchette's own admission his novel has no revolutionary function, what hope should we invest in claims about the transience of bourgeois rule—especially in the face of rebellion that is individualized and hence in Engels's terms easily crushed? Rather than trying to answer this question head-on, I'd like to focus attention on the question of Aimée's revolutionary potential and how during the course of the novel this is increasingly ensnared by the power she ostensibly opposes.

It is understandable that scholars would want to claim Manchette as protest writer—as Claire Gorrara puts it, a writer of 'powerful narratives of protest'[67]—but exactly what his novels are protesting against and what protest means in a culture and at a moment where the revolution, by the time Manchette published *Fatale*, seemed an increasingly distant prospect, still needs to be teased out. To do this, it is helpful to think about *Fatale* in relation to Dashiell Hammett's *Red Harvest*,[68] and not just because of Manchette's self-acknowledged debt to Hammett

---

[64] David Platten, 'Violence and the Saint: Political Commitment in the Fiction of Jean Amila', in David Gascoigne (ed.) *Violent Histories: Violence, Culture and Identity in France from Surrealism to the Néo-Polar* (Bern: Peter Lang, 2007), p. 176.
[65] Atack, *May 68 in French Fiction and Film*, p. 123.
[66] Manchette qtd in 'Foreword by David Peace', in Jean-Patrick Manchette, *Fatale* (London: Serpent's Tail, 2015), pp. vi, vii–viii. Peace credits the translation to Manchette's son Doug Headline.
[67] Gorrara, 'Narratives of Protest', p. 313.
[68] Gorrara asserts *Red Harvest* is a novel 'to which [*Fatale*] could be very productively compared'. See 'Narratives of Protest', p. 322.

whom he described as 'the best novelist in the world, since 1920'.[69] There are the some obvious points of connection between the two novels cemented by Manchette's appreciation for Hammett in particular and American hard-boiled crime fiction in general. The nomenclature of the towns is similar—Bléville and Personville—as is the *poisoning* effects of capital, blé being slang for money. As in *Red Harvest*, too, *Fatale*'s elites, whose activities blur the distinction between legal and illegal, turn on each other, with a little help from Aimée, until no one is left alive, including Aimée who has reaped her own bloody harvest and who in this respect recalls the Continental Op. To push this last point, I want to take Manchette's assessment of Hammett—that his characters 'have only lying rotters to deal with' and that 'the pleasure they take in cleaning up a city or an affair is bitter, for the more they clean up, the more general filthiness of the world appears'[70]—and apply the resulting logic to *Fatale*.

In light of my reading of *Red Harvest* (see Chapter 5) and the Op's fraught complicity with the state in its expanded or ethical form, as interpreted by Gramsci as the interpenetration of civil and political society, it is intriguing to see how far the comparisons with *Fatale* extend. In Hammett's novel, the Op's self-professed independence and neutrality is gradually eroded by his proximity to the Personville czar, Elihu Willsson, and the Continental Detective Agency, which forces him to uphold order in such a way as to strip him of ethical pretension. Aimée is not beholden to another person but nor is she a free spirit or a politically motivated vigilante. In a revealing afterword, Jean Echenoz describes how Manchette identified the passage where Aimée pulls out 'fistfuls of banknotes' and rubs them 'against her sweat-streaked belly and against her breasts and her armpits and between her legs and behind her knees',[71] as the novel's 'primal scene'.[72] As such, Aimée is motivated by and beholden to money and by implication to what money buys or represents, namely capital, though not in a straightforward manner.

Aimée might try and comfort herself with the thought she just kills 'assholes' by insinuating herself into wealthy circles and exploiting 'the conflicts that invariably arose among them' (p. 68). In this respect at least, there is an ethical aspect to her character, hence her reluctance to follow through with her plan to kill Baron Jules (who detests the 'assholes' more than she does and who has compiled incriminating dossiers on the town's players). But, as per the contracts she has drawn up with 'the pillars of Bléville's prosperity' (p. 22), kill him she does, and having done so, Aimée consciously or otherwise strengthens the position of the town's 'assholes'. Up to this point and notwithstanding her regret at having killed the baron, Aimée's work, the contracts she executes, her professionalism, her meticulous attention to detail, her restraint and control over her body, her rational self-interest, and ability to defer gratification and save for the future establish her as capitalist subject par excellence. What still needs to be considered is the implications of her 'blood simple'

---

[69] Manchette, 'Foreword by David Peace', p. v.
[70] Manchette, 'Foreword by David Peace', p. x.
[71] Manchette, *Fatale*, trans. Donald Nicholson-Smith (New York, NY: New York Review of Books, 2011), p. 6.
[72] See Jean Echenoz, 'Afterword', *Fatale*, p. 97.

rampage at the end of the novel and her assassination of the same 'assholes' who hired her to kill Jules for money: i.e. whether this constitutes resistance and if so resistance to what?

From the outset there is nothing self-consciously political about Aimée's actions, even if her decision to kill her abusive husband could be construed as a political act. When Baron Jules spouts his Marxist–Hegelian rhetoric about poverty being a consequence of 'the increase of constant capital as compared with variable capital' (p. 39), her response is incomprehension. On the face of it Manchette wants us to see Aimée's killing spree as penance: a *volte fa*ce brought on by her realization that she has committed a grave wrong by shooting Jules and in doing so buttressing the authority and logic of capital—for we, like her, see the hollowness of Lorque and Lenverguez's claims about capitalism as socially useful (for example their celebration of a new business venture 'capable of toppling the barriers of social class because it contributes to the prosperity of all, of workers, of business owners, of those in the service sector', p. 16). The reference to the workers reminds us that they are wholly absent in the novel, notably at the end when we are told that they were sleeping 'FOR JUST A WHILE LONGER' (p. 90); hence if we are to see Aimée's killing as a political act, as a solo initiative, it is destined to achieve very little. Just as Engels realized as early as 1843, citing the ease with which such individual acts of criminality-as-protest were 'crushed' by the 'immense superiority' of the state,[73] Gorrara nicely observes that 'Aimée's resolutely non-intellectual and individualistic quest for natural justice is equally flawed as a sustained form of radical protest'.[74] But it also should remind us of a similar absence in *Red Harvest*: hence we need to ask whether Aimée's individualized violence resembles the Op's and whether the relationship between Aimée and Bléville's ruling elite, in the absence of wider working-class agitation, must be construed as antagonistic.

To put this another way, if the bloodletting in *Red Harvest* is best understood as a containable if admittedly nasty struggle between different factions of capital, rather than a genuine 'crisis of authority' for the state, could we apply the same logic to *Fatale*? Here it is worth bringing Poulantzas back in, not least because his great work, *State, Power, Socialism* (1978), one that owes a significant debt to Gramsci and that pushes against classical Marxism in ways that Manchette may have approved, was first published a year after *Fatale*. Instead of seeing power as an instrument, 'a quality attached to a class "in-itself", understood as a collection of agents', Poulantzas argues that it 'depends upon, and springs from, a relational system of material places occupied by particular agents' and hence the state 'is a site and a center of the exercise of power, but it possesses no power of its own'.[75] In this sense, the fact that Aimée assassinates all of the 'assholes' (before being shot by Lorque's wife) cannot be seen as an assault against power or indeed against the state (which possesses no power) because power is structurally embedded in the system which of course remains untouched. Eschewing an instrumentalist account of

---

[73] Friedrich Engels, *The Condition of the Working Class in England*, ed. Victor Kiernan (London: Penguin, 1987), p. 224.
[74] Gorrara, 'Narratives of Protest', p. 323.
[75] Poulantzas, *State, Power, Socialism*, pp. 147, 148.

capital and the state for a relational one allows Poulantzas to develop a Gramscian 'war of position' argument (e.g. the struggle between competing power blocs) well suited to Manchette's dyspeptic vision of the haute bourgeoisie turning on itself. But here it makes most sense, following Hammett, to see Aimée not as destroyer per se but as catalyst and symptom of the volatile, fractious nature of capital and, since the conditions that made social relations in Bléville are unaltered at the end, of the state's capacities, as Poulantzas would have it, for safeguarding the long-term interests of capitalism, even as the day-to-day affairs of the state are temporarily threatened by the nakedness of Aimée's violence. This, then, is an example of the bitterness produced by 'cleaning up a city': the fact that this cleansing work produces more 'general filthiness', not more order, and certainly not Manchette's hoped-for 'move away from the bourgeois moment in order to rebuild a Unitarian world'. All clean and ready to go to the dogs again, as Hammett would say.

It may well be true, as Susannah Lee argues, that the 'néo-polar', which Manchette named and brought into existence, 'is a literature of killing sprees, of absence of narrative closure... and, as often as not, a corpus of characters who could not care less about social cohesion';[76] but in an irony or indeed an absurdity that Manchette could only have intended, the killing spree in *Fatale* leads not to social anarchy but an inevitable return of the status quo. For both Manchette and Himes, this knowledge and its implications for their dwindling faith in the capacities of the crime novel to straightforwardly oppose entrenched power would push their work into more surreal and despairing territory. But what of Sjöwall and Wahlöö? What of their novels which move carefully from the fleshing out of realistic characters who act in rational ways to solve crimes to a wider interrogation of the tectonics of contemporary capitalism and its symbiotic relationship with the state? As Winston and Mellerski rightly point out, theirs is certainly an indictment of this system, rather than a disinterested portrait.[77] It is an indictment of the amoral viciousness of the business world, personified by Victor Palmgren who is assassinated in *Murder at the Savoy* and whose firms 'crushed everyone and everything around them' (p. 205), and of the capitalist parasitism of film director Walter Petrus, in *The Terrorists* (1975), who traps young girls in a cycle of drug dependence before exploiting them in his pornographic films. For the first half of the series, Sjöwall and Wahlöö are able to keep in check this tension between the demands of procedure, where investigations are carried out and solutions reached, and an awareness of how the executive decisions of the higher-ups inevitably favour the rich and powerful. But as the series progressed they found it increasingly hard to hold the component parts of their procedural novels together and with this would come a loosening of the genre's rationalist epistemology, the need for everything to cohere.

In his 1972 work *Counter-revolution and Revolt*, Herbert Marcuse argues that 'the extension of exploitation to a large part of the population' makes the 'unifying force' of capitalism, paradoxically, 'a force of disintegration' and under the weight

---

[76] Lee, 'May 1968, Radical Politics and the *Néo-Polar*', p. 75.
[77] Robert P. Winston and Nancy C. Mellerski, *The Public Eye: Ideology and the Police Procedural* (Basingstoke: Macmillan, 1992), p. 17.

of this pressure the centre cannot hold, a situation that in turn breeds intensified repression and discontent which is 'unpolitical, diffuse [and] unorganized'.[78] This is the socio-political context for the later works of Sjöwall and Wahlöö, Himes, and Manchette. As we'll see, their frustration at this intensified repression and the piecemeal, chaotic nature of the discontent it produced manifested itself most obviously in sudden, violent intrusions of the absurd into narratives prized for their verisimilitude.

THE POLITICAL ABSURD: HIMES, SJÖWALL AND WAHLÖÖ, MANCHETTE 2

One of the pivotal moments for the unfolding account of 'radical' crime fiction in this chapter is the arrival of Himes in Europe, and not just anywhere in Europe but specifically in Paris. Central to this account, and to the book as a whole, has been a claim about the development of a politically committed crime fiction as a transnational and transcontinental phenomenon. But Himes's passage from America to Europe and more pointedly his turning to crime fiction for the first, at the insistence of Marcel Duhamel, editor of Gallimard's 'Série Noire' imprint, gives us a particularly acute example of this melding of influences: the US hard-boiled style with its ideology of violence,[79] reinvented by a black American writer and, at Duhamel's urging, laced with streaks of French surrealism. Himes left the US because 'there was nothing to keep [him] any longer',[80] but he didn't necessarily find freedom—from racism, the logic of the market, or from himself—in France. In interviews and letters, Himes was always equivocal about his complicated relationship with his new home. 'I don't know exactly what I expected from Paris, but whatever it was I didn't get it', he wrote in the spring of 1953,[81] shortly before penning the outline to a novel that would eventually be published as *A Case of Rape* (1980): an indictment of racial prejudice in the French justice system after four black American men are accused of raping a white woman. Yet, elsewhere he is kinder to his adopted country and specifically to Paris—the 'city I most like in the world'.[82] 'Yes, here a Negro can find a sense of normality. He can calm down a little', he told François Bott in 1964.[83] What he did find in France, in Paris, was an influential editor, in Duhamel, a former surrealist, who urged him to dispense with the psychological realism and stream-of-consciousness of his first novel *If He*

---

[78] Herbert Marcuse, *Counter-revolution and Revolt* (London: Penguin, 1972), pp. 16, 25.
[79] Michael Denning has written most persuasively about the ideology of violence in Himes's Harlem novels; see 'Topographies of Violence: Chester Himes's Harlem Domestic Novels', *Critical Texts: A Review of Theory & Criticism*, 5 (1988), p. 10. Himes himself described the American detective story as 'plain and simple violence in narrative form': Fabre and Skinner, *Conversations with Chester Himes*, p. 47.
[80] Himes, *The Quality of Hurt: The Autobiography of Chester Himes Vol. 1* (New York, NY: Thunder's Mouth Press, 1995), p. 139.
[81] Himes qtd in Belas, 'Chester Himes's The End of a Primitive', p. 380.
[82] Himes qtd in Belas, 'Chester Himes's The End of a Primitive', p. 380.
[83] Fabre and Skinner, *Conversations with Chester Himes*, p. 15.

Hollers Let Him Go (1945) and not to worry about 'making sense'.[84] Himes also found sufficient distance from Harlem to write about it both as 'real' ('I write about black crimes in a black ghetto' as a 'kind of reporter'[85]) and as a place scarred and transfigured by the related absurdities of racism and poverty.

It is hard to determine with any real clarity whether there is political intent informing Himes's early experimentations with surrealism or absurdism, or whether intent on Himes's part matters or not. To talk about the 'political absurd' may even be something of a tautology because, at least in a French context, as Eburne tells us, surrealism, from the 1920s onwards, with its 'affected indifference to truth and justice' and its stylistic and moral excesses 'out of step with serious political commitment' but nonetheless providing 'access to unconscious revolutionary desires'[86] was always a political movement. Still, whether we call Himes's realistic anti-realism 'absurd' or 'surreal', my aim here is to trace Himes's developing political consciousness vis-à-vis the consequences of this preoccupation. In doing so I'd like to cement a new critical tendency, if not to claim Himes as 'French' then to lift his work out of a specifically American context and, quoting Eburne, to see not what his fiction loses in translation but what it gains: 'an involvement in French thinking about modes of writing that frustrate instrumentality through their irretrievable lapses and excesses of meaning'.[87] To qualify this claim a little: France may have been the cradle of the surrealist movement but, as novels by Sciascia and Dürrenmatt demonstrate, a preoccupation with the limits of rationality and intrusions of the absurd into ostensibly 'realistic' stories about law and policing can't be located exclusively in the crime stories of any one country. Indeed the excesses and lapses of meaning Eburne claims as characteristics of Himes also find their way into Manchette's late novels and even into the procedural 'realism' of Sjöwall and Wahlöö.

Returning first of all to Himes, we should perhaps distinguish between the baroque excesses of his early Harlem novels where the emphasis is on the unravelling of 'reality' into what Himes calls 'a cesspool of buffoonery'[88] and, as Eburne so nicely puts it, on a 'form of caricature whose deliberate misrepresentations articulate unforeseen connections'[89] and the later novels, notably *Blind Man with a Pistol*, where epistemological breakdown bears more heavily on the operation of law and the viability of genre. Overlaying the series as a whole is a much quoted formulation, borrowed from Camus and expressed most cogently in the second volume of Himes's autobiography, *My Life of Absurdity*, that suggests how the absurdity of racism gathers its own logic and momentum:

> Not only does racism express the absurdity of the racists but it generates absurdity in the victims. And the absurdity of the victims intensified the absurdity of the racists, ad infinitum. If one lives in a country where racism is held valid and practiced in all

---

[84] Duhamel qtd in Jonathan Eburne, 'The Transatlantic Mysteries of Paris: Chester Himes, Surrealism, and the Série Noire', *PMLA*, 120:3 (May 2005), p. 818.
[85] Fabre and Skinner, *Conversations with Chester Himes*, p. 26.
[86] Eburne, 'The Transatlantic Mysteries of Paris', p. 808.
[87] Eburne, 'The Transatlantic Mysteries of Paris', p. 808.
[88] Himes, *My Life of Absurdity: The Autobiography of Chester Himes Vol. 2* (New York, NY: Doubleday, 1976), p. 126.
[89] Eburne, 'The Transatlantic Mysteries of Paris', p. 811.

ways of life, no matter whether one is a racist or a victim, one comes to feel the absurdity of life.[90]

This then is the bottom line for Himes, the fundamental truth of existence for black and white alike under conditions of racism, but there are limits, at least initially, to how far and widely he wants to extend the logic of this claim. The opening of *The Real Cool Killers* is indicative. The 'cesspool of buffoonery' is initially contained in a Harlem bar. A 'little knifeman' tries to take on 'Big Smiley's axe', an action that results in his arm being 'cut off just below the elbow as though it had been guillotined' and that causes blood to spout 'from his jerking stub as though from a nozzle of a hose' even as the knifeman is searching for his missing hand and the knife in it (pp. 735, 736). It then spills out onto the street and gathers its own absurd momentum, becoming a 'macabre pantomime' (p. 852) or 'three ring circus' (p. 867). Absurdities generate further absurdities: a gang of black youths dressed as Arabs with 'bright green turbans, smoked glasses and ankle-length white robes...jabbering and gesticulating like a cage of frenzied monkeys' (p. 738) while a big white man with his throat cut is chased down the street by another black man as Sonny Pickens fires at him with a 'blue-steel revolver' which turns out to be a toy. Yet seen in the context of the novel as a whole, these absurdities, funny as they are, can still, as per Himes's formulation, be traced back to the twin effects of racism and of course capitalism—dissembling being a form of what Stephen Soitos, following Henry Louis Gates, calls 'signifying' or 'double consciousness'[91] and the vicious fighting over scraps being a consequence of class inequality and relentless poverty. And in the personae of Grave Digger and Coffin Ed, Himes gives us figures of authority capable of seeing through the grotesque pantomime and, despite their own flirtations with excess (e.g. excessive violence and rage), of drawing the necessary conclusions.

There is a corresponding scene at the start of Himes's final (completed) Harlem novel *Blind Man with a Pistol*: another white man in Harlem, this time, without any underpants and with blood spurting 'from the side of his throat where his jugular had been cut' (p. 36). It is a spectacle that again brings 'colored people' out of their 'black, dark tenements' including, as witnessed by Coffin Ed and Grave Digger, a black man 'with a red fez stuck on his head' (p. 34); but this time the general reaction and even the language used by Himes to describe this reaction is muted (e.g. there's no repeat of the exuberance associated with seeing a white man bleed in *The Real Cool Killer*: 'the greatest show on earth...greater than Emancipation Day', pp. 867, 868). Shortly afterwards, the disorder, conceived as absurd pantomime, spreads to a nearby tenement where a bogus doctor, called on to administer a sperm elixir to a one-hundred-year-old black Mormon with more than fifty children, is stabbed by a 'short muscular black man in a red fez' (p. 49). Here, though, the capacities of Himes's detectives to see through and decipher the grotesque pantomime of violent excess falter in the face of its sheer ubiquity. These

---

[90] Himes, *My Life of Absurdity*, Vol. 2, p. 1.
[91] Stephen Soitos, *The Blues Detective: A Study of African American Detective Fiction* (Amherst, MA: University of Massachusetts Press, 1996), pp. 33–7.

two scenes segue into more generalized disorder, the trope of absurdist spectacle incorporating the supposedly 'serious' realm of political protest, with various groups including the Brotherhood, the Black Jesus movement, and the Black Muslims beating lumps out of each other on a public holiday to celebrate Nat Turner, misrecognized as a jazz musician or prizefighter. 'It was all really funny, in a grotesque way... Best show they'd had in a month of Sundays' (p. 105). Rather than standing apart from, and indeed seeing through the falsity, Coffin Ed and Grave Digger join in the fray, this time to no effect. In an acute analysis of the novel, Lee Horsley reads this failure as 'narrational breakdown' marked by 'temporal confusion, the non-solution of crimes, the refusal to subordinate any of the proliferating plots to a master plot, the "leakage" between plots and the tendency of characters to metamorphose into one another'.[92] Faced by a world, and a plot, that is disintegrating in front of them, even the ability to see the contours of power and the links between money and politics desert Himes's detectives. 'Ask your boss', Michael X says, alluding to corruption in the police department. The logical end point of this absurdist vision is, as Horsley suggests, total collapse: of plot, protest, reason, authority, character, and law. Thus when a blind man unconnected to the story starts to shoot indiscriminately in a crowded subway car, causing further mayhem, Coffin Ed and Grave Digger, marginalized and defeated, and shooting at rats on a building site, can do little more than point out the obvious: 'It's all out of hand' (p. 195).

Himes's preoccupation with absurdity has been the subject of a great deal of critical scrutiny but much less attention has been paid to the more subtle but nonetheless significant intrusions of the absurd into the crime narratives of Sjöwall and Wahlöö, and Manchette—and indeed the political implications of these intrusions. For my argument is that we need to widen and extend Himes's formulation about the absurdity of life under racism to think about the consequences, for individuals, society, and indeed the structures of the crime story, of having to negotiate ever more concentrated conglomerations of power.

Turning to Sjöwall and Wahlöö first of all, it has become almost *de rigeur* to comment on the related claims of the ten 'Report of a Crime' novels to procedural realism and political commitment.[93] Only Nestingen, to my knowledge, has given much thought to the novels' occasional but significant melodramatic excesses or what I am calling intrusions of absurdity. Nestingen's enquiry opens by considering the comic interventions of two patrol policemen, Kristiansson and Kvant, in *The Laughing Policeman*, as they contrive not to discover mass murder committed on a Stockholm public bus and he rightly asks 'What mode of narration is at work here? Realism? Melodrama?' Arguing that 'realism and melodrama often work complementarily' in Scandinavian crime fiction,

---

[92] Lee Horsley, *Twentieth-Century Crime Fiction* (Oxford: Oxford University Press, 2005), pp. 211–12.
[93] See, for example, Barry Forshaw, *Death in a Cold Climate: A Guide to Scandinavian Crime Fiction* (Basingstoke: Palgrave Macmillan, 2012), pp. 16–17; Nestingen and Arvas, 'Introduction', p. 3; Messent, *The Crime Fiction Handbook* (Oxford and Malden, MA: Wiley-Blackwell, 2013), pp. 177–83.

Nestingen claims that melodrama—which 'well suits the project' of dramatizing 'the protagonist's participation in state institutions changed by neoliberalism'— is also a means of simplifying 'conflicts by reducing them to subjective moral dramas' and compensating 'for the state's and the genre's incapacity to provide reassurance and certainty about the social order'.[94] While I am more than happy to endorse the first part of this formulation I think that Nestingen often misrecognizes absurdity as melodrama, a move which allows him to dismiss or overlook its potential for political engagement. Rather than simplifying conflicts by 'reducing them to subjective moral dramas', the eruptions of absurdity that puncture the realistic sheen of the novels work in the opposite way, i.e. they draw our attention to the larger structural/systemic forces that increasingly shape people's lives. It is worth looking at how Sjöwall and Wahlöö deploy Kristiansson and Kvant in the rest of the series to see how this logic develops and to explore its implications.

Having featured in *The Fire Engine That Disappeared* where they fail 'out of sheer idleness or stupidity'[95] to follow up on a 'false alarm' call to the fire service, they are found at the beginning of *Murder at the Savoy*, a novel that is often and perhaps not uncoincidentally noted for ushering in a more pronounced political turn in Sjöwall and Wahlöö's crime writing.[96] In this novel the shape and trajectory of the entire plot is thrown by their inability to perform a simple task: pick up and arrest a suspect just landed at Arlanda airport in Stockholm. Their initial explanation for their delay in getting to the airport is that they had to caution a man 'riding a bicycle' who 'shouted insults at us' (p. 23); but it quickly transpires that they were eating hot dogs outside the car while a three-year-old boy on the back of his father's bike sang, 'Daddy, this little pig' (p. 23). This not only draws attention to the absurdity of their initial explanation but also, as Michael Carlson tells us, is reflexive comment on the book's Swedish title, *Polis, Polis, Potatismos*, itself a riff on an anti-police protest chant in the 1960s ('polis, polis, potatisgris', meaning 'police, police, potato pig');[97] Sjöwall and Wahlöö's clever revision of *potatisgris* to *Potatismos* (meaning mashed potato) part of an emerging absurdist undercurrent in their work. Still, this sly reference, even if it is an appropriate description doesn't prepare us for what happens to the 'two blond giants from Skåne' (p. 151) in *The Abominable Man*. Initially their appearance three-quarters of the way through the novel would seem to usher in another moment of comic relief: they try to confront a contrary vagabond called the Rump who brandishes a pickled pig's foot in their faces and

---

[94] Nestingen, 'Unnecessary Officers: Realism, Melodrama and Swedish Crime Fiction in Transition', *Scandinavian Crime Fiction* (2011), pp. 171, 172, 175.

[95] Sjöwall and Wahlöö, *The Fire Engine That Disappeared*, trans. Joan Tate (London: Fourth Estate, 2011), p. 153.

[96] Dawn Keetley challenges the critical consensus that the first three or four Beck novels are apolitical and makes a good case for considering 'the "private"... crimes of the early novels and the political crimes of the later novels' as part of the same critical impulse ('Unruly Bodies: The Politics of Sex in Maj Sjöwall and Per Wahlöö's Martin Beck Series', *Clues: A Journal of Detection*, 30:1 (Spring 2012), p. 55). Still, I would want to argue that the later novels, especially after *Murder at the Savoy*, do demonstrate a more explicit effort to expose and confront the cosy relationship between state and capital.

[97] Michael Carlson, 'Introduction' in Sjöwall and Wahlöö's *Murder at the Savoy*, pp. vii–viii.

proceeds to taunt them with references to their hooves and curly tails. In an absurdist twist, the Rump wants to be taken in by the police in order to waste their time and once they realize this, the two cops pay him to get out of their car, Kvant even driving him to the nearest alcohol shop.

Up to this point the absurdity is mild and containable. After all, the two cops have been the butt of Sjöwall and Wahlöö's jokes since *The Man on the Balcony* (1967). But then Kristianson, the pig's foot still is in his hand, is shot by a sniper perched on top of a tall building and an unfolding scene of mayhem, worthy of Himes, ensues, disorder fuelling further disorder as the sniper fires at will at arriving police officers and others; Kollberg is seized by 'a strong sense of unreality' as he sees Kvant, returned from his trip to the alcohol shop, killed as the first bullet 'emerged neatly halfway between Kvant's Adam's apple and his collar' (p. 162). The resulting spectacle, heightened by the arrival of a 'mass of motorcycle policemen, two fire engines and a traffic surveillance helicopter' (p. 185) and described as an 'absurd and desperate situation' (p. 190), is not an ameliorist one—part of the society of spectacle imagined by Guy Debord who was a significant influence on Manchette. Rather, it is an incendiary political act; the sniper, Åke Eriksson, a former policeman, is not simply deranged but someone who has been driven to extremity by a culture of systematic abuse of power and cover-up organized around the figure of Stig Nyman who is the 'abominable man' of the novel's title (p. 71). Here, then, the melodramatic excesses of the scene, which culminate when Eriksson shoots down a police helicopter, are not, as Nestingen argues, 'compensation', part of a move to simply reduce complex political dramas, but quite the opposite: they are violent, unruly intrusions into the orderly world of the procedural which in turn draw attention to the 'problem' caused by concentrations or conglomerations of power. In a neat absurdist twist, the act provokes the kind of excessive response from the police that confirms, rather than refutes, the underlying 'problem'—which as we are told is rooted in the institutional reforms of the mid-1960s, ushered in under the guise of 'nationalization' but a ruse to centralize power and bypass accountability.

This move reaches its apotheosis in the next novel of the series, *The Locked Room*, notably in a scene where a raid by members of the special bank robbery squad led by Bulldozer Olsson goes horribly and comically wrong. The intention is to surprise two notorious bank robbers but the police are so pumped up that the situation quickly and disastrously unravels: first Larsson who 'flung himself at the door' with 'inconceivable celerity' meets no resistance and flies 'straight across the room like a bolting crane' before, unable to stop, exiting another window and 'dangling five storeys up... with the larger part of his body outside the window' (pp. 124–5); then Zachrissson enters the room, sees the mayhem, fires at the ceiling, shoots a police dog, and then perforates a hot water pipe which strikes him 'full in the face' (p. 126), at which point another policeman wielding a loaded sub-machine gun trips over Rönn and is bitten by the injured dog before the tear-gas specialists hurl two grenades into the room (which of course is empty, no sign of the robbers anywhere). The grenades explode just as another bullet, fired by the dog-handler, hits the 'tear-gas man in the upper shoulder'—only then does Bulldozer himself enter and declare, to the deserted apartment, 'throw away your guns and come out with your hands up' (p. 127).

It's a very funny scene but it serves a serious purpose. The trope of disorder, perpetrated by heavy-handed policing, generating further disorder, is repeated later in the novel, when a Vietnam demonstration, planned by people quite understandably 'indignant about the bombing of North Vietnam' but vilified by the security forces as 'dangerous communists' is corralled by the chief of police himself 'straight into a large and extremely disgruntled crowd of football fans' (pp. 223–4) at which point mayhem ensues. The novel's ultimate absurdity is that this heavy-handed policing produces a suspect in the bank robbery case who we know is innocent but who is found guilty, while Martin Beck's quiet, methodical approach in another, apparently unrelated murder enquiry identifies the same suspect, who this time is guilty of the crime but who is not punished, because the police chief condemns Beck's sound assumptions as 'absurd' (p. 294). It is not the Swedish welfare state per se that is under attack but a system of criminal justice founded upon excessive and unchecked power, whereby 'well-heeled murderers are allowed to wreck...lives' and 'order others about merely because they happen to be better off' (*Laughing*, p. 215).

The extent to which these absurdist eruptions in what are ostensibly 'realistic' crime stories requires us to examine the basis of this claim to reality is made particularly relevant by Manchette's affiliation with Situationism and especially the Situationist credo of *détournement*—whereby pre-existing cultural representations are re-routed or hijacked and reworked in order to turn, or to try to turn, the society of spectacle (and its preference for images over 'reality') against itself and expose its inherent exhaustion and emptiness.[98] Manchette's *3 to Kill* borrows heavily from the archives of US popular culture—not, though, from US popular culture in its most debased form or that which bears the strongest imprint of what Adorno and Horkheimer referred to as the 'culture industry'.[99] Rather Manchette's *détournement*, in this novel at least, takes jazz, film noir, and hard-boiled crime fiction as its source texts—forms that have already sought to negotiate critical positions vis-à-vis mainstream culture (a version of *détournement* or a politicized move to avoid being wholly recuperated by this culture). For example the movie playing on the TV just after George Gerfaut has been attacked and nearly killed at the beach is Sam Fuller's *Pickup on South Street* (1953) a hysterical denouncement of excessive state power masquerading as an anti-communist, McCarthyite tract. In the same way, *3 to Kill* would seem, at first glance, to be an unremarkable narrative about an innocent man who witnesses a murder and is hunted down by the two killers, a narrative gleaned from the pages of the crime novels George reads, stripped down and reassembled in a form that does not seem to be very different from its source texts. But dig a little deeper and a more overtly political crime story emerges.

---

[98] See Guy Debord, *The Society of Spectacle*, trans. Donald Nicholson-Smith (New York, NY: Zone Books, 1994).
[99] See Theodor W. Adorno, *The Culture Industry: Selected Essays on Mass Culture*, ed. J.M. Bernstein (London and New York, NY: Routledge, 2001).

George's desires, at least at first, are shaped and limited by his smooth incorporation into the world of capital or as Manchette famously puts it 'the social relations of production'[100]—Scotch, bourbon, jazz, his Mercedes, and comfortable family life standing in for what he has given up: a former existence as left-wing 'militant' (p. 23). This flat, affectless landscape is punctured only by contained eruptions of the absurd—news stories that contrast the 'realistic' (e.g. 'Tanks and air power had been deployed against six thousand rebellious Bolivian peasants') with the ridiculous (e.g. 'An Eskimo had been shot and killed while trying to divert a Boeing 747 to North Korea', p. 26). Manchette then wrenches his protagonist from his comfortable existence and thrusts him into the domain of the crime story—the hard-boiled crime story refracted again through Manchette's complex political affiliations. George's predictable existence is shattered by the two gunmen and absurdities, reconfigured as narrative contingencies, proliferate. Here, cause and effect conjure not the rational epistemology of the enquiring detective but a chaotic world where action and counteraction gather their own grotesque momentum and where one thing leads to the next in a random and contingent manner: George, pursued to a petrol station, is attacked and turns the tables on his attackers, killing one and destroying the petrol station in the process; he then escapes on a passing train, is assaulted and thrown off the train by a vagabond, and ends up wandering through the French countryside, with a broken ankle, before being rescued by a Portuguese logger.

In a nod to Debord's pre-Situationist, Letterist maxim—'Never Work!'[101]—Manchette allows George to recuperate in a remote mountain village, far removed from time–space imperatives of modern capitalism (for example a year passes with George barely noticing and he spends his time either being taken care of by an elderly man or, after the man's death, tending house for his granddaughter). But George's quasi-existentialist insistence that 'I am free...I can make whatever I want of my existence' (p. 106) is exposed and curtailed by the remaining gunman who tracks him down and kills the granddaughter. George, then, is thrust back into the domain of the crime story which, from Manchette's perspective, can only be re-routed or hijacked so far, precisely because the crime story, even in the hands of leftist writers like Hammett and Sciascia cannot escape its securitarian tendencies. In the end, Manchette's vision is aligned neither to the consumer culture to which George returns nor to Debord's faith in the revolutionary potential of *détournement*. Instead the political possibilities of *3 to Kill* are limited by the form Manchette has inherited.

Manchette's novel, and especially the ending (where George, 'racing around Paris at 145 kilometers per hour' with 'diminished reflexes' can only escape his circumstances if the 'relations of production' which 'contain the reason' why he is doing this are destroyed (p. 134)—unlikely in the extreme) wonders, in line with

---

[100] Manchette, *3 to Kill*, trans. Donald Nicholson-Smith (San Francisco, CA: City Light Books, 2002), p. 6.
[101] McKenzie Wark points out that Letterism argued against the division of work and leisure time and instead 'sought a quite different concept of time, resolutely based on non-work'. See *The Beach Beneath the Street: The Everyday Life and Glorious Times of the Situationist International* (London and New York, NY: Verso, 2011), p. 25.

Marcuse, about the possibilities of radical political change, given the extent to which political protest, by the mid-1970s, had been incorporated into the same landscape of consumer capitalism that ensnares George.[102] At the same time, Marcuse's shift of emphasis from *One-Dimensional Man* (1964), where this process of assimilation is presented as totalizing or inevitable, to *Counter-revolution and Revolt* (1972), where the disintegrating tendencies of the productive forces opens up the possibility for more widespread social disruption finds its corollary in Manchette's late novels: the absurdist violence analogizing these disintegrating tendencies.[103] But against Marcuse's renewed optimism regarding the revolutionary potential of an expanded and revitalized political left, Manchette and indeed Sjöwall and Wahlöö, and Himes would steer their last crime novels into more despairing political terrain and in doing so their desire to remain politically committed and continue to write crime novels informed by this commitment would be tested to the limits.

THE REVOLUTION NEXT TIME: SJÖWALL AND WAHLÖÖ, HIMES, MANCHETTE 3

There is a fascinating symmetry between the trajectory of these crime writers' lives, beyond their dwindling faith in the potential of radical politics, faced by the political and economic retrenchments of the 1960s and 1970s, to institute lasting social change. All of them lived and wrote through a period of unprecedented social and political tumult and sought to find ways, with varying degrees of success, of incorporating not just the riotous, violent atmosphere of the era but also its, and their, revolutionary hopes into a genre that, despite its elasticity, would not easily accommodate them. Just as Himes wrote his ten Harlem detective novels between the late 1950s and the mid-1970s, Sjöwall and Wahlöö wrote ten novels in their 'Report of a Crime' series between 1965 and 1975.[104] Manchette's crime writer oeuvre, meanwhile, is bookended by *L'Affaire N'Gustro* (1971) and *The Prone Gunman* (1981). But for the purpose of this final section of the chapter, it is to the affinities, and differences, between their final novels—*The Prone Gunman*, Sjöwall and Wahlöö's *The Terrorists* (1975) and Himes's *Plan B*, started in 1967 and continued in the early 1970s before being published unfinished, first in French in 1983, and posthumously in the US in 1993—that I want to turn. Particularly for Sjöwall and Wahlöö, and Himes, the prospect of their series coming to an end would present potential headaches but also real opportunity: no more would they have to care about leaving things in place for the next instalment. For Sjöwall and

[102] David Platten makes some highly productive links between *3 to Kill* and Marcuse's *One-Dimensional Man* in *The Pleasures of Crime: Reading Modern French Crime Fiction* (Amsterdam: Rodopi, 2011), pp. 95–6.
[103] Marcuse, *One-Dimensional Man: Studies in the Ideology of Advanced Society* (London: Routledge and Kegan Paul, 1964), pp. 252–7; *Counter-revolution and Revolt*, pp. 15–16.
[104] Per Wahlöö died in June 1975, having completed along with Sjöwall the tenth Martin Beck novel, *The Terrorists*, but the critic Bo Lindin makes it clear that they only ever intended to write ten novels in the series. See Lindin qtd in Winston and Mellerski, *The Public Eye*, p. 17.

Wahlöö the focus would be on the nature and effectiveness of political protest and its characterization by some as criminality; and the efforts by Beck and his colleagues to negotiate, not always successfully, the resulting contradictions. For Manchette it would be on failure and despair—the implications for the genre, with its typical orientation towards action and struggle, of having a central character who is defeated almost from the outset. And for Himes it would be to explore the subject of revolution and to ask whether, for America's black population, meaningful social transformation could only be achieved through organized violence. In all cases, and under pressure from incompatible generic and political imperatives, the genre would be pushed to breaking point and beyond.

Just prior to the publication of *Roseanna* (1965), the first novel in the 'Report of a Crime' series, Per Wahlöö wrote *Murder on the Thirty-First Floor* (1964), a novel set in an unnamed country in the near future where harmony is fostered by the products of a single publishing–media monopoly, effectively under state control. The crime here is a bomb threat made against this conglomerate's HQ, a building known as the Skyscraper, and it is Chief Inspector Jensen's job to find the person who has made the threat. That he does so, within the time allotted to him, and is unmoved by the man's explanation—to combat the 'murder of countless ideas, the murder of the capacity to form an opinion, of freedom of expression'[105]—attests to his, and by extension, the genre's function as the state's (un)willing executioner. But true to his Marxist beliefs, Wahlöö adds a powerful kicker: the man who made the threat has sent another letter to the Publisher which on Jensen's advice is ignored but the final pages has the Chief Inspector realizing his mistake and rushing towards the Skyscraper just as a bomb is about to detonate. In a 'standalone' novel, Wahlöö could end on such a note—with a justified revolutionary act tantalizingly deferred—but this kind of grand gesture would be harder to pull off in the 'Report of a Crime' novels: because to have such an attack succeed, and with it the loss of 'innocent' lives, would require Beck and his team to utterly fail, a move that would, in turn, unravel the logic of the series. Jensen can fail because he is no more than an apparatchik of a totalitarian order but Beck and his team, though defenders of the establishment in part, are also capable of independent, even anti-capitalist, anti-statist thinking. With *The Terrorists*, then, the challenge would be to try and do justice to these seemingly incompatible sentiments—the revolutionary potential of violent protest on the one hand and the politics of progressive social democracy, as exemplified by Beck and his team, on the other.

At first glance, *The Terrorists* would not seem to be especially keen to throw its weight behind revolutionary causes. One of the main plot lines requires Beck and others to foil an attempt by a terrorist group, ULAG, to assassinate an unpopular right-wing US Senator. In this role Beck is sequestered, grudgingly but wanting to do a good job, into the inner sanctum of the state, together with the National Commissioner of Police, the chief of Security Police, and the head of the National Police Administration. Our sympathies are unequivocally with Beck, not least because ULAG, set up to support white regimes in southern Africa, lacks popular

---

[105] Wahlöö, *Murder on the Thirty-First Floor*, trans. Sarah Death (London: Vintage, 2011), p. 190.

legitimacy, even if another of their ambitions ('the creation of distrust and general political unease'[106]) links it to revolutionary causes in the broadest sense. Thus when Beck, Larsson, Röhn, and others thwart the assassination attempt, having heeded the lessons from a similar incident in an unnamed South American country, Sjöwall and Wahlöö would seem to be moving their final novel towards the political centre: the senator may have been 'one of the most active forces behind the strategic bombing in North Vietnam' (p. 167) but since his visit is a state one, he must be protected. But other plot lines impinge and threaten to destabilize this move. For a start, an unrelated investigation into the murder of a film director, Walter Petrus, uncovers a more familiar landscape of abuse and exploitation. Then another more daring intervention occurs, one which requires explanation. Earlier in the novel, Rebecka Lind, who has little knowledge of the 'real' world and who is accused of robbing a bank (when in fact she just went there to ask for money), is found not guilty: her lawyer successfully presenting her as someone 'not interested in politics other than that she finds society...incomprehensible and its leaders either criminal or insane' (p. 39). During the visit by the US Senator, and just after the ULAG action has been neutered, Lind steps out of the crowd and assassinates the Swedish prime minister because he has ignored her letters requesting help. The act may be an individual one, and hence easily contained, but given who has been killed, it has revolutionary implications, not least because her defence lawyer seeks to explain it in exactly these terms—terms which question the legitimacy of the state, especially in its administration of justice, and which the series as a whole has endorsed:

> What this young woman did yesterday was a political act, even if unconscious...Recently—no; for as long as I can remember, large and powerful nations within the capitalist bloc have been ruled by people who according to accepted legal norms are simply criminals, who from a lust for power and financial gain have led their peoples into an abyss of egotism...and a view of life based entirely on materialism and ruthlessness towards their fellow human beings. (p. 266)

This is Sjöwall and Wahlöö, wearing their Marxist–Leninist credentials on their sleeves, speaking through the defence lawyer, but crucially it is not the position of the novel as a whole. The judicial system may not be able to recognize Rebecka's act as political—she is put under an arrest order and dispatched 'to a State Psychiatric Institute for long-term evaluation' where she takes her own life 'by throwing herself against a wall with such force that her skull was shattered' (pp. 267, 268). But nor it seems is the rest of the novel interested in developing this claim as a political argument. Instead, the focus reverts to Beck's hunt—successful as it turns out—for the ULAG terrorists and in the end the rule of law (which elsewhere has been shown to be inadequate and partial) is endorsed, precisely because there are 'good' policemen like Beck to enforce it and because there are no real alternatives. As such, the much discussed ending, where Kollberg, who resigned from the police at the end of the previous novel because 'he saw that the police as an organization

---

[106] Sjöwall and Wahlöö, *The Terrorists*, trans. Joan Tate (London: Harper Perennial, 2007), p. 143.

devoted itself to terrorizing...socialists and those who can't make it in our class society' (p. 165), places the letter X at the end of a word while playing a version of Scrabble to make the word Marx, requires our consideration. Right at the end, Sjöwall and Wahlöö would seem to be shoring up their Marxist credentials but the larger implications of such a move aren't entirely apparent. On the one hand, we might agree with Nestingen's claim that the state in their work is depicted as 'criminal' in so far as 'state officials and bureaucrats...collude with their friends, who belong to economic or political elites, and who are sometimes involved in crimes themselves'.[107] On the other hand, the state, as it is embodied by Beck and his team of detectives, is the last and perhaps only bulwark against the relentless march of capital, a force capable of exposing and keeping a check on those like Petrus whose exploitative practices speak to or about capitalism's worst excesses. Without the police, without Beck and his team, Sjöwall and Wahlöö imply, where would we be? Notwithstanding the fact that related moves in Marxism would also refute straightforward relationship between the base and superstructure, or between the forces of production and, in this case, the police,[108] the complicated and at times contradictory politics of Sjöwall and Wahlöö's crime novels, especially regarding the rule of law and legitimacy of the state under capitalism, would not easily accommodate revolutionary sentiment. For Manchette and Himes, meanwhile, the crisis of faith regarding the capacities of writing, crime or otherwise, to directly affect political change would take them into ever bleaker and, in Himes's case, more confrontational territory.

Himes's decision to turn away from his early career as 'protest' novelist to write *The End of a Primitive* (1956) and then his Harlem domestic novels was informed, to a greater or less extent, by a growing awareness of the limits of writing, protest or otherwise, as a vehicle for instigating genuine social transformation. 'I don't think that all the books and speeches of any writer can have any direct influence on racism, or the other problems experienced by black people in the United States', he declared in an interview in 1970, restating this view a year later: 'I've never believed literature could change anything.'[109] But despite Himes's hostility to the doctrines of the US Communist Party and to Marxism as it was understood and practised in the years after the Second World War, he remained, like Marx himself, committed to the idea of organized rebellion and direct confrontation—'sweep[ing] away by force the old conditions of production' as Marx put it in *The Communist Manifesto*.[110] Only, for Himes, it wasn't just the class system that needed to be dismantled, if necessary by force; rather it was racism as a mode of social organization or race and class as interlocking axes of oppression that he fantasized about sweeping away. Political writing, for Himes, might have been an oxymoron but he

---

[107] Nestingen, 'Scandinavian Crime Fiction and the Facts'.
[108] Pawling traces this move right the way back to Marx and his assertion in *Grundrise* of the 'unequal development of material production and that of the arts' but points out that it finds its clearest articulation in the work of twentieth-century Marxists like Lukács and Jameson. See, *Critical Theory and Political Engagement*, pp. 154–5.
[109] See Fabre and Skinner, *Conversations with Chester Himes*, pp. 28, 103.
[110] Marx, *Essential Writings of Karl Marx*, p. 180.

did not entirely lose faith in the potential of writing 'to be a force in the world'[111] and with *Plan B*, he set out to imagine what a violent collective black uprising might look like, how it might come about, what consequences it would have, and what the implications for the viability of the crime story would be. In doing so, the novel reverses the tone and logic of his other Harlem domestic novels, replacing the grotesque humour and disorganized violence characteristic even of *Blind Man with a Pistol* with clear-eyed intent and direct political action. 'I believe in rebellion', Himes declared while writing *Plan B*, 'although up to now it has really been disorganized and ridiculous.' Ipso facto, as he said a little later, 'If there must be violence, I believe it should be organised violence.'[112] This is the *raison d'être* of *Plan B* and in imagining a scenario where widespread organized political and above all uncontainable violence takes place as a challenge to the dominant social and economic order, Himes would realize one of the most disorientating and destabilizing crime novels ever written—but one paradoxically that he could not finish for exactly these reasons and that would constitute, as Himes himself predicted, something akin to 'literary suicide'.

The novel opens conventionally enough, with an act of domestic violence perpetrated by T-Bone Smith against his wife, causing her death. Coffin Ed and Grave Digger arrive at the crime scene, a crumbling Harlem tenement building, and on this occasion Digger's rage causes him to lash out against and kill the perpetrator, something that precipitates his suspension from the police, a dynamic familiar from *The Real Cool Killers* and *The Heat's On*. What they ignore or overlook is the object which caused the argument between T-Bone and his wife in the first place—an automatic rifle sent anonymously through the post with the instructions 'LEARN YOUR WEAPON...!!! WARNING!!! DO NOT INFORM THE POLICE!!! FREEDOM IS NEAR!!!'[113] With nothing to investigate, they disappear from the narrative, at least until the end, even when the targeted violence exercised by a black gunman against white police officers sets in motion a series of acts and counteracts that threaten to unravel first New York and then the entire country. Initially, in this particular scene, it is business as usual for Himes—Eighth Avenue in Harlem, where black 'residents just sit in their squalor and swelter' (p. 48) is described in typical terms, fusing material and embodied decay:

> It stank from the yearly accumulations of thousands of unlisted odors embedded in the crumbling walls, the rotting linoleum, the decayed wall paper... the rancid face creams and cooking fats, the toe jam, the bad breath from rotting or dirty teeth, the pustules of pus. It stank from gangrenous sores, maggoty wounds, untended gonorrhoea, body tissue rotten from cancer or syphilis. (p. 51)

But once the shooting starts, Himes's aim, like the sniper's, narrows, focuses, and assumes a wholly new, dispassionate register, perhaps not shorn of such grotesque excesses (for we are told that 'a row of 7.62 calibre rifle bullets... passed through

---

[111] Fabre and Skinner, *Conversations with Chester Himes*, p. 89.
[112] Fabre and Skinner, *Conversations with Chester Himes*, pp. 28, 93–4.
[113] Himes, *Plan B*, ed. Fabre and Skinner (Jackson, MS: University Press of Mississippi, 1993).

[Pan and Van's—two white policemen] diaphragms... pounding the drooping blonde heads into splinters of bone and blobs of soft gray brain tissue', p. 55), but without any accompanying humour. Rather Himes's aim is to record, as fully and precisely as possible, the violence and its far-reaching consequences: the arrival of a tank to blow up the sniper and the reaction of the white cops once the sniper has been obliterated—'killing people for the sheer pleasure of killing; killing black people who died with the fatalism of animals' (p. 65).

Himes abandons the project of having proxy detectives investigate a particular crime or crimes, e.g. who did what to whom. Instead the issue of how this organized violence is orchestrated, by whom, for what ends, and what results it produces, leads him to explore the genealogies, extending back to slavery, of a piece of land in the Deep South and of a black man, Tomsson Black, who we come to suspect is behind the dispatching of weapons and the spread of revolutionary violence. In doing so, Himes puts to the sword a few (related) liberal fantasies that even the most supposedly 'radical' crime novels—by Manchette, Sjöwall and Wahlöö, and even Himes, prior to *Plan B*—hadn't been able to fully dislodge: first, that the apparatus of criminal justice, however coercive, skewed, corrupt, or inadequate it might be, is nonetheless capable of containing excessive violence and disorder; and second, that capitalism, as a mode of economic and social organization, is as inviolate as it is inevitable—as Mark Fisher neatly puts it, 'it is easier to imagine the end of the world than it is to imagine the end of capitalism.'[114]

With Ed and Digger, described by Fabre and Skinner as 'symbols of integration',[115] and the only effective keepers of the peace in Harlem, expunged from the narrative, the centre does not and cannot hold. In their absence the law ends up legitimizing a de facto apartheid where blacks are either rounded up and locked away or killed by lynch mobs. In such a climate, and with the law openly abandoning its commitment to neutrality, the killings inevitably proliferate. We are told about black men, for Himes's vision of revolution is problematically a male-only one, 'from all classes, from all levels of education... from all economic levels' (p. 127) 'running amok and shooting white people right-left-and center' (p. 124), eliciting white demands for prisons to be built 'and that all blacks be locked up in them' (p. 146) and ultimately leading to the bombing of black underground hiding places. The result is the unspooling of the nation and the destruction of its attendant myths about freedom, equality, and democracy. The escalating violence, verging on civil war, also threatens the conditions of possibility for the capital's survival—the obliteration not just of market confidence but also of the infrastructure of the business world: 'important areas of economic, cultural, and commercial activity, such as Wall Street and Rockefeller Center—suddenly found themselves without water, lights and telephones' (p. 186).

In a clever Marxist twist, or indeed an ironic comment on Marxism, capital, quite literally, plants the seeds of its own imminent destruction. Long before

---

[114] Mark Fisher, *Capitalist Realism: Is There No Alternative?* (Winchester and Washington, DC: Zero Books, 2009), p. 2.
[115] Fabre and Skinner, 'Introduction', *Plan B*, p. xxix.

Coffin Ed and Grave Digger belatedly return at the end of the novel to investigate the activities of Chitterlings Inc., we have been told how Black earned a million dollar grant from the philanthropic Hull Foundation, ostensibly to establish a meat processing business in the Deep South with the purpose of assimilating 'indigent blacks' into the working population and hence into the lifeblood of the 'capitalist nation, where all life forces derive from wealth' (p. 163). Of course, the business is just a ruse for soliciting sufficient capital to buy and distribute the automatic rifles and set in motion a chain of events that threatens to bring down the system. 'The very structure of capitalism began to crumble', Himes tells us with glee. 'Confidence in the capitalist system had an almost fatal shock' (p. 182). The word 'almost' here is key because right at the point where Himes has, if only in his own head, brought the capitalist state to its knees, he loses his nerve or his way or both and the spectre of genre returns, like the repressed, to (re)impose its own ambivalent vision of order, or order masquerading as disorder, on proceedings.

With Pandora's box well and truly open, there is no possibility of putting things back in their places but nor can Himes entirely dispense with his two detectives, even if he has a surprise in store for them and us. Tasked with going undercover and finding out who is procuring the automatic rifles and sending them to the black population, they immediately identify Black's Chitterlings Inc. as 'the only organization in the world that fitted the bill' (p. 194); but the conclusion, which is unfinished and which the editors 'reconstructed from a detailed outline found with the rest of the manuscript' (p. 192), is insufficiently worked out to be effective. Confronting Black, Coffin Ed and Grave Digger turn on each other, with Grave Digger, sympathetic to Black's project, shooting his partner in the head and Black killing him. It is an incredibly bold move but the repercussions for the story, the escalating violence and impending civil war, and for the genre as a whole are not elaborated and hence the shock, visceral and immediate as it is, fails to translate into the thing which Himes is most striving for: a way of using the crime novel to successfully articulate a vision of black revolution. 'I've tried to imagine what would happen', Himes remarked in 1969, admitting this failure. 'But I've had to stop. The violence shocks even me.' A year later, speaking about his inability to finish the novel, he told Fabre, 'it shocked me to discover that I'd inadvertently ended the careers of Coffin Ed and Grave Digger, because it amounted to literary suicide. Maybe this is the reason I couldn't complete the book.'[116]

Himes's detectives, paragons of integration and upholders of law despite their misgivings, must die for the revolution to succeed, but in killing them off, Himes does in effect commit 'literary suicide'. The genre, elastic as it is, would only bend so far. But there is another explanation for his failure to finish *Plan B*. When it was first published, as unfinished, in France in 1983, with Himes in ill health, the reception, as Fabre and Skinner indicate, was generally favourable; but there is something utterly incongruous about his vision of organized black revolution, begun in the radical ferment of the late 1960s, appearing for the first time in the early 1980s following the social, economic, and political retrenchments ushered in by Reagan in the US, by

---

[116] Fabre and Skinner, *Conversations with Chester Himes*, pp. 22, 136.

Thatcher in Britain, and by Mitterrand in France. In other words, perhaps the reason Himes couldn't finish *Plan B* is because his commitment to truth telling, to writing the novel 'as a documentary',[117] allowed him to see the disjuncture: between his own fantasy of violent revolution and what had come to pass in the 1970s and early 1980s—i.e. what compelled Manchette to write *The Prone Gunman* and what made it so hard for Sjöwall and Wahlöö to square the circle between their own Marxist–Leninist sympathies and both the securitarian tendencies of the genre and a growing realization, as the 1970s advanced, that the revolution, any revolution, had missed its shot. The fantasy of violent uprising may have been a comfort to Himes in his declining years but the reality, as the later works of Manchette, and Sjöwall and Wahlöö, tell us, was precisely the opposite: the intensification of what Nicos Poulantzas referred to as 'authoritarian statism' and the further surrender of public interests to the imperatives of private individuals and corporations.[118]

In an interview in 1980, just before he published *The Prone Gunman*, Manchette declared, 'The polar for me, was—and still is—the novel of violent social intervention. I set off in that direction encouraged also by my experience as a leftist.'[119] The key words here—'still is'—suggest some kind of continuum between the novel he was about to publish and his earlier works. But while as Platten rightly points out 'the *raison d'être* of the political struggle' in his last three published novels ebbs away 'as the behaviour of his protagonists...is increasingly regulated by the laws of the market',[120] (already complicating his 'leftist' politics), there is considerable difference between the agitation and rage demonstrated by George Gerfaut (*3 to Kill*) and Aimée Joubert (*Fatale*), even if this ultimately services the interests of capital and the capitalist state, and Martin Terrier's quietism, even if he kills a small army sent to persuade him against retiring as state-sanctioned assassin. Instead of the heady days of May 1968, the election of François Mitterrand looms over the novel, which for Manchette and indeed Guy Debord, his old Situationist compadre, was, as McKenzie Wark admirably puts it, 'not the longed-for entry of socialists into the state, but the final entry of the state into the Socialist Party'.[121]

Martin Terrier has no political allegiances, no ambition beyond accruing enough money to retire (and to woo his former hometown 'sweetheart') and, in a move borrowed from Hammett's behaviourist method, as demonstrated in *The Maltese Falcon* and *The Glass Key*, no inner life at all: what little we glean about him is inferred from what he does, his actions and behaviour, rather than what he thinks which is not just concealed from us but, as we come to suspect, is nothing because he is incapable of

---

[117] Fabre and Skinner, *Conversations with Chester Himes*, p. 22.
[118] Andreas Kalyvas describes Poulantzas's concept of authoritarian statism as 'the subordination of the legislative branch to the executive...the abolition of the separation of powers, the rise of the administrative-bureaucratic state, the crisis of the rule of law...and the significant accentuation of state repression'. See 'The Stateless Theory: Poulantzas's Challenge to Postmodernism', in Aronowitz and Bratsis (eds), *Paradigm Lost*, p. 124.
[119] Manchette qtd in Annissa Belhadjin, 'From Politics to the Roman Noir', *South Central Review* 27:1&2 (Spring, Summer 2010), p. 62.
[120] Platten, *The Pleasures of Crime*, p. 95.
[121] Wark, *The Spectacle of Disintegration* (London and New York, NY: Verso, 2013), p. 157.

contemplation beyond what he must do in order to survive, an animal instinct that can only ever be reactive to circumstances. His violence, when he or Anne, his childhood crush who turns out to be as blank as he is, are threatened, is robotic and devoid of all political content: having killed people to contract because he's been paid to do so, he kills people, in the present of the novel, because they are trying to kill him. This is the logic of Debord's spectacle finally come home to roost. As the nature of his former work and employer come into focus, i.e. that he is product of the Cold War and of an expansionist CIA agenda, the issue of escape, of ever finding a position outside power, is rendered increasingly moot. At stake is the question of who controls the past and the future. Terrier's past is the property of his CIA paymasters but, without the capacity to think and to act as autonomous subject, so is his future, rendering him trapped in a perpetual present, one where, as Fisher's account of capitalist realism makes clear, the old struggle between *détournement* and recuperation *has* played itself out and where Martin's needs have been '*pre-corporated*': extending Debord's understanding of the spectacle, they have been pre-emptively shaped by the pacifying logic of capitalist culture.[122]

Even the ability to find pleasure in the private realm has been squeezed out of him. Unable to satisfy Anne he returns to find her 'straddling' his handler 'and fucking him',[123] a revelation that shocks him into silence, robbing him of another basic function. 'I can't speak anymore', he writes on a pad of paper. 'Complete aphonia. I think it's because of the psychological shock. But I don't understand it' (p. 101). Therefore, at the end of the novel, when Martin, defeated from the outset, is shot in the head but does not die, trapped quite literally in a perpetual present, little changes for him, as he himself acknowledges. Left to wait tables and abandoned by Anne who 'grew tired of three-minute coitus' (p. 153), Martin's babbling is recorded by CIA agents and turned by an academic into a book of memoirs in which it is stated that his leftist ideals 'had not withstood the test of reality' (p. 150) but that is rejected by his former CIA bosses 'on the grounds that it was perfectly ridiculous' (p. 151). Rather than going out in a blaze of uneasy violence, as Aimée Joubert does in *Fatale,* Terrier, assuming the 'prone firing position' goes to sleep and Manchette, *agent provocateur* of the néo-polar, the violent novel of social intervention, is left only to reflect on its inadequacies, on the hollowness of writing as a form of protest and the ease with which it is ensnared by a power that is as ubiquitous as it is all-encompassing. One suspects Manchette isn't blaming the *néo-polar* per se, for his resignation has more to do with the subjection of writing to the exigencies of the marketplace. As Philip Anderson astutely asserts, 'He too is pinned down, with nowhere to go, and nothing to say, subjected in silence to the overt and covert power structures of the world he implicitly shares with his characters.'[124] Still, since the *raison d'être* of the crime story, or at least the kind central to this chapter and indeed this book, has been to

---

[122] Fisher, *Capitalist Realism*, p. 9.
[123] Manchette, *The Prone Gunman*, trans. James Brook (San Francisco, CA: City Lights Books, 2002), p. 98.
[124] Philip Anderson, '*Roman Noir* and Subjectivity: The Last Three Novels of Jean-Patrick Manchette', *Australian Journal of French Studies*, 43:1 (2006), p. 72.

interrogate and negotiate these same power structures, Manchette's final statement is one of failure, an admission of the difficulties of using the genre, with its awkward, uncomfortable proximity to the state and capital, to do the political work he once believed or hoped it could; to hijack and re-route culture for revolutionary ends.

But nor is his final novel, in and of itself, a capitulation to the market, to Debord's society of spectacle—'the autocratic reign of the market economy which had acceded to an irresponsible sovereignty'[125]—even if Terrier himself succumbs to it. Instead, in its off-key strangeness and its refusal to pass judgement on its protagonist or allow us to infer, in any clear-cut way, the meaning of particular actions, Manchette's final novel constitutes not so much a hijacking or re-routing of the crime novel for revolutionary ends as a sly negotiation with power in order not to be subsumed by it. Unlike Himes's tactic in *Plan B*, borrowed from Marx whether he cares to acknowledge it, of direct confrontation, Manchette's realization of the impossibility of finding a position outside of the power of the state and capitalism from which to confront its workings leads him to create an entirely passive figure whose passivity, paradoxically, requires us as readers to think very carefully about the circumstances which have produced it—the 'new techniques of government' that Debord wrote about in 1988 which possess 'all the means necessary to falsify the whole of production and perception'.[126]

Much of the crime fiction examined in this chapter, following or recalibrating Marx, is committed to tackling or laying bare the ills of a political and judicial system, ostensibly set up to serve socially democratic ends, but in fact beholden to the interests of modern capitalism. With *The Prone Gunman*, Manchette, who had started out as a Marxist–Leninist, finally found a way of moving beyond the language of revolution and counter-revolution and recognizing that his reflections on the limits of what the crime novel could do politically might also constitute a subdued form of political resistance. As such, there is something distinctly Foucauldian about this last novel, even though Manchette, with one eye on Debord, remains much more committed than Foucault to locating power in what Debord calls the 'autocratic reign of the market economy' and its links to 'an irresponsible sovereignty'. In *The Prone Gunman*, it is less the case that Terrier is an example of Foucault's self-policing subject but rather that the novel as a whole demonstrates or enacts a form of 'counter conduct'—the idea, developed by Foucault in his later works, e.g. *Security, Territory, Population*, of locating 'more diffuse and subdued forms of resistance' and of seeking not to beat the enemy or capture the state but rather to find ways of bypassing the centre and creating alternative modes or visions of being in the world and hence other ways of governing.[127] For the next generation of crime writers, the task of identifying, let alone tackling power, still located in the practices of government and corporations but

---

[125] Guy Debord, *Comments on the Society of the Spectacle*, trans. Malcolm Imrie (London and New York, NY: Verso, 1990), p. 2.
[126] Debord, *Comments on the Society of the Spectacle*, p. 10.
[127] Michel Foucault, *Security, Territory, Population: Lectures at the Collège de France, 1977–78*, trans. Michel Senellart (Basingstoke: Palgrave Macmillan, 2007), p. 200.

rendered even more amorphous by the new conditions of globalization and the flows of goods, people, and money across state borders would be even more daunting. But the lesson of Manchette's final novel would prove to be both salutary and instructive. For here was a novel that managed to turn its protagonist's capitulation to power into a subtle form of resistance and that would give writers as diverse and politically 'committed' as David Peace and Dominique Manotti a language for, and a means of, perpetuating the dissident energies of the crime story into the contemporary era.[128]

---

[128] It is, strictly speaking, incorrect to claim that Manchette and Manotti belong to different generations, given they were both born in 1942. But while Manchette's later works, concluding with *The Prone Gunmen*, belong to this post-1968 era and find most common ground with writers like Himes and Sjöwall and Wahlöö, Manotti's novels like *Lorraine Connection* and *Affairs of State*, I want to argue, published in the 1990s and 2000s, speak about or to a set of more contemporary preoccupations: e.g. the ongoing effects of global capitalism and the attendant transformation of sovereignty.

7

From Sovereignty to Neoliberalism
Crime Fiction in the Contemporary World

The close, some might say incestuous, relationship between crime fiction and the state which has been the subject of this book should not lead us to assume that the genre as a whole, or particular examples of the genre, are able to collectively give us an authoritative sense of what the state is. If the best definition of the state is famously provided by Max Weber—'a human community that (successfully) claims *monopoly of the legitimate use of physical force* within a given territory'[1]— then the crime stories considered here unpick, though not wholly so, the logic and related claims of this definition. For what, these stories ask, if this claim is *not* successfully articulated or indeed achieved? What if the state, challenged by other bodies, is unable to exercise its monopoly over the use of physical force? What happens when the state's legitimacy is questioned—both because its links to private bodies (corporations and/or individuals) are excavated and because its actions are injurious to certain sections or classes of the populace while offering unconditional protections to others? And what if the state's claim to territorial boundedness, and its pursuit of a policing mandate within clearly demarcated jurisdictional limits, is called into question by the growing transnationalization of crime and indeed policing? The contemporary crime story grapples with these dilemmas and in doing so poses very significant questions against the state's policing mandate and its justice provisions; but at the same time it remains wedded, always uneasily, to the state, to the conditions of possibility established by the state (e.g. that modern political life is made possible by the state), and to the idea or ideal of the law as a universal good and security, as Loader and Walker put it, as an 'indispensable ingredient of any good society'.[2] The unruly, often uncontainable collision between these incommensurate and even wholly contradictory impulses (which constitutes the *prima facie* of the type of crime story that is central to my account of the genre's development) finds its most complex manifestation in contemporary crime stories precisely because the state and state sovereignty, as are traditionally understood, are under most threat in this period.

Essentially what I am talking about is not the state per se but state sovereignty, defined by R.B.J. Walker, one of its most perceptive and far-reaching critics, as 'the

---

[1] Max Weber, *From Max Weber: Essays in Sociology*, eds H.H. Gerth and C. Wright Mills (London: Routledge and Kegan Paul, 1985), p. 78.
[2] Ian Loader and Neil Walker, *Civilizing Security* (Cambridge: Cambridge University Press, 2007), p. 4.

legal expression of the character and legitimacy of the state' and an expression of 'the claim by states to exercise legitimate power within strictly delimited territorial boundaries'.[3] This Weberian formulation, which as James Sheptycki notes in the context of crime and policing, implies 'the existence of a bounded...and named territory within which a policing mandate is executed',[4] continues to cause problems,[5] not least because international crimes such as financial fraud, drug and people trafficking, and smuggling necessarily exceed state limits and because it is increasingly hard to distinguish between the operations of the licit and illicit economies. The crime story is both attuned to the implications of these problems (e.g. when crimes exceed jurisdictional borders or where the probity of the entire state apparatus is called into question by its wilful overlooking of the ever-deepening interpenetration of capital and organized crime) and yet is not always fully or easily able to think beyond the state precisely because it remains so embedded in the state's practices and jurisdictional limits. In an era where the flows of people, goods, money, and capital across national borders are quickening and intensifying, and where it is increasingly hard to distinguish between licit and illicit activities, the issue of whether the crime novel has been able to adapt to, and reflect upon, these deterritorializing impulses and the fracturing and diffusion of sovereignty is a key point of departure for this chapter.

Elizabeth Anker argues that '[t]o exist in a post-Westphalian world is to witness the waning of the nation-state and its formal legal domain, as state influences are ever more subordinated to agonistic forces' such as 'the neo-liberal economic order'.[6] In one sense, she is quite right to draw attention to the numerous ways in which sovereignty has been superseded by other articulations of power not necessarily or solely linked to the state (e.g. Foucault's bio-power). But while the contemporary crime novel is happy to acknowledge significant ruptures in the plate-tectonics of power formations and to draw attention to the ongoing transfer of power from state institutions to private corporations under the auspices of neoliberal reforms,[7] it is less willing to characterize sovereignty only as 'waning' or somehow fatally in decline. As recent works by Don Winslow and David Peace demonstrate, for example, anti-leftist manoeuvrings or drug prohibition initiatives from the 1970s onwards or indeed post-9/11 enhancements of security provisions by state agencies

---

[3] Walker here is describing the 'normative' view of sovereignty in order to dissect and problematize it. See R.B.J. Walker, *Inside/Outside: International Relations as Political Theory* (Cambridge: Cambridge University Press, 1993), p. 165.

[4] Sheptycki qtd in Peter K. Manning, 'Policing New Social Spaces', in J.W.E. Sheptycki (ed.) *Issues in Transnational Policing* (London and New York, NY: Routledge, 2000), p. 177.

[5] Walker argues that the problems associated with traditional or normative definitions of sovereignty are more self-evident in 'accounts of the world beyond the secure confines of territorial jurisdiction' (Walker, *Inside/Outside*, p. 166): for me, the international crime novel or the crime novel that focuses on the transnational dimensions of criminality would be a good example of the self-evident nature of this problem.

[6] Elizabeth S. Anker, 'In the Shadowlands of Sovereignty: The Politics of Enclosure on Alejandro Gonzáles Iñárritu's Babel', *University of Toronto Quarterly*, 82:4 (Fall 2013), p. 953.

[7] David Harvey defines neoliberalism as follows: 'Masked by a lot of rhetoric about individual freedom, liberty, personal responsibility and the virtues of privatization, the free market and free trade, it legitimized draconian policies designed to restore and consolidate capitalist class power.' See Harvey, *The Enigma of Capital and the Crisis of Capitalism* (London: Profile, 2011), p. 10.

have led to intensification of state power, rather than its withering away.[8] Yet, as Loader and Walker make clear, there is also much evidence to support the view that 'the political and legal sovereignty of the state over its bounded territory...is being eroded by flows of capital, people, information, goods and economic power that criss-cross and undermine territorial borders' and that 'the state's monopoly over legitimate coercion...is giving way in the face of the emergent claims...of private security interests working beyond the state, forms of "grassroots" communal policing below the state, and transnational security networks operating above the state'.[9]

Perhaps these two positions—the simultaneous waning and intensification of sovereignty—are not as far apart as we might think and are actually related, insofar as both speak to or about sovereignty as performance: this performative aspect attesting to the ways in which the heightened or exaggerated projection of state power necessarily conceals, often barely so, its fragility, and underscoring Lauren Berlant's astute description of sovereignty as 'fantasy misrecognized as an objective state'.[10] If this tension—and the shift back and forth between contested articulations of sovereign power and what we might call the emergence of newer forms of neoliberal governance—constitutes the jumping-off point for this chapter, we should not see it as entailing an uncomplicated passage of one condition to another; i.e. the wholesale usurping of sovereignty with another form of totalizing power. Wendy Brown argues that neoliberalism 'must be conceived of as more than a set of free market economic policies that dismantle welfare states and privatize public services'; i.e. that we also need to emphasize how these policies have a direct effect on 'the organization of the social, the subject, and the state'.[11] But in making these connections, we need to be careful about overdetermining the capacities of neoliberal practices for producing homogeneous societies and subjects. As Berlant puts it, the term 'neoliberal' is best understood as a 'heuristic' for 'pointing to a set of delocalized processes that have played a huge role in transforming postwar political and economic norms of reciprocity and meritocracy since the 1970s' but not a 'world-homogenizing' system 'whose forces are played out to the same effect, or affect, everywhere'.[12]

This important qualification helps to set up the basic architecture of the chapter, whereby the continuing presence and effects of sovereignty, as intensified and waning, and the passage back and forth between sovereignty and neoliberalism, or sovereignty as neoliberalism, is explored through a consideration of a wide range of contemporary crime novels from around the globe. If the focus remains primarily

---

[8] See, for example, H. Richard Friman and Peter Andreas (eds), *The Illicit Global Economy and State Power* (Lanham, MA: Rowman & Littlefield, 1999); and Peter Andreas and Ethan Nadelman, *Policing the Globe: Criminalization and Crime Control in International Relations* (Oxford: Oxford University Press, 2006).
[9] Loader and Walker, *Civilizing Security*, pp. 18–19.
[10] Lauren Berlant, *Cruel Optimism* (Durham, NC and London: Duke University Press, 2011), p. 97.
[11] Wendy Brown, 'American Nightmare: Neoliberalism, Neoconservatism, and De-Democratization', *Political Theory*, 34:6 (December 2006), p. 693.
[12] Berlant, *Cruel Optimism*, p. 9.

on European and US examples, in order to reflect and consolidate the geographical frame of the book as a whole, some effort is made to extend this lens to include other locales and traditions (e.g. South Africa, Mexico, Japan) though of course there is much more work that needs to be done in this particular area. The larger point of course is that the effects of this complicated passage back and forth between sovereignty and neoliberalism are felt and depicted differently by this diverse group of crime writers and novels: there are—because of the novels I have chosen to look at—clear shared areas of concern and interest, to do with the precarity of life in the neoliberal economy and the growing interpenetration of the domains of crime, politics, and business; but the precise ways in which these concerns or interests are dealt with, and play out, in the novels themselves differ from text to text.

Given the enormous spread of crime fiction right the way across the globe, this chapter could not hope to adequately map and explain this proliferation, nor offer an equitable account of this spread not just throughout Europe, Australia, and the Americas but also into Asia and Africa as well. Instead I have been much more judicious in my selections, choosing to look at crime novelists and novels that best exemplify, though in not necessarily synonymous ways, the aforementioned preoccupations and tensions. In the first section, The State of Emergency and Parapolitics, I look at the attempts by David Peace and Eoin McNamee to recover the recent past (e.g. Britain and Ireland in the 1970s and early 1980s) and to excavate the state's hidden archive and, in doing so, to think about the state's coercive capacities, especially at moments of crisis or emergency, where it is no longer possible to distinguish between norms and exceptions.

One important consequence of the resulting crisis of sovereignty (which in turn becomes constituted of what sovereignty is) is the related parcelling out of security initiatives to individuals, private contractors, and paramilitary groups, whereby these parties represent both the emerging contours of what Wilson and others have termed 'parapolitics'[13] and also the beginnings of neoliberal forms of governance (whereby the state cedes authority to other bodies). In the second section, Sovereignty, Neoliberalism, Gender, beginning with Margie Orford's Cape Town-based Claire Hart novels, I consider the gendered nature of sovereignty and the links unearthed by the novels between state power and misogynistic violence, but I also think about what the traditional public/private dichotomy (which arguably produces a gendered sovereignty in the first place) means in the context of the transfer of public power into private control. The exact nature of crime in Natsuo Kirino's *Out* (1997) and Dominique Manotti's *Lorraine Connection* (2006) and its linkages to the workplace and the larger neoliberal economy, especially the kind of low-paid, factory work performed by women and immigrants, allows us to think about the nature of 'precarity' (i.e. as a political and economic condition suffered by the working poor and an affective environment) and whether this transfer of power has produced a neoliberal female subjectivity capable of more than merely surviving in the global economy.

---

[13] See Eric Wilson (ed.) *Government of the Shadows: Parapolitics and Criminal Sovereignty* (London: Pluto, 2009).

The third section, Capitalist Noir, is organized around this trope—the idea that the interpenetration of crime, politics, and business is now so pervasive that it produces a bleak, potentially totalizing imaginary whereby all expressions of deviance and violence, however shocking, can be understood as an inevitable symptom of free market rationality. While crime novels by Pierre Lemaitre and Lauren Beukes use the genre to project, in grotesque and deliberately excessive ways, the exploitative, destructive impulses of contemporary capitalism, they also offer a legal and judicial framework, in the form of a good cop, for addressing the problem. More far-reaching examples of 'capitalist noir' can be found in novels by James Sallis and Massimo Carlotto where the effects of what Carlotto calls 'strategic alliances between entrepreneurs, financial policing bodies, politics and organized crime'[14] can be seen to saturate and affect all aspects of life and from which there is no refuge. The issue of what it means to be a political or even leftist crime novelist in an era where it is impossible to imagine an alternative to capitalism is the jumping off point for this section.

In the final section of the chapter, Borders, Sovereignty, and the Globe, the internationalization of the contemporary crime fiction genre, and its capacities for interrogating the ever quickening flows, legal and illegal, of people, goods, and capital across state borders, take centre stage. Don Winslow's hybrid crime/espionage novel *The Power of the Dog* (2005) and China Miéville's sf/crime 'crossover' novel *The City & The City* (2009) are used to explore the implications of this questioning of borders, territorial integrity, and jurisdictional norms, and to consider whether their questioning of the formal and geographical limits of the genre has enabled them to better map the complex passage back and forth between spectacular articulations of state power on the one hand and the usurping of this power by other interests and procedures of governance on the other.

THE STATE OF EMERGENCY AND PARAPOLITICS: DAVID PEACE AND EOIN MCNAMEE

It is perhaps appropriate for this book that David Peace's *GB84* (2004) reimagines the 1984 miners' strike as 'The Third English Civil War',[15] and that the novel itself is haunted by spectres of the original English civil war: 'Roundheads lead their horses around the road. Bloody. In retreat' (p. 112). For it was in response to the destruction unleashed by this particular conflict that Hobbes wrote *Leviathan*, arguing that power could not be shared, or sovereignty divided, because this would lead to internal discord and thereby to war, 'contrary to the end for which all Sovereignty is instituted'.[16] The spectre of Hobbes, where our story of crime and detection began, hovers over the novel, as well as the frames and language of war,

---

[14] Massimo Carlotto, 'Eulogy for Jean-Claude Izzo', in Jean-Claude Izzo, *Total Chaos*, trans. Howard Curtis (New York, NY: Europa, 2013), p. 12.
[15] David Peace, *GB84* (London: Faber and Faber, 2004), p. 137.
[16] Thomas Hobbes, *Leviathan*, ed. Richard Tuck (Cambridge: Cambridge University Press, 1996), p. 130.

which in Hobbesian terms is a consequence of the failure of sovereign power to enforce its indivisibility: in *GB84* flying pickets and police reinforcements are mobilized, bridgeheads are achieved, battlefields are staked out and fought on. For Hobbes, as Norberto Bobbio tells us, the sovereign cannot be challenged on moral or even legal grounds because whatever the sovereign commands is right,[17] and as such we can usefully see Carl Schmitt's definition of sovereignty ('Sovereign is he who decides on the exception'[18]) as an extension of Hobbesian thought. For Schmitt, the Weimer jurist and critic of weak, divisible government, the sovereign can be located in the law because it is through the law that the sovereign rules, and yet can also be located outside of the law in order to suspend the law in times of emergency, a paradoxical move that in turn becomes constitutive of what sovereignty is.[19]

In Peace's novel, the same double manoeuvre is attempted, so that the law is at times invoked by Margaret Thatcher and her government to sanction their move to break the strike ('Today is their day in court. The first of many days', p. 96), and yet Peace also wants to draw attention to the exceptional or emergency nature of the state's power, and to underscore its repressive, anti-democratic character: the bypassing of the legislature by the executive, the subversion of the press for propaganda purposes and the deployment of the police *en masse*, and the use of special 'emergency' policing powers, against organized labour.[20] Peace's evocation of Schmitt, whether consciously intended or not, may seem like an odd move, given Peace's leftist political leanings, but Schmitt's appeal, as Loader and Walker explain, lies in his ability to draw out 'the deep antagonisms that constitute political life and the role of extra-legal violence in constituting democratic politics that aim to be free of violence'.[21] Further excavating this link between Peace and Schmitt, Matthew Hart argues that *GB84* wants to excavate the 'deep sociological fracture' whereby the multitude splits and 'devolves into something like civil war' and where power is depicted as 'indivisible and antagonistic'—not, that is, to wallow in the viciousness but to reflect upon and perhaps even lament what has been produced by this 'existential antagonism' and by the sovereign's recourse to extra-legal violence as a constitutive element of its power.[22]

The antagonisms in Eoin McNamee's Blue trilogy—*The Blue Tango* (2001), *Orchid Blue* (2010), and *Blue is the Night* (2014), three novels that shine a light into the dark corners of legal and political machinations in the north of Ireland after the Second World War and prior to the onset of the Troubles—are less visible but just as pernicious. *Orchid Blue* revisits the circumstances behind Robert

---

[17] Norberto Bobbio, *Thomas Hobbes and the Natural Law Tradition* (Chicago, IL and London: University of Chicago Press, 1993), p. 57.
[18] Carl Schmitt, *Political Theology: Four Chapters on the Concept of Sovereignty*, trans. George Schwab (Chicago, IL and London: University of Chicago Press, 2005), p. 5.
[19] See Schmitt, *Political Theology*, p. 13.
[20] For a fuller account of the state's repressive arsenal, see Paddy Hillyard and Jane Percy-Smith, *The Coercive State: The Decline of Democracy in Britain* (London: Fontana, 1988).
[21] Loader and Walker, *Civilizing Security*, p. 84.
[22] Matthew Hart, 'The Third English Civil War: David Peace's "Occult History" of Thatcherism', *Contemporary Literature*, 49:4 (Winter 2009), pp. 590, 591.

McGladdery's execution by the state for the murder of Pearl Gamble in 1961. It posits that the presiding judge, Lord Justice Lancelot Curran, 'sabotaged' McGladdery's defence as recompense for the murder of his own daughter, Patricia, nine years earlier—the subject of *The Blue Tango*. 'There was not one shadow of doubt that McGladdery would pay for the happenings of that night nine years before', Curran's election agent and political fixer Harry Ferguson muses.[23] In *Blue is the Night*, most of which is set in 1949, Curran, this time as prosecuting counsel for the Crown, takes on and dissects Robert Taylor who is accused of murdering Mary McGowan, a respectable Catholic woman. Taylor is Protestant and while he is most likely guilty, mob justice and political expediency decree that a Protestant cannot hang for killing a 'Papist': 'The people that run this city. They won't let one of their own be convicted for something like this.'[24] Curran's determination to see Taylor convicted could be construed as an ethical act, given Taylor's likely guilt, but his remark in *Orchid Blue* that '[j]ustice is a by-product of our system of law, not an end' (p. 234) would suggest otherwise. In this sense, his determination to see Taylor hang is best characterized as a high-stakes game of cards because he knows that Ferguson will do all he can to 'nobble' the jury (in order to secure a 'not guilty' verdict), something that will, in turn, save Curran's career. 'If he wins', Ferguson explains, 'it'll be seen as turning against his own side. Then he's finished' (p. 51). The spectre of a shadowy cabal of Protestant men—the 'people who run this city'—making sovereign decisions, e.g. about who gets to live and die, in consort with 'the mob', in order to ward off further agitation, characterizes sovereignty in Schmittian terms as the exception. But in light of this cabal's recourse to violence at once characterized as legal and extra-legal, and the unashamed partiality and sectarianism of its interventions, McNamee's novels ask probing questions about the legitimacy of these arrangements and about the illegality of the judicial order.

In his 'Critique of Violence' (1921) Walter Benjamin claims that the 'in the exercise of violence over life and death... law reaffirms itself' and at the same time reveals itself to be 'rotten' but he goes on to argue that, despite this rottenness, legal decisions are visible and subject to scrutiny, and that by contrast police violence is not connected to 'general law' or is not even subject to it:

> [T]he 'law' of the police really marks the point at which the state... can no longer guarantee through the legal system the empirical ends that it desires at any price to attain. Therefore the police intervene 'for security reasons' in countless cases where no clear legal situation exists.[25]

What McNamee's Blue trilogy shows us is that law's power is just as formless as the police's because courtroom 'decisions' are in fact determined by private negotiations struck up behind closed doors for reasons that have less to do with law than general security arrangements in the north of Ireland (which in McNamee's work

---

[23] Eoin McNamee, *Orchid Blue* (London: Faber and Faber, 2010), pp. 256, 234.
[24] McNamee, *Blue is the Night* (London: Faber and Faber, 2014), p. 28.
[25] Walter Benjamin, *Reflections: Essays, Aphorisms, Autobiographical Writings*, ed. Peter Demetz, trans. Edmund Jephcott (New York, NY: Schocken Books, 1986), pp. 286–7.

becomes a euphemism for Protestant rule). As such, the vision we get of the Stormont class, in effect a rump Protestant mini-state, is of 'an affluent and corrupted bourgeoisie'[26]—a class within a class where decisions are reached in Belfast's private clubs, always with the interests of this rump in mind, and where no distinctions are made between the executive, judiciary, and policing domains, all boats pulling or being pulled in the same direction. The 'state of exception' which is invoked to justify and which in turn constitutes the claims of sovereignty becomes a measure that, in McNamee's hands, allows us to see its partiality and degeneracy. In effect, the power of the police and judiciary 'is not violence fenced in and directed by reason and law, but violence beyond reason and law'.[27]

In one sense, then, Peace and McNamee draw attention to the expansion and intensification of sovereign power in direct response to internal threats which in turn legitimate its recourse to extra-legal violence. In *GB84*, for example, Peace delineates the symbiotic manoeuvrings of the judiciary, executive, and policing in order to break the miners' strike and safeguard the long-term interests of the political and economic establishment. Still, as Anker points out, the very fact that 'the properties historically tied to nation-state sovereignty are being progressively transferred to other organizations and energies' (e.g. the market) requires that we 'speak of multiple sovereignties that coexist, exerting a surplus of demands that at times coalesce and at others diverge and compete'.[28] The fact that the prime movers in *GB84*'s war against the miners do not operate with the official sanction of public office (i.e. they are not part of the official police force or security service), but in the case of Stephen Sweet, industrialist and free market champion, represent the interests of the emerging neoliberal economic order, means that it may be more helpful to talk about parapolitics than about the political order, as it is traditionally understood. In other words we're talking about the multiplication of sovereignty which in turn exposes the 'strange, powerful, clandestine and apparently structural relationship between state security-intelligence apparatuses, terrorist organisations and transnational organised criminal syndicates' with a view of 'sustaining illiberal and anti-democratic features of the system'.[29]

If Sweet, as Mrs Thatcher's 'bagman', coordinates the police response to the union's use of flying pickets, Neil Fontaine, a former member of the security services and now a freelance operative, is the link between Sweet and the murky, clandestine world of private contractors and counter-espionage. One of the novel's italicized sections focuses on the exploits of David 'the Mechanic' Johnson, who is forcibly sequestered into the counter-insurgency effort, as part of a team who patrol the Yorkshire–Nottingham border in order to deter pickets from disrupting the flow of coal from pits still operating despite the strike.[30] '*The Mechanic and his*

---

[26] McNamee, *The Blue Tango* (London: Faber and Faber, 2001), p. 254.
[27] Loader and Walker, *Civilizing Security*, p. 83.
[28] Anker, 'In the Shadowlands of Sovereignty', p. 953.
[29] Robert Cribb, 'Introduction' in Wilson (ed.) *Government of the Shadows*, p. 1.
[30] Peace also details the violence of the pickets against miners who have returned to work. In one passage he writes: 'The pickets caught the man in his own front room. The pickets set about him with their bats and steel-toe-capped boots... The pickets broke his ankle. The pickets broke his shoulder' (*GB84*, p. 344).

men step forward. They punch the pickets. Bridge of their noses. Kick them. Their balls. The Mechanic and his men put bags on their heads. Tight. Handcuff their hands behind their backs' (p. 98). The Mechanic is one cog in a dense counter-insurgency network, so dense in fact it can't be fully perceived, which also includes Malcolm Morris, government eavesdropper and key player in *Operation Vengeance—Imported from Ulster. Updated for Yorkshire* (p. 127), a refrain repeated throughout *GB84*, as if to underline the connections between parapolitics during the miners' strike and the British state's long war against the Provisional IRA:

> MI5. MI6. Special Branch. The RUC. The army and the SAS –
> Until everything became one long, long scream –
> One long, long scream of places, names, terror and treachery –

Derry. The Bogside. Belfast. The Lower Falls. The Shankill Road. Chichester-Clark. Faulkner. Stormont. McGuirk's Bar. Bloody Sunday… The Miami Showband. Tullyvallen Orange Hall. Whitecross. Kingsmills. Mrs Marie Drumm. Captain Robert Nairac. (p. 417)

As Hart points out, this method—at the level of the sentence—'leads to a pattern of allusions and rhythmical associations between the individual and the social, the national and the international' and allows us to think about how 'personal ethical rot legitimizes wider social crimes'.[31] The focus on ethics, and on the ethical issues raised by representing 'real' events and people from the recent past, requires us— and both Peace and McNamee—to address the reasons behind this move: why do so and how to avoid turning people's lives, experiences, and indeed pain into entertainment? Peace is adamant that 'true crime—and its social and political consequences—is the key to unlock the hidden history' and that 'because crimes happen to actual people in actual places at actual times in history, the crime novel has the opportunity to ask why such crimes happen to those certain people at certain times in certain places'.[32] But what does that mean for *GB84*? What 'crimes' have been committed and why? By whom and for what reasons? And what kind of 'hidden history' is Peace seeking to construct? For McNamee, writing about *GB84* at its time of publication and referencing his novel, *The Ultras*, the answer lies in Peace's excavation of 'the real political field' and of an 'eerie, covert infrastructure falling into place':

> The mass denial of civil liberties, the use of spies, agents provocateurs, psyops, the compliant judiciary, the compliant and subverted media. It's hard not to get a sense of something huge and shambling and reeking of malign intent lurking in the political undergrowth. Something that had its genesis in the north of Ireland in the 1970s.[33]

Here, and in *The Ultras*—which revisits the same Ulster that Malcolm Morris references in *GB84* and particularly the Miami Showband massacre and the disappearance of British army captain Robert Nairac—the frames of crime and war are

---

[31] Matthew Hart, 'An interview with David Peace, conducted by Matthew Hart', *Contemporary Literature*, 47:4 (Winter 2006), p. 548.
[32] 'An interview with David Peace', p. 559.
[33] McNamee, 'Hand-held narrative', *Guardian*, 30 April 2004, http://www.theguardian.com/books/2004/apr/30/news.comment, accessed 15 May 2014.

fused and in doing so, Peace and McNamee ask what happens when internal and external security agendas converge and political power is not bound by the formal requirements of law. The resulting recourse to the 'exceptional' invokes Schmitt's foundational definition—e.g. that this, as Aradau and van Munster note, is not just the stirring up of moral panics so that 'state elites can further their interests' but rather is 'a general concept in the theory of the state'.[34] But the focus in these novels on parapolitics, rather than on politics per se puts greater pressure on the distinction between crime and war and on the horrific 'crimes' perpetuated by the security services, broadly defined, at a time of so-called war in order to apparently safeguard democracy.[35]

McNamee's *The Ultras* is an eerily resonant account of what is troubling about the state's extra-legal violence, not least because the truth about what happened in the past can never be fully recovered and is dependent on one's perspective, on the 'processes of seeing' which as Robert Nairac's eye-surgeon father tells the young Robert, 'were fraught'.[36] This difficulty is written into the structure of the narrative; former RUC officer Blair Agnew has in the present of the novel (i.e. 1999) compiled his own archive on Nairac's disappearance in 1975 (and the assassination of the Miami Showband) and is seeking to re-examine his own complicity in the events leading up to both events. 'Since his own memories about his presence at several atrocities prove…unreliable', Stefanie Lehner notes, Agnew 'turns to the official archive' but finds its records 'destroyed, misplaced…blacked out'.[37] The omniscient narrator can move—unofficially of course—in and out of the past but what we get is more collage or mosaic than official record, fragments rather than facts. Hence McNamee's account of the difficulties of writing *The Ultras*—'[t]he harder you looked, the less you saw. The ground continuously gave way'[38]—is folded into the novel's self-reflexive and self-undermining logic, even at the level of syntax. For example, this is left behind by Agnew's daughter, part of her last will and testament: 'I can't help thinking about Robert I look at his photograph I look into his eyes. I can't see anything there. Maybe that is the meaning of the word ultra. That you are ultra secret and do not give anything away no matter what' (p. 255).

But for McNamee, the task is 'learning how to see properly' because 'if you describe what you see in front of you, that gives your words authority'[39] and while

---

[34] Claudia Aradau and Rens van Munster, 'Exceptionalism and the "War on Terror": Criminology Meets International Relations', *British Journal of Criminology*, 49:5 (2009), p. 689.

[35] Jeff Huysmans writes about this paradox in the post-9/11 context when 'security knowledge and technology that is meant to protect liberal democracy against violence seriously risks to undermine it'—'Minding Exceptions: The Politics of Insecurity and Liberal Democracy', *Contemporary Political Theory*, 3:3 (2004), p. 322.

[36] McNamee, *The Ultras* (London: Faber and Faber, 2004), p. 7.

[37] Stefanie Lehner, *Subaltern Ethics in Contemporary Scottish and Irish Literature* (Basingstoke: Palgrave Macmillan, 2011), pp. 102, 103.

[38] Interview with Eoin McNamee, Open Book Toronto, http://www.openbooktoronto.com/cbforrest/blog/%E2%80%9C_writer_you_make_your_own_weather%E2%80%9D_irish_crime_writer_eoin_mcnamee_style_voice_and_i, accessed 15 May 2014.

[39] McNamee qtd in Arminta Wallace, 'Turning True Crime into True Blue Fiction', *Irish Times*, 22 March 2014, http://www.irishtimes.com/culture/books/turning-true-crime-into-true-blue-fiction-1.1730683, accessed 27 August 2015.

he may not be able to see and describe everything at the same time, what we get in *The Ultras* is a unsettling collage of related people and events, unsettling because there *is* a connection between them, even if it remains beyond our grasp. The Gemini Health Club in North Belfast, run by David Erskine, in fact a brothel where secret cameras film clients for blackmail purposes; Theipval barracks where 'MRU, PsyOps, 14th Int, MI5' all 'shared the corridor' (p. 26); Clyde Knox, MI6, an authority on 'disorientation techniques in interrogation' and 'sensory deprivation' (p. 27); Nairac, a liminal figure who traverses the North–South border and whose allegiances remain unknown and unknowable; Agnew, a rogue cop who moves in these circles; 'an atmosphere of barely contained psychosis' (p. 87) and the need for an 'atrocity to move things along' (p. 167). The convergence of all these fragments is the assassination of the Miami Showband, Nairac's presence at the massacre, and his disappearance soon after, 'the idea of getting out of control now, spiralling downwards' (p. 216).

What is being recovered here is not simply a truth about the willingness of the security-intelligence services to use extra-legal violence but rather an articulation about what happens when this violence spirals out of control, when its point or purpose cannot even be fathomed. This is not necessarily the state—and the state of exception—imagined by Schmitt, where authoritarianism and the suppression of some civil liberties is the price to pay for security, but something more inchoate, sovereignty turned inwards and privatized, a world where no one makes decisions and where the state, though strengthened in one sense by the context of war, in fact recedes, in the sense that one cannot discern its shape, its role, its mobilizations. To bring Peace's *GB84* back in, what is being recovered, from the perspective of the twenty-first century, an era of New Labour and the Celtic Tiger, is an important moment in the state's transformation under neoliberalism. The overriding sense is *not* how much better or safer the present is (despite the fact that there is, as McNamee remarks, nothing now 'to compare to that feeling of constitution extremity'[40]), but that the neoliberal reforms of our current epoch,[41] with their emphasis on the privatization of public institutions and assets and the relentless privileging of free trade and individual freedom over collective rights and responsibilities, are not the triumph of 'common-sense' thinking or the working out of the 'natural order'. Instead, as we see in *GB84*, this neoliberal logic has its own dark history, and had to be brought into the world using extra-legal violence and via the politicized state's eagerness to contract out its work to paramilitary and parapolitical bodies.

To the question of what, if anything, can be done in the face of what Hart calls this 'violent triumph of neoliberalism',[42] Peace and McNamee offer some insights but no proselytizing, no false revolutionary sentiment. *GB84* ends with the defeat of the miners and by implication the entire political left. The politics of

---

[40] McNamee, 'Hand-held Narrative'.
[41] In line with this claim, David Harvey defines neoliberalism as a 'class project that coalesced in the crisis of the 1970s'. See *The Enigma of Capital*, p. 10.
[42] 'An interview with David Peace', p. 549.

direct confrontation attempted by the miners, hewn from the rock of Marxist revolutionary sentiment, fails miserably, even if the (Marxist) analysis of the situation is spot on ('an unprecedented and wholesale operation involving unlawful actions of the police, organized violence against the miners... and their communities by means of an unconstitutionally and nationally controlled police force', p. 265). As the crime novels of Himes, Manchette, and Sjöwall and Wahlöö make clear (see Chapter 6), the genre, with its complex and ambivalent relationship to the state, would not easily accommodate revolutionary thinking in general and Marxist analysis in particular, despite a shared sense of the state's willingness to act in favour of those with deepest pockets.[43] It would be wrong to blame the miners' failure in *GB84* on the novel's representative leftist figure, Terry Winters, but he is too naive, and too focused on the minutiae, to really see what is happening to him, to the miners, and to the country. Instead, and if we turn to McNamee's Blue trilogy, it is to the insider, the figure compromised by his or her associations with power, the state's unwilling executioner, that we must turn for a sense of how to effectively intervene in the world—not necessarily to change it for the better but to register small victories in a larger landscape of defeats.[44]

Take, for example, the case of Eddie McCrink, the police detective charged with finding Pearl Gamble's murderer in *Orchid Blue*: McCrink may do his job and fit up Robert McGladdery for the noose but his growing interest in Lance Curran and his wife Doris, and their possible involvement in their daughter's murder nine years earlier, is too direct and too clumsy to bear any fruit. Compare this to the much cannier, much slyer approach of Harry Ferguson who harbours similar suspicions but uses his insider status, his proximity to the Currans and those with power, to get closer to the truth, something, McNamee implies at the end of *Blue is the Night*, that indicates a quiet subversion of extant power relations. 'The phone would ring again... Men who bade him come to them that they might show how they had mastered the world when the truth was that they always had attended on his will' (p. 259). What is being excavated here is an era marked both by the ascendency of 'authoritarian statism' and paradoxically by the growing transfer of power and authority to other bodies, other entities: sovereignty transformed by the emerging logic of neoliberalism. In the face of this power, the crime novel can bear witness to crisis and attendant abuses of power but its protagonists, even ones as canny as Ferguson, are too immersed in the grubbiness to do more than see—another way of speaking about the tension that has always been central to the genre.

---

[43] In David Peace's *Nineteen Seventy Four* (London: Serpent's Tail, 1999), we see techniques of torture employed during police interrogations which serve, directly or otherwise, the interests of the capitalist classes.

[44] Here, as in Chapter 6, it might be more helpful to talk about 'more diffuse and subdued forms of resistance' rather than direct confrontation—see Michel Foucault, *Security, Territory, Population: Lectures at the Collège de France, 1977–78*, trans. Michel Senellart (Basingstoke: Palgrave Macmillan, 2007), p. 200.

SOVEREIGNTY, NEOLIBERALISM, GENDER: MARGIE ORFORD, NATSUO KIRINO, AND DOMINIQUE MANOTTI

One of the problems of focusing on crime fiction's complex relationship to sovereignty, even if the focus is on the ways in which the genre unsettles straightforward understandings of the authority and jurisdictional limits of state power, is a tendency to overlook the quieter operations of power in the domestic and/or private domains. And yet, if one can generalize that female crime writers have traditionally preferred to explore the intricacies of the private world of home, family, and money as opposed to trying to directly address and comment on the inner logic of the criminal justice system, the move by contemporary female crime writers like Karin Slaughter, Margie Orford, and Carol O'Connell, following earlier efforts by P.D. James and Ruth Rendell, to reclaim the public (and, say, the operation of the police and justice system) as the main point of departure for their works, has brought into focus a blind spot that has troubled my account of the genre's development: the gendered nature of sovereignty and the extent to which this results in the occlusion or downplaying of male efforts to silence or marginalize women—both through an appeal to procedural norms that are themselves gendered and an unthinking sanctioning of misogyny.

In the first part of this section, I want to think about the effects of Margie Orford's willingness to confront the pervasiveness of this misogyny in South African society and more specifically in the policing and legal system and hence the gendered character of sovereignty. But the move by some contemporary crime novels to explore the implications of the transfer of public power to private corporations, ushered in by neoliberal reforms,[45] has, I want to suggest in the second part, some potentially far-reaching consequences for this account of the relationship between gender and sovereignty. On the one hand, Natsuo Kirino's *Out* and Dominique Manotti's *Lorraine Connection*, both of which start with similarly bleak accounts of the precarious nature of low-paid factory work carried out by women and ethnic minorities, mourn the loss of a usable 'public' sphere (where these women could have petitioned for equal rights, etc.) and detail, with great unease, the underlying precarity of low-paid labour in the neoliberal economy. At the same time, these novels are keen to think about whether the waning and fragmentation of sovereignty affords their female subjects the opportunity to recast their labour perhaps not in straightforwardly emancipatory terms but rather to reflect on what Wendy Brown calls 'the problem of freedom'—that which is never quite achievable or the permanent struggle against what 'will otherwise be done to and for us'.[46]

---

[45] Robin Truth Goodman argues that in 'a neoliberal age, the problem of state sovereignty characterizes the police as a public authorization interrupted constantly, and antagonistically, by regimes of private production'. See *Policing Narratives and the State of Terror* (Albany, NY: State University Press of New York, 2009), p. 13. The articulation of this problem, she rightly claims, becomes one of the central issues for the paradigmatic crime stories of the era.

[46] Wendy Brown, *States of Injury: Power and Freedom in Late Modernity* (Princeton, NJ: Princeton University Press, 1995), p. 25.

Margie Orford's Cape Town-based crime novels, featuring Clare Hart, a profiler and police auxiliary, make subtle but penetrating connections between individual cases of abuse and exploitation perpetrated against women and children and the larger structures of power that govern social relations and safeguard patriarchal dominance. In *Water Music* (2013) Clare is called on to investigate the circumstances behind the discovery of a traumatized child and possible links to the disappearance of a teenage girl and, as the story unfolds, the murders of another child and a woman in her thirties who has whip scars on her back. The unfolding plot might implicate a single deviant figure—a farmer called Noah Stern whose wife, when she is confronted about his crimes, tells Clare, 'This is not a safe country for girls'[47]—and set in place a fairly hackneyed denouement where Clare, along with the missing teenager, is held captive by Stern and must engineer her escape. But the map 'with the forest of pins' attached to the wall of the Section 28 office where Clare works—the red pins showing 'where injured children have been found' and green pins indicating 'the ones that didn't make it' (p. 41)—tells its own story: not only that South Africa is very much *not* a safe country for children but more disturbingly that the violent mistreatment of children, and women, is becoming routinized and is being downgraded as a priority by the policing and political establishment. Section 28, we find out, is 'a clause in the Constitution that guarantees children their rights' (p. 37) but the office set up to oversee this process is, in the novel, being 'dissolved' or to use the language of neoliberalism or downsizing, '[e]xpertise in this area is being redeployed' in order to prioritize 'economic stability' (p. 39) and 'the preservation of law and order' (p. 181). What this tells us is that, in the face of evidence to the contrary—the continuing and ongoing brutalization of women and children that Clare must investigate here, and in other novels in the series—the state's priorities lie elsewhere. In doing so, Orford, with great subtlety and skill, suggests how sovereignty—the legal expression of the authority of the state—might be gendered, insofar as the policing priorities proposed by the political establishment pay little heed to those most affected by male violence and its normalization in the 'new' South Africa. One should add that the presence of Clare Hart, who describes herself as 'almost a cop' (p. 79) and the good work undertaken by Section 28, however imperilled it is, attests to the continuing relevance of the state as a politically progressive force in contemporary society and a necessary bulwark against the relentless march of neoliberal economic reforms.

Elsewhere in Orford's series, notably *Gallows Hill* (2011) where an investigation into the remains of women and children discovered on a construction site brings into focus the close relationship between big business and policing elites, the notion that the public power of the police, itself always already gendered, is at times beholden to regimes of private production, in turn has profound implications for the construction of female subjectivity. Historically of course the dichotomy between public and private, as Carole Pateman maintains, 'is central to almost two centuries of feminist writing and political struggle; and it is, ultimately, what the

---

[47] Margie Orford, *Water Music* (London: Head of Zeus, 2014), p. 269.

feminist movement is about'.[48] Or, as Ruth Gavison puts it, even 'feminists who advocate versions of the "no difference" claims agree that, in our social reality, pervasive differences exist between public and private, and that these differences, real and perceived, greatly affect the situation of women'.[49]

Turning my attention to two contemporary crime novels, written by Natsuo Kirino and Dominique Manotti, both of which situate the low-paid factory work undertaken by women and immigrants in the context of a larger narrative about public and private criminality, I want to trace and interrogate two related moves. First, the continuing relevance of the public/private dichotomy in an era of economic neoliberalism, whereby the retreat of the state and its protocols about fair workplace practices has resulted in deepening patterns of exploitation, especially for the low-paid, mostly female workers who constitute these novels' subjects. And second, the notion that crime in these novels might relate to more than individual acts of deviance and that by exploring connections between crime, solidarity, and protest, Kirino and Manotti open up a space to think about workplace resistance, via the public activities of the unions and attempts to reclaim the private realm of deregulated labour for potentially progressive ends.

Kirino's *Out*, first published in Japan in 1997 but not translated into English until 2004, follows the entwined paths of four female workers employed in a 'boxed lunch factory...in the middle of the Musashi-Murayama district [in Tokyo], facing a road that was abutting the grey wall of a large automobile plant'.[50] The grimy industrial landscape and 'the exhaust fumes from the Shin-Oume Expressway' (p. 1) is reflected in the monotonous nature of the work itself: from 'midnight until five-thirty without a break' standing 'at the conveyor belt making boxed lunches' (p. 1). In one sense, the description of the production line and division of labour, where each worker is assigned to a particular task, is evocative of Marx's account of estranged labour whereby 'the worker is related to the product of his labour as to an alien object' which in turn leads to his or her alienation.[51] Certainly there is no affective connection between workers and the process or object of their labour. One can quite literally feel the life dripping from Masako Katori as each meal makes 'its way down the line, assembled in so many small increments' (p. 10). In another sense, however, the 'scene' is a contemporary one: the labour force, comprising part-time, female, and overseas workers, and paid a subsistence wage, are the economic losers of the 'flexible' labour market and of the neoliberal economic reforms. Drawing upon delineations of these reforms provided by Saskia Sassen and David Harvey, Chris Breu points out that Kirino's novel traces how the 'neoliberal transformation of global cities like Tokyo' produce 'an "economic polarization" in which the managerial and financial class fractions benefit from a

---

[48] Carol Pateman, *The Disorder of Women: Democracy, Feminism and Political Theory* (Cambridge: Polity, 1989), p. 118.
[49] Ruth Gavison, 'Feminism and the Public/Private Distinction', *Stanford Law Review*, 45:1 (November 1992), p. 21.
[50] Natsuo Kirino, *Out*, trans. Stephen Snyder (London: Vintage, 2004), p. 1.
[51] Karl Marx, *Economic and Philosophic Manuscripts of 1844*, trans. Martin Milligan, ed. Dirk J. Struik (London: Lawrence & Wishart, 1973), p. 108.

major increase in real wages...workers in the manufacturing sector...experience "the informalization and casualization of work"'.[52] For Kirino's female subjects, the move into the public domain of work is not an emancipatory one. Nor does their daily retreat into the private realm of family offer them respite: Masako has to deal with rejection by her husband and teenage son; Yayoi has to cope with a husband who beats her; and Yoshie is weighed down by a spoiled daughter and infirm mother-in-law. All carry the burden of the household chores. As such, the factory functions as mirror of the home, whereby all four women are corralled by the related logic of capitalism and patriarchy into subject positions that mutually reinforce their subordinate status. This is an age-old story of course but what marks *Out*'s portrait of workplace and domestic subjugation as distinctly modern is its linking of the precarity of these four women and the extent to which, as Harvey puts it, 'neoliberal economic practices mobilize this insecurity in unprecedented ways',[53] to their entire world, or affective environment, so that a sense of exploitation and violence shapes every aspect of their existences.

The novel pivots around a murder: Yayoi strangles her abusive husband and Masako agrees to help get rid of the corpse. The act itself, unpremeditated but nonetheless 'thrilling' (p. 61), is less transgressive than the cutting up and disposing of the corpse, which Masako treats 'as just one more unpleasant job' (p. 80) and for which she solicits the labour of her co-workers, Yoshie ('the skipper') and Kuniko, having first agreed a fee. 'Four hundred for the Skipper and one for Kuniko. She's just going to help us get rid of the bags. I think they'll settle for that,' Masako informs Yayoi (p. 120). Kirino's move here is to treat what is, for all intents and purposes, a criminal act or series of criminal acts (e.g. aiding and abetting, perverting the course of justice, and manslaughter, if not murder itself) as work, where everyone has a specific role to perform, something that analogizes the factory's division of labour and in turn requires us to consider not just crime as work but also work as crime—the production line, with its unequal exchange between labour and wages, as a form of criminality.

But what kind of labour is this? Certainly the work, cutting up the body, is unpleasant, perhaps more so than making lunch boxes, but treating the act as work allows Kirino to drain it of sensationalism and connect it to the duties undertaken in the factory. Still if for Kirino, the production line and division of labour is implicated in the exploitative nature of capitalist production, especially for the low-paid women who make up the majority of the workforce, does the same apply to this other type of deregulated labour? Here it is worth turning our attention back to the nature of the public/private split, and its implications for women in the factory, in order to tease out the complexities of Kirino's associations. For J.S. Mill and liberal theory in general, individual freedom depends on the separation of public and private and the privileging of the latter over the former, so that free, equal beings can make their own decisions, and can choose to bring their own

---

[52] Christopher Breu, 'Work and Death in the Global City: Natsuo Kirino's *Out* as Neoliberal Noir', in Andrew Pepper and David Schmid (eds) *Globalization and the State in Contemporary Crime Fiction* (Basingstoke: Palgrave Macmillan, 2016).
[53] Harvey qtd in Berlant, *Cruel Optimism*, p. 192.

labour to the marketplace. But, as feminists such as Pateman have long argued, 'the profound ambiguity of the liberal conception of the private and public obscures the social reality it helps to constitute'—in other words, 'the dichotomy between the private and public obscures the subjection of women...within an apparently universal, egalitarian, individualist order'.[54] Kirino's female workers, of course, do not freely bring their labour to the factory but are compelled, by circumstances and a lack of opportunities elsewhere, to perform menial work for low wages.[55] Moreover the affective environment, conditioned as it is by a general sense of precarity, produces subjects that are always under threat, always one step or stroke of bad luck from dissolution. It is notable, for example, that all the women, except for Masako, owe money, either to each other or to loan companies that underline the parasitic nature of modern capitalism and where there is little to distinguish between the work of the T Credit and Loan company and street-level loan sharking businesses run by the yakuza. Still Kirino is equally keen not to dismiss the move by Masako and the other women back into the home, to dismember corpses for money, as just another form of subjugation. After all, Masako is more of a partner in this venture than employee, and their privately contracted labour, whose rates of remuneration are far higher than they could ever earn packing lunch boxes, has important consequences for their and our conceptions of freedom.

The notion of corpse disposal as a fledging business or 'start-up' emerges when Jumonji, a debt collector who, in pursuing one of the women, stumbles upon the truth of what has happened to Yayoi's husband, and persuades them to take on other cases, other corpses to be disposed of. 'I would drum up the business,' Jumonji tells Masako. 'Once we took delivery of a shipment, you would cut it up and then I'd get rid of it' (p. 333). If the lunch box factory is one example of the intensification of the inequalities between wage relations and labour power under conditions of neoliberalism (i.e. where the practice of hiring part-time, female, and foreign workers to create a flexible labour force, is, one could argue, a ruse to cut wages and reduce union participation), what can be said about this other venture? In one sense, it is also a product or indeed consequence of neoliberal economics: Jumonji who finds the 'units' and negotiates a fee, contracts the work to Masako for a percentage of this fee who in turn sub-contracts the work to Yoshie and Kuniko for a cut of her fee. In other words, this is an example of changes in the labour market to create more flexible, specialist, and non-unionized forms of employment. But Kirino, clearly no advocate or celebrant of the neoliberal move 'to bring all human action into the domain of the market'[56] wants to at least consider whether the passage for these women from the factory into the home, not as a form of re-domestication but rather as private contractors who have a significant stake, financial and operational, in the success of the venture, could be construed as something other than power reasserting itself in new ways—i.e. as something

---

[54] Pateman, *The Disorder of Women*, p. 120.
[55] They only 'enjoy' parity with male workers from abroad, like Kazuo Miyamori, who is half-Japanese, half-Brazilian and whose loneliness and misery at the 'mindless, backbreaking work' (p. 154) mirrors their own subjugation.
[56] Harvey, *A Brief History of Neoliberalism* (Oxford: Oxford University Press, 2007), p. 3.

other than an ostensibly emancipatory move that in fact mirrors, to quote Brown, 'the mechanisms of power of which [it is] an effect and which [it] purport[s] to oppose'.[57]

For a start, the operation is not premised on the kind of exploitative wage relations to the labour power characteristic of the lunch box factory or capitalist production generally: each 'worker' is paid different amounts, depending on his or her 'responsibilities' and 'experience' but the arrangement is more akin to a profit share, even if, when it comes to the work itself, 'there was really very little difference between this job and the one they did at the factory' (p. 368). One needs to be careful about how far to push this claim about female solidarity—after all Kuniko seeks to blackmail Yayoi in order to grab a larger share of the pot and yields information about the initial murder to Jumonji in return for the cancellation of her debt. But when Yoshie approaches Masako for a loan, after she realizes she's been robbed by her daughter, Masako refuses to act as a bank ('you'd have no way to pay me back... It's bad policy to make loans like that') and instead gives her the money. 'You've been a great help in all of this,' she says, adopting an approach that no capitalist venture would ever try to copy (p. 403).

There is only so far that Kirino can or wants to push the crime–business analogy—to present crime, i.e. the cutting up and disposal of dead bodies, as work and work, i.e. cutting up bodies *and* packing lunch boxes, as crime, even if this merging mirrors the connections elsewhere in the novel between licit and illicit operations (e.g. loan companies/loan sharking operations; bars/gambling dens; escort services/prostitution rings). Contra these blurrings, Kirino gives us an out-and-out sociopath, Mitsuyoshi Satake, who has sadistically killed a woman for pleasure and who in the present of the novel, once he's been mistakenly accused of murdering Yayoi's husband, turns on the four women, and especially Masako, to exact his revenge. Critics of the novel are split about the implications of the climactic scene in which Satake ties up, rapes, and try to kill Masako in a disused factory (before she turns the tables and kills him). Amanda Seaman reads the novel in general and the ending in particular as evidence of 'a deeply conservative nature' that is symptomatic of the genre with its 'interest in establishing order and preserving social harmony' and sees Masako's final act as a form of escape, rather than a way of addressing society's gendered and economic ills.[58] Conversely Raechel Dumas argues that 'Kirino's decision to set the rape of Masako within the abandoned bentō factory' connects what would seem to be a personal struggle to 'a public space—a space explicitly designed for the purpose of exploiting its workers'.[59] Chris Breu agrees, stating that an image of Masako in a disused factory 'tied to a conveyor belt like the one on which she usually works' and described as 'an enormous concrete coffin' becomes 'a condensation of the various forms of violence

---

[57] Brown, *States of Injury*, p. 3.
[58] Amanda Seaman, 'Cherchez La Femme: Detective Fiction, Women, and Japan', *Japan Forum*, 16:2 (2004), p. 189.
[59] Raechel Lynn Dumas, 'Domesticity, Criminality and Part-Time Work: The Labouring Body in Natsuo Kirino's *Auto*', http://pqdtopen.proquest.com/doc/873456736.html?FMT=ABS, accessed 27 August 2015.

associated with neoliberalism'—e.g. where Masako 'literally becomes the commodity to be consumed and then thrown away'.[60]

These latter claims seem to carry more weight but the bigger question for me, and indeed for Breu, is exactly what kind of freedom is being proposed. Certainly *Out* is scornful of the freedoms promised either by liberalism (e.g. where individuals can freely exchange their labour in the marketplace for financial remuneration) or neoliberalism (e.g. where the market becomes the main catalyst for bringing about freedom) but its insistence on considering freedom not just as a philosophical problem but rather in Brown's words as something that is 'responsive to social forces and institutions—the sites and sources of domination'[61] permits a harder-nosed and more wary appreciation of the limits and potential of individual action. The fact that Masako's freedom isn't some kind of generic inevitability, i.e. it isn't something that inevitably accrues from the working out of the plot, but, to quote Brown again, is 'suffused not just with ambivalence but with anxiety, because it is flanked by the problem of power on all sides' means that *Out* offers a damning verdict on the claims of neoliberalism and a way of moving the 'feminist' crime novel beyond its 'kick ass' incarnations—whereby the unattached female private investigator, in effect, does as she likes within certain limits[62] and where little attention is paid to 'the powers that situate, constrain and produce subjects as well as the will to power entailed in practicing freedom'.[63]

In *Lorraine Connection*, emphasis is also placed on the menial, precarious, alienating, and life-threatening nature of production-line work, this time in a factory owned by Korean multinational Daewoo in the fictional industrial town of Pondange in Eastern France. As in *Out*, those labouring on the shop floor are predominantly working-class women and/or immigrants, mostly from North Africa, the 'precariat'[64] of the globalized, neoliberal economy. Pondange is in the grip of a post-industrial blight and the Daewoo factory, described as 'a hastily erected sheet-metal cube on wasteland in the bottom of a valley overgrown with weeds' is poor compensation for the demise of the 'Lorraine blast furnaces'—once 'one of the world's most powerful iron and steel industries'.[65] The work itself is dull and monotonous ('The women, also looking grey in the short overalls, lean forward, their eyes constantly moving from the aggressive oblong-shaped bases of the cathode tubes filing past them', p. 3) and is part of a global supply chain, with the cathode ray tubes, once finished, dispatched 'to Poland, where they will be given

---

[60] Breu, 'Work and Death in the Global City'.   [61] Brown, *States of Injury*, p. 7.

[62] For me, Sara Paretsky's VI Warshawski novels would be an example of this kind of crime fiction whereby the separation afforded between the private eye and the conglomerations of power being investigated allow over-simplistic politicization, i.e. whereby Warshawski is comfortably able to oppose the intertwined ills of patriarchy, sovereignty, and capitalism without having to consider her own complicity in extant relations of power.

[63] Brown, *States of Injury*, p. 25.

[64] Guy Standing describes the precariat as a 'growing number of people across the world living and working precariously, usually in a series of short-term jobs, without recourse to stable occupational identities or careers, stable social protection or protective regulations relevant to them'; see *The Precariat: The New Dangerous Class* (London: Bloomsbury, 2011).

[65] Dominique Manotti, *Lorraine Connection*, trans. Amanda Hopkinson and Roz Schwartz (London: Arcadia Books, 2009).

plastic casings and become television sets' (p. 3). What Manotti shows so well is how the neoliberalizing agenda at the global scale, whereby the decision to bring the Daewoo factory to Pondange was instituted by a French private consultant, Maurice Quignard, acting 'on behalf of the European Development Plan committee' and with the support of huge 'EU and French subsidies' (p. 14), is intimately connected to the dire conditions on the shop floor. Fears that the factory might close and relocate to Eastern Europe mean that the type of national and EU regulations (e.g. health and safety statutes) that otherwise might safeguard the workers from harm are routinely ignored. Hence early in the novel one of the female workers, Émilienne, is electrocuted and her unborn child killed and, prior to the start of the novel, a Korean engineer was decapitated in another shop floor 'accident'.

Here Manotti is cleverly playing with the trope of the dead body that typically sets in motion the crime story—the decapitated Korean engineer or Émilienne's unborn child—so that the production line, and by implication the unequal exchange between labour power and wages which the capitalist mode of production depends on, to reverse Moretti's formulation, is in fact implicated as 'criminal'.[66] But Manotti's target is not simply the factory or the production line or indeed the unequal exchange between labour power and wages which is responsible for creating and perpetuating the class divisions that are still very apparent in Pondange. Rather, her point is that the work itself, producing cathode ray tubes, is merely a ruse or a 'stage set' (p. 135) for securing vast EU and state subsidies which are then 'transferred' to Daewoo Poland 'by falsifying the purchase and sales ledgers' (p. 188). Here and in the events that follow, notably the destruction of the factory by arson, and the wider political context, involving Daewoo's bid to acquire a major French armaments company, Manotti's concern is to use the crime story as a vehicle to unravel the complex entanglements between 'factory and finance' and unearth what might have happened in the late 1990s because as Manotti makes clear the basic building blocks for the story really took place:

> The first element of the story is in 1996. Juppé [Alain Juppé, Prime Minister at the time] wanted to give Thomson to Daewoo...the state puts money into Thomson and then cedes it to Daewoo for a franc...In 1999 Daewoo went bankrupt. Then it's one surprise after another...Daewoo's owners had fled because the South Korean official receiver discovered that he took off with two and a half billion dollars...South Korea puts out an arrest warrant, they find him in France and France refuses to extradite him because he has French citizenship...The idea that he gave money to Chirac and Juppé for the presidential campaign gains currency...In 2003, the last Daewoo factory burns down and four days later they arrest the arsonist; it's an Arab factory worker...and I tell myself that's too much.[67]

---

[66] As I have noted in Chapter 4, Franco Moretti argues: 'Like popular economics, detective fiction incites people to seek the secret profit in the sphere of circulation, where it cannot be found—but in compensation, one finds theft, con-jobs, frauds, false pretences, and so on. The indignation against what is rotten and immoral in the economy must concentrate on these phenomena. As for the factory—it is innocent, and thus free to carry on.' See *Signs Taken for Wonder: Essays in the Sociology of Literary Form*, trans. Susan Fischer, David Forgacs, and David Miller (London and New York, NY: Verso, 1983), p. 139.

[67] Manotti qtd in Anissa Belhadjin, 'From Politics to Roman Noir', *South Central Review*, 27:1&2 (Spring, Summer 2010), pp. 74–5.

At stake here is not just the 'criminal' negligence of the production line but the criminality of the entire system of globalized trade whereby the perceived sanctity of entrepreneurial freedom is used by multinationals like Daewoo and their European advisors to justify and also conceal what is effectively a 'long firm' scam, and where the role of the French state and the EU, as Harvey says about neoliberalism, 'is to preserve an institutional framework appropriate to such practices'.[68] Manotti's point is that such practices are by no means the exception—indeed, the scheme may be 'fraudulent' but 'a large number if not all the multinationals operate in a similar fashion' (p. 168). One consequence is an ever-widening gap between those who directly profit from the scam or those, like Quignard, who may be 'an unpaid advisor' to Daewoo but who is likely to accrue 'financial rewards' from the company's successes, and the factory workforce who struggle to make ends meet and who are denied their annual bonuses on the grounds that the company's financial liquidity is poor. As Manotti puts it, 'The criminal is no longer a lone individual. It is the world of suffering, poverty, violence, and corruption in which we live that produces criminals.'[69]

Manotti is famously reluctant to see her crime novels labelled under the category of '*polar féminin*'. As Angela Kimyongür points out, she writes using a gender-neutral pseudonym, often with a male policeman as the lead and 'the adoption of socio-political themes in her work would seem to suggest that gender is not a primary concern'.[70] But as Kimyongür rightly notes, Manotti's interest in the position and plight of women only makes sense in the context of a much larger, more complex landscape of discrimination and marginalization, one that sees gender considered alongside race/ethnicity and class as competing and overlapping axes of oppression. The women in the Daewoo factory are not exploited simply because they are women: they are also working class and have no other options. Their position is no more or less precarious than that of Nourredine and other male workers of North African/Arab descent who have to face the additional challenge of confronting racial and/or religious prejudice. Faced with these injustices, the 'bloody Arabs' and 'women' condemned by the factory's human resources manager at the start of the novel as 'dross' (p. 5) manage to collectively organize and take strike action, after Émilienne's electrocution, and once one of the most popular female workers Rolande Lepetit is fired for lashing out against her section foreman. But compared to Kirino, Manotti is more circumspect about the likelihood of anything positive (e.g. freedom or otherwise) emerging either from the strike or from covert manoeuvrings against Daewoo's owners and supporters. The strike is effective only insofar as it generates negative publicity for Daewoo, who in league with a French arms manufacturer Matra, are bidding to the French government to acquire 'France's biggest military-electronics concern, a publically-owned company' (p. 47). It is also emblematic of freedom that has hitherto been denied to the workers. '[W]e all started walking around the factory,

---

[68] Harvey, *A Brief History of Neoliberalism*, p. 2.
[69] Manotti qtd in Angela Kimyongür, 'Dominique Manotti and the Roman Noir', *Contemporary Women's Writing* 7:3 (November 2013), p. 238.
[70] Kimyongür, 'Dominique Manotti and the Roman Noir', p. 235.

freely, the bosses had disappeared. I thought I'd go mad with joy. I felt as though I existed. I thought it was easy, and that I was changing my life' (p. 107). With so much at stake, however, the fightback is savage: the factory is burnt down and the strike comes to an end. At which point, the women not only lose their jobs but also their central roles in the unfolding narrative, as the focus shifts from the site of the factory to the task of proving corporate malpractice and to the struggle between two multinationals over the right to acquire this state-owned military electronics concern—where 'the links between factory and finance'[71] are brought to the fore.

The unfolding investigation into the Daewoo fraud, then, is not without significance for these women, for it brings into focus the extent to which these corporations, while affirming a commitment in public to producing goods, like cathode ray tubes, in particular places, e.g. Pondange, and providing much-needed jobs for the local population, are, in private, looking to develop complex international arrangements, to quote Goodman, 'outside of the state's regulatory and oversight apparatus, that is, outside sovereignty'.[72] Indeed, if sovereignty itself is gendered, as Orford suggests, what is outside or beyond sovereignty's regulatory framework doesn't necessarily offer a space for gendered imbalances of power to be readdressed. In the face of the increasingly fraught distinction between public and private under neoliberalism (for example public bodies being privatized, public governance depending on private finance initiatives, the space for private reflection and action being eroded, etc.), Manotti turns the *raison d'être* of the crime story—making public private knowledge—against the conglomerations of public/private power which pose a threat, direct or otherwise, to the factory workers because of the private knowledge about the Daewoo scam they have acquired. Here, as per her complex feminist credentials, Manotti is less interested in shoring up the private as a site for female freedom or arguing for female workers' full access to the public world of equality, rights, contract, citizenship, etc. than in showing the difficulties of identifying and confronting these new formations of power which seek to appropriate public and private worlds in their ever expanding reach. It is certainly true that one of the female workers, Rolande Lepetit, makes a successful transition from the fixed milieu of the factory to the mobile realm of international finance and with the assistance of Montoya, a private investigator for the insurance industry, manages to use information procured from Daewoo's accountant to divert 'a tidy sum, nearly a million francs' from one of the company's shell accounts into her and Montoya's private possession (p. 177). But theirs is a private rather than public victory and their private investigation into the bribing of public officials in return for their support of the Daewoo/Matra bid is used as leverage by a rival multinational to force its way back into the bidding process. The end result is the triumph of one multinational over another, hardly a cause for unequivocal celebration.

---

[71] Manotti qtd in Belhadjin, 'From Politics to Roman Noir', p. 75.
[72] Goodman, *Policing Narratives*, pp. 14–15.

CAPITALIST NOIR: PIERRE LEMAITRE, LAUREN BEUKES, JAMES SALLIS, AND MASSIMO CARLOTTO

Let us assume for a moment that examples of misogyny or sexual violence against women in crime fiction are linked, directly or otherwise, to either the power structures of the state or the imperatives of the market, i.e. we see this violence as reflecting the logic of exploitation under capitalism. In these instances, precisely because the violence cannot be dismissed as the product of a single deviant individual, the political intent of these works comes into sharper focus. If Kirino ties Masako's brutality, via the location of the abandoned factory, to the destructive potential of global capital, Pierre Lemaitre's *Alex* (2013)—initially published in France under the same title in 2011—attempts a similar manoeuvre: in this case, linking a case of incest, ostensibly a family matter in which Alex, as a twelve-year-old girl, is repeatedly and violently raped by her adult stepbrother, to the wider logic of accumulation or profit, when it emerges that the stepbrother has 'rented' her to his acquaintances for the same purpose. In the context of the novel, where Alex is kidnapped and effectively tortured—she is held in a cage suspended from the ground so that rats may devour her—because she has, prior to this, killed the torturer's son, and other people as well, what establishes the framework for the narrative as a whole is not so much the original act of abuse but rather its 'monetization'. For much of the novel, the violence—whether directed against Alex or perpetrated by her—is not explained, or is not given full explanation, though we, along with Police Commandant Camille Verhœven come to suspect that Alex is avenging a wrong that has been done to her.

Without logic or explanation the violence becomes not just horrific but almost unreadable, for we have nothing to explain it. Indeed the descriptions of Alex caged, and surrounded by rats quite literally waiting to devour her, and of Alex, once she has escaped, pouring battery acid down the throat of her victims while they are still alive and watching as the acid dissolves the flesh to 'a liquefied pulp of pink and white'[73] run the risk of reducing the violence to an albeit horrific banality.

While reading these acts as they happen, we are tempted, and perhaps even encouraged, to see them as symptom of some nameless contemporary condition, but it is only at the end of the novel, when Verhœven links Alex's violence to the abuse she suffered as a child, i.e. her victims are those she was 'rented' out to by her stepbrother, that the profit motive and indeed motif comes into focus. At this point the mystery of symptom is cleared up and it is for this reason that I want to read the novel's horrific web of tit-for-tat depravity as a partial example of what I am calling 'capitalist noir'. Lemaitre is, very definitely, a political crime novelist, with leftist sympathies, but like other novelists considered in this section, e.g. Lauren Beukes, James Sallis, and Massimo Carlotto, the issue of what it means to be a political or leftist crime writer in an era where capitalism is not just inevitable

---

[73] Pierre Lemaitre, *Alex*, trans. Frank Wynne (London: Maclehose, 2013), p. 223.

but where 'it is impossible even to imagine a coherent alternative to it'[74] is central to its treatment of crime. To put this another way these writers, unlike their counterparts who grew up in the direct shadows of the revolutionary tumult of the 1960s, demonstrate no faith in the idea that capitalism can be directly confronted and overturned.[75] Rather their opposition takes the form of narratives that hyperbolically show the worst excesses and depravities of capitalism, and where characters, sometimes main characters, are imagined as symptoms of these excesses, in order to draw readers' attention to these same excesses and depravities as part of an intentionally politicized and politicizing move.

However, in the case of Lemaitre's *Alex*, the twinned logic of violence and exploitation is not a totalizing one. For alongside the narrative of tit-for-tat or dog-eat-dog violence, and offsetting some of its horrors, is the story of the police enquiry. Some effort is made to implicate Verhœven in the horrors of what he is investigating—not just that he wants to kill the stepbrother but also that 'deep down he is just like everyone else' insofar as Alex, even for him, 'is just a means to an end' (pp. 326, 336)—but restitution is made, the brother-in-law is charged for his crimes, and some kind of normality is restored. The criminal justice system, battered and dysfunctional as it may be, is just about up to the task required of it, even if it is only Verhœven and his small team of helpers who make the difference. The police, as the state's representatives, are significant players in the struggle against, or indeed to ameliorate, the worst excesses of 'capitalist noir'—a point that should not be forgotten when we think about the state's ambivalent relationship to capital. In other words, those who assume the erasure or diminution of the state as part of the neoliberalizing turn, or who point to the state's ongoing surrender to the forces and interests of capital, should remember that the state can and does still play an important role in confronting and reversing the injustices produced by the marketization of social life.

The same logic is identifiable in Lauren Beukes's *Broken Monsters* (2014) but while the police in this novel, especially the female lead detective Gabi Versado, also stand in opposition—morally, ethically—to the crimes being investigated, and do in the end catch the killer, the polluting effects of what the killer has unleashed, and what he is beholden to and is symptom of, are not as easily contained. Beukes is South African but has chosen to set *Broken Monsters*, her fourth novel, in Detroit in the United States, and it is not difficult to see why: bankrupt, violent, racially segregated, and economically deprived and with whole neighbourhoods abandoned, along with the now ruined monuments to its former industrial grandeur, Detroit is shorthand for the extremities of capitalism. It is the literal embodiment of its boom/bust cycles, its exploitative and destructive impulses, and what Alain Badiou calls its nihilism or 'the absence of any other project than its

---

[74] Mark Fisher, *Capitalist Realism: Is There No Alternative?* (Winchester and Washington, DC: Zero Books, 2009), p. 2.

[75] It is a moot point whether writers like Sciascia, Himes, and Manchette believed that revolutionary acts might lead to political change but their writing, while despairing in the end about the potential for such change, is also imbued with the spirit of the revolutionary zeitgeist of their era.

perpetuation'.[76] In the novel, the dreams which 'summon[s] shapes up out of the darkness'[77] and which drive artist Clayton Broom to commit unspeakable acts of violence (e.g. he murders and then cuts in half an eleven-year-old boy and then melds the torso with the lower half of a deer) are implicated in the circulation of capital; what Harvey calls 'a process in which money is perpetually sent in search of more money'.[78] As Broom himself puts it, 'Money makes the rules. This is what things *cost*. This is what you have, where you are, what you are, what you can be. Money is a dream that has made itself definitive' (p. 85).

If value, for Marx, is to be understood primarily as '"abstract human labour... objectified... or materialized" in the commodity',[79] it is interesting to speculate what is objectified in Broom's artworks, especially since Beukes, throughout the novel, is quick to deny art's autonomy or separation from the market. Rather she shows us the processes of commodification by which art is assimilated into the market and in turn expresses its hidden desires and energies. Hence we see aspiring journalist Jonno Haim not merely trying to delineate the 'new' art scene for a YouTube audience but rather reporting, quite literally, as the art itself is being produced, thereby reducing the gap between the creative act and its inevitable commodification to nothing. 'I'm at the Powerhouse District in Detroit,' Jonno gushes straight to camera, 'where a group of visionary artists have spent the last three months working hard to transform these derelict *death-traps*... into astonishing works of art' (p. 171). The idea expressed here is that art has the power to appropriate and transform—and in a sense to breathe new life into—the decaying ruins of the nation's once vibrant industrial heartland. But the fact that this new art scene is linked to and made possible by the reinvention of entrepreneurial or neoliberal capitalism (Detroit, we are told, 'is friendlier to start-ups: lower overheads, tax incentives, hungry talent, cheap office space', p. 210), suggests it is capital that is breathing new life into art. Hence when we ask what is being abstracted in Broom's artworks, we should pay some attention to their beauty—the 'found-objects' of post-industrial ruin melded and transformed into an 'army of the beautiful deformed' (p. 199)—that can't easily be measured according to their exchange value.

That said the absent present in the work, what has been abstracted, is both the human labour that has gone into its creation but also more pertinently the destructive violence that informs and is informed by the ever quickening circulation of capital. The ruin of Detroit as an industrial powerhouse and its latter-day transformation into a 'creative' hub for the technology-driven, immaterial economy are both premised on the kind of creative destruction first characterized by Marx in a famous passage from *The Communist Manifesto* and where the human cost of the destruction, of the violence unleashed by the free market, is borne first and foremost

---

[76] Alan Badiou, *Infinite Thought: Truth and the Return of Philosophy*, trans. and ed. Oliver Feltham and Justin Clemens (London and New York, NY: Continuum, 2003), p. 161.
[77] Lauren Beukes, *Broken Monsters* (London: HarperCollins, 2014), p. 37.
[78] Harvey, *The Enigma of Capital*, p. 40.
[79] Marx qtd in Harvey, *A Companion to Marx's Capital* (London and New York, NY: Verso, 2010), p. 19.

by the ghosts of Detroit's once-vibrant industrial plants now left to rot: the workers. To Marx's assertion that '[a]ll old-established national industries have been destroyed or are daily being destroyed' and are being 'dislodged by new industries, whose introduction becomes a life and death question for all civilized nations',[80] Beukes gives us Detroit where the destruction of the automotive industry—under the conditions of globalization that Marx describes—has laid bare whole neighbourhoods. Crucially, though, the attendant violence has not been abstracted in the production of value; rather it flows through the city's hidden arteries—'a world beneath the world that is rich and tangled with meaning' (p. 112)—and is channelled via figures such as Broom.

If this gives Broom too much signifying potential, Beukes holds open the possibility that he might just be a sick, deluded murderer, in which case his capture by Versado would close down some of the more troubling implications of the violence he unleashes or perhaps is unleashed through him. The exact nature of the novel's resolution, therefore, requires close examination. It takes place in the abandoned Fleischer Body Plant where Broom, as artist and murderer, has transformed 'eight stories of automotive ruin' (p. 470) into a vast installation where what has been left behind—robot arms...canted at crazy angles on their heavy stands, wiring dangling like guts' (p. 469) or 'a wall of newspapers piled high to the ceiling, hardened with damp, like papier-mâché' (p. 477)—merges with what has been made: a murdered policeman 'wired to one of the big industrial pillars, his arms outstretched in benediction, wearing a spiky halo of beams as if in a medieval painting, gold wires stuck into his scalp' whose face has been 'sheared cleaned off' and replaced with 'an ornately carved wooden door embedded in the skull' (pp. 478, 479).

In one sense, the ending is fairly conventional: Versado kills Broom and saves her teenage daughter who has been caught up in the escalating turmoil. In another sense, however, the violence that Broom enacts—such as when Jonno Haim's girlfriend, Jen, is torn apart by 'a torrent of crows with their slashing beaks and battering wings...squirming out of her chest' (p. 441)—has no obvious explanation. Indeed, when Versado shoots Broom, her daughter sees 'something else spilling out of the ruin of his head...a great cloud, like gray cotton candy, condensing in the air' (pp. 490–1), a storm extending up to the ceiling of 'misshapen feathery smears' (p. 492) which intensifies when Haim starts to stream footage via his mobile phone (we're told a 'black angel steps into the room with a door embedded in its face' p. 494) and which only collapses when the live feed is turned off, 'birds fall[ing] out of the air and shatter[ing] like so much glass' (p. 496). Here, then, the process of assimilation or commodification deepens, rather than dilutes, the mania and the result is a phantasmagoria of violence—spectres not of Marx but of capital, of what has been destroyed and abandoned. After the event, efforts are made to provide rational explanation—'witnesses' testimony,' we are told, 'interviewed separately, confirm[s] that many of them experienced vivid and subjective hallucinations'

---

[80] Marx, *The Communist Manifesto*, in *The Essential Writings of Karl Marx* (St Petersburg, FL: Red and Black, 2010), pp. 164–5.

(p. 504)—but such manoeuvres, managed by the state, cannot wholly contain or neutralize the polluting effects of what Broom's Dream represents and perhaps even brings to life.

If Beukes's black vision coalesces with what I am calling capitalist noir—that is, the noir equivalent of what Jacques Rancière characterizes as 'a disenchanted knowledge of the reign of the commodity and the spectacle' in which we are inevitably 'absorbed into the body of the beast, [and] where even our capacities for subversive, autonomous practices and the networks of interaction that we might utilize against it, serve the new power of the beast'[81]—we need to be careful how far we push this association. Certainly Broom's Dream—his 'art' and the violence it enacts—can be seen in this light, as apparently subversive, autonomous practice quite literally serving the 'new power of the beast'—but Broom is but one individual and the novel as a whole counters this noirish vision of the destructive potentialities of contemporary capitalism with an accompanying narrative about the 'good' cop who vanquishes the Dream, if not the threat posed by it. To paraphrase Slavoj Žižek, what isn't questioned in such stories 'is the democratic-liberal framing of the fight' against such threats or excesses, or indeed 'the institutional set-up of the (bourgeois) democratic state'.[82] Therefore in order to discern what capitalist noir is or looks like in its most complete articulation we need to look beyond even these dark fables, *Alex* and *Broken Monsters*, to where the effects of capital's violence and exploitative nature and the absence of any alternative vision and the inadequacy, absence, or complicity of the judicial system in the face of such a totalizing logic, leak into every aspect of story and characterization. If Mark Fisher describes 'capitalist realism' as what happens to cultural practice when capitalism's colonization of the 'dreaming life of the population is so taken for granted that it is no longer worthy of comment',[83] capitalist noir is the nightmarish end point of this idea, i.e. where even the most horrific acts of violence raise barely an eyebrow, except, that is, in the minds of readers, because such acts are symptomatic of a politico-economic order seen as inevitable—inevitable because capitalism is presented as inevitable and because the criminal justice system is powerless to intervene or is wholly beholden to the same logic.[84]

James Sallis's *Drive* (2005) would not seem, at first glance, to be a promising example of capitalist noir, given it is centred around the activities of an extreme outsider; that is to say, a figure—known only as Driver because this speaks to his function first as stunt and then as getaway driver—who would not seem to be assimilated into any system and who, we're told, 'existed a step or two to one side

---

[81] Jacques Rancière, *The Emancipated Spectator*, trans. Gregory Elliot (London and New York, NY: Verso, 2009), pp. 32, 33.

[82] Slavoj Žižek, 'Good Manners in the Age of Wikileaks', *London Review of Books*, 33:2 (20 January 2011), p. 9.

[83] Fisher, *Capitalist Realism*, pp. 8–9.

[84] This type of crime fiction has its own genealogy and one finds an earlier articulation of this phenomenon in Hammett's *The Maltese Falcon*; but here, in the figure of Sam Spade, we find some kind of antidote to the debasing effects of capital, even if Spade himself is, to some extent, complicit in the pursuit of gain and self-interest that defines almost every aspect of social existence.

of the common world, largely out of sight, a shadow, all but invisible'.[85] Indeed it is tempting to see Driver's hyper-violent struggle with the 'dogs of war' unleashed on him by an organized crime syndicate he's unwittingly stolen from as a political act and Driver as a reluctant social bandit—someone whose violence against the established order, in whatever form, assumes political significance in the context of the larger structures of oppression that are undoubtedly present in Sallis's Los Angeles. As James Buccellato puts it, '[b]y contextualizing acts of social banditry as part of a larger antagonistic relationship between predatory capitalists and local populations, it becomes possible to fuse the identity of the outlaw with political meaning'.[86] In one sense, Driver belongs to what we might call the underclass—a restless, unmoored, transient population that inhabits the peripheries, the outer fringes of the great sprawls of Los Angeles and Phoenix, a world of seedy motels and rental units, 'dive' bars, diners, discount malls, chain restaurants, and 'ugly, cheap-looking, wobbly' things (p. 114). Indeed it is the atomized nature of this world—the fact that Driver comes to prefer 'older apartment complexes' where 'tenants loaded up in the middle of the night and rode off never to be heard from again' (pp. 18–19) and where any interaction with neighbours 'absolutely did *not* happen' (p. 20)—which stymies the development of a collective political consciousness and in turn compels figures like Driver to enact their opposition to the existing order through individualized acts of violence.

This, at least, would be one way of reading Driver's violence—the retaliatory manoeuvres he makes against the organized crime syndicate he has crossed. But to see Driver's violence as politicized, at least in a straightforward sense, is to miss the way in which *Drive* as a novel functions as a much more oblique reflection of contemporary socio-economic arrangements. Moreover it is to miss the extent to which Sallis, as crime and espionage novelist, uses and contorts the familiar tropes of genre to further a form of socio-political critique that does not easily reveal its hand.[87] Certainly Driver ascribes no political inferences to what he does: 'I drive. That's *all* I do' (p. 14). But nor, I think, can we see him as a quasi-existentialist figure, someone who has chosen his life, circumscribed as it is, and has found an accompanying sense of freedom. Instead, it is more helpful to see him as symptom of an emerging socio-economic order aligned and maybe even synonymous with neoliberalism. As such the claim that Driver 'existed a step or two to one side of the common world' (p. 18) needs to be revised slightly. The 'common world' here would seem to refer to normal life—defined in terms of security, work, family,

---

[85] James Sallis, *Drive* (Orlando, FL: Harvest, 2006), p. 18. All subsequent citations refer to this edition.
[86] James A. Buccellato, 'Sign of the Outlaw: Liberal Boundaries, Social Banditry, and the Political Act', *New Political Science*, 34:3 (September 2012), p. 278. Also see Eric Hobsbawm, *Primitive Rebels: Studies in Archaic Forms of Social Movement in the 19th and 20th Centuries* (Manchester: Manchester University Press, 1971).
[87] Sallis is the author of five private eye novels featuring Lew Griffin including *The Long-Legged Fly* (1996) and *Black Hornet* (2003) where the familiar coordinates of the genre, and of plot and character in general, gradually disappear and a series of spy novels, including *Death Will Have Your Eyes* (1997), where the job the spy does segues slowly and inexorably into an ever-deepening examination of self, conscience, and existence.

progress, and prosperity—but that in terms of the novel as a whole simply doesn't exist. Rather Sallis gives us an unsettling simulacrum of this world but where all familiar coordinates have been stripped away. The police are invisible; there is no social welfare provision; the state is notable only for its absence; healthcare provision is non-existent (Driver even has to set up his own private 'plan' in the form of the Doc who 'spent a lifetime dispensing marginally legal drugs... before he got shut down and moved to Arizona' (p. 63) and who Driver pays with 'a wad of bills' to stitch him back up); and the work that Driver does, both as stunt and getaway driver, perfectly analogizes the kind of deregulated, flexible, contract-based labour central to the operations of the neoliberal economy. As such, the freedom that Driver claims to enjoy, based on an ability to go where he likes and contract his own labour and choose his own life (p. 155), is akin to what neoliberalism purports to give us (i.e. greater flexibility, choice, etc.) but, as Harvey points out, is in fact a ruse or mask to conceal the concentration of power and resources in the hands of an ever-shrinking elite.[88]

The unusual 'cut up' narrative structure Sallis deploys, where chapters are arranged out of chronological order, further unsettles our straightforward understanding of cause and effect and hence the idea that Driver's actions have clear-cut precedents or explanations. Instead, insofar as life is understood as 'upset, movement and agitation' (p. 143), Driver's violence is best seen not as an explicit political act—a reaction to oppression, where there is clear-cut cause and effect—but as an inchoate symptom of an underlying socio-economic condition he can neither wholly discern nor do anything about: except to recognize his so-called freedom as 'upset, movement and agitation'. In other words, his actions—the coolly effective manner in which he kills people who are trying to kill him—reflect what Fisher calls 'a deeper... more pervasive, sense of exhaustion, of cultural and political sterility' whereby the system of which Driver is symptomatic, for example capitalism in its neoliberal phase, shows no sign of going away and indeed 'has colonized the dreaming life of the population' and of Driver to such an extent 'that it is no longer worthy of comment'.[89] The apparent effectiveness of Driver's rampage against the organized crime syndicate is not, therefore, a blow struck against power but rather the re-routing of power in a different form or via a different conduit. This perhaps explains why Driver admits that he 'mourns' the death of kingpin Bernie Rose, even if he can't quite explain to himself or us why he feels this sadness. At the moment of his apparent victory, the fact that Driver's retaliatory violence has produced nothing but the continuation of what came before, i.e. no epiphany and no catharsis, speaks exactly to or about this condition I'm calling capitalist noir: a violent, sometimes gratuitously so, blood-soaked social vision where there is no alternative to capitalism, where no one can articulate or organize effective opposition, and where reader and character are left with little or indeed no hope that the situation will ever be any different.

Still, the idea that Driver could be construed—mistakenly in my view—for an oppositional figure, or at least as someone capable of lamenting the situation he

[88] Harvey, *The Enigma of Capital*, p. 10.   [89] Fisher, *Capitalist Realism*, pp. 7, 9.

ultimately finds himself in, means that *Drive* is not perhaps the most complete articulation of what capitalist noir is. For this, I'd like to turn to the Italian crime writer, Massimo Carlotto, and two of his novels featuring criminal-turned-restaurateur Giorgio Pellegrini—*Arrivederci amore, ciao* (2000), translated from the Italian by Lawrence Venuti as *The Goodbye Kiss* (2006), and *Alla fine di un giorno noioso* (2011) translated by Antony Shugaar as *At the End of a Dull Day* (2013). The fact that Carlotto's novels, and especially these examples, are extraordinarily bleak goes without saying. Or, to put this another way, who could read these stories about everyday psychopaths scheming and murdering their way towards some undefined end point without compunction and where the law has caused this situation or is complicit in its perpetration or at best is powerless to prevent it, and arrive at a different conclusion? What concerns me is not that these novels are bleak per se but the precise nature of their bleakness: their seamless conjoining of political and criminal economies—what Carlotto, in a eulogy for the French crime writer Jean-Claude Izzo, called 'an endless spiral in which legal and illegal economies merge in a single model'[90]—so that crime is characterized not as an interruption or challenge to the smooth running of the system, or even a sign that the system is broken, but rather as an indication that everything is working perfectly well, that is, according to the logic of the market.[91]

The shift from what Fisher calls capitalist realism—where capitalism is 'so taken for granted that it is no longer worthy of comment'—to capitalist noir is best analogized by seeing crime as capitalism and capitalism as crime, and by the attendant implications for the moral basis of our actions. In *A Contribution to the Critique of Political Economy* Marx famously claimed, '[t]he mode of production of material life conditions the general processes of social, political and intellectual life. It's not the consciousness of men that determines their existence, but the social existence that determines their consciousness.'[92] In other words the capitalist mode of production determines the *general* character of our society, and the consciousness and indeed morality of its citizens. If there is no interruption between the realms of crime and capitalism in Carlotto's work, i.e. that they are not merely synonymous but effectively part of the same continuum, it stands to reason that the further intensification of what a local politician in *The Goodbye Kiss* calls the 'locomotive' 'economic model of the northeast' where 'the legal and illegal economies were merged in a single system',[93] must generally produce ever more aberrant patterns of moral behaviour. It is not the case that everyone will steal, cheat, and even kill but insofar as the pursuit of self-interest, by whatever means necessary, has been normalized across the whole of society, we shouldn't be surprised or shocked when

---

[90] Massimo Carlotto, 'Eulogy', in Jean-Claude Izzo, *Total Chaos*, trans. Howard Curtis (New York, NY: Europa, 2013), p. 12.
[91] Barbara Pezzotti skilfully shows how capitalism, in Carlotto's work, 'has assumed the typical features of the mafia and, ultimately, how all distinctions between the two have blurred'. See 'Crime and Capitalism: Giorgio Scerbanenco's and Massimo Carlotto's Italian Domestication of American Hard-Boiled Fiction', *Clues: A Journal of Detection*, 32:2 (Fall 2014), p. 52.
[92] Marx, *A Contribution to the Critique of Political Economy*, trans. S.W. Ryazanskaya, ed. Maurice Dobb (Moscow: Progress Publishers, 1970), pp. 20–1.
[93] Carlotto, *The Goodbye Kiss*, trans. Lawrence Venuti (New York, NY: Europa, 2006), p. 108.

individuals such as Giorgio Pellegrini commit heinous acts in order to improve their own position.

If we swap Marx's capitalist and landowner, in his formulation in the preface to the first German edition of *Capital*, for businessman/criminal, Carlotto is by no means depicting such figures in 'rosy colours' but individuals are dealt with 'only in so far as they are personifications of economic categories, the bearers...of particular class relations'.[94] To be offended, morally or otherwise, by Pellegrini's actions is to miss the point. This is not a *carte blanche* justification to anyone wishing to scheme and kill their way to greater wealth; but Carlotto's point is that criminality in the Italian north-east, and by extension everywhere in developed capitalist societies, is so widespread that it barely merits comment and should be seen as the norm rather than as the exception, i.e. Pellegrini, brutal, violent, and exploitative as he is, is actually a man of his time and place, a symptom of the logic of accumulation. As such he offers us an extremely uncomfortable vision of the saturation of capitalist principles across all spheres of existence and where hope—if there is hope—is enacted at the level of the reader and the sense of what Barbara Pezzotti astutely terms 'moral rebellion': 'thanks to the "active" relationship between the author and his readers, Carlotto's books become expressions of and useful instruments for "moral rebellion" in Italian society'—and, I would add, across those societies affected by the seemingly unstoppable march of capitalism in its neoliberal phrase.[95]

Carlotto, seemingly, sets the two halves of his masterpiece, *The Goodbye Kiss*, against one another. In the first half, he traces Pellegrini's easy and unproblematic abandoning of the 'camaraderie and freedom' of the anarchist movement, a move engineered by Carlotto, one suspects, to indicate his unease about the usefulness or viability of the politics of direct revolutionary confrontation that characterized the writing context of an earlier generation of crime novelists. Rather what Carlotto shows us is Pellegrini willingly selling out his former comrades, in order to secure his own freedom, and his uncomplicated absorption into the 'new' economy where '[a] ton of cash was floating around, and mostly everybody was oozing confidence' (p. 28). Initially 'out of place' he very quickly adapts to the dog-eat-dog strictures of this new economy's dark mirror and proceeds to cheat, scheme, kill, and to do whatever is necessary in order to secure his own economic advantage. In this part of the novel his activities—prostitution and the exploitation of women and armed robbery (where Pellegrini also assassinates his accomplices in order to cover his tracks)—are a long way from the realm of 'respectability'; but crucially while Pellegrini acknowledges that he is 'disgusting' he also claims his actions 'caused [him] no shame' (p. 41): in this sense, his modus operandi—'[a]ways pick the easiest, quickest and cleanest method' (p. 75)—speaks to or about exactly the kind of hard-headed pragmatism that is required in the world of business.

---

[94] Marx, *Capital: A Critique of Political Economy Vol. 1*, ed. Ernest Mandel, trans. Ben Fowkes (London: Penguin, 1990), p. 92.
[95] Pezzotti, *Politics and Society in Italian Crime Fiction: An Historical Overview* (Jefferson, NC: McFarland, 2014), p. 166.

The second half of the novel, meanwhile, charts Pellegrini's move into this world—he opens a restaurant—and of what his counsellor and mentor, Sante Brianese, who oversees his legal rehabilitation, calls 'white collar crime, purely financial' (p. 108). But rather than leaving the 'institutional set of the (bourgeois) state', to quote Žižek, untouched and unquestioned, and to imply that the liberal-democratic state can and indeed will 'extend democratic control to the economy',[96] the collusion of Brianese and the entire juridico-political apparatus in facilitating the cross-pollination of '[c]rime, business, politics (p. 108) attests to the deep-rooted, systemic nature of the problem. In a fascinating riff on the topic of determinism, Pellegrini seeks, with some success, to adapt to his new environment, and learn to play the role of petit-bourgeois restaurateur and caring boyfriend, even if it is just a role: 'I got a taste of the pleasure to be had from sharing something with a woman' (p. 110). The implications of Marx's claim about the mode of production conditioning the general character of society is never far away, but rather than seeing Pellegrini's inevitable reversion to type, i.e. he realizes that his fiancée can link him to the murder of a cop and in any case is 'fed up with playing the role of sweetheart' (p. 141), as proof of his natural depravity, Carlotto suggests that Pellegrini's most horrendous act, poisoning his fiancée and watching her die a slow, agonizing death, is simply what needs to be done in order to secure his new-found respectability. The collusion of the legal process—in the end he is not imprisoned for his crimes but rewarded with his official rehabilitation—confirms this point.

The interchangeability of crime and business is underscored at the start of the sequel, *At the End of a Dull Day*, where the exploitative nature of a 'high-end' prostitute ring Pellegrini has set up is described in the functionalist language of economics. 'Never more than four girls at a time…and we replaced them after exactly six months',[97] with the resulting air of discretion allowing Pellegrini to charge 'extra', and hence accrue large profits, even if '[i]t was damned expensive to keep up certain standards of quality' (p. 23). What is being abstracted here is the women's labour; but by foregrounding, rather than concealing, the violent and indeed coercive underpinnings of the exchange between wages and labour power—Pellegrini's dependence on 'a shiny pair of brass knuckles' and his matter-of-fact revelation that, after six months, the women were shipped off, like cattle, 'to the Maghreb region of northwest Africa or to Spain' for a life of enforced servitude (p. 22)—Carlotto allows us to see what crime and hence capitalism really is. That said the language of classical Marxist political economy only takes us so far. For what is being described, particularly in this novel, is not a world dominated by the old 'productive forces' but the flexible, networked, deregulated world of the neoliberal economy.

Facing the consequence of a complex financial scam that involves Brianese, who has risen to political power in consort with the now disgraced former Italian prime minister Silvio Berlasconi, and the Calabrian mafia, Pellegrini, who has been

---

[96] Žižek, 'Good Manners in the Age of Wikileaks'.
[97] Carlotto, *At the End of a Dull Day*, trans. Antony Shugaar (New York, NY: Europa, 2013), p. 18.

robbed himself, channels the entrepreneurial zeal of what he calls 'an astounding wave of creativity' or 'creative criminality' in contrast to the 'dull, repetitive crimes committed by the capitalist establishment' (p. 122), to retrieve his money. Here the Calabrian mafia, with its dependence on hierarchical organization and procedures which in turn 'absolutely forbid any independent thinking' (p. 141), is easily outmanoeuvred by Pellegrini's 'creative criminality' but the apparent celebration of creativity and entrepreneurialism here should not be seen as an endorsement of the logic of neoliberalism. In one sense, what Carlotto shows us, here and in *The Goodbye Kiss* and responding to a similar set of conditions as Kirino and Manotti, is the nature of contemporary precarity—as it seeps into every aspect of social existence and affects the professional and managerial class, e.g. Brianese who would formerly have been protected, and Pellegrini who in a perverse way benefits from the erosion of security.[98] But we need to be careful about how far we celebrate Pellegrini's success since in effect it speaks about or to the replacement of one form of coercive parasitism with another. In other words, his decision to give up the prostitution ring, 'which demanded a special dedication to logistical structure and hierarchical organization' and embrace what he calls the emerging 'order of the creative local economy' (p. 182) simply attests to the mutation of capitalist activity and the extent to which it continues to induce what Berlant, following Harvey, calls 'scenes of productive destruction—of resources and of lives being made and unmade according to the dictates and whims of the market'.[99] We may be cheering in the end for Pellegrini but we are not allowed to forget we are also cheering for a monster.

BORDERS, SOVEREIGNTY, AND THE GLOBE: DON WINSLOW AND CHINA MIÉVILLE

If the contemporary crime novel remains bound, uneasily and anxiously, to the idea and reality of the state, it is also wedded, again ambivalently, to the territory and therefore to the jurisdictional limits that the state lays claim to.[100] Crime fiction is always located *somewhere*: Orford is synonymous with Cape Town in South Africa, McNamee with the north of Ireland. These places in turn become emblematic of the states they are part of, so that the delineation of the investigative process in *Water Music* or *Blue is the Night* sheds light on the operation of the state's provision

---

[98] Lauren Berlant describes precarity as 'more than economic': that is, 'it is structural in many senses and permeates the affective environment' so that its effects are felt by 'everyone whose bodies and lives are saturated by capitalist forces and rhythms'. See *Cruel Optimism*, p. 192.

[99] Berlant, *Cruel Optimism*, p. 192. Berlant refers to Harvey's claim that 'neoliberal economic practices mobilize this instability in unprecedented ways' (p. 192).

[100] Abraham and van Schendel claim: 'Territorial control is intrinsically linked to other normative characteristics of the modern state—its claim to a monopoly of legitimate violence and its sovereign ability to establish the law. The scope of the law and the boundaries of legitimate violence are "contained" by the territory the state lays claim to. Without territory there is no modern state; a claim to statehood must begin from the political control of land.' See Willem van Schendel and Itty Abraham (eds) *Illicit Flows and Criminal Things: States, Borders and the Other Side of Globalization* (Bloomington and Indianapolis, IN: Indiana University Press, 2005), p. 13.

for justice and therefore on the state itself. Even where crime fiction moves across state borders and explores the transnationalization of crime and policing, such as Manotti's *Lorraine Connection* or, as we will see in this final section of the chapter, Don Winslow's *The Power of the Dog*, these novels are still located somewhere, within or across sovereign jurisdictions, and do not want to wholly disregard the notion of a policing mandate being executed within clearly defined jurisdictional limits. Yet, as Elizabeth Anker puts it and as the crime novels of Sallis and Carlotto demonstrate, to 'exist in a post-Westphalian world is to witness the waning of the nation-state and its formal legal domain, as state influences are ever more subordinated' to, say, multinational corporations or organized crime networks and hence the 'gradual supplanting of national sovereignty requires that we...speak of multiple sovereignties that co-exist'[101] (e.g. the sovereignty of states, of supranational institutions, of competing non-state organizations, of markets, etc.).

This, then, is the paradox of sovereignty at the heart of the crime novels under examination in this chapter. The state proliferates, the state recedes. Even as the state seeks to reassert itself in the face of competing threats, or to determine what counts as 'exceptional' (i.e. in order to sanction extra-legal violence) its authority is unravelled. Its borders are more porous, more traversed by goods, people, and capital than ever before, its claims to territorial boundedness harder to justify. Its monopolistic ambitions are under ever greater threat from capitalism and organized crime-as-capitalism and its legitimacy as public body standing above or apart from society is increasingly difficult to reconcile with its complex embeddedness in and with the affairs of multinational corporations and the selling of security to private contractors. The state has always been under threat, its projections of authority a mask for its anxieties, its duties or responsibilities contracted out to private bidders, and its claims to legitimacy, monopoly, and territorial integrity coming under threat. Perhaps it is just a matter of degree: that the tensions and paradoxes that inform and in turn constitute contemporary crime fiction's enquiries into crime, law, and justice putting ever greater pressure on the idea of state sovereignty, even as the novels themselves remain wedded to the conditions of possibility established by the state.

We could think about the crossing and recrossing of borders in Don Winslow's *The Power of the Dog*, by people, money, drugs, and guns and about what van Schendel and Abraham describe as 'the neo-liberal dream of a borderless economy'[102] on the one hand, and about Winslow's account of the vast sums being poured by state bodies into border security efforts right across the Americas on the other. We could point to those heightened instances of state-sponsored violence in Peace's *GB84* or McNamee's *The Ultras*, together with the manoeuvre, brilliantly scrutinized by both writers, to contract out violence—characterized as extra-legal—to private bodies. And we could think about the virtual absence or disappearance of the state in *Drive* or the interpenetration of politics, crime, and business in *The Goodbye Kiss*. In each example, as Lauren Berlant puts it, sovereignty—understood as 'a condition

---

[101] Anker, 'In the Shadowlands of Sovereignty', p. 953.
[102] van Schendel and Abraham, *Illicit Flows and Criminal Things*, p. 24.

of and blockage to justice'—is, at bottom, 'a fantasy misrecognized as an objective state' which in turn can only offer 'an affective sense of control in relation to the fantasy of that position of security'.[103] Or as Marx put it, all that is solid melts into air.

In the field of international relations (IR), moves to explore the deterritorialization of sovereignty, i.e. what happens when sovereignty is no longer bound to territory, have produced fascinating studies that contest assumptions about the international as an orderly realm made up of fully autonomous nation states and explore the implications for understandings about the workings of power.[104] Walker, for example, points out that 'the most interesting forms of contemporary analysis begin with the observation that both states and capital participate in spatio-temporal processes that are radically at odds with the resolutions expressed by the principle of state sovereignty'.[105] In turn, these moves have had far-reaching implications for understandings of policing and security—i.e. the idea that national police forces exercise their mandates within clearly delineated territorial borders. Rather policing by a single, unified power, for example, Loader and Walker argue we have seen a 'repositioning of the state in relation to a plurality of agents and agencies now involved in the "governance of security"',[106] while Les Johnston talks about 'a changing morphology of governance in which partly fragmented states interact with commercial, civil and voluntary bodies both within and across national jurisdictional boundaries'.[107]

In this final part of the chapter, I want to think about whether or to what extent contemporary crime novels in general, and Don Winslow's *The Power of the Dog* and China Miéville's *The City & The City* in particular, have been able to find a structure and language adequate to the task of representing the rupturing and transformation of sovereignty—in effect to construct what Fredric Jameson would term a cognitive map that seeks to make visible the intertwined vessels of multiple sovereignties and global capitalism across national borders.[108] Certainly we should not assume that contemporary crime fiction, even when it directly tackles the topic of crime and policing's transnationalization, has been successful at destabilizing 'normative' understandings of state sovereignty.

As I have argued in a journal article entitled 'Policing the Globe', a good deal of crime fiction which takes place in a single location or sovereign jurisdiction and tells the story of a discrete investigation into a particular crime, runs the risk of

---

[103] Berlant, *Cruel Optimism*, p. 97.
[104] See Stuart Elden, *Terror and Territory: The Spatial Extent of Sovereignty* (Minneapolis, MN: University of Minnesota Press, 2009); Michael Hardt and Antonio Negri, *Empire* (Cambridge, MA and London: Harvard University Press, 2000); Walker, *Inside/Outside*.
[105] Walker, *Inside/Outside*, p. 155. [106] Loader and Walker, *Civilizing Security*, p. 120.
[107] Les Johnston, 'Transnational Private Policing', in J.W.E. Sheptycki (ed.) *Issues in Transnational Policing* (London and New York, NY: Routledge, 2000), p. 38.
[108] The term cognitive mapping was first developed by Fredric Jameson as a response to the obscuring impulses of late capitalism; i.e. part of a critical move to map, and hence make visible, the totality of power relations in an era of late or global capitalism. See 'Cognitive Mapping' in C. Nelson and L. Grossberg (eds) *Marxism and the Interpretation of Culture* (Urbana-Champaign, IL and London: University of Illinois Press, 1990).

falling into what John Agnew calls the 'territory trap'[109] whereby potentially disruptive questions about jurisdictional domains and the boundaries of legitimate violence are '"contained" by the territory the state lays claim to'.[110] My decision to focus on *The Power of the Dog* and *The City & The City* is intended to draw attention to the ways in which the genre has, I think, successfully probed the territorial limits of sovereignty, and hence of a shift from police to policing and from government to governance. To start with, their narrative reach and open-endedness and their geopolitical mobility, together with a refusal to lose sight of what Ellen Meiksins Wood calls 'the unique *ability* of nation-states to organize the world for global capital',[111] mean that their accounts of policing and power in the contemporary era isn't reducible to the working of discrete judicial systems. It is also no coincidence that both novels are organized around or in relation to state borders (e.g. in *The Power of the Dog* the US–Mexico border is central and in *The City & The City* the border in question separates, and doesn't separate, the fictional city states of Besźel and Ul Qomo, on the eastern fringes of Europe). Rather than depicting borders as indivisible and sacrosanct, both novels' account of borders as porous and easily crossed in turn allows for a far-reaching questioning of the politico-jurisdictional limits of sovereignty—not least because, as van Schendel and Abraham put it, it is in the borderlands that 'state territoriality is dramatized and state sovereignty paraded' and contested and, hence, it is here or indeed there, in the spaces between states, that the 'spatiality of social relations is forever taking on new shapes'.[112]

The idea of sovereignty as performance, or what Lauren Berlant calls 'self-legitimating performativity',[113] is central to Winslow's treatment of the spectacular and highly visible character of US power in *The Power of the Dog* and its follow-up *The Cartel* (2015);[114] except that there is nothing self-legitimating about Winslow's depiction of the performativity of sovereignty. Rather by connecting state violence and its corollary in the actions of the drugs gangs to practices of torture—e.g. the covert training by US special forces of anti-Communist paramilitaries in Colombia which leads to the massacre of entire villages: '[h]eadless bodies...washed up on the shore like fish waiting to be cleaned'[115]—the novel asks far-reaching questions about the legal precedents for such actions and the interchangeability of state and criminal bodies.[116] Indeed, while David Holloway argues that the thriller 'legitimises

---

[109] John Agnew, 'The Territory Trap', *Review of International Political Economy*, 1:1 (1994), p. 53.

[110] van Schendel and Abraham qtd in Andrew Pepper, 'Policing the Globe; State Sovereignty and the International in Post-9/11 Crime Fiction', *Modern Fiction Studies*, 57:3 (Fall 2011), p. 409. Also see Pepper, 'Henning Mankell: Political Reactionary', *Moving Worlds*, 13:1 (2013), pp. 90–101.

[111] Ellen Meiksins Wood, 'A Manifesto for Global Capitalism?', in Gopal Balakrishnan (ed.) *Debating Empire* (London and New York, NY: Verso, 2003), p. 65.

[112] van Schendel and Abraham, *Illicit Flows and Criminal Things*, p. 46.

[113] Berlant, *Cruel Optimism*, p. 97.

[114] Winslow's follow-up or sequel to *The Power of the Dog*, *The Cartel* was only published in the middle of 2015 and too late to play a part in my analysis here.

[115] Don Winslow, *The Power of the Dog* (New York, NY: Vintage, 2006), p. 490.

[116] The potentially paradoxical idea of the state as criminal—paradoxical because the state defines what is criminal—is explored in Penny Green and Tony Ward's *State Crime: Governments, Violence, and Corruption* (London: Pluto, 2004).

human rights abuses by the West, particularly state-sanctioned torture, by depicting the West, rhetorically, as the virtuous bringer of rights',[117] *The Power of the Dog* stakes out a counterposition: the main export the US can offer, in addition to its illegal (under international law) intelligence-gathering techniques, is the same liberation of markets that is responsible for helping drug kingpin, Adán Barrera, to turn his ailing cartel into a highly successful 'vertically integrated polydrug operation' (p. 418).

The 'lessons of the Reagan Revolution' (that the Barreras 'could make more money by lowering taxes than raising them because the lower taxes allowed more entrepreneurs to come into the business and make more money and pay more taxes', p. 309) are deployed to restructure a 'criminal' operation, to the point it becomes hard to tell it apart from a legitimate capitalist enterprise. That is, it's hard to distinguish between the accumulative tendency of capital which as David Harvey points out is 'a process in which money is perpetually sent in search of more money' and which of course is aided by trade agreements like NAFTA (e.g. ensuring 'continuity of flow in the circulation of capital'[118]) and the workings of the international drug trade which is also facilitated by free trade agreements and the adoption of neoliberal economic policies. Here it is not simply the case that the licit and illicit economies are so bound up together that it is impossible to disaggregate them (e.g. 'the cartel's financial operations are fully enmeshed with those of Mexico's wealthiest and most powerful business concerns', p. 418) but rather, following Carlotto, that capitalism becomes a form of organized criminality and vice versa. As Robert Saviano puts it in a foreword to Anabel Hernández's book on the Mexican drug gangs, *Narcoland* (2013), the 'rules of drug trafficking…are also the rules of capitalism'.[119]

At first glance, Miéville's *The City & The City* would seem to occupy much securer, less unsettled ground. Besźel and Ul Qoma are two, separate, territorially bounded city states with their own political authorities, legal jurisdictions, and policing/security apparatuses. The novel also begins in conventional, for a crime novel, manner: with the discovery of a corpse. Because the body is discovered on Besź soil, the investigation is led by Inspector Tyador Borlú of the Besź Extreme Crime Squad. But when it emerges that the victim was part of an archaeological dig in Ul Qomo and the investigation moves there, Borlú is invited by his Ul Qoman counterpart Qussim Dhatt to consult on the case but is told he has no jurisdictional authority or 'policing powers'.[120] In this sense the investigation is an international one—part of 'an exciting new era of cross-border policing' (p. 137)—where jurisdictional complications pose questions against without necessarily unravelling the sovereign claims of Besźel and Ul Qoma. There is only one official border checkpoint between the city states—inside Copula Hall, straddling

---

[117] David Holloway, 'The War on Terror Espionage Thriller, and the Imperialism of Human Rights', *Comparative Literature Studies*, 46:1 (2009), p. 20.
[118] Harvey, *Enigma of Capital*, pp. 40, 41.
[119] Roberto Saviano, 'Foreword', trans. Paolo Mossetti in Anabel Hernández, *Narcoland*, trans. Iain Bruce (London and New York, NY: Verso, 2013), p. viii.
[120] China Miéville, *The City and The City* (London: Macmillan, 2009), p. 164.

'a considerable chunk of land in both cities' (p. 157)—and to pass through it you need the appropriate paperwork and the approval of both states' border authorities. The border marks the limits of both states' territorial claims and hence shores up their respective claims to sovereignty. And yet it is not this simple. In actuality the two city states are bound together in a more complex, intimate manner, overlaid on top of one another almost, in the manner of palimpsest. As such there are numerous intersections, or rather points at which Besźel and Ul Qoma are 'cross-hatched', where citizens from each place could, if they so desired, simply walk from one to the other but where they have been trained, by custom, indoctrination, and fear, not to see, to actually 'unsee', their cross-hatched neighbour.

This border is better understood as an invisible membrane, more a state of mind than a physical mark on the landscape, and where the sovereignty being performed is much more vulnerable to 'breach' as a result. Indeed because transgression is—potentially at least—so easy and by implication so commonplace, the two city states have formed an Oversight Committee, a supranational body comprising officials from both places which looks into such breaches, as they are called, and that is in turn subject to an external authority (external, that is, to both states) simply known as 'Breach'. Breach is a policing body that does not derive its authority from the sovereignty of either Besźel or Ul Qoma but that stands from both, a superordinate authority if you like, which allows Miéville to tease out the same 'paradox of international law' he explored as a legal theorist; i.e. that 'force is determining, but determining between relations which cannot be understood except as equal in fundamentally constitutive and constituting ways'.[121] This has important implications for our understanding of sovereignty.

If the interpenetration of Besźel and Ul Qoma is in part enabled by Miéville's generic mash-up, yoking together the procedural realism of the traditional crime novel with its dependence upon claims about jurisdictional limits and speculative or sf fiction where these limits do not have the same purchase, Winslow gets around the problem of the crime novel's situated-ness using a related manoeuvre. In other words, his novel is able to so well interrogate the problem of borders, i.e. as markers of sovereign limits and as lines easily crossed by people, goods, and capital, because he draws, generically speaking, from both the crime novel, where a policing mandate is typically executed within a delineated territory and jurisdiction, and the thriller or espionage novel where the security work being undertaken is more open-ended, speculative, and necessarily crosses national borders. Here the convergence of crime and war and policing and security—aptly analogized by Didier Bigo as the 'möbius ribbon of internal and external security(ies)'[122] i.e. where the domains of the police and military/intelligence services cannot be separated, permits the same thoroughgoing critique of the territorial limits of sovereignty undertaken by Miéville.

---

[121] Miéville, *Between Equal Rights: A Marxist Interpretation of International Law* (Chicago, IL: Haymarket Books, 2005), p. 8.
[122] Didier Bigo, 'The Möbius Ribbon of Internal and External Security(ies)' in Mathias Albert, David Jacobson, and Yosef Lapid (eds) *Identities, Borders, Orders: Rethinking International Relations* (Minneapolis, MN and London: University of Minnesota Press, 2001), p. 91.

This last point requires further elucidation. *The Power of the Dog*'s focus on internal security arrangements within Mexico and the US, and on attempts by state institutions like the Central Intelligence Agency (CIA) and the Drug Enforcement Administration (DEA) to forge links with counterparts in Mexico and beyond as part of a global policing initiative, and at the same time on the inevitably more successful efforts of internationally connected drug cartels to smuggle drugs, money, and guns across state borders, poses serious questions against sovereignty's claim to territorial integrity.[123] While national defence interests are still orientated towards protecting state borders (for example to secure the state against external threats), what Winslow's novel shows us, contra these efforts and definitions, is that 'states and capital participate in spatiotemporal processes that are radically at odds with the resolutions expressed by the principle of state sovereignty'.[124]

The Mexican–US border is both physical reality and arbitrary marker—a heavily fortified line that establishes the state's limits and creates separate economic markets and political jurisdictions, and a boundary so often crossed and recrossed that it becomes a marker of very little. Early in *The Power of the Dog*, Art Keller, a DEA agent working in Mexico, stumbles across what he refers to as 'the Mexican trampoline' with 'cocaine bouncing from Medellín to Honduras to Mexico to the States' and weapons flowing back in the other direction to arm the Contras fighting against the leftist government in Nicaragua (p. 136). Elements in the CIA are actively conspiring with the Barrera brothers to facilitate the importation of cocaine into the US in return for their assistance in procuring guns (from the New York mafia) to help the Contras' insurgency. Hence one kind of border transgression—the smuggling of cocaine—is encouraged in order to deter a more troubling (from the perspective of those tasked with safeguarding the US 'national interest') manifestation of the same thing (i.e. keeping Communists out). 'What if Mexico falls to the Communists, Arthur?' a CIA chief asks Keller. 'Cuba is dangerous enough—now imagine a two-thousand-mile border with a Russian satellite' (p. 176). Later, though, in response to an act of war by the Barreras—they kidnap, torture, and kill a DEA agent—the Americans, we learn, 'closed the border, leaving thousands of trucks stranded on the road, their loads of produce rotting in the sun, the economic cost staggering' (p. 158).

This, of course, is only a temporary measure and while border crossings are depicted, to quote van Schendel and Abraham, as 'high militarized gateways',[125] to secure the state's territorial integrity, the legal and illegal flow of goods, money, and people through these gateways speaks to exactly the kind of disjuncture between the principle of state sovereignty and the spatio-temporal processes of global capital that Walker refers to. Winslow's point is not that sovereignty retreats or even disappears in the context of such transgressions—for the plans implemented by elements within the CIA, DEA, and the White House to combat left-wing insurgency across Latin America, in consort with the special forces, organized crime,

[123] I explore this issue at greater length elsewhere—see Pepper, 'Policing the Globe', pp. 403–24.
[124] Walker, *Inside/Outside*, p. 165.
[125] van Schendel and Abraham, *Illicit Flows and Criminal Things*, p. 14.

and even the Catholic Church, is evidence of the state's enhanced security/policing apparatus—and is not necessarily at odds with the relaxation of border controls, under the North American Free Trade Agreement (NAFTA), to ensure the 'smooth flow of traffic between Mexico and the United States... [a]nd with it, the smooth flow of drug traffic' (p. 401). Rather it is that, like the flow and accumulation of capital and goods (licit or otherwise) that the state wants to facilitate, sovereignty operates in the novel as an absent presence or a present absence, a means of differentiating between 'them' and 'us' but where the constitutive elements of both categories is forever in flux, dependent as much on contingency or fast-changing circumstances as on fixed geopolitical realities.

Much of this chapter has been devoted to exploring how contemporary crime fiction, with its historical affiliations with and to the state, explores not just the nature but also the limits of state sovereignty—in an era marked by the encroaching power of global capital and the encroaching logic of neoliberalism. As such it mirrors corresponding moves by legal, IR, and political theorists, to map these same manoeuvres and indeed these same limits. As Michael Hardt puts it, 'With the decline of national sovereignty there is even less distinction between inside and outside—and therefore there is the tendency toward the formation of a global space of sovereignty that has no outside.'[126]

In *Empire* (2000), Hardt together with Antonio Negri, provides some useful clarification: this decline of national sovereignty 'does not mean that sovereignty has declined' but rather that it 'has taken a new form, composed of a series of national and supranational organisms united under a single logic of rule'.[127] There are more than passing similarities between Hardt and Negri's idea of 'Empire' and Miéville's notion of Breach. Breach mirrors and appropriates the language of sovereignty, of norms and exceptions—i.e. its power, evoking a Schmittian sense of the Sovereign, is described as 'limitless', 'frightening' (p. 83) and later as 'secretive' and 'unique' (p. 96)—but, like 'Empire', it is not locatable in a particular sovereign jurisdiction. It is, to quote Hardt and Negri, 'a decentered and deterritoralizing apparatus of rule'.[128] The idea of a 'space of sovereignty that has no outside' finds affinity with Winslow's and Carlotto's vision of the 'crime-society dyad' conjoined in a single model and while, on one level, organized crime is conceived by both writers as openly violent, predatory, and acquisitive, e.g. enacting a form of conquest, there is also a move—linked to Hardt and Negri's idea of 'Empire'—to show new forms of 'creative criminality' as flexible, inclusive, incorporating, and open-ended.[129] Despite its brilliant interrogations of sovereignty, the contemporary crime novel, it would be fair to say, has struggled to delineate what lies beyond or outside the state (except other states) or, again with notable exceptions, to find an appropriate form and language to depict the openness and mobility of global

---

[126] Michael Hardt, 'Sovereignty', *Theory & Event* 5:4 (2002), http://muse.jhu.edu/login?auth=0&type=summary&url=/journals/theory_and_event/v005/5.4hardt.html, accessed 19 June 2014.
[127] Hardt and Negri, *Empire*, pp. xi–xii.   [128] Hardt and Negri, *Empire*, p. xii.
[129] Hardt and Negri describe 'Empire' not as a form of conquest linked to territory and colonial rule but as a system of rule that operates by 'progressively incorporate[ing] the entire global realm within its open, expanding frontiers'. See *Empire*, pp. xii–xiii.

capital. Miéville's Breach is a good example of the former—of a power that is described as both 'nothing' and 'commonplace' (p. 296), and is at once everywhere and nowhere—but the fact he is not interested in using Breach to analogize the patterns and logic of the global market suggests a parting of ways with Hardt and Negri, something that in turn requires us to reflect back on Miéville's Marxist account of international law.

In Miéville's novel, Borlú's investigation into Geary's murder results in his pursuit of a man who has just assassinated her friend Yolande from within Besźel while she is about to cross from Ul Qomo to Besźel—and crucially while Borlú is stranded in Ul Qomo. Hence, '[t]his was not, could not be a chase. It was only two accelerations. We ran, he in his city, me close behind him, full of rage, in mine' (pp. 284–5). Hence when Borlú shoots him—as he 'stepped toward space where no one in Ul Qomo could go' (p. 285)—the act is doubly transgressive in so far as he has shot a man, not necessarily in self-defence, and that the bullet has travelled across the border, resulting in the intervention of Breach, a 'force shoving me effortlessly out of my place, past candles of Beszáel and the neon of Ul Qomo, in directions that made sense in neither city' (p. 286). Borlú is taken and held by and in Breach, so that being 'in both cities had gone from being in Besźel and Ul Qomo to being in a third place, that nowhere-both, that Breach' (p. 306). Miéville has to give Breach some kind of physical form—'anonymous bedrooms, kitchens, offices, outdated-looking computers' and '[t]erse men and women' sitting in these anonymous rooms 'bickering and voting in their fast and loose way on issues alien to me' (p. 317). The fact that Miéville associates Breach not simply with universal and universalizing 'emergency' powers but also with vigorous, if arcane, debate and voting suggests the law, as it is manifest in Breach and whose remit is in fact described as very 'precise', operates in as fair and equitable manner as it can do and according to some kind of due process. The move by Borlú at the end of the novel to join Breach is the logical culmination of development as cop. And yet, we are told, 'my task is changed: not to uphold the law or another law, but to maintain the skin that keeps law in place. Two laws in two places, in fact' (p. 373)—a defence of the law which in turn leads Borlú to describe himself as a 'liberal' (p. 373). Borlú, that is, but not Miéville who, we must not forget wrote *A Marxist Theory of International Law* organized around Marx's observation, 'between equal rights, force decides'. In this sense, Breach's liberal credentials come under severe scrutiny because, as Miéville himself remarks, the 'international rule of law is not counter-posed to force and imperialism: it is an expression of it'[130]—a rather different account of power than we get in 'liberal-cosmopolitan writers' and for that matter in *Empire*. In Miéville's novel, given the role that the US corporation Sear and Cone plays in orchestrating violence for its own ends, in consort with Besź law, this could be interpreted, as per Balakrishnan's retort to Hardt and Negri's *Empire*, as vindication of 'the indispensable role of territorially organized state

---

[130] Miéville, *Between Equal Rights*, p. 8.

power in the reproduction of capitalist social relations'.[131] But we also should not lose sight of the fact that Breach is not the expression of a single sovereign jurisdiction and that in its reliance on performance, on its ubiquity and visibility, being seen to act, it again reveals sovereignty's limits as a descriptive and analytical concept. Breach may be real but this reality is founded upon what Berlant, aptly, calls a 'fantasy of sovereign performativity and state control over geographical borders'.[132]

On the outer edges of Europe, at some indeterminate point of the twenty-first century, what should, by now to us, be the highly recognizable logic of the crime story is playing out in yet another variation—testament, if ever one was needed, to the inventiveness and elasticity of the formula. Even as sovereignty, the legal character and authority of the state within particular territorial limits, is being questioned, unpicked, put back together again, the crime story, in Miéville's hands, as in Gay's and Defoe's hands three hundred years earlier, wants and needs to find ways, always new ways, of recognizing and defending the potentiality of the law, of the justice system, to do some kind of 'good' while at the same time underscoring its failures—its reliance on force and its proximity to capital. This is not to imply that nothing has changed in the intervening three hundred years, i.e. that we can seamlessly map Miéville's *The City & The City* back onto Gay's London, but rather to point out that the crime story, in its idiosyncrasies and multiplicities, has proven itself more than capable of tracing and interrogating the nature and limits of state sovereignty over this period of time.

---

[131] Gopal Balakrishnan, 'Introduction', in Balakrishnan (ed.) *Debating Empire*, p. xii. In fact this is Balakrishnan paraphrasing the claims of Ellen Meiksins Wood.
[132] Berlant, *Cruel Optimism*, p. 96.

Conclusion

There are obvious benefits and drawbacks associated with pursuing the kind of 'long' argument attempted in this book; e.g. that the development of crime fiction as a recognizable genre over a three hundred year period, in Britain, France, and the United States predominantly, is tied to the consolidation of the modern state. My general claim is simple: it is the contradictions that emerge when the state assumes responsibility for administering criminal justice which fuel the subsequent development of the genre. This in turn allows us to unearth or delineate a radical genealogy of crime writing but the point requires some important qualifications.

As I made clear in the introduction, this is not a history of crime fiction and the claims made here do not apply equally to all crime novels—but rather to a tradition, admittedly a long and well-established tradition, in which crime is seen as rooted in the social and economic circumstances of its time. Radical, in this sense, does not mean crime fiction that pursues a set of revolutionary claims or necessarily seeks to promote or further progressive politics—crime fiction has always shied away from directly advocating political causes, even as it shines a light into the dark corners of society's ills and inadequacies. The term 'radical' speaks to or about a willingness to bring the contradictions thrown up by the state's provision for law and justice into explosive conflagration, rather than trying to find ways of ameliorating and resolving them. This is not to make a pejorative judgement on crime novels that pursue either goal but simply to point out a difference; and to make clear that my book has focused almost exclusively on the former.

Meanwhile the expanded historical and geographical frame has put to the sword a number of misplaced assumptions about the genre (for example that its development needs to be primarily understood in Anglo-American terms; that this development can be understood in terms of a move from 'conservative' classic crime fiction to 'radical' hard-boiled crime fiction) and has opened up national crime fiction traditions to instructive transnational and international comparisons, a move that is just beginning to gain critical momentum and that this book will, I hope, play a part in developing. In this process, some important context-based particularities will inevitably be lost and as such there remain some compelling reasons why excavating discrete crime fiction traditions in their specific national contexts should not be abandoned, but instead pursued alongside the comparative approach adopted here. Such studies, with their tighter, thicker focus, are also better placed to assess the vexed question of readership than the kind of 'long' study I have attempted: the complex, multifarious reasons why people read crime fiction and the emergence of new reading habits and communities over time.

In seeking to make connections between crime novels and national crime fiction traditions across time and space, I am not aiming to collapse the very important differences between these texts and traditions, as for example how these relate to the contrasting practices of judicial systems in discrete countries and even to the nature of state power itself. One might argue, for example, that crime fiction in Latin America is better able or more willing to explore the brutalities and violence of state power than US or European examples because right the way across Latin America people arguably regard, and have always regarded, state violence as the norm rather than as an exception. If the comparativist approach taken here runs the risk of overlooking such differences, it compensates by bringing these different texts and national traditions into productive dialogue.

This study wasn't conceived as an historical survey or overview and as such there are, inevitably, glaring omissions and blind spots: entire national crime fiction traditions are either overlooked or referred to in passing and particular crime writers, considered elsewhere as indispensable to an understanding of the field, are passed over here. Aside from Brecht, there is nothing about German crime/krimi fiction, for example, and there is nothing or little about emerging crime fiction cultures in Australia, South Africa (apart from Orford and Beukes), India, Japan (apart from Kirino), and right the way across Latin America, from Mexico and Cuba to Colombia and Argentina.

In other words, the business of exploring 'the international dimensions of crime fiction by framing the genre within a world-literature framework'[1] needs to be pushed much further than I've been able to do. Thinking about the Anglo-American tradition, there is no place for, or no mention of, Chandler and Christie, and though Sjöwall and Wahlöö are a very significant presence in the book, more recent practitioners of Swedish noir, such as Henning Mankell and Stieg Larsson, are not considered. I would have liked to have said more about emerging crime fiction traditions in Germany, Italy, Ireland, Australia, Japan, and elsewhere but felt it prudent to focus my critical attention on the transnational affinities between works produced in England and France in the eighteenth and nineteenth centuries, and continental Europe (predominantly France) and the US in the twentieth century—while of course expanding this lens at certain moments to include, for example, Belgium-born Simenon, Brecht, Sjöwall and Wahlöö, and more recently writers such as Carlotto, Beukes, McNamee, and Kirino.

There is admittedly something a little arbitrary about these decisions, especially when looking at the contemporary crime fiction genre, where, for example, the case for considering Swedish noir, with its international dimensions and its far-reaching interrogations of the interpenetration of state institutions, organized crime, and multinational corporations, is just as compelling as for the 'capitalist noir' of Sallis and Carlotto. (That said, I would stand by my claim that these latter examples constitute the richest and most far-reaching manifestations of this particular phenomenon.)

---

[1] Stewart King, 'Crime Fiction as World Literature', *Clues: A Journal of Detection*, 32:2 (Fall 2014), p. 8.

As in all critical studies, omissions were forced upon me by the necessary limits of word count; I would have liked, for example, to have written about the British noirist Derek Raymond, who remains an absent presence in the book—his 'European' outlook, his jaundiced account of the functioning of state-police bureaucracy, and his willingness to see crime in an expansive social and political context would have fitted very well and in some senses Raymond is the missing link between 'radical' crime writers like Manchette, Himes, and Sjöwall and Wahlöö from the 1960s and 1970s and their contemporary counterparts like Peace and Manotti. In other cases, the omissions were easier for me to justify: Hammett, for example, was preferred over Chandler because his examination of the intersections between public and private are more pervasive and acute than Chandler's; and there was no place for Christie who has no interest in the state's administration of justice, beyond the fact that the police are, by and large, absent from her stories. Indeed the continuing influence of Doyle over successive generations of British crime fiction, and his relentless privileging of the private over the public, was given—in Chapter 4—as a reason for my shift of focus away from British to continental European crime fiction in the twentieth century.

This brief afterword, then, is both an opportunity to applaud the excellent work already being undertaken by crime fiction scholars across the globe, too numerous to mention by name, excavating and opening up discrete, national crime fiction traditions, and to draw attention to the growing emphasis on cross-cultural comparison and on the internationalization of crime fiction (and not just as a contemporary phenomenon). But it is also to admit to what hasn't perhaps been paid enough attention here: the development of what has been a dominant strain of crime fiction criticism in the past quarter century—the study of race, ethnicity, and gender—into my account here of the genre's negotiations with state sovereignty and capitalism. This aspect has, in my defence, not been wholly lacking—the focus on Himes in Chapter 6 and on the complex intersections between race, capital, and state power opens up some new territory, I hope; in Chapter 7 due consideration is given to works by Orford, Kirino, and Manotti where the nature of low-paid female labour, and the relationship between work and crime, is examined in the context of larger structural transformations occurring in the global economy.

Still, as Robin Truth Goodman's *Policing Narratives and The State of Terror* demonstrates, there is much more scope for exploring the nature of public and private power and its gendered and racial dimensions—how the state both enables and regulates the lives of its diverse citizens and non-citizens within and beyond its borders—and for thinking about the ways in which crime fiction registers 'the changing relationships between what constitutes the nation-state and its outside or its "others", particularly at a time when global economic power is offsetting traditional expectations of what the nation-state can do'.[2] If the efforts made in this book to acknowledge and explore these dimensions have been limited in scope, it

---

[2] Robin Truth Goodman, *Policing Narratives and the State of Terror* (Albany, NY: State University of New York Press, 2009), p. 1.

only remains for me to admit to these limits and to encourage further explorations of the complex intersections between race, ethnicity, and gender in crime fiction and the changing relationships between the state and the international in an era of global capitalism and neoliberalism (whereby freedom and free expression are both encouraged and also regulated, managed, etc.).

Certainly, looking ahead to future trends and directions in crime fiction, while the state and state sovereignty will remain a central feature of, and condition of possibility for, crime fiction, for decades to come, increasingly, I think, writers will explore, and continue to explore, how the claims of states inside and outside their borders—the claims of law and justice that have always been central to crime fiction—are modified, revised, augmented, and transformed by the exigencies of global capital, the encroaching transformations ushered in by neoliberalism, continuing changes to the global economy, and perhaps most importantly of all by the new policing and security practices best described by Ian Loader: where 'the sovereign state—hitherto considered focal to both provision and accountability in this field—is reconfigured as but one node of a broader, more diverse "network of power"'.[3] In all of this, I suspect that the crime novel will need to adapt, as it has always had to, and incorporate aspects of other genres, notably the thriller, the spy–espionage novel, and science fiction, if it is to successfully map and interrogate what Loader calls 'plural, networked policing'—'private policing forms secured through government to transnational arrangements above government to markets in policing and security beyond government to policing initiatives engaged by citizens below government'[4]—but this is a story, and an argument, for another place and another time.

---

[3] Ian Loader, 'Plural Policing and Democratic Governance', *Social & Legal Studies*, 9:3 (2000), p. 323.

[4] Loader, 'Plural Policing and Democratic Governance', p. 324.

Select Bibliography

In this bibliography I have included only those texts I have referred to in detail. I have given the date of original publication in square brackets, followed by the details of the particular edition I have used. The page references cited in the body of the chapters refer to these editions. Where I have used a writer's selected works, compiled over a number of years, I have not provided a date of original publication.

PRIMARY SOURCES

Adams, Charles Warren ([1865] 2012). *The Notting Hill Mystery*. London: The British Library.
Allain, Marcel and Souvestre, Pierre ([1911] 2006). *Fantômas*, intro. John Ashbery. London: Penguin.
Balzac, Honoré de ([1834] 1999). *Père Goriot*, trans. A.J. Krailsheimer. Oxford: Oxford University Press.
Braddon, Mary Elizabeth ([1861–2] 1998). *Lady Audley's Secret*. Oxford: Oxford University Press.
Carlotto, Massimo ([2000] 2006). *The Goodbye Kiss*, trans. Lawrence Venuti. New York, NY: Europa.
Carlotto, Massimo ([2011] 2013). *At the End of a Dull Day*, trans. Antony Shugaar. New York, NY: Europa.
Collins, Wilkie ([1868] 1986). *The Moonstone*. London: Penguin.
Defoe, Daniel ([1722] 1722). *The Life and Actions of Lewis Dominique Cartouche*, 2nd edn. London: J. Roberts.
Defoe, Daniel ([1725] 2004). *Defoe on Sheppard and Wild*, intro. Richard Holmes. London: Harper Perennial.
Doyle, Arthur Conan ([1905] 1981). *The Return of Sherlock Holmes*. London: Penguin.
Doyle, Arthur Conan ([1892] 2007). *The Adventures of Sherlock Holmes*. London: Penguin.
Dürrenmatt, Friedrich (1982). *Friedrich Dürrenmatt: Plays and Essays*, ed. Volkmar Sander. New York, NY: Continuum.
Dürrenmatt, Friedrich ([1958] 2000). *The Pledge*, trans. Joel Agee. New York, NY: Berkley Boulevard.
Faber, Michael ([2002] 2003). *The Crimson Petal and the White*. Edinburgh: Canongate.
Fielding, Henry ([1743] 2003). *The Life of Mr Jonathan Wild the Great*, ed. Hugh Amory. Oxford: Oxford University Press.
Gaboriau, Emile ([1866] 1903). *The Widow Lerouge*. New York, NY: Charles Scribner's Sons.
Gaboriau, Emile ([1868] 1904). *Monsieur Lecoq*. New York, NY: Charles Scribner's Sons.
Gay, John ([1728] 1986). *The Beggar's Opera*. London: Penguin.
Gayot de Pitaval, François ([1734] 1744). *A Select Collection of Singular and Interesting Histories*. London: A. Miller.
Godwin, William ([1794] 1998). *Caleb Williams*, ed. David McCracken. Oxford: Oxford University Press.

Green, Anna Katharine ([1878] 2010). *The Leavenworth Case*. London and New York, NY: Penguin.
H.D., late Clerk to Justice R—(1725). *The Life of Jonathan Wild from his Birth to Death*. London: T. Warner.
Hammett, Dashiell ([1931] 1982). *The Glass Key*, in *The Four Great Novels*. London: Picador.
Hammett, Dashiell ([1929] 1982). *Red Harvest*, in *The Four Great Novels*. London: Picador.
Hammett, Dashiell ([1930] 1992). *The Maltese Falcon*. New York, NY: Vintage.
Himes, Chester ([1959] 1997). *The Real Cool Killers*, in Robert Polito (ed.), *Crime Novels: American Noir of the 1950s*. New York, NY: Library of America, pp. 731–876.
Himes, Chester ([1969] 1986). *Blind Man with a Pistol*. London: Allison & Busby.
Himes, Chester ([1965] 1988). *Cotton Comes to Harlem*. London: Allison & Busby.
Himes, Chester ([1961] 1992). *The Heat's On*. London: Allison & Busby.
Himes, Chester (1993). *Plan B*, ed. Michel Fabre and Robert E. Skinner. Jackson, MI: University Press of Mississippi.
Kirino, Natsuo ([1997] 2004). *Out*, trans. Stephen Snyder. London: Vintage.
Lauren Beukes (2014). *Broken Monsters*. London: HarperCollins.
Lemaitre, Pierre ([2011] 2013). *Alex*, trans. Frank Wynne. London: Maclehose.
Leroux, Gaston ([1907] 2006). *The Mystery of the Yellow Room*. Mineola, NY: Dover.
McNamee, Eoin ([2000] 2001). *The Blue Tango*. London: Faber and Faber.
McNamee, Eoin (2004). *The Ultras*. London: Faber and Faber.
McNamee, Eoin (2010). *Orchid Blue*. London: Faber and Faber.
McNamee, Eoin (2014). *Blue is the Night*. London: Faber and Faber.
Manchette, Jean-Patrick ([1976] 2002). *3 to Kill*, trans. Donald Nicholson-Smith. San Francisco, CA: City Light Books.
Manchette, Jean-Patrick ([1981] 2002). *The Prone Gunman*, trans. James Brook. San Francisco, CA: City Lights Books.
Manchette, Jean-Patrick ([1977] 2011). *Fatale*, trans. Donald Nicholson-Smith. New York, NY: New York Review of Books.
Manotti, Dominique ([2006] 2009). *Lorraine Connection*, trans. Amanda Hopkinson and Roz Schwartz. London: Arcadia Books.
Miéville, China (2009). *The City & the City*. London: Macmillan.
Morrison, Arthur ([1897] 2003). *The Dorrington Deed-Box*. Rockville, MD: James A. Rock & Company.
Orford, Margie ([2013] 2014). *Water Music*. London: Head of Zeus.
Peace, David (2004). *GB84*. London: Faber and Faber.
Poe, Edgar Allan (1991). *Selected Tales*. Oxford and New York, NY: Oxford University Press.
Sallis, James ([2005] 2006). *Drive*. Orlando, FL: Harvest.
Sciascia, Leonardo ([1966] 1992). *To Each His Own*, trans. Adrienne Foulke. Manchester: Carcanet.
Sciascia, Leonardo ([1961] 2013). *The Day of the Owl*, trans. Archibald Colquhoun and Arthur Oliver. London: Granta.
Simenon, Georges ([1952] 2004). *Monsieur Monde Vanishes*, trans. Jean Stewart. New York, NY: New York Review of Books.
Simenon, Georges ([1933] 2005). *Tropic Moon*, trans. Marc Romano. New York, NY: New York Review of Books.
Simenon, Georges ([1932] 2006). *The Bar on the Seine*, trans. David Watson. London: Penguin.

Simenon, Georges ([1931] 2006). *Lock 14*, trans. Robert Baldick. New York, NY: Penguin.
Simenon, Georges ([1938] 2006). *The Man Who Watched the Trains Go By*, trans. Stuart Gilbert, rev. David Watson. London: Penguin.
Simenon, Georges ([1931] 2006). *The Yellow Dog*, trans. Linda Asher. London: Penguin.
Simenon, Georges ([1933] 2007). *The Engagement*, trans. Anna Moschovakis. New York, NY: New York Review of Books.
Sjöwall, Maj and Wahlöö, Per ([1968] 2002). *The Laughing Policeman*, trans. Alan Blair. London: Orion.
Sjöwall, Maj and Wahlöö, Per ([1971] 2007). *The Abominable Man*, trans. Thomas Teal. London: Harper Perennial.
Sjöwall, Maj and Wahlöö, Per ([1975] 2007). *The Terrorists*, trans. Joan Tate. London: Harper Perennial.
Sjöwall, Maj and Wahlöö, Per ([1975] 2011). *Cop Killer*, trans. Thomas Teal. London: Fourth Estate.
Sjöwall, Maj and Wahlöö, Per ([1969] 2011). *The Fire Engine That Disappeared*, trans. Joan Tate. London: Fourth Estate.
Sjöwall, Maj and Wahlöö, Per ([1972] 2011). *The Locked Room,* trans. Paul Britten Austin. London: Fourth Estate.
Sjöwall, Maj and Wahlöö, Per ([1970] 2011). *Murder at the Savoy*, trans. Joan Tate. London: Fourth Estate.
Vidocq, François-Eugène (1828). *Memoirs of Vidocq, Principal Agent of the French Police Written by Himself.* London: Whittaker & Co.
Voltaire ([1759] 1998). *Candide and Other Stories*, trans. and notes, Roger Pearson. Oxford: Oxford University Press.
Wahlöö, Per ([1964] 2011). *Murder on the Thirty-First Floor*, trans. Sarah Death. London: Vintage.
Wallace, Edgar (2010). *The Casefiles of Mr J. G. Reeder*. Ware, Hertfordshire: Wordsworth Editions.
Winslow, Don ([2005] 2006). *The Power of the Dog*. New York, NY: Vintage.

SECONDARY SOURCES

Adkins, Lisa (2005). 'The New Economy, Property and Personhood'. *Theory Culture Society*, 22:1, pp. 111–30.
Agnew, John (1994). 'The Territory Trap'. *Review of International Political Economy*, 1.1, pp. 53–80.
Alder, Bill (2011). 'Maigret, Simenon, France: Social Class and Social Change in the 1930s Maigret Narratives of Georges Simenon'. *Clues: A Journal of Detection*, 29:2, pp. 47–57.
Alder, Bill (2012). *Maigret, Simenon and France: Social Dimensions of the Novels and Stories*. Jefferson, NC: McFarland.
Anderson, Philip (2006). '*Roman Noir* and Subjectivity: The Last Three Novels of Jean-Patrick Manchette'. *Australian Journal of French Studies*, 43:1, pp. 70–9.
Andreas, Peter and Nadelman, Ethan (2006). *Policing the Globe: Criminalization and Crime Control in International Relations*. Oxford: Oxford University Press.
Anker, Elizabeth S. (2013). 'In the Shadowlands of Sovereignty: The Politics of Enclosure on Alejandro Gonzáles Iñárritu's Babel'. *University of Toronto Quarterly*, 82:4, pp. 950–73.
Aradau, Claudia and van Munster, Rens (2009). 'Exceptionalism and the "War on Terror": Criminology Meets International Relations'. *British Journal of Criminology*, 49:5, pp. 686–703.

Aronowitz, Stanley and Bratsis, Peter (2002). *Paradigm Lost: State Theory Reconsidered*. Minneapolis, MN and London: University of Minnesota Press.

Ascari, Maurizio (2007). *A Counter-History of Crime Fiction: Supernatural, Gothic, Sensational*. Basingstoke: Palgrave Macmillan.

Atack, Margaret (1999). *May '68 in French Fiction and Film: Rethinking Society, Rethinking Representation*. Oxford: Oxford University Press.

Badiou, Alan (2003). *Infinite Thought: Truth and the Return of Philosophy*, trans. and ed. Oliver Feltham and Justin Clemens. London and New York, NY: Continuum.

Bastien, Pascal (2005). 'Private Crimes and Public Executions: Discourses on Guilt in the *Arrêts Criminels* of the Eighteenth-Century Parliament of Paris', in Amy Gilman Srebnick and René Lévy (eds), *Crime and Culture: An Historical Perspective*. Aldershot and Burlington, VT: Ashgate, pp. 141–62.

Beattie, J.M. (2004). *Policing and Punishment in London, 1650–1750: Urban Crime and the Limits of Terror*. Oxford: Oxford University Press.

Beccaria, Cesare ([1765] 1986). *On Crimes and Punishments*, ed. David Young. Indianapolis, IN: Hackett.

Becker, Lucille (1999). *Georges Simenon Revisited*. New York, NY: Twayne.

Belas, Oliver (2010). 'Chester Himes's The End of a Primitive: Exile, Exhaustion, Dissolution'. *Journal of American Studies*, 44:2, pp. 377–90.

Belhadjin, Annissa (2010). 'From Politics to the Roman Noir'. *South Central Review*, 27:1&2, pp. 61–81.

Bell, Ian A. (2003). 'Eighteenth-century Crime Writing', in Martin Priestman (ed.) *The Cambridge Companion to Crime Fiction*. Cambridge: Cambridge University Press, pp. 7–17.

Benjamin, Walter ([1935] 1983). *Charles Baudelaire: A Lyrical Poet in the Era of High Capitalism*, trans. Harry Zohn. London: Verso.

Benjamin, Walter (1986). *Reflections: Essays, Aphorisms, Autobiographical Writings*, ed. Peter Demetz, trans. Edmund Jephcott. New York, NY: Schocken Books.

Benjamin, Walter (1998). *Understanding Brecht*, trans. Anna Bostock. London: Verso.

Benjamin, Walter (2005). 'Travelling with Crime Novels', trans. Aaron Kelly, in Kelly (ed.), *The Thriller and Northern Ireland Since 1969*. Aldershot and Burlington, VT: Ashgate, pp. 165–6, App. A.

Bentham, Jeremy (2002). *Rights, Representation and Reform: Nonsense upon Stilts and Other Writings*, ed. Philip Schofield, Catherine Pease-Watkin, and Cyprian Blamires. Oxford: Clarendon Press.

Berlant, Lauren (2011). *Cruel Optimism*. Durham, NC and London: Duke University Press.

Bielecki, Emma (2013). 'Fantômas's Shifting Identities: From Books to Screen'. *Studies in French Cinema*, 13:1, pp. 3–15.

Biet, Christian (2008). 'Judicial Fiction and Literary Fiction: The Example of the Factum'. *Law and Literature*, 20:3, pp. 403–22.

Bigo, Didier (2001). 'The Möbius Ribbon of Internal and External Security(ies)', in Mathias Albert, David Jacobson, and Yosef Lapid (eds), *Identities, Borders, Orders: Rethinking International Relations*. Minneapolis, MN and London: University of Minnesota Press, pp. 91–116.

Bobbio, Norberto (1993). *Thomas Hobbes and the Natural Law Tradition*. Chicago, IL and London: University of Chicago Press.

Bratlinger, Patrick (1998). *The Reading Lesson: The Threat of Mass Literacy in Nineteenth-Century British Fiction*. Bloomington, IN: Indiana University Press.

Brecht, Bertolt (2005). 'On the Popularity of Crime Novels', trans. Aaron Kelly, in Kelly (ed.), *The Thriller and Northern Ireland Since 1969*. Aldershot and Burlington, VT: Ashgate, p. 167, App. B.
Brecht, Bertolt ([1928] 2005). *The Threepenny Opera*, trans. Ralph Manheim and John Willett. London: Methuen.
Breu, Christopher (2005). *Hard-Boiled Masculinities*. Minneapolis, MN: University of Minnesota Press.
Breu, Christopher (forthcoming). 'Work and Death in the Global City: Natsuo Kirino's *Out* as Neoliberal Noir', in Andrew Pepper and David Schmid (eds), *Globalization and the State in Contemporary Crime Fiction*. Basingstoke: Palgrave Macmillan.
Brown, Wendy (1995). *States of Injury: Power and Freedom in Late Modernity*. Princeton, NJ and London: Princeton University Press.
Brown, Wendy (2006). 'American Nightmare: Neoliberalism, Neoconservatism, and De-Democratization'. *Political Theory*, 34:6, pp. 690–714.
Buccellato, James A. (2012). 'Sign of the Outlaw: Liberal Boundaries, Social Banditry, and the Political Act'. *New Political Science*, 34:3, pp. 271–94.
Buci-Glucksmann, Christine (1980). *Gramsci and the State*, trans. David Fernbach. London: Lawrence & Wishart.
Carlotto, Massimo (2013). 'Eulogy for Jean-Claude Izzo', in Jean-Claude Izzo (ed.), *Total Chaos*, trans. Howard Curtis. New York, NY: Europa, pp. 9–13.
Cassuto, Leonard (2009). *Hard-Boiled Sentimentality: The Secret History of American Crime Stories*. New York, NY: Colombia University Press.
Chandler, Raymond (1995). *Later Novels and Other Writings*, ed. Frank McShane. New York, NY: Library of America.
Clarke, Clare (2010). 'Horace Dorrington, Criminal-Detective: Investigating the Re-Emergence of the Rogue in Arthur Morrison's *The Dorrington Deed-Box*'. *Clues: A Journal of Detection*, 28:2, pp. 7–18.
Clarke, Clare (2014). *Late Victorian Crime Fiction in the Shadows of Sherlock*. Basingstoke: Palgrave Macmillan.
Cobley, Paul (2000). *The American Thriller: Generic Innovation and Social Change in the 1970s*. Basingstoke: Palgrave Macmillan.
Cohen, Michael (1998). 'Godwin's *Caleb Williams*: Showing the Strains in Detective Fiction'. *Eighteenth-Century Fiction*, 10:2, pp. 203–20.
Collins, Jim (1992). *Uncommon Culture: Popular Culture and Post-Modernism*. London and New York, NY: Routledge.
Comaroff, Jean and John (2004). 'Criminal Obsessions after Foucault: Postcoloniality, Policing and the Metaphysics of Disorder'. *Critical Inquiry*, 30:4, pp. 800–24.
Copjec, Joan (1998). 'The Phenomenal Nonphenomenal: Private Space in Film Noir', in Copjec (ed.), *Shades of Noir: A Reader*. London and New York, NY: Verso, pp. 167–97.
Damrosch, David (2003). *What is World Literature?* Princeton, NJ and London: Princeton University Press.
Debord, Guy (1990). *Comments on the Society of the Spectacle*, trans. Malcolm Imrie. London and New York, NY: Verso.
Debord, Guy ([1967] 1994). *The Society of Spectacle*, trans. Donald Nicholson-Smith. New York, NY: Zone Books.
Denning, Michael (1982). 'Beggars and Thieves: *The Beggar's Opera* and the Ideology of the Gang'. *Literature and History*, 8:1, pp. 41–52.
Denning, Michael (1988). 'Topographies of Violence: Chester Himes's Harlem Domestic Novels'. *Critical Texts: A Review of Theory & Criticism*, 5, pp. 10–18.

Diawara, Manthia (1993). 'Noir by Noirs: Towards a New Realism in Black Cinema'. *African-American Review*, 27:4, pp. 525–37.
Dubois, Page (2005). 'Oedipus as Detective: Sophocles, Simenon, Robbe-Grillet'. *Yale French Studies*, 108, pp. 102–15.
Eburne, Jonathan (2005). 'The Transatlantic Mysteries of Paris: Chester Himes, Surrealism, and the Série Noire'. *PMLA*, 120:3, pp. 806–21.
Eburne, Jonathan (2008). *Surrealism and the Art of Crime*. Ithaca, NY and London: Cornell University Press.
Emsley, Clive (2002). 'The Origins and Development of the Police', in Eugene McLaughlin and John Muncie (eds), *Controlling Crime*. Milton Keynes and Philadelphia, PA: Open University Press, pp. 11–52.
Engels, Friedrich ([1843] 1987). *The Condition of the Working Class in England*, ed. Victor Kiernan. London: Penguin.
Evans, Mary (2009). *The Imagination of Evil: Detective Fiction and the Modern World*. London and New York, NY: Continuum.
Fabre, Michel and Skinner, Robert E. (eds) (1995). *Conversations with Chester Himes*. Jackson, MS: University Press of Mississippi.
Faller, Lincoln B. (1987). *Turned to Account: The Forms and Functions of Criminal Biography in Late Seventeenth- and Early Eighteenth-Century England*. Cambridge: Cambridge University Press.
Farrell, Joseph (1995). *Leonardo Sciascia*. Edinburgh: Edinburgh University Press.
Femia, Joseph V. (2004). *Machiavelli Revisited*. Cardiff: University of Wales Press.
Fisher, Mark (2009). *Capitalist Realism: Is There No Alternative?* Winchester and Washington, DC: Zero Books.
Fornabai, Nanette (2005). '"Fantômas", Anthropometrics, and the Numerical Fictions of Modern Criminal Identity'. *Yale French Studies*, 108, pp. 60–73.
Foucault, Michel (1988). 'The Dangerous Individual', in Lawrence D. Kritzman (ed.), *Politics, Philosophy, Culture: Interviews and Other Writings 1977–1984*. London and New York, NY: Routledge, pp. 125–51.
Foucault, Michel ([1975] 1991). *Discipline and Punish: The Birth of the Prison*, trans. Alan Sheridan. London: Penguin.
Foucault, Michel (1991). 'Nietzsche, Genealogy, History', in Paul Rabinow (ed.), *The Foucault Reader*. New York, NY: Penguin, pp. 76–100.
Foucault, Michel (2004). *Society Must be Defended: Lectures at the Collège de France, 1975–76*, trans. David Macey. London: Penguin.
Foucault, Michel (2007). *Security, Territory, Population: Lectures at the Collège de France 1977–1978*, ed. Michel Senallart, trans. Graham Burchell. Basingstoke: Palgrave Macmillan.
Freedman, Carl and Kendrick, Christopher (1991). 'Forms of Labor in Dashiell Hammett's Red Harvest'. *PMLA*, 106:2, pp. 209–21.
Friman, H. Richard and Andreas, Peter (eds) (1999). *The Illicit Global Economy and State Power*. Lanham, MD: Rowman & Littlefield.
Gavison, Ruth (1992). 'Feminism and the Public/Private Distinction'. *Stanford Law Review*, 45:1, pp. 1–45.
Gay, Peter (1959). *Voltaire's Politics: The Poet as Realist*. Princeton, NJ: Princeton University Press.
Ginzburg, Carlo (1989). *Clues, Myths and the Historical Method*, trans. John and Anne C. Tedeschi. Baltimore, MD and London: The Johns Hopkins University Press.

Gladfelder, Hal (2001). *Criminality and Narrative in Eighteenth-Century England*. Baltimore, MD and London: The Johns Hopkins University Press.
Godwin, William ([1793] 1971). *Enquiry Concerning Political Justice*, ed. K. Codwell Carter. Oxford: Oxford University Press.
Goodman, Robin Truth (2009). *Policing Narratives and the State of Terror*. Albany, NY: State University Press of New York.
Gorrara, Claire (2000). 'Narratives of Protest and the *Roman Noir* in Post-1968 France'. *French Studies*, 54:3, pp. 313–25.
Gorrara, Claire (2003). 'Cultural Intersections: The American Hard-Boiled Detective Novel and Early French Roman Noir'. *Modern Humanities Research Association*, 98:3, pp. 590–601.
Gorrara, Claire (ed.) (2009). *French Crime Fiction*. Cardiff: University of Wales Press.
Goulet, Andrea (2005). 'The Yellow Spot: Ocular Pathology and Empirical Method in Gaston Leroux's *Le mystère de la chambre jaune*'. *SubStance*, 34:2, pp. 27–46.
Gramsci, Antonio (1971). *Selections from the Prison Notebooks of Antonio Gramsci*, ed. Quintin Hoare and Geoffrey Nowell-Smith. London: Lawrence & Wishart.
Gramsci, Antonio (1985). *Selections from Cultural Writings*, ed. David Forgas and Geoffrey Nowell-Smith. London: Lawrence & Wishart.
Green, Penny and Ward, Tony (2004). *State Crime: Governments, Violence, and Corruption*. London: Pluto Press.
Greenberg, David F. (ed.) (1981). *Crime and Capitalism: Readings in Marxist Criminology*. Palo Alto, CA: Mayfield Publishing Company.
Gunning, Tom (2003). 'The Exterior as Interieur: Benjamin's Optical Detective'. *boundary 2*, 30:1, pp. 105–30.
Gunning, Tom (2005). 'Lynx-Eyed Detectives and Shadow Bandits: Visuality and Eclipse in French Detective Stories and Films before WW1'. *Yale French Studies*, 108, pp. 74–88.
Hardt, Michael and Negri, Antonio (2000). *Empire*. Cambridge, MA and London: Harvard University Press.
Hart, Matthew (2006). 'An Interview with David Peace, Conducted by Matthew Hart'. *Contemporary Literature*, 47:4, pp. 546–69.
Hart, Matthew (2009). 'The Third English Civil War: David Peace's "Occult History" of Thatcherism'. *Contemporary Literature*, 49:4, pp. 573–96.
Harvey, David (2001). *Spaces of Capital: Towards a Critical Geography*. Edinburgh: Edinburgh University Press.
Harvey, David (2007). *A Brief History of Neoliberalism*. Oxford: Oxford University Press.
Harvey, David (2010). *A Companion to Marx's Capital*. London and New York, NY: Verso.
Harvey, David (2011). *The Enigma of Capital and the Crisis of Capitalism*. London: Profile.
Heise, Thomas (2005). '"Going Blood-Simple Like the Natives": Contagious Urban Spaces and Modern Power in Dashiell Hammett's *Red Harvest*'. *Modern Fiction Studies*, 51:3, pp. 485–512.
Heise, Thomas (2007). 'Harlem is Burning: Urban Rioting and the "Black Underclass" in Chester Himes's *Blind Man with a Pistol*'. *African-American Review*, 41:3, pp. 487–506.
Held, David (1984). 'Central Perspectives on the Modern State', in Gregor McLennan, David Held, and Stuart Hall (eds), *The Idea of the Modern State*. Milton Keynes and Philadelphia, PA: Open University Press, pp. 29–79.
Higginson, Pim (2005). 'Mayhem at the Crossroads: Francophone African Fiction and the Rise of the Crime Novel'. *Yale French Studies*, 108, pp. 160–76.
Higginson, Pim (2011). *The Noir Atlantic: Chester Himes and the Birth of the Francophile Crime Novel*. Liverpool: Liverpool University Press.

Hilfer, Tony (1992). *The Crime Novel: A Deviant Genre*. Austin, TX: University of Texas Press.
Hillyard, Paddy and Percy-Smith, Jane (1988). *The Coercive State: The Decline of Democracy in Britain*. London: Fontana.
Himes, Chester (1976). *My Life of Absurdity: The Autobiography of Chester Himes Vol. 2*. New York, NY: Doubleday.
Himes, Chester ([1972] 1995). *The Quality of Hurt: The Autobiography of Chester Himes Vol. 1*. New York, NY: Thunder's Mouth Press.
Hobbes, Thomas ([1653] 1996). *Leviathan*, ed. Richard Tuck. Cambridge: Cambridge University Press.
Hobsbawm, Eric (1971). *Primitive Rebels: Studies in Archaic Forms of Social Movement in the 19th and 20th Centuries*. Manchester: Manchester University Press.
Hobsbawm, Eric (2003). *Bandits*. London: Abacus.
Hoffman, Josef (2013). *Philosophies of Crime Fiction*, trans. Carolyn Kelly, Nadia Majid, and Johanna da Rocha Abreu. Harpenden: No Exit Press.
Holloway, David (2009). 'The War on Terror Espionage Thriller, and the Imperialism of Human Rights'. *Comparative Literature Studies*, 46:1, pp. 20–44.
Horsley, Lee (2005). *Twentieth-Century Crime Fiction*. Oxford: Oxford University Press.
Howell, Philip (1998). 'Crime and the City Solution: Crime Fiction, Urban Knowledge and Radical Geography'. *Antipode*, 30:4, pp. 357–78.
Howson, Gerald (1987). *It Takes a Thief: The Life and Times of Jonathan Wild*. London: Cresset.
Hume, L.J. (1981). *Bentham and Bureaucracy*. Cambridge: Cambridge University Press.
Hundert, E.J. (1996). *The Enlightenment's Tale: Bernard Mandeville and the Discovery of Society*. Cambridge: Cambridge University Press.
Jann, Rosemary (1990). 'Sherlock Holmes Codes the Social Body'. *ELH*, 57:3, pp. 605–708.
Johnston, Les (2000). 'Transnational Private Policing', in J.W.E. Sheptycki (ed.), *Issues in Transnational Policing*. London and New York, NY: Routledge, pp. 21–42.
Kalifa, Dominique (2004). 'Crime Scenes: Criminal Topography and Social Imaginary in Nineteenth-Century Paris'. *French Historical Studies*, 27:1, pp. 175–94.
Kalifa, Dominique and Flynn, Margaret Jean (trans.) (2005). 'Criminal Investigators at the Fin-de-siècle'. *Yale French Studies*, 108, pp. 36–47.
Kayman, Martin (1992). *From Bow Street to Baker Street: Mystery, Detection and Narrative*. Basingstoke: Macmillan.
Kimyongür, Angela (2013). 'Dominique Manotti and the Roman Noir'. *Contemporary Women's Writing*, 7:3, pp. 235–52.
King, Stewart (2014). 'Crime Fiction as World Literature'. *Clues: A Journal of Detection*, 32: 2, pp. 8–19.
Knight, Stephen (1980). *Form and Ideology in Crime Fiction*. Basingstoke: Macmillan.
Knight, Stephen (2004). *Crime Fiction 1800–2000: Detection, Death, Diversity*. Basingstoke: Palgrave Macmillan.
Krajenbrink, Marieke and Quinn, Kate (eds) (2009). *Investigating Identities: Questions of Identity in Contemporary International Crime Fiction*. Amsterdam: Rodopi.
Lehner, Stefanie (2011). *Subaltern Ethics in Contemporary Scottish and Irish Literature*. Basingstoke: Palgrave Macmillan.
Leps, Marie-Christine (1992). *Apprehending the Criminal: The Production of Deviance in Nineteenth-Century Discourse*. Durham, NC and London: Duke University Press.

Linebaugh, Peter (2003). *The London Hanged: Crime and Civil Society in the Eighteenth Century*. London: Verso.
Lloyd, David and Thomas, Paul (1998). *Culture and the State*. London and New York, NY: Routledge.
Loader, Ian (2000). 'Plural Policing and Democratic Governance'. *Social & Legal Studies*, 9:3, pp. 323–45.
Loader, Ian and Walker, Neil (2007). *Civilizing Security*. Cambridge: Cambridge University Press.
Loughrey, Bryan and Treadwell, T.O. (1986). 'Introduction', in John Gay, *The Beggar's Opera*, ed. Bryan Loughrey. London: Penguin, pp. vii–xxxviii.
McCann, Sean (2000). *Gumshoe America: Hard-Boiled Crime Fiction and the Rise and Fall of New Deal Liberalism*. Durham, NC and London: Duke University Press.
Machiavelli, Niccolo ([1532] 1999). *The Prince*, trans. George Bull. London: Penguin.
Mandel, Ernest (1984). *Delightful Murder: A Social History of the Crime Story*. London: Pluto.
Mandel, Ernest (1990). 'Introduction', in Karl Marx, *Capital: A Critique of Political Economy. Vol. 1*, trans. Ben Fowkes. London: Penguin, pp. 11–86.
Mandeville, Bernard (1725). *An Enquiry into the Causes of Frequent Executions at Tyburn*. London: J. Roberts.
Mandeville, Bernard ([1714] 1725). *The Fable of the Bees or, Private Vices, Publick Benefits*. London: J. Tonson.
Marable, Manning (2000). *How Capitalism Underdeveloped Black America: Problems in Race, Political Economy, and Society*. London: Pluto Press.
Marcus, Stephen (1975). *Representations: Essays on Literature and Society*. New York, NY: Random House.
Marcuse, Herbert (1964). *One-Dimensional Man: Studies in the Ideology of Advanced Society*. London: Routledge and Kegan Paul.
Marcuse, Herbert (1972). *Counterrevolution and Revolt*. London: Penguin.
Marx, Karl ([1863] 1969). *Theories of Surplus-Value Part I*, trans. Emile Burns, ed. S. Ryazanskaya. London: Lawrence & Wishart.
Marx, Karl ([1859] 1970). *A Contribution to the Critique Political Economy*, trans. S.W. Ryazanskaya, ed. Maurice Dobb. Moscow: Progress Publishers.
Marx, Karl ([1843] 1970). *Critique of Hegel's Philosophy of Right*, trans. Annette Jolin and Joseph O'Malley, ed. Joseph O'Malley. Cambridge: Cambridge University Press.
Marx, Karl ([1852] 1972). *The Eighteenth Brumaire of Louis Bonaparte*. Moscow: Progress Publishers.
Marx, Karl (1973). *Economic and Philosophic Manuscripts of 1844*, trans. Martin Milligan, ed. Dirk J. Struik. London: Lawrence & Wishart.
Marx, Karl ([1894] 1981). *Capital: A Critique of Political Economy, Vol. 3*, intro. Ernest Mandel, trans. David Fernbach. London: Penguin.
Marx, Karl ([1867] 1990). *Capital: A Critique of Political Economy, Vol. 1*, ed. Ernest Mandel, trans. Ben Fowkes. London: Penguin.
Marx, Karl (2010). *Essential Writings of Karl Marx: Economic and Philosophic Manuscripts, Communist Manifesto, Wage Labor and Capital, Critique of the Gotha Program*. St Petersburg, FL: Red and Black Publishers.
Marx, Karl and Engels, Friedrich ([1845] 1965). *The German Ideology*, trans. and ed. S. Ryazanskaya. London: Lawrence & Wishart.
Matzke, Christine and Mühleiser, Susanne (2006). *Postcolonial Perspectives: Crime Fiction from a Transcultural Perspective*. Amsterdam: Rodopi.

Messent, Peter (2010). 'The Police Novel', in Charles J. Rzepka and Lee Horsley (eds), *A Companion to Crime Fiction*. Oxford and Malden, MA: Wiley-Blackwell, pp. 175–86.
Messent, Peter (2013). *The Crime Fiction Handbook*. Oxford and Malden, MA: Wiley-Blackwell.
Miéville, China (2005). *Between Equal Rights: A Marxist Interpretation of International Law*. Chicago, IL: Haymarket Books.
Miliband, Ralph (1973). *The State in Capitalist Society*. London: Quartet Books.
Mill, John Stuart ([1859] 1987). *On Liberty*, ed. Gertrude Himmelfarb. London: Penguin.
Miller, D.A. (1988). *The Novel and the Police*. Berkeley and Los Angeles, CA: University of California Press.
Moretti, Franco (1983). *Signs Taken for Wonder: Essays in the Sociology of Literary Form*, trans. Susan Fischer, David Forgacs, and David Miller. London and New York, NY: Verso.
Moretti, Franco (2000). 'Conjectures on World literature'. *New Left Review*, 1, pp. 54–68.
Morton, James (2005). *The First Detective: The Life and Revolutionary Times of Vidocq*. London: Ebury Press.
Nestingen, Andrew (ed.) (forthcoming). 'Scandinavian Crime Fiction and the Facts: Social Criticism, Epistemology, and Globalization', in Andrew Pepper and David Schmid (eds), *Globalization and the State in Contemporary Crime Fiction*. Basingstoke: Palgrave Macmillan.
Nestingen, Andrew and Arvas, Paula (eds) (2011). *Scandinavian Crime Fiction*. Cardiff: University of Wales Press.
Nestingen, Andrew and Arvas, Paula (eds) (2011). 'Unnecessary Officers: Realism, Melodrama and Swedish Crime Fiction in Transition'. *Scandinavian Crime Fiction*, pp. 171–81.
Nickerson, Catherine Ross (ed.) (2010). *The Cambridge Companion to American Crime Fiction*. Cambridge: Cambridge University Press.
Parmalee, Patty Lee (1981). *Brecht's America*. Columbus, OH: Ohio State University Press.
Pateman, Carole (1989). *The Disorder of Women: Democracy, Feminism and Political Thought*. Cambridge: Cambridge University Press.
Pawling, Christopher (2013). *Critical Theory and Political Engagement: From May '68 to the Arab Spring*. Basingstoke: Palgrave Macmillan.
Peace, David (1999). *Nineteen Seventy Four*. London: Serpent's Tail.
Peace, David (2015). 'Foreword by David Peace', in Jean-Patrick Manchette, *Fatale*. London: Serpent's Tail, pp. v–xii.
Pepper, Andrew (2010). '"Hegemony Protected by the Armour of Coercion": Dashiell Hammett's *Red Harvest* and the State'. *Journal of American Studies*, 44:2, pp. 333–49.
Pepper, Andrew (2011). 'Early Crime Writing and the State: Jonathan Wild, Daniel Defoe and Bernard Mandeville in 1720s London'. *Textual Practice*, 25:3, pp. 473–91.
Pepper, Andrew (2011). 'Policing the Globe; State Sovereignty and the International in Post-9/11 Crime Fiction'. *Modern Fiction Studies*, 57:3, pp. 401–24.
Pepper, Andrew (2013). 'Henning Mankell: Political Reactionary'. *Moving Worlds*, 13:1, pp. 90–101.
Pezzotti, Barbara (2014). 'Crime and Capitalism: Giorgio Scerbanenco's and Massimo Carlotto's Italian Domestication of American Hard-Boiled Fiction'. *Clues: A Journal of Detection*, 32:2, pp. 51–61.
Pezzotti, Barbara (2014). *Politics and Society in Italian Crime Fiction: An Historical Overview*. Jefferson, NC: McFarland.

Pfeil, Fred (1990). *Another Tale to Tell: Politics and Narrative in Postmodern Culture*. London and New York, NY: Verso.
Platten, David (2007). 'Violence and the Saint: Political Commitment in the Fiction of Jean Amila', in David Gascoigne (ed.), *Violent Histories: Violence, Culture and Identity in France from Surrealism to the Néo-Polar*. Bern: Peter Lang, pp. 175–98.
Platten, David (2009). 'Origins and Beginnings: The Emergence of Detective Fiction in France', in Claire Gorrara (ed.), *French Crime Fiction*. Cardiff: University of Wales Press, pp. 14–35.
Platten, David (2011). *The Pleasures of Crime: Reading Modern French Crime Fiction*. Amsterdam: Rodopi.
Porter, Dennis (1981). *The Pursuit of Crime: Art and Ideology in Detective Fiction*. New Haven, CT: Yale University Press.
Poulantzas, Nicos (1978). *State, Power, Socialism*. London: NLB.
Priestman, Martin (ed.) (2003). *The Cambridge Companion to Crime Fiction*. Cambridge: Cambridge University Press.
Rancière, Jacques (2009). *The Emancipated Spectator*, trans. Gregory Elliot. London and New York, NY: Verso.
Rancière, Jacques (2009). 'A Few Remarks on the Method of Jacques Rancière'. *Parallax*, 15, pp. 114–23.
Reynolds, Elaine A. (1998). *Before the Bobbies: The Night Watch and Police Reform in Metropolitan London, 1720–1830*. Basingstoke: Macmillan.
Rolls, Alasdair and Walker, Deborah (2009). *French and American Noir: Dark Crossings*. Basingstoke: Palgrave Macmillan.
Ruggiero, Vincenzo (2000). *Crime and Markets: Essays in Anti-Criminology*. Oxford: Oxford University Press.
Ruggiero, Vincenzo (2003). *Crime in Literature: Sociology of Deviance and Fiction*. London and New York, NY: Verso.
Ruggiero, Vincenzo (2004). 'Review of *The Cambridge Companion to Crime Fiction*'. *Modernism/modernity*, 11:4, pp. 851–3.
Ruggiero, Vincenzo (2009). 'On Liberty and Crime: Adam Smith and John Stuart Mill'. *Crime, Law, Social Change*, 51:3–4, pp. 435–50.
Rzepka, Charles J. (2005). *Detective Fiction*. Cambridge: Polity.
Rzepka, Charles J. and Horsley, Lee (eds) (2010). *A Companion to Crime Fiction*. Malden, MA and Oxford: Blackwell.
Sartre, Jean-Paul ([1947] 1967). *What is Literature?* trans. Bernard Frechtman. London: Methuen.
Sartre, Jean-Paul ([1946] 2007). *Existentialism and Humanism*. London: Methuen.
Saviano, Robert (2013). 'Foreword', trans. Paolo Mossetti, in Anabel Hernández, *Narcoland: The Mexican Drug Lords and Their Godfathers*, trans. Iain Bruce. London: Verso, pp. vii–x.
Scaggs, John (2005). *Crime Fiction*. London: Routledge.
Schmid, David (1995). 'Imagining Safe Urban Space: The Contribution of Detective Fiction to Radical Geography', *Antipode*, 27:3, pp. 242–69.
Schmitt, Carl ([1922] 2005). *Political Theology: Four Chapters on the Concept of Sovereignty*, trans. George Schwab. Chicago, IL and London: University of Chicago Press.
Seaman, Amanda (2004). 'Cherchez La Femme: Detective Fiction, Women, and Japan'. *Japan Forum*, 16: 2, pp. 185–90.
Shapiro, Michael J. (2010). *The Time of the City: Politics, Philosophy and Genre*. London and New York, NY: Routledge.

Sheptycki, J.W.E. (ed.) (2000). *Issues in Transnational Policing*. London and New York, NY: Routledge.

Shorley, Christopher (2009). 'Georges Simenon and Crime Fiction between the Wars', in Claire Gorrara (ed.), *French Crime Fiction*. Cardiff: University of Wales Press, pp. 36–53.

Shpayer-Makov, Haia (2011). *The Ascent of the Detective: Police Sleuths in Victorian and Edwardian England*. Oxford: Oxford University Press.

Shpayer-Makov, Haia (2011). 'Revisiting the Detective Figure in Late Victorian and Edwardian Fiction: A View from the Perspective of Police History'. *Law, Crime and History*, 2, pp. 165–93.

Simonsen, Karen-Margrethe and Stougaard-Nielsen, Jakob (eds) (2008). *World Literature, World Culture: History, Theory, Analysis*. Aarhus, DNK: Aarhus University Press.

Skinner, Quentin (1989). 'The State', in Terence Ball, James Farr, and Russell L. Hanson (eds), *Political Innovation and Conceptual Change*. Cambridge: Cambridge University Press, pp. 90–131.

Soitos, Stephen (1996). *The Blues Detective: A Study of African American Detective Fiction*. Amherst, MA: University of Massachusetts Press.

Standing, Guy (2011). *The Precariat: The New Dangerous Class*. London: Bloomsbury.

Summerscale, Kate (2008). *The Suspicions of Mr Whicher or The Murder at Road Hill House*. London: Bloomsbury.

Thomas, Ronald R. (1999). *Detective Fiction and the Rise of Forensic Science*. Cambridge: Cambridge University Press.

Thompson, E.P. (1975). *Whigs and Hunters: The Origin of the Black Act*. London: Allen Lane.

van Schendel, Willem and Abraham, Itty (eds) (2005). *Illicit Flows and Criminal Things: States, Borders and the Other Side of Globalization*. Bloomington and Indianapolis, IN: Indiana University Press.

Walker, R.B.J. (1993). *Inside/Outside: International Relations as Political Theory*. Cambridge: Cambridge University Press.

Walz, Robin (2000). *Pulp Surrealism: Insolent Popular Culture in Early Twentieth-Century Paris*. Berkeley, CA and London: University of California Press.

Wark, McKenzie (2011). *The Beach beneath the Street: The Everyday Life and Glorious Times of the Situationist International*. London and New York, NY: Verso.

Wark, McKenzie (2013). *The Spectacle of Disintegration*. London and New York, NY: Verso.

Weber, Max (1985). *From Max Weber: Essays in Sociology*, ed. H.H. Gerth and C. Wright Mills. London: Routledge and Kegan Paul.

Whitton, Kenneth S. (1990). *Dürrenmatt: Reinterpretation in Retrospect*. Providence, RI and Oxford: Berg.

Wilson, Eric (ed.) (2009). *Government of the Shadows: Parapolitics and Criminal Sovereignty*. London: Pluto Press.

Winston, Robert P. and Mellerski, Nancy C. (1992). *The Public Eye: Ideology and the Police Procedural*. Basingstoke: Macmillan.

Worthington, Heather (2005). *The Rise of the Detective in Early Nineteenth-Century Popular Fiction*. Basingstoke: Palgrave Macmillan.

Žižek, Slavoj (2011). 'Good Manners in the Age of Wikileaks'. *London Review of Books*, 33:2, pp. 9–10.

Index

Adams, Charles 79, 81, 99–103
Adkins, Lisa 84
Adorno, Theodor 148
Adorno, Theodor and Horkheimer, Max 193
Agnew, John 241
Alder, Bill 156, 160
Allain, Marcel and Souvestre, Pierre 7, 105, 127–30
Ambroise, Claude 171
Anderson, Philip 203
Anglo-American critical tradition 6, 8, 9, 133, 167, 248
Anker, Elizabeth 207, 213, 239
Aradau, Claudia and Van Munster, Rens 215
art and capitalism 229–32
Ascari, Maurizio 4, 12
Atack, Margaret 9, 183

Badiou, Alan 229
Bailey, Quentin 62
Balzac, Honoré de 74–6, 140
Bastien, Pascal 19, 28–9
Bastille (prison) 58
Beccaria, Cesare 27, 52–6, 58–9, 66, 69
Becker, Lucille 141
Bell, Ian A. 21
Benjamin, Walter 8, 105, 107, 153–4, 157, 158, 212–13
Bentham, Jeremy 23, 53, 57, 58, 60, 64, 66, 68, 69, 72
Berlant, Lauren 3, 10, 15, 208, 238, 239, 241, 247
Berman, Marshall 128
Bertillon, Alphonse 107, 112
Beukes, Lauren 210, 228, 229–32, 249
Bielecki, Emma 128
Biet, Christian 24–5, 28, 47
Bigo, Didier 243
Bitter Lemon Press 9
Black Act of 1724 (Britain) 21, 58
Black Mask magazine 139
Bobbio, Norberto 28, 32, 38, 211
Bourbon (House of) 67
Bow Street Runners (London) 94
Braddon, Mary Elizabeth 14, 81, 84, 95, 96–7, 98, 100
Bratlinger, Patrick 61, 62
Brecht, Bertolt 7, 8, 48–9, 133, 135, 136, 137–40, 168, 249
Brecht, Bertolt and Hammett, Dashiell 148–55
Breu, Christopher 132, 220, 223, 224

Briggs, John 94
Brown, Wendy 15, 208, 218, 223, 224
Buccellato, James A. 233
Buci-Glucksman, Christine 151
Burke, Edmund 58

Caillois, Roger 64
Cain, James M. 102
Calas, Jean 50–1
Camus, Albert 173, 188
Carlotto, Massimo 210, 228, 235–8, 239, 242, 245, 249
Cartouche, Louis-Dominique 20, 22, 33, 38, 39, 40–1, 48, 63
Cassuto, Leonard 180
Central Intelligence Agency, *see* CIA
Chandler, Raymond 132, 249, 250
Child, Lee vii
Christie, Agatha 4, 133, 249, 250
CIA 204, 244
Clarke, Clare 109, 110, 116, 127
Cobley, Paul 4
Cohen, Michael 17, 52, 54, 56
Collins, Paul 100
Collins, Wilkie 95, 99
Comaroff, Jean and John 1
Communism 135, 137
Connolly, Michael vii
Conrad, Joseph 173
Copjec, Joan 71
crime
  and business/capitalism 7, 17, 20, 38, 39–40, 41–5, 100–3, 115–27, 136, 138, 149–55, 156, 158–9, 162–5, 171–3, 184–7, 194, 207, 209, 210, 221–2, 225–7, 229–32, 235–8, 239, 242, 245
  and finance and speculation 123–7, 144, 162–4, 225–7, 237–8
  and greed/exploitation 20, 30–1, 40, 45, 98, 100–1, 109, 122, 123–7, 137, 144, 162–3, 180–2, 184, 197
  and insurance 100–3
  and parapolitics 209, 213–17, 239
  and poverty 19–20, 24, 40, 43–5, 88, 109, 122, 152–3, 209, 221
  and rebellion 12, 21, 28, 34, 40, 45, 54, 55, 58–9, 62, 64–5, 83, 150
  and war 214–15, 241–2
crime fiction
  and absurdity 7, 169, 170, 175, 182, 186, 187–95
  and bureaucracy 7, 71–2, 73, 76

crime fiction (*cont.*)
  and capitalism/exploitation 7, 11, 12, 14,
    20, 41–5, 48, 82–4, 99–103, 115–27,
    132–3, 136–9, 141, 148–9, 158–9, 210,
    220–1, 223–4, 224–7, 228–38, 245
  and colonialism 162–5
  and complicity and defeat 131–2, 140, 141,
    154–5, 156–65, 170, 182–7, 193–5,
    203–4, 217
  and conservatism 2–3, 23–8, 46–8, 62, 80,
    95–6, 97, 110, 112, 134, 140, 142, 143
  and contradictions/tensions 1–2, 5, 7, 11,
    14, 17, 18, 23, 24, 27–8, 29, 33, 36–40,
    46, 49, 51, 52, 55–6, 61–2, 63, 64–5,
    72–5, 76, 89–92, 109, 111, 127–30,
    132–3, 134, 141, 144, 154–5, 158–9,
    161–2, 164–5, 169–70, 172, 176, 182–4,
    186, 197–8, 202, 206–8, 211, 229–31,
    240, 245, 247, 248
  and definitions 12, 21, 45, 51, 52, 56, 61
  and detection 50–1, 60–1, 63, 64–5, 67,
    70–2, 78–9, 86–7, 95, 100–1, 107–8,
    109–12, 114, 139–40, 145, 154, 157–8,
    173–5, 177–8, 242–3
  and development/genealogy 3–6, 12–13, 45,
    51, 52, 56, 61, 64, 65, 73, 76, 78, 80, 81,
    87, 92, 103, 108, 114, 127, 130, 153,
    165, 248
  and early criminal biographies 4, 19, 20,
    23–30, 33–41
  and existentialism 142, 143, 146, 163,
    168, 233
  and gender 14, 81, 84, 96–9, 104–5, 133,
    209, 218–27, 228–9, 250–1
  and hard-boiled viii, 7, 82, 84, 131–3,
    184, 193
  and individualism 1, 3, 53, 57, 60, 68, 80,
    82, 88, 95, 97, 108, 112–13, 115–17,
    119, 121, 122, 128, 131–2, 140, 143,
    151, 156, 232–4
  and law and justice 1–2, 28–9, 31, 42, 52,
    54–5, 56–7, 60, 63, 68, 69, 73, 75, 93–9,
    99–103, 117–20, 147–8, 157–8
  and liberalism 15–16, 23, 32, 81–2, 84, 88,
    91, 97, 103, 112–13, 115–17, 121, 126
  and Marxism vii–viii, 11, 16, 17, 48, 82–3,
    84, 89, 104–5, 122–7, 132, 134, 137–8,
    144, 145, 160, 164, 168–70, 175, 178,
    180, 183–5, 196, 217, 220, 230–1
  and modernity 105, 127–30
  and narrative breakdown 170, 189–90,
    195–6, 200–4
  and the panopticon 77, 85–6, 105–7,
    110, 116
  and political commitment vii–viii, 11–16,
    41–5, 83–4, 121–7, 132, 135, 137–41,
    145, 148, 165, 166, 168, 169–70, 175,
    176, 183–4, 186–7, 190, 191, 195,
    198–9, 202, 228–9, 232, 234, 248
  and race 14, 167, 179–82, 187–8, 198–202,
    229–30, 250–1
  and revolution 166–70, 183, 190, 195–205,
    216–17, 236
  and science and technology 110, 112,
    113–14, 127–9
  and translation 9–11
  and transnationalism viii, 6–11, 13, 133,
    155, 166–70, 187–8, 208–10, 238–47,
    249–50
crime fiction in
  England (Britain) 5, 6, 7, 9, 13,
    17, 19, 21, 23–8, 30–3, 35–8,
    39–40, 41–5, 48, 54, 56–63,
    82–3, 93–9, 105, 106, 109–27,
    133–4, 138, 209, 210–11, 213–14,
    216–17, 250
  France 6, 9, 12, 13, 19, 22, 24,
    28–30, 33–4, 38–9, 40–1, 46–7,
    52, 56, 63–76, 85–93, 103, 106,
    109–15, 127–30, 133, 140–8, 155–65,
    166, 169, 182–6, 193–5, 202–4, 224–7,
    228–9
  Ireland (north) 209, 211–17, 238
  Italy 170–3, 235–8
  Japan 220–4
  Latin America 249
  Mexico 242, 244
  South Africa 209, 218–19, 229, 238
  Sweden 176–9, 190–3, 196–8, 249
  United States 6, 7, 9, 13, 14, 84, 93,
    98–9, 103, 133–5, 138, 140–65, 169,
    179–82, 188–90, 198–202, 229–35,
    241–2, 244–5
crime scenes 77–8, 85, 87, 99, 107

Damrosch, David 8, 10
Debord, Guy 192, 194, 202, 203, 204
Defoe, Daniel 4, 5, 8, 14, 21, 22, 31–2,
  33–41, 78
Delamare, Nicolas 21
Denning, Michael 43–4, 45
Detroit (city) 229–32
Diawara, Manthia 179
Dickens, Charles 95, 96, 106
Doyle, Arthur Conan 4, 5, 6, 7, 8, 14, 17, 80,
  91, 105, 106, 108, 109–21, 122, 125,
  126, 127, 133, 250
Duhamel, Marcel 187
Dumas, Alexander 139
Dumas, Raechel Lynn 223
Dürrenmatt, Friedrich 7, 169, 173–5, 188

Eburne, Jonathan 167, 188
Echenoz, Jean 186
Engels, Friedrich 14, 82–3, 84, 90, 101, 102,
  135, 183, 185
EU 225–7
Europa Publishing 9

European Union, *see* EU
Evans, Mary 4

Faber, Michael 104–5
Fabre, Michel and Skinner, Robert E. 201
factory (in crime fiction) 209, 218, 220–2, 223, 224–5, 226–7
Faller, Lincoln B. 25, 26
Farrell, Joseph 170, 175
Femia, Joseph V. 67, 68, 74
Fielding, Henry 48–9
Fisher, Mark 203, 232
Foucault, Michel 5, 6, 13, 16, 20, 28, 64–5, 85, 103, 105, 106, 110, 204, 207
Freedman, Carl and Kendrick, Christopher 151, 158
French Revolution 13, 56, 57, 62, 66–7
Fryer, Bob 101
Fuller, Sam 193

Gaboriau, Emile 8, 74, 79, 81, 85–93, 99, 133
Galbraith, John Kenneth 175
Galton, Francis 112
Gates, Henry Louis 189
Gavison, Ruth 220
Gay, John 7, 14, 21, 33, 41–5, 46, 48, 127, 133, 152
Gayot de Pitival, François 22, 29–30, 46–7
Gide, André 8
Ginzburg, Carlo 107, 109, 111, 112, 114
Gladfelder, Hal 21, 27, 28
Godwin, William 7, 8, 17, 51, 52, 53–6, 56–63, 76, 78, 127, 168, 172, 173
Goodman, Robin Truth 227, 250
Gorrara, Claire 8, 183, 185
Gothic (in crime fiction) 61, 96
Goulet, Andrea 113–15
Gramsci, Antonio 3, 14, 48, 84, 90, 136, 137, 139–40, 149, 150–2, 156, 159
Gray, John 146, 148
Green, Anna Katharine 14, 79, 81, 96, 98–9
Greenberg, David F. 80
Gunning, Tom 105, 107, 109

H.D. (late clerk to Justice R—) 31, 33, 37–40, 46, 48
Hammett, Dashiell viii, 5, 7, 8, 11, 84, 128, 130, 131–3, 134, 135, 136–40, 180, 183–4, 186, 202, 250
and Brecht, Bertolt 148–55
and Simenon, Georges 140–8, 155–65
Hardt, Michael 245
Hardt, Michael and Negri, Antonio 245–6
Harlem (New York City) 8, 179–82, 188–90, 195, 199
Hart, Matthew 211

Harvey, David 124, 159, 165, 181, 220, 221, 226, 230, 238, 242
Helvetius, Claude 53
Higginson, Pim 167
Highsmith, Patricia 128
Himes, Chester 7, 166, 167, 168, 169, 176, 179–82, 186, 187–90, 192, 195, 196, 198–200, 217, 250
Hoare, Quintin and Nowell-Smith, Geoffrey 151
Hobbes, Thomas 4, 14, 19, 22, 23–4, 26, 28, 30–1, 33, 37, 38, 47, 52, 53, 58, 126, 152, 210, 211
Hobsbawm, Eric 43, 59, 153
Hoffman, Josef 17
Holloway, David 241
Horsley, Lee 2, 4, 7, 134, 144, 190
House of Un-American Activities 137–8
Howell, Philip 82
Howson, Gerald 19, 20
Hugo, Victor 74
Hume, L.J. 60
Humm, Peter 147

immigration (in crime fiction) 224–5, 226
Izzo, Jean-Claude 235

James, P.D. 218
Jameson, Fredric 240
Jann, Rosemary 106, 110
Jeannerod, Dominique 9
Jessop, Bob 181
Johnston, Les 240
Joyce, Stephen 110

Kalifa, Dominique 9, 78, 85
Kayman, Martin 4, 12, 19, 23, 42
Kersh, Gerald 133
Kimyongür, Angela 226
King, Stewart 8–10
Kirino, Natsuo 209, 218, 220–4, 226, 238, 249, 250
Knight, Mark 110
Knight, Stephen 4, 61, 96
Knopf, Blanche 138
Kracauer, Siegfried 157, 158

Larsson, Stieg 9, 249
Lee, Susannah 186
Lehner, Stefanie 215
Lemaitre, Pierre 210, 228–9
Leroux, Gaston 105, 108, 109–15
liberalism 14, 22–3, 32, 81–4, 107–9, 116–17, 135, 167, 200
Linebaugh, Peter 14, 22, 23, 44
Lloyd, David and Thomas, Paul 152
Loader, Ian 251
Loader, Ian and Walker, Neil 1, 206, 208, 211, 240

Locke, John 53
London (city) 4, 5, 8, 19–23, 33–45, 109, 110, 120–1, 123, 168

McCann, Sean 15, 81, 132, 148, 156, 167
Machiavelli, Niccolo 24, 38, 46, 67, 68, 69, 70, 72, 73, 170
McNamee, Eoin 209, 211–13, 214–17, 238, 239, 249
Manchette, Jean-Patrick vii–viii, 8, 166, 167, 168, 169, 176, 182–7, 190, 192, 193–5, 196, 198, 202–5, 217, 250
Mandel, Ernest 80, 124
Mandeville, Bernard 14, 21, 22, 23, 30–3, 39
Mankell, Henning 9, 249
Manotti, Dominique 12, 205, 209, 218, 220, 224–7, 238, 239, 250
Marable, Manning 180–1
Marcus, Stephen 152
Marcuse, Herbert 186–7, 195
Marx, Karl 15, 23, 77, 78–9, 82, 83, 88, 89–90, 92, 101, 102, 103, 123, 124, 125, 126, 127, 135, 139, 144, 149, 173, 181, 198, 204, 220, 230–1, 235, 236, 237, 240, 246
Marxism 1, 6, 14, 16, 22–3, 169, 175, 200–1, 202, 246
Maza, Sara 21
Meiskins-Wood, Ellen 241
Messent, Peter 4, 176
Metropolitan Police (London) 94, 95, 134
Middlesex Justice Act (1792) 94
Miéville, China 210, 240, 241, 242–3, 245–7
Miliband, Ralph 175
Mill, John Stuart 14, 17, 23, 88, 97, 108, 112, 113, 115, 116, 117, 119, 120, 127, 221
Miller, D.A. 85, 94, 105, 106, 107
Mitterand, François 202
monopoly capitalism 136, 150, 153, 156–7, 159–61
Montesquieu, Baron de 58
Moretti, Franco 10, 80, 86, 88, 91, 104, 105, 106, 110, 116, 121, 225
Morrison, Arthur 7, 17, 109, 115, 116, 117, 121–7
Morton, James 65, 66

NAFTA 242, 245
Negri, Antonio 6
neoliberalism 3, 191, 207–9, 213, 216–17, 218, 222–4, 226–7, 229, 234–5, 237–8, 239, 242
Nestingen, Andrew 9, 190–1
Nestingen, Andrew and Arvas, Paula 179
Newport rising (1839) 94
Nicolson-Smith, Donald 10
Nietzsche, Friedrich 128
North American Free Trade Agreement, *see* NAFTA

O'Connell, Carol 218
Ordinary of Newgate 25, 26, 35
Orford, Margie 209, 218–19, 227, 238, 249, 250
organized crime 20, 31–2, 37–41, 43–4, 46, 122–3, 150–5, 170–3, 233–5, 237–8, 242, 244–5

Padovani, Marcelle 172
Panek, Leroy 176
Paris (city) 4, 5, 11, 19–23, 28–30, 33, 38–9, 40–1, 63, 65, 68, 70, 72, 74, 85, 142, 143, 145, 146, 158, 166, 168, 187–8
Parmalee, Patty Lee 149
Pateman, Carol 84, 219–20
Pawling, Christopher 168
Peace, David vii, 8, 205, 207, 209, 210–11, 213–14, 215, 216–17, 239
Peterloo massacre (1819) 94
Pezzotti, Barbara 9, 236
Pfeil, Fred 179
Pinkerton detective agency 137
Platten, David 9, 110, 113, 183
Poe, Edgar Allan 4, 6, 7, 63, 77–80, 128, 134
policing 5, 7, 20, 26, 36, 39, 40, 44, 69, 70, 71, 73, 74, 76, 79, 80, 84, 86, 93–4, 98, 106, 111, 112, 115, 118, 127, 129, 147–8, 152–3, 155–7, 159–60, 163, 174–5, 176, 179, 180–2, 188, 212–14, 229, 231–2, 242–3
  and class 61, 74–5, 92–3, 93–4, 95, 96–9, 102, 136, 150, 153, 156–7, 159–61, 182–3, 185, 198–9, 211
  and criminality 63–4, 65, 67, 69–70, 71, 72–3, 74–6, 146–8
  global 240–7
Polito, Robert 166, 167
Porter, Dennis 80, 132
Poulantzas, Nicos 181, 185–6, 202
precarity 209, 220–4, 225–6
private property 54, 58–9, 64, 74
public/private 1, 3, 4–5, 14, 20, 30, 32, 36, 40, 80, 81–4, 86, 88, 93–9, 104–9, 113, 125, 207, 218, 219–20, 223–4, 227, 239, 250
Punter, David 21

race and capital 179–81, 190, 200–1
Rancière, Jacques 11, 232
Rankin, Ian vii
Raymond, Derek 250
Reagan, Ronald 201, 242
Rendell, Ruth 218
Robespierre, Maximilien 66
Rousseau, Jean-Jacques 62
Ruggiero, Vincenzo 42, 43, 44, 119, 152
Rush, Norman 162, 164
Russian Revolution 135, 136, 137
Rzepka, Charles 4, 144, 145, 148

Sallis, James 210, 228, 232–5, 239, 249
Salzini, Carlo 157
Sartre, Jean-Paul 143, 145, 148, 168
Sassen, Saskia 220
Saviano, Robert 171, 242
Scaggs, John 176
Schmid, Conrad 90
Schmid, David 3
Schmitt, Carl 211, 212, 215
Schutt, Sita A. 66
Sciascia, Leonardo 130, 169, 170–3, 174, 175, 188
Seaman, Amanda 223
sensation novels 96–9, 100, 104
Shapiro, Michael 171–2, 173
Sheptycki, J.W.E. 207
Shorley, Christopher 140
Shpayer-Makov, Haia 93, 94
Simenon, Georges viii, 8, 11, 132, 133, 134, 136, 137, 140, 168, 249
Simenon, Georges and Hammett, Dashiell 140–8, 155–65
situationism 169, 183, 193, 194, 202
Sjöwall, Maj and Wahlöö, Per viii, 7, 130, 167, 169, 176–9, 186–7, 188, 190–3, 195, 196–8, 202, 217, 249, 250
Skinner, Quentin 24
Slaughter, Karin 218
Smith, Adam 69, 108, 115
social banditry 43, 44, 58–9
Soitos, Stephen 189
sovereignty 3, 14–17, 20, 21, 23, 28, 33, 54, 62, 206–10, 238–47
 and contradictions 2, 13, 15, 20, 38, 49, 53–6, 58–9, 68, 73–4, 152, 206–9, 210–11, 227, 238–40, 241, 243–5, 247, 250–1
 and gender 209, 218–27, 250
 and state of emergency 209, 211–17, 239, 246
state
 and capital 1–2, 4–5, 11, 13, 30–2, 37, 42, 44, 54, 57, 75–6, 80, 84, 92, 102, 107, 108, 111, 112, 114, 127, 133, 137, 138, 141, 145, 148, 151–2, 163–5, 168, 169, 170–3, 175–87, 200, 212–14, 225–7, 240, 244–5, 246, 249
 and civil society 13, 14, 22, 23, 31, 32, 39, 82, 92, 96–9, 100–2, 104, 105, 108–9, 111, 125, 135–6, 149, 151–2, 159–60
 and criminal justice system 1, 12, 17, 20, 21, 26, 29–30, 34, 38, 44, 48, 49, 50–1, 55–6, 58, 59–60, 64–5, 68–9, 73–4, 77–8, 80, 85, 86, 88, 89, 96–7, 103, 107–8, 115, 117, 129–30, 174–5, 176–7, 181–2, 192–3, 197–8, 200, 206, 207, 212–13, 218, 229, 232

bureaucratic reform, organisation 67–8, 71–2, 73, 79, 84, 85, 87–8, 89–90, 92, 105, 111–12, 114
 consolidation and expansion 135, 136, 149, 150, 157, 159, 164, 175–6, 184
 definition 206–7, 238–9, 240
 foundations 19–30
 institutions and imaginary 77–8, 81, 85, 90, 99, 101, 103, 107, 108, 111–12, 114, 117, 128
 penal reform 51–63, 64, 69–70, 73
 unreformed 23–7, 53–4, 57, 58, 60, 66, 69
 violence 7, 11, 20, 27, 41, 55–6, 58, 72–3, 149–50, 151, 154, 162, 192, 199–201, 202, 203
Sue, Eugene 82
Summerscale, Kate 95
Sûreté (police) 63, 64, 65, 68, 72, 93
surrealism 169, 187–8

Thatcher, Margaret 202, 211, 213
Thomas, Ronald 81, 110, 117
Thompson, E.P. 14, 19, 21, 22, 23, 42, 44, 48
Trollope, Anthony 106
Troubles (N. Ireland) 211–17

utilitarianism 53, 57, 67–8, 69, 72

van Schendel, Willem and Abraham, Itty 239, 241, 244
Venuti, Lawrence 10
Vidocq, Eugène François 5, 6, 7, 8, 51, 63–74, 75, 76, 78, 87, 127, 133, 168
Voltaire 50–2, 53, 58, 69, 170, 172, 173
Von Mueller, Eddy 176

Wahlöö, Per 196
Wall Street Crash (1929) 135, 144
Wallace, Edgar 133
Walpole, Robert 32, 42
Wark, McKenzie 202
Watz, Robin 128
Weber, Max 206
Westphalia (treaty) 4, 19, 207, 239
Whicher, Jack 95
Wild, Jonathan 3, 8, 20, 22, 31–2, 33–41, 46, 48, 63
Wilson, Eric 209
Winslow, Don 207, 210, 239, 240, 241–2, 243, 244–5
Winston, Robert P. and Mellerski, Nancy C. 186
World War One 135, 136
World War Two 168, 211
Worthington, Heather 93
Wright, Richard 181

Žižek, Slavoj 232, 237

Printed and bound by CPI Group (UK) Ltd, Croydon, CR0 4YY